THE MOST ANCIENT OF SCIENCES . . .

This remarkable book offers convincing proof of
the validity of astrology. Here is authentic testimony
of scientists, economists, astronomists—of people
who have plotted their way to wealth by the use
of horoscopes. Also included is evidence of the use
of astrology in the prediction of major historical
events such as the death of John F. Kennedy
and of the astonishing but proven phenomenon
of the astral twin. But most importantly, this
comprehensive and entertaining guide gives *you*
all the information you need to write your own
personal horoscope, to read the message that is
clearly written in the stars about your character,
talents, potentials, and future.

JOSEPH F. GOODAVAGE was a renowned
astrologer and the author of more than twenty books
on the subject of astrology.

# WRITE
# YOUR
# OWN
# HOROSCOPE

## By
## Joseph F. Goodavage

### FOURTH REVISED EDITION

### *Foreword by Linda Goodman*

A SIGNET BOOK

For Maria and Danny
who have enriched my live

SIGNET
Published by the Penguin Group
Penguin Books USA Inc., 375 Hudson Street,
New York, New York 10014, U.S.A.
Penguin Books Ltd, 27 Wrights Lane,
London W8 5TZ, England
Penguin Books Australia Ltd, Ringwood,
Victoria, Australia
Penguin Books Canada Ltd, 10 Alcorn Avenue,
Toronto, Ontario, Canada M4V 3B2
Penguin Books (N.Z.) Ltd, 182–190 Wairau Road,
Auckland 10, New Zealand

Penguin Books Ltd, Registered Offices:
Harmondsworth, Middlesex, England

Published by Signet, an imprint of Dutton Signet,
a division of Penguin Books USA Inc.
*Write Your Own Horoscope* previously appeared in a somewhat different form in an
NAL BOOKS edition.

First Printing, November 1968
36  35  34

REGISTERED TRADEMARK—MARCA REGISTRADA

Printed in the United States of America

# ACKNOWLEDGMENTS

No individual could ever learn everything needed to put together the material you'll find in these pages. I owe a great debt to all the scientists, astrologers and scholars of the past for preserving the remnants of what was once known about this ancient science.

I'd also like to thank *Saga* magazine and its editor, Martin Singer, for permission to reprint the major part of "Space-Time Forecasting." Thanks also to the editors of *Science & Mechanics* for their permission to use "How the Stars Influence Your Health" as another chapter, to *The Mercury Hour* for permission to use their preface to my article, "Response to 'The Inaccuracy of Astrological Research,'" and to Ruth Hale Oliver for permission to use her letter in the Winter 1977 issue of *The Mercury Hour*.

For their help in the preparation of the manuscript, my thanks to my wife, Evelyn, and to Frances Jacoby.

# FOREWORD

I first saw Joe Goodavage's name in the mid-1960s on the cover of his marvelous book, *Astrology, the Space Age Science*. That book has become an occult classic; it was exciting for me to read because it showed a Western writer was aware of a crucial issue regarding the harmony of polarity, the North-South mystery.

Briefly stated, this principle is first evident in small physical ways. Water runs down a drain clockwise in the northern hemisphere, and counter-clockwise in the southern hemisphere. On a larger scale, hurricanes and tornadoes turn *counter*-clockwise in the northern hemisphere and clockwise in the southern hemisphere. This harmonic polarity reflects the harmony of a functioning Universe and astrologers have long recognized the contrasting directions of the Universe when they charted the heavens: the planets move clockwise in the astrological cycle, while the "Ages"—the influence of Aquarius in our Age of Aquarius—move counter-clockwise.

Joe's great contribution on this issue was to point out that spiritual enlightenment moves eastward—counter-clockwise—while civilization moves westward, or clockwise. This is a crucial distinction for anyone concerned about the fates of nations. I won't go into a detailed discussion of the implications of this distinction (for that you can turn to my book *Linda Goodman's Star Signs* and start reading at page 380). But I will say that Joe Goodavage's insights were a real inspiration for me and I've always been grateful to him for that.

I know I'm not the only one who found Joe's writing inspiring. In April, 1990, just a few months after Joe passed away, I received a letter from a woman who had been reading my books for years. Like me, she had been a student of astrology early in her life; she'd read *Sun Signs* when it was first published, but hadn't yet truly begun to explore. Then one day, she read this book, *How to Write Your Own Horoscope:* "And puff! It rekindled the fire left unattended but still smoldering from being introduced to Astrology through . . . *Sun Signs*." Since that time she tells me she's owned three copies.

That woman found Joe Goodavage through her high school English teacher, who encouraged her students to read, read, read. I'm glad to know that happened in 1973 because I felt for a long time that Joe's work was important enough that we ought to be exposing our young people to it. In fact, in 1987 in *Star Signs* I wrote that *Astrology, The Space Age Science* "ought to be required reading for all schools." I went even further:

I'd like to say that Goodavage's books should be one of the "bibles" of all New Age thinkers. They are packed with colorful confetti of esoteric knowledge, and chorded with ancient wisdom, backed up by scientific data for the skeptical. If these splendid books were made required reading in schools, the education system would be powerfully transformed, as would the students exposed to it.

Perhaps that's what Joe did best—excite people to learn more. He was always learning himself. Our own studies took us down different paths, and he and I reached some very different conclusions on some important points about fundamental issues. But no matter what those disagreements were, I'll always remember that thrill I had when I first saw one of Joe's books. And I know from my mail that Joe's work still has that effect on many people.

May it inspire you, too, to brighter things.

Love and magic,

—*Linda Goodman*
*1990*

# CONTENTS

# INTRODUCTION

In 1975, 186 scientists—eighteen of them Nobel laureates—virtually declared all-out war against astrology and all other forms of "obscurantism, irrational thinking and superstition." The first broadside appeared in the Fall issue of *The Humanist* magazine. Whether or not editor Paul Kurtz anticipated it, the attack detonated an explosive controversy. Scientists who signed the declaration condemned astrology as nonsense and hogwash, and used other, less complimentary terms.

To me, the most interesting fact to emerge about the original 186 (apparently there are many more now) signers of the anti-astrological manifesto is that none of those gentlemen had ever made a serious study of astrology—*or ever intended to*. When a man's position in life depends upon his having a certain opinion, you can bet your eyeteeth *that* is the opinion he will have.

Those scientists "knew" without study that astrology is a false doctrine. The members of Professor Kurtz's *Committee for the Scientific Investigation of Claims of the Paranormal* have never undertaken *any* such investigation.

Herein lies an interesting revelation about freedom of scientific inquiry that I can tell you from personal experience: It once occurred to me that the simplest, most direct method of *disproving* astrology's validity "once and for all" was to locate people with identical horoscopes, compare their life patterns, personality traits, and—*most important*—the outstanding events in their lives: incidents such as major illnesses, accidents, surgery, scars, time and place of marriages, birth of children, divorces, long trips, occupations, promotions, changes of domicile, and the like.

It *seemed* easy enough, but after several years of intensive investigation I realized I'd been getting nowhere. Then I received an unexpected free-lance assignment from the old New York *Herald Tribune.* It was to cover part of a three-year, citywide study in Philadelphia, part of which was to determine whether atmospheric conditions had anything to do with physical and mental health or well-being.

Under the nominal leadership of the American Institute of Medical Climatology (AIMC), the cooperation of Philadelphia's fire and police departments, some major industries, the University of Pennsylvania, and several large hospitals was enlisted in a long-range scientific project. Weather, the Institute discovered, influenced people in various strange ways according to the ever-changing ion content of the atmosphere. In the course of my interviews with various members of the Institute, one of the bonus correlations made (particularly by policemen, firemen, and workers in mental hospitals) between human behavior and lunar phase put me back on the search for Time Twins.

During one particularly stimulating session with Forrest P. Speicher, the chief research scientist at Philco, I learned more about cycles than I'd ever known or suspected. Philco had participated in the three-year study and had manufactured a large negative ion generator, the Ionotron 8000. According to Dr. Igho H. Kornblueh at the Frankford Hospital (then one of the directors of the AIMC), patients suffering from third-degree burns over 90 percent of their bodies were markedly relieved of excruciating agony when exposed for long periods to negative ionization of the air they breathed inside oxygen tents.

I observed the pain-relieving qualities of negative ionization several times; in some cases, patients suffering from cancer were—after just a half hour of breathing negatively charged ions—able to go for long periods without pain-killing narcotics. After Dr. Kornblueh treated one of my closest relatives (a terminally ill cancer patient) and successfully relieved her of pain, I told him (and later, Forrest Speicher) of my astro-twin research. Dr. Kornblueh invited me to become a member of the AIMC.

Interested, Forrest Speicher gave me a letter of introduction—something to the effect that as a science reporter and technical writer I was engaged in research with the AIMC to determine the possibility of parallelism in the incidence of various illnesses in the lives of children born at approximately the same time in the city

Furthermore, to reach sociological and scientific conclusions, it was necessary that I locate the individuals in these cases by first collecting data from the Protocol of the Delivery room and then trying to trace the individuals for a medical interview concerning the illnesses and nature of such illnesses of the children involved, and any cooperation in giving me this help would be appreciated.

Because isolated instances of such parallelism of somatic function had been noticed, he said they were most anxious to learn whether these cases were anomalies or were more common than believed.

But once again the enormity of trying to trace the few people born at the same time and place proved a much bigger job than I could handle. However, because of the rare conjunction of all five inner planets at the time of a total solar eclipse (in Aquarius) on February 4 and 5, 1962, I decided to concentrate on children born during the first week of February of that year. The unusual nature of the cosmic pattern, I figured, should satisfy both friend and foe of astrology—whichever way the chips fell.

Meanwhile, I was busy gathering material from magazines, newspapers, science journals, and other sources. Scores of intriguing items were added to my files—some of them downright mind-blowing.

\* \* \*

For example:

*The New York Times*, March 18, 1973: A story bylined Robert McG. Thomas, Jr., told of two men named James Edward Taylor, one a Health Department inspector and the other a Postal Service employee, who were giving each other (and the Internal Revenue Service) an unusual headache. The former lived in Manhattan and the other in Brooklyn. "Not only do both men have the same names," wrote McG. Thomas, "they also have the same birth date, July 23, 1919, and were born in the same state, Virginia.

"But what causes the problem with the Internal Revenue Service is that both men have the same Social Security number. . . .

"The Taylors, who were born 154 miles apart and had never met, did not become aware of each other until 1960, when their problems began. That was because of a mix-up with the Motor Vehicles Bureau. . . . That is not really surprising, considering that both men were issued the same license number. . . ."

\*       \*       \*

Intriguing? Read on.

From an old Robert Ripley "Believe-It-or-Not!" syndicated feature came "The Strangest Parallel in All History!" "King Umberto I (1844-1900) of Italy had a double named Umberto Santini, and they looked exactly alike. They were born in Torino on the same day. Umberto became a restauranteur on the day Umberto became king. Both had wives named Margherita, each had a son named Vittorio, and both died in Monza, Italy, of gunshot wounds on the same day—the monarch by assassination, and his double by a gun accident!"

\*       \*       \*

New York *World-Telegram*, March 25, 1964: *2 Friends, Born on Same Day, Die on Same Day in Auto Crash*. San Leandro, Calif., March 25 (AP)—The lives of Fred V. Schockley, Jr. and Barrett Woodruff seemed drawn together from the very start:

"Both were born on July 19, 1944. Fred in Nebraska, Barrett in Oakland.

"The Schockleys moved to Oakland and the two boys became classmates in elementary school and high school and they entered Oakland City College together.

"But the greatest thing they had in common was that they were friends.

"Monday night they double-dated.

"They dropped their dates at their homes and then headed for Oakland.

"The car swerved out of control, stuck a divider in the middle of the freeway, then smashed into a trailer-truck.

"Both young men were thrown out.

"Both were dead."

\*       \*       \*

And . . .

*The New York Times*, November 12, 1966: *"2 Students
Are Alike in Name and Birthday.* Bethany, Kans. (AP)
—Two young natives of Sweden had never heard of each
other until they came to this Kansas town and learned they
had the same names and birthdays."

Goran Lundberg, it seemed, had learned about the other
Goran Lundberg after seeing his name in a newspaper. Both
Lundbergs were in the United States on scholarships and
were born on September 25th.

\*     \*     \*

Sometimes the "coincidences" seemed ominous and fright-
ening: *"Two Born Same Day Die in Collision.* Eureka,
Calif., September 10, 1956 (AP)—Donald Brazill and Donald Chapman, born the same day 23 years ago, died at the
same time early Sunday when they met in a head-on auto-
mobile collision on U.S. 101 south of Eureka. Mr. Brazill of
Ferndale and Mr. Chapman of Eureka had their 23rd birthday anniversaries Sept. 5."

Both Donalds, according to a local newspaper, were de-
capitated. According to a foe of astrology two decades later,
Brazill merely perished with a crushed skull, and Chapman
of a cerebral hemorrhage.

\*     \*     \*

The parade of these "coincidences" seemed almost end-
less: New York *Daily News*, February 22, 1964—"Two women
whose lives touched in an almost unbelievable sequence of
similarities will reach a final coincidence in a Yonkers
cemetary today.

"Lifelong friends, the two—both named Julia—were born
in the Portuguese coastal village of Caldas da Rianha before
the turn of the century.

"They attended the same school and both married men
named Joaquim. One came to this country as a teenager and
married Joaquim Frade in Chicopee, Mass. The other wed
Joaquim Leal in Portugal and came here in 1920. They had
wed in the same year, 1914.

"Both couples had daughters named Celeste. Now mar-
ried, the daughters live at the same address, 112 Saratoga
Ave., Yonkers, where Mrs. Frade made her home. Mrs.
Leal formerly lived in Yonkers. . . ."

The list of parallel events went on and on, ending with each woman's heart attack and death in different hospitals and services in different Catholic churches. Both were buried in St. Joseph's Cemetery in Yonkers.

\*       \*       \*

Several more from the now-burgeoning file—groundwork for what is to come:

New York *Sun*, June 18, 1941: "Wilkesbarre, Pa., June 18 (AP)—The enlistment of Joseph David Williams caused Army recruiting officers to remember that another Joseph David Williams had enlisted in January.

"Service records showed each was born December 28, 1922. Both had blue eyes, brown hair and ruddy complexions. Both had four teeth missing—exactly the same ones. Both lived on Market Street here and each had a brother whose name was Daniel.

"They listed mother and brother Daniel as beneficiaries in the event of accident.

"They were not related."

Fifty times as many cases (space prohibits including some of the longest, most baffling reports) seemed unerringly to indicate the working of an unknown natural law.

\*       \*       \*

*"Born November 13, 1944. Died June 22, 1964.* Durham, N. H. (UPI)—This incredible coincidence occurred Monday when two outstanding students were killed in a $50,000 fire that swept a three-story Phi Kappa Alpha fraternity house at the University of New Hampshire.

"Both George A. Blunden, Jr. of Gorham, N.H. and Douglas Fillebrown of Portsmouth, N.H. were born on the same day. And their bodies were found in the charred rubble of the blaze.

"A dozen other students scrambled to safety."

\*       \*       \*

New York *Daily News*, July 15, 1964—"The city's two top commissioners—Police boss Michael J. Murphy and Fire boss Edward Thompson—were born on July 19, 1913, in adjoining neighborhoods in Queens, borough of commissioners."

I obtained the official biographical records of both men and found about a dozen additional important coincidences of events in the lives of commissioners Thompson and Murphy.

Another pair of New York's finest—one a cop and the other a fireman—were former classmates at Manhattan College. Police officer Redmond O'Hanlon (who won $26,000 on the TV show, "$64,000 Question") and fireman Vincent Murphy married twins Teresa and Marguerite O'Connell and settled into marital bliss on Staten Island.

Whether by accident, "coincidence," or the design of nature, the sisters then proceeded to present their respective husbands with six children in identical order both in time and gender.

"The kids range in age from three months to twelve years," O'Hanlon observed. "A mathematical expert tells me there are incredible odds against this similarity in the arrival of our progency."

*        *        *

In Morristown, Tennessee, nearly everyone who sees Mr. and Mrs. Leo A. Lunsford is certain they are brother and sister. In fact, they look exactly like twins.

"Not only do we look alike," says Lunsford, "but the amazing thing about us is the fact that we were born only hours apart.

"I was born on July 23, 1923, at 11 p.m. and Sara was born July 24, 1923, at 4 a.m.—just five hours later."

The Lunsfords, according to the *National Enquirer*, which published their picture with the story, said they had been happily married for sixteen years and had never dated anyone else.

"They were married 45 days after their first date.

"Both feel that they have grown to look more and more alike over the years."

*        *        *

At the age of three, Ung-yong Kim of Seoul, Korea, applied for admission to Grand High School in Van Nuys, California. Kim was at the time (1965) a mental giant. The Intelligence Quotient for genius is 160. On one test, Kim scored 175; on another, 200; and on a third, 210. How's this little ditty of philosophical insight by a three-year-old?

> *First it costs four and a half thousand*
> *When grandmother does not buy, the price*
> *Mysteriously becomes three and a half thousand*
> *I can only laugh.*
> *The market man is lying.*
> *In the market everybody tells lies.*

Kim's formidable intellect sometimes seems to overwhelm him, but he has proven himself capable of wit and charm while still hardly more than a baby, when he began abstract drawing and painting and interpreting difficult Korean airs for the voice and instrument.

Why is the "Einstein of Seoul" of interest to us?

*Because his father and mother, both university lecturers, were born precisely at 11 P.M., on May 23, 1934, in Seoul.*

When the story appeared in *Parade* magazine, Kim's relatives were characterized as "superstitious" for wondering whether his gigantic intellect could be connected with the fact that his parents are Time Twins.

*            *            *

From time to time in the long search for the "Children of Aquarius" (if you happen to know anyone born any time during the first week of February, 1962, please let them know that I would appreciate hearing from them), I would weave several of these out-of-this-world stories into an article for one of the Sunday supplements or magazines.

Therefore, when *The Humanist* published its criticism of astrology, the story was immediately picked up by the wire services and printed in just about every newspaper in the country. Barry Farber at New York's WOR wasted no time inviting Professor Kurtz to discuss the cause of all the scientific hullabaloo on his syndicated radio show. And because he knew of my own research and writings on the Time Twin phenomenon (I'd been a guest perhaps a dozen times previously), Mr. Farber also invited me.

It developed into an uncomfortable and embarrassing preshow confrontation. Professor Kurtz was willing to appear with another guest, it seemed, until he realized I'd written scientific as well as astrological articles and books. When he discovered I was the author of *Astrology: The Space-Age*

*Science*\* and had done extensive research on the Time Twin
phenomenon, Professor Kurtz flatly refused to appear on
the same show with me. Farber was distressed, embarrassed, and angry about the whole episode, and did his best
to salvage the time (two or three hours of taping), but
finally wound up asking us to return separately.

Kurtz went on alone and unchallenged. It was a dull
show. I came back and did the same a week or so later. It
was probably equally dull. (I enjoy good debates.)

\*       \*       \*

The November, 1975 issue of *Chemistry* observed:

"At a time when a host of problems such as nuclear-weapon proliferation, food and energy crises, and genetic
engineering are on our doorstep, some members of the
scientific establishment have turned their attention to astrology. They don't say that astrology is responsible for our
problems but do claim that astrology leads people to abandon free will and rationality.

"The scientists voicing criticism number 186 and include
18 Nobel laureates. Their signed statement, published in
*The Humanist*, was drafted by Bart J. Bok, former president
of the American Astronomical Society. In fact, most of the
signers are astronomers, but many other disciplines, except
astrology, are represented."

After noting that astrology has persisted throughout world
history, believed and practiced by some of the greatest
minds the human race has produced, the editorial concluded:

"What prompted issuance of the statement is not clear.
No wholesale abandonment of modern scientific precepts
appears to be threatening the science establishment, though
a growing popularity of the occult among students may be a
consideration. Of course, astrology has been around for
longer than modern science, and probably enjoys a wider
audience. But modern science does not owe its success to
popularity ratings. Scrapping with occult artists is not likely
to damage astrologers—nor is it likely to benefit modern
science."

\*New York: The New American Library, 1967.

Wise words.

Backing out of a debate is one thing. Suppression, however, is a horse of another color, which the first chapter will demonstrate

# 1

## The Facts About Time Twins

Armed with a large file of astro-twin "coincidences," I happened to receive (from a keenly interested reader) a list of fifty children born in Tucson during the stellium-eclipse of February, 1962.

In the early afternoon of September 2, 1975, I called the editor of the *Arizona Star* in Tucson, and outlined my data and the contradiction it posed to the attack on astrology by Professors Bok and Kurtz.

\*     \*     \*

I followed up with this letter:

*September, 2, 1975*

Frank Johnson, Ed.
*Arizona Star*
Tucson, Arizona

*Re: Time Twins data vs Bok statement*

Dear Frank:

Nice talking to you today. I decided, after hanging up, to send you two of the names of the parents of children born during that alignment of all five inner solarian planets during a total solar eclipse in Aquarius in 1962 (Feb. 4–5, 1962).

As I said, I've been engaged in satisfying my curiosity on

this subject for 15 years, and the data isn't all in. It's *extr-e-e-e-mely* difficult to trace people born maybe 25–40 years ago, and even when you do, more often than not only one will co-operate.

Those 186 "scientists" who signed the statement against the "pretentious claims of astrological charlatans" (who could disagree with that?) could never have done any hard research. Their option is just that—a collective whim, nothing more. If just one would adhere to the (stated) *true* spirit of science by actual hard and diligent research in an unbiased way, if their statement were backed by some sort of facts instead of a collective emotional spasm, they wouldn't need a quorum of 186 (how'd they go about that, anyway—and *why*?), including 18 Nobelists, to present a convincing argument.

Those are bullying tactics, and therefore suspect. I happen to have some hard data, extracted at great expense and difficulty over a long period. What do you think my chances are of getting those learned gentlemen to give *me* a fair hearing? The answer to that is in the question itself.

Here are the names of the parents of two unrelated children born close to the aforementioned date: A.2 C. Mr. & Mrs. Phillip G. Eisel, 3315 N. Euclid, Tucson—a boy born 9:52 A.M. in Tucson on 2/2/62. And . . . Mr. & Mrs. Kenneth Johnson, 4526 E. 12—a boy born 9:55 A.M. on 2/2/62.

I've never had the chance to check these out myself, but I'll include two sets of questionnaires and two copies of the letter from the AIMC stating the objective of the research. From long, hard experience and great expense I'd say that chances are that at least one family has moved, broken up or something, and would not be easy to find, but it can be done.

From your point of view, this is a blockbuster of a circulation-boosting story, no matter which way the cookie crumbles. I have 48 more cases born at the same approximate time in Tucson in case you want to go all out on this for a Sunday feature or a series.

Even if you don't, it might be interesting to hear Bart Bok's reaction to the proposal if it is presented like this: Astrology must stand or fall on the evidence of parallelism in the lives and events of people born at the same time and place (i.e., with almost identical horoscopes).

I'd appreciate very much hearing from you whichever way you decide to go with this.

Best wishes,

*Joe Goodavage*

\*     \*     \*

Frank Johnson didn't reply. Then, on September 8, 1975, the invitation to appear with Professor Kurtz on the Barry Farber Show was aborted by Professor Kurtz. I wrote to him the next day (actually to see if he'd be interested in Real Universe evidence that contradicted his dearly cherished opinions). Here's what I wrote:

*September 9, 1975*

Paul Kurtz, Editor
*The Humanist*
State University of New York at Buffalo
4244 Ridge Lea Road
Amherst, New York, 14226

Dear Professor Kurtz:

I was surprised and disappointed yesterday by your refusal to appear with me on the Barry Farber show. Twelve to fifteen years ago, when astrology was in disrepute, I faced many panels of scientists on radio and television debates and at various universities.

The point you've completely overlooked in presenting Bok's "Objections to Astrology" was the possibility of an equally valid viewpoint—one not based on Opinion and/or Authority (as is most of astrology), but on previously unsuspected real Universe data.

While writing a science piece on assignment for TRUE magazine in 1963, I became interested in the effect of weather on health and joined the American Institute of Medical Climatology (see enclosed letter). At the time the entire city of Philadelphia was engaged in a three-year study of the moon's influence and effect on rainfall. Under the aegis of the AIMC I began studying the lives of people born at the same time and place to determine whether there was an unaccountable tendency for the same sort of major events to happen to them at the same time or not. If not, then astrology could be discredited once and for all because it based its credence entirely on the horoscope.

My initial search yielded positive results of "parallelism," which were reported in magazine articles and in the first chapter of the book I gave you. Since then, the results have been more refined and specific.

In all fairness—after publishing "Objections to Astrology"— can you refuse to give equal attention to an alternate view that is backed by hard data? I note that neither Bok nor Jerome presented any new evidence or proof to back their assault, but instead relied on Opinion and Authority—the same mistake they're indirectly accusing the astrologers of committing.

My aim is not to defend astrology, but to present the truth as I have found it. It's no use, apparently, to present it to either side in the dispute; if they'd wanted such data it was there for fifty years or more for the taking.

If my cases of parallelism are purely anomalistic and a further study of other genetically unrelated Time Twins yields the exact opposite data, I will be just as satisfied to have it judged once and for all on the facts instead of bias or the emotional opinions of experts who know little or nothing about a subject they're condemning. I hold the same opinion about those who practice and defend astrology without ever checking the basic premises to question its validity.

I agree that astrology has never been conclusively proven on a purely scientific basis, and neither has it been disproven. I'm perfectly willing to present the results of my search in Bart J. Bok's own territory: fifty Time Twins all born at the time of the five-planet conjunction and total solar eclipse (in the zodiacal sign of Aquarius) on February 4 and 5, 1962 in Tucson, Arizona.

I suggest that the locations and identities of the families of those children be given to one or two disinterested or objective observers to be investigated on their own terms. I further suggest that you print my letter and this open challenge in your magazine.

Now that *The Humanist* has acted as the catalyst of what must by now be a tidal wave of reaction, pro and con, I'm sure that you—as a responsible editor and journalist—will want to examine ALL the facts, not just one set of opinions.

You can be certain that before long you will receive the signatures of several thousand astrologers to back a set of (lengthy) arguments citing the Opinion and Authority of experts in *their* field.

Sooner or later however, the facts will out. I was not prepared to present my data for another eighteen months, but your action prompts me to make this premature announcement.

With all good wishes,

*Joseph F. Goodavage*

\*      \*      \*

About a week later I wrote to Dr. Kornblueh, who had been keenly interested in and extremely helpful with my work. It had been a long time since we'd been in touch, and strongly suspecting what I was up against, I needed at least some moral support.

September 15, 1975

Igho H. Kornblueh, M.D.
American Institute of Medical Climatology
1618 Allengrove Street
Philadelphia, Pennsylvania 19124

Dear Igho:

I am writing at this time to ask whether the Institute is still interested in the results of more than a decade of my private research into the question of birth synchronism and possible parallelism of events in the lives of genetically unrelated children born at the same time and place.

This is particularly interesting in view of Professor Bart J. Bok's current statement in *The Humanist* (which attacks astrology and is signed by 186 scientists, 18 of them Nobel Prize winners).

My initial data indicates that Professor Bok and his supporters may be entirely wrong. In any case, no one—neither scientists nor astrologers—has ever undertaken the kind of research outlined in the copy of the letter (enclosed) signed by Forrest Speicher of the AIMC over a decade ago.

I would appreciate a statement of the AIMC's continued interest in the results of this study.

Many thanks,

Joe

\*   \*   \*

I also wrote to Professor Bart J. Bok on the same date:

September 15, 1975

Bart J. Bok
Professor Emeritus of Astronomy
University of Arizona
Tucson, Arizona

*Re:* "Objections to Astrology" (*The Humanist*—September/October, 1975)

Dear Professor Bok:

Your valiant and sincere effort to promote rationality about astrology is admirable. Your cause, however, can be much better served by a relatively simple, crucial test based on astrology's own chief instrument—the horoscope. Such a test, moreover, would be acceptable to scientists, understandable to laymen, and would put the question to rest for all time to come—for those who accept Nature's verdict.

The symbolic representation of the angular positions of the planets for a specific meridian is the horoscope, few of which are believed to be alike except for twins. According to the basic tenets of astrology, children born at the same time and place, even when genetically unrelated, must have an overwhelmingly significant number of life events and psychological characteristics in common because they share the same horoscopes. Although my initial research seemed to support this view, it was gleaned from newspapers and other periodicals which, on being checked, turned out to contain minor errors.

Since then, I have been sending questionnaires to the parents of children born during the most significant astrological moment of recent history—the five-planet conjunction and total solar eclipse of February 4–5, 1962. If astrology has no validity, these children should have no more in common than a control group chosen at random.

The volume of data I'd hoped for is short of my expectations, and the issue is still unresolved. However, it seems to me that only the unhinged would refuse to accept the verdict of the facts. Since you are ardently dedicated, intellectually honest, and committed to full disclosure of the facts about astrology, I would like to invite your participation in a novel test: I will furnish—either to you or anyone you designate—the names and addresses of fifty children born in the Tucson area during the stellium-eclipse of February 4–5, 1962—for an impartial investigation and comparison of major life events.

Sincerely,

*Joseph F. Goodavage*

* * *

When there was no response, I wasn't too surprised, but a month later, I received an interesting answer from one of astrology's most stalwart foes.

Professor Bok wrote that he had heard indirectly and from several sources about my earlier studies of identical twins, and felt that the subject was indeed worth following up. He approved highly of the project as outlined in my letter, but asked to be left out of the test picture for the very simple reason that he was a Professor Emeritus and living on limited pension funds. These funds were decreasing in value each year, and while he had a little secretarial help from the University of Arizona during his retirement, he was unable to take on any large-scale studies relating to astrology.

His energies and time were to be used for his continuing research on star birth and the Milky Way, the two fields of astronomy in which he had done the most work of the past decade. However, he assured me that he would read with greatest interest and care any results that might come forth from my work. He also stated that he thought my project was an excellent one.

Altogether, I considered this a fair letter from a man who had "paid his dues" and accomplished a great deal of important work—a fact I respected.

*   *   *

To my surprise, the editor of *The Humanist* (with whom Professor Bok, among others, had been in contact), wrote me on October 30, 1975 (the day after my birthday), that Professor Bok had sent a copy of my letter of September 15, 1975, and that he was going to publish it in the November/ December issue of *The Humanist*.

He asked me to send him the names of people born in the Tucson area on February 4–5, 1962, a period I had indicated as an astrologically significant time. Moreover, if I could do exactly the same for the Buffalo, New York area, he might be able to get a group of students and researchers at the State University of New York at Buffalo to conduct the research.

All he wanted from me was to instruct them in the method of locating "astral twins" in the western New York, Buffalo, Erie and Niagara counties areas, and they might be able to conduct an astrological test of my thesis. On the surface the message was very courteous and objective, clearly implying that *The Humanist* was deeply and sincerely interested only in obtaining honest answers.

This time he admitted having read my book, but found the data on astral twins that I had cited inconclusive and the controls virtually nil. This came as no surprise, although he did agree that some sort of tests that I had suggested might be useful.

I promptly provided him with all fifty of the names and addresses of children born in Tucson during the first week of February, 1962, but could not come up with the same data for the Buffalo, New York area, simply because there are not that many people born in the same place at the same time—about six to eight per minute in the entire continental United States. Apparently Kurtz decided this was a cop-out, and the correspondence dribbled off to nothing. He took no action whatever on the twenty-five sets of astro-twins I had sent him.

But he was preparing his *coup de grace* for astrology, for Time Twins and me. In the Winter issue of *The Humanist*, six cases of parallelism, chosen from the hundreds I had gleaned from various sources and written about in various books and magazines, appeared under the title "The Inaccuracy of Astrological Research."

The contradictory "evidence" was something less than objective, scientific, or even fair. Much of the piece was devoted to personal criticism when it could have (and *should* have) been spent unearthing original cases, new material, and trying to deal strictly with the evidence rather than personally attacking the author.

By early 1977 it became painfully obvious that no one connected with *The Humanist* intended to give the evidence a fair hearing. Therefore, when I responded to the attack, I also enclosed copies to several other publications, one of them the astrological magazine called *The Mercury Hour*. Editor Edith Custer of *The Mercury Hour* published my letter to Kurtz with my "Response to 'The Inaccuracy of Astrological Research' " with this preface:

*          *          *

"In the Nov./Dec., 1976 edition of *The Humanist* magazine there appeared an article in which the cases of time-twins cited in the well-known book, ASTROLOGY: THE SPACE-AGE SCIENCE, and other sources by Joseph Goodavage are attacked as all false. I wrote to Joe, who is a subscriber to the MH, and asked his views on the article. He sent me, along with his permission to print it in its entirety, his rebuttal to Paul Kurtz, editor of *The Humanist*. He also sent me 15 pages of (photocopies of) newspaper clippings, many relating to the stories he had originally quoted. The one related to Mrs. Hanna of Montvale and Mrs. Osborne of Allendale, sharing the same hospital room and giving birth on the same day to girls, appeared in one of Ripley's "Believe It or Not" columns. It seems rather unusual that the mothers didn't bother to deny the story when it appeared but denied most of it after being contacted years later. The New York *Daily News*, July, 1964, carried these words: 'The city's two top commissioners—Police boss Michael J. Murphy and Fire boss Edward Thompson—were both born on July 19, 1913, in adjoining neighborhoods in Queens.' The story of King Umberto I (1844–1900) also appeared in one of Ripley's columns."

*          *          *

I subsequently wrote to Professor Kurtz that I had read the Nov./Dec. 1976 issues, and enclosed my "Response to 'The Inaccuracy of Astrological Research,' " along with fifteen pages of photocopies of news clips indicating just a small segment of my research—the pages were longer than legal size.

I also included a copy of the letter supporting the continuation of the studies by the American Institute of Medical Climatology, typed and signed by Forrest P. Speicher, a copy of the Time Twin questionnaire, and Isaac Asimov's initial suggestions for continuing the research in *Analog* magazine.

"I'm sure," I wrote, "that publication, either in full or part, will be an interesting and valuable new addition to the pro- and anti-astrological viewpoints you've been publishing. Especially so, I think, since your Committee for the Scientific Investigation of Claims of the Paranormal is dedicated to the ideal of pursuing the truth—even when the facts may be distasteful or contradictory to previously held beliefs.

"As you will see by examining the enclosed material, the attack fails to vitiate the facts. Moreover, I know you will recognize the value of a test that will put the question of astrology to rest once and for all.

"I fully intend to abide by the verdict of Nature. I'm certain that you feel the same and that you will treat the enclosed with the same courtesy shown to contributors with whom you agree.

"Thank you,

"*Joseph Goodavage*"

"Response to 'The Inaccuracy of Astrological Research' "

*By Joseph Goodavage*

"This obscure and humble 'writer of pseudo-scientific features for various pulp magazines' (as I have been characterized in the November/December 1976 issue of *The Humanist*), was intrigued by the interpretation of the results of a long, hard crusade to discredit my research on twins and Time Twins.

"From nearly a hundred published reports, the writer's entire case consists of six obvious errors gathered from several of my books and magazine articles (four of which I freely acknowledged during a newspaper interview published in his own territory some time ago). The reason: all my original data was acquired through newspaper reports, magazine articles, science journals, and press releases during almost two decades of seeking some basis for otherwise unexplainable 'coincidences' I noticed recurring in the lives of twins. This study was later extended to include published (i.e., newsworthy) reports among unrelated people who experienced such 'unnatural' sychronicities of events that it became almost too shattering for conservative thinkers to contemplate. Far too many people who had undergone these parallelisms were born in the same year, month, and on the same date for it to be pure 'coincidence.'

"The available data from the media was (and is) a prodigious undertaking for a long researcher. I discarded scores of cases due to various inaccuracies, inconsistencies, even typographical and other errors, including (as armchair researcher Charles Fort observed) 'the lies, yarns, hoaxes and superstitions found everywhere, not excluding prestigious scientific journals.'

"Even after allowing an error factor in the neighborhood of ten to fifteen percent, a dim but discernible pattern clearly existed between time of birth and major events (including death) in the lives of people born at the same time and place.

"I hereby submit fifteen pages of photocopies of more than forty-five such unexplainable 'coincidences' among twins and Time Twins. By itself, this sample from my files is sufficient evidence to provide rational support for my theory. It is more than enough to neutralize any subjective or irrational rejection of the evidence. This is in fact intellectually persuasive proof. Even thousands of such cases, however, are just a modest beginning.

"More scientific, less vulnerable proof exists, available to anyone sincerely searching for answers derived from Real Universe data—hard evidence, not theory. (In the interest of honesty, rationality, and objectivity, the material on the first four to six pages, at least, should be published as is—including the biographical sketches of former New York Police and Fire Commissioners Michael J. Murphy and Edward Thompson, both born July 19, 1913 in the same neighborhood.) The writer's enthusiasm should demand that he disprove thirty or forty of these cases rather than choose six.

"It's worthwhile here to give some consideration to the familiar adage that 'A man convinced against his will is of the same opinion still.' That perverse tendency to gullibility and nincompoopery in the humans species applies equally to ALL zealots and cultists. (Not you and I of course—just all those other crackpots.) However, having had some intimate experience with it, I'm on familiar terms with this obtuse human characteristic and the formidable obstacle it has presented to every real inventor and true discoverer in history. Character assassination, calumny, imprisonment—even death—was usually their fate.

"Because of this I decided some years ago to focus my efforts on a very special group of people who—by definition—must be perfectly acceptable candidates to both friend and foe of astrology. One of the most unusual celestial events of modern times occurred on February 4 and 5, 1962, when Mercury, Venus, Mars, Jupiter, and Saturn aligned at the time of a total solar eclipse—all in the Zodiacal sign Aquarius. In several articles and books I made a 'call for data' from parents of children born during the first week of February, 1962 (deliberately extending the time period on both sides of the 4th and 5th so as to catch the anticipated 'fallouts' I'd receive).

"I've been collecting detailed questionnaires from those parents, and now from some of the kids themselves. One of the best-known foes of astrology, scientist and author Isaac Asimov, agreed last year to participate in an additional search (titled Crucial Experiment II) in *Analog* magazine for as many more cases of 1962's Time Twins as a published questionnaire would attract. Editor Ben Bova quickly discovered the complexities and obstacles encountered in this kind of research.

"Because of the minuscule response, Crucial Experiment II (which should have been at least as long as our very successful Crucial Experiment I—on astrometeorology—in 1963 and 1964) was scrubbed. But having been going it alone, making every conceivable mistake and encountering myriad obstacles for over a decade, I wasn't too surprised or disappointed.

"Since then I've read *The Humanist*'s editor's 'Special Report: Astrological Fallout' in the November/December 1975 issue. Paul Kurtz commented on the current epidemic of obscurantism by pointing out that the meaning of scientific enterprise has not been adequately conveyed to the general public:

'Our educational system has not succeeded in cultivating an appreciation for the standards of objective thinking or dispassionate inquiry. Yet the key point of the scientific method is that, unless one has sufficient evidence or reasons for a belief, one ought to suspend judgment.'

"With no quibbling about what constitutes 'sufficient evidence or reasons' I must agree. The Scientific Method as endorsed and taught is an excellent albeit not exclusive way of determining the validity of certain facts and theories. I'm reminded of George Bernard Shaw's riposte when asked what he thought of Christianity. "It's a wonderful idea," he said. "Too bad nobody has ever tried it."

"Item: Michel Gauquelin's interesting and useful studies notwithstanding, no scientists has ever applied the Scientific Method to the study of astrology.

"My own decade-long struggle to compile a statistical survey of a specific group—the aforementioned children born early in February, 1962—will become quite profitable during the next three years. For openers, those kids are now mostly high-school freshmen. Many have (or will have) lived sufficiently long to have had uniquely individual human experiences. By the time I've compiled a few thousand questionnaires of the many matching Time Twins, perhaps we can determine (statistics being a valid scientific tool) whether time and place of birth are indeed significantly important in determining psychological and/or psychological factors of human existence.

"One way or another, it is of no small consequence to know—for sure. Naturally, I admit to a certain bias: I've seen enough of these completed questionnaires to convince me that a pattern exists—Opinion and Authority with unsubstantiated, contradictory theories notwithstanding. People who can be intimidated by such unfounded negativism never accomplish very much. As John W. Campbell put it, 'My interest is in the progress of the human species. Anyone who opposes this is my enemy and I will do everything in my power to sabotage that person.'

"Ditto.

"To follow the facts regardless of where they lead is our

mutually *stated* objective. In this sense it would be singularly gratifying for *The Humanist* to support said objective by positive action. Rather than encourage bias or hysteria against an idea about which no one has produced a shred of rational (let alone scientific) evidence, I urge that—in accordance with the *stated* objectives of your Committee for the Scientific Investigation of Claims of the Paranormal—you publish the enclosed questionnaire—or provide valid reasons for refusing to do so.

"The subjective attack and its publication by *The Humanist* has renewed my determination to see this through to the very end. Whether 186 or 186,000 scientists oppose or condemn my work is immaterial and unimportant. But let one scientist or anyone else provide hard evidence, incontestable proof, that no undetected forces, no undiscovered energies, exist in the terrestrial and celestial environment which influence human life, and I will recant—in fact, I'll publicly retract everything I've said or written in favor of astrology.

"It seems very strange that no concrete proof to discredit this hypothesis has been found or announced by any scientist anywhere at any time.

"On the other hand, I'm presenting an array of natural evidence clearly indicating that such forces and energies exist, and that humankind is profoundly affected by them. Do we ignore it in favor of pursuing the usual nincompoopery (prejudging without adequate proof), or do we live up to our word?

"Your move."

\*     \*     \*

Kurtz moved, but not directly. I didn't hear from him again.

Then, in a letter dated April 26, 1977, the AIMC advised me that I was illegally continuing to use the name of the Institute. They demanded an immediate statement from me that I had ceased all such references, and threatened legal action if I continued my research. The letter was signed by a new Executive Vice President and Director, with carbon copies signed to Forrest P. Speicher and another member.

Since I hadn't heard from Dr. Kornblueh and was unable to contact him, I assumed he'd died. I ignored the letter from the AIMC, however, just on general principles. Four days later there was another letter on the AIMC letterhead, this one signed by Margaret Kornblueh, who had become one of the Institute's officers, replacing, I suspected, her husband. The gist of the letter was that I had falsely implied that the AIMC had authorized my research and that the undated letter *"allegedly"* written by F. P. Speicher was *not* an authorization and hereby disavowed.

Mrs. Jennie Goodavage never raised any boys stupid enough not to protect themselves in the clinches. I *still have the original of the letter* on the AIMC letterhead, typed and signed by Forrest P. Speicher, so the question of deliberate suppression of my work is *not only* legitimate but fairly typical of establishment scientists throughout history when their comfortable theories are threatened.

In conclusion, here are some observations on the subject by Ruth Hale Oliver, one of the most scholarly and intelligent astrologers in the business. They appeared in the Winter, 1977 issue of *The Mercury Hour*.

\*       \*       \*

"I think astrologers should be alerted by the material sent in by Joseph Goodavage . . .

"There was the recent attack on astrology and astrologers, in *The Humanist*. The 186 signers should have known better, and, to their credit, some scientists did refuse to sign the pronouncement and a handful even deplored it.

"This was followed up by a paper in which Goodavage's work on Time Twins was 'demolished,' which is legitimate, but, in addition, Joe was personally villified with name-calling hardly worthy of objective, truth-seeking scientists. His letter of protest was ignored, and he was given no chance to rebut those who 'demolished' his work.

"If astrology is really such quackery and superstition as the scientists claim, why are they exercised about it? Why do they mount this all-out attack? I think they fear astrology not as a superstition but as a heresy.

". . . Scientists do not care that many uneducated and superstitious people believe in astrology. They are deeply disturbed that any of their own college students have an open mind on the subject, that many people with degrees, and some of them with degrees in science, have an open mind on the subject, that some of them are testing it, and some have a modicum of belief in it. They are also perturbed that much of the generally literate public is sympathetic to the subject. They are disturbed that this unorthodox system of thought is not confined to the scientific community, but lies outside of it. If basic new theories are to be accepted, it can only be done by scientists—no one else should be allowed to present evidence which in any way contradicts current scientific dogma.

"But there is another basic question raised by Goodavage's material. It is book-burning, witch-hunting and the suppression of freedom of thought and expression. Even if scientists believe that astrology is pure nonsense, how can they have the nerve to try to eradicate it and to suppress the work of those who believe in it, and/or who are simply testing its tenets? I think the 186 should seriously consult their souls on this very matter."

*      *      *

At this juncture I'm more convinced than ever that astrology represents some part of a large cosmic pattern. It may lie beyond science today (as did the Sun-centered system of Copernicus when many "scientists" believed the Earth was flat).

So if enough of those born during the first week of February, 1962 will write me for a questionnaire, the broadside will, I assure you, be returned—in spades.

**2**

# What Is a Horoscope?

At the exact moment and from the specific location of your birth, the Sun, Moon and all the planets of the solar system were in specific places. Your horoscope is a map, "picture" or diagram of the heavens for that all-important event. The electromagnetic, gravitational pattern of the solar system at the time of your birth indelibly marks your personality and character. Let's say it happened in the fall—October 15, to be exact. You may call yourself a "Libran." If in November, a "Scorpion." What you *mean* by this is that the Sun was transiting through a certain Sign of the celestial Zodiac for an entire month. Many people were born all over the world during that month, but at the same time and place of *your* birth, chances are that very few or no other babies were born.

That map of the heavens as seen from a specific location on the Earth on a certain date in a certain month—in a specific year and at a certain hour and minute—is one of the most important factors in making you unique in the world. Chances are that no one with your horoscope has existed for 25,000 years and no one will be born with your horoscope for another 25,000 years. That's how long it takes for all the planets to return to their same positions, in their same signs and same relationships to each other.

In addition to the sun's being in any of the twelve astrological Signs, there are almost limitless ways for horoscopes to be different. If you have the sun in Gemini, you will learn here how this factor may be modified if the Moon was in the Sign Leo at your birth. Moreover, Jupiter might be in Sagittarius and/or Saturn might be in Capricorn, Mercury, never straying far from the Sun, must be in the Sun's Sign or the one before or after it. The chart of the heavens for your birth is one of the most important and valuable documents you will ever own, and you'll learn how to calculate it in these pages. Properly used, it can be worth more to you than insight, understanding, vocational counseling or money.

By learning how to set up and interpret even one horoscope, you will already have saved anywhere between five and twenty times the price of this book!

Nearly everyone thinks he knows what a horoscope is. Most people believe it is a prediction they read in the daily newspaper. But these are merely limited Sun Sign readings—interpretations based broadly on the daily position of the fast-moving Moon with respect to any of the twelve Signs of the Zodiac.

The same limitation applies to the monthly "guidance" articles in those astrology magazines you see on the newsstands. Most of them presume to reveal usually positive secrets about your future health, wealth and love. I don't intend these remarks as a blanket condemnation of this kind of entertainment. In fact those "readings" are what often attract people who then become really interested and eventually do serious research in better methods of astrological prediction.

All mass-produced so-called "horoscopes" apply to you as an individual only in a *general* way. They thrive as a publishing phenomenon because there are many people primarily concerned with their personal interests, who derive some kind of satisfaction from reading what the future might bring. Subjectively, the whole universe performs an orbit about each of us, and we tend to view ourselves in a most kindly light. My point is that no one, regardless of his objectivity, is able to see himself from the "outside." Although most books on astrology provide this kind of insight, they, too, concentrate solely on your favorable chances.

In all likelihood this is the quality that has made astrology such a perennially popular subject. Until the last few centuries only the horoscopes of kings, emperors and noblemen were considered of sufficient importance to be calculated and interpreted specifically and carefully. In time the rich and influential became astrology's foremost patrons; then came military men and politicians. Now you can probably find a competent professional astrologer somewhere in your own town. According to the astrologer's reputation and the amount of work done on a chart, the fee for a horoscope of you as an individual will vary between fifteen and one hundred dollars. The skills necessary to become a competent professional have never been fully determined, but *anyone* with average intelligence can learn to calculate a horoscope. Knowing how to *interpret* properly the myriad possibilities in a chart is another question entirely. Depending on the individual, it can take months or years. Good astrologers are forever learning something new.

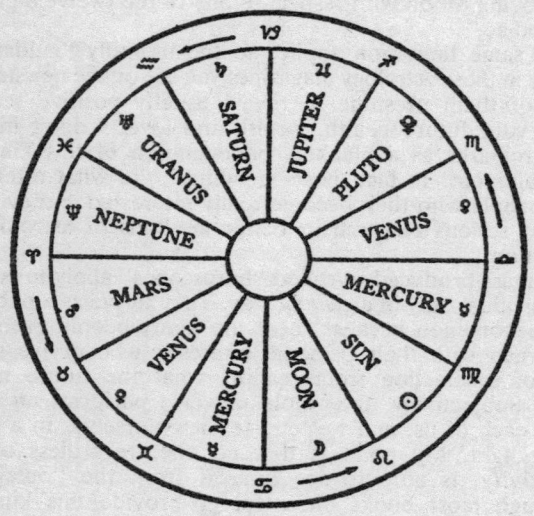

*Natural order of the zodiac, beginning with Aries (♈) on the ascendant. The ruling planet of each sign is in the Sign it rules, i.e., the influence of the Sign and planet are most nearly alike.*

Generally speaking, the radix, or horoscope, is an Earth-centered wheel divided into 12 radiating segments or "houses" and Signs. The houses always remain in the same positions, but the "spokes" of the wheel, the configuration of stars from your place of birth, at its exact time, can be in any of the twelve Signs. Often they overlap. Into these Signs and houses, symbols for the planets are placed; this part of horoscopy (ideally) is done with great mathematical and astronomical exactness. When you consider that there are 360 degrees to a circle (30 degrees to a Sign), 60 minutes to a degree and 60 seconds of arc to one minute of arc, it can become very exact indeed.

And yet in spite of this wonderful exactitude, some of the most excellent *personal* astrologers simply skip the use of logarithms or precision mathematics and scribble out a chart in a few minutes—using only *proportionate* math. Let's say they have an ephemeris (table of planetary positions), traditionally set up for noon, Greenwich time. If the birth time is six P.M., they simply add *one-fourth* of each planet's 24-hour motion to arrive at what are roughly the correct positions of the celestial bodies. You need not perform intricate logarithmic calculations here. By checking the lists of dates at the end of each chapter on each of the planets, you will not only learn where each was located at your birth, but *also what each position means.*

In the last paragraph I stressed the term "personal" astrologer. There are many different kinds of astrologers—including some who practice astrology but call it something else—like "solar biology" or "astrogeophysics," sometimes "geoastrophysics." It all boils down to the fact that there are areas of specialization within astrology that almost no one hears about. Take medical astrology, for example. There are only a few dozen medical doctors in the United States able to diagnose ailments according to the rules and aphorisms of Hippocrates, the medical astrologer of classic Greek antiquity. But they are largely concentrated in two groups—one in the east, notably New York, and the other in the west, mainly Southern California. Small as these groups are, they have stimulated a good deal of scientific research into what biologists once called "biological clocks." As a result, it is becoming more fashionable now to concede that many of the mechanisms which control living things are exogenous, i.e., emanating from terrestrial and extraterrestrial sources.

Another specialization in astrology is astro-meteorology—the prediction of weather on a seasonal or yearly basis by the setting up of charts of the heavens for the exact moment the sun crosses the equinoxes and solstices, the dates on which the seasons change—the four cardinal points of the celestial compass. This is a very ancient art and is probably the first use ever made of astrology. Chapter 16 will give you the details about how accurate this branch of the science of the stars can be when used with technical proficiency. It should also provide some insight into the workings of the Scientific Establishment. America's largest long-distance communications network times its short-wave broadcasts according to the advice of a staff astronomer who reports on favorable planetary conditions, i.e., when the angular positions of the planets cause clear weather.

Sub-specializations of astro-weather prediction include the forecasting of earthquakes, volcanic eruptions, drought and disease epidemics. Specific examples of how this is done appeared in *Astrology: The Space Age Science*.

Two founders of the American Federation of Astrologers, John Hazelrigg and G. J. McCormack, were successful in getting a fair description of astrology into the *New International Encyclopedia* in the 1940s:

Astrology is the study of the influence of the Sun, Moon, planets, stars on all things terrestrial, including man. It is based on experience in observing that world events coincide with mathematical patterns between, and cycles of, celestial bodies. Likewise, events in the lives of people coincide with changing relationships of celestial bodies to positions they held at birth. These can be accurately predetermined mathematically. Their manifestation is modified both by environment and heredity.

Originally there were two basic kinds of astrology, Natural and Mundane. Natural astrology is that branch out of which astronomy has grown. Mundane astrology is a study of planetary influences at times of earthquakes, epidemics, wars, good times, etc. As a result, natal astrology came into being, dealing with horoscopes of kings and rulers, and later, everyone.

In more recent times, like other sciences, astrology has

been divided into specialized fields, such as astro-psychology, -meteorology, -pathology, horary astrology, etc. Although often objected to as a pseudo-science, investigation has shown that these objections usually result from the misuse or adaptation of a few astrological principles for the purposes of attempting to tell fortunes. This is not the function of genuine astrology or sincere astrologers. Perhaps the greatest moral step forward for the proper application of astrology was through the formation of an American organization dedicated to investigation, research and education, which also established a code of moral ethics, and later an examination system with high tenets for those who profess to be astrologers.

History of Astrology. As archeological research penetrates ever farther into antiquity, it pushes back the birthdate of astrology. The earliest graphic records, the Chinese Trigrams of Fui-Hi, indicate that astrology was then well-defined in China. It antedates written records in India when Hindu astrology was first passed down by word of mouth. Study of the Hebrew Scriptures, the Old Testament of the Christian Bible, indicates the active use of astrology by the Hebrews. Western astrology grew from that of the Middle East. Isaac Newton pointed out its use by the first dynasties of Eygpt, quoting from Diodenos that the Chaldeans learned it from the Egyptians. Akkadian celestial observations date back to 4310 B.C.; the Tablets of Sargon I (circa 3800 B.C.) clearly show the Chaldeans were competent astrologers.

It later moved to Greece. Hippocrates, the "Father of Medicine," correlated the climactic periods in acute diseases to the motion of the Moon. From Greece, astrology moved to Rome and Arabia. But it did not originate in a single country. The earliest records of Mexico, Central and South America, and many other people of antiquity indicate astrological science developed proportionately to the advancement of the level of civilization of those people.

As predestination took over the philosophy of the Dark Ages, astrologers became fatalistic. All the great minds of ancient and modern history—from Hippocrates through Ptolemy, from Copernicus through Newton—first became astrologers. As man began to rid himself of the shackles of fatalism, astrology became less and less an attempt to tell fortunes. It was a method of interpreting celestial *influences* affecting the life of man.

In all fields of human endeavor and knowledge there are and have been charlatans. It would be eminently unfair to write a history of law, medicine or religion depicting disbarred lawyers, medical quacks and unfrocked clergymen. It is equally one-sided to refer to those who have misused astrological knowledge as though they were typical. No one knows what might have developed in place of the Copernican system, if Copernicus had not attended the great astrological school established at Craco by the King of Poland.

Terms in Astrology. Astrology has four principal terms: Zodiac, House, Planets and Aspects. There are many more, but these are basic. The zodiac with which the Western astrologer deals is the Sun's apparent path in the heavens which is inclined at an angle of 23° 27' to the celestial equator. Its twelve divisions are the signs of the Zodiac. The Houses are twelve equal divisions of space at a given time from a specific point on Earth. They relate to twelve major departments of life. The planets are those of our solar system. For the sake of convenience, however, astrologers refer to the Sun, a *fixed* star, and the Moon, Earth's natural satellite, as "planets." Aspects are the cyclical and geometric interrelationship of the celestial bodies. Some of these angular relationships are favorable, some adverse, and other are variable. Such aspects have been shown to be highly significant in medical and psychological studies, in the transmission and receiving of radio signals and in barometric changes.

Both officially and unofficially, nations and leaders, both of the past and present, have successfully employed the talents of astrologers. Sixteen years before the Great Fire of London, astrologer William Lilly predicted the disaster. In the same year (1651) Lilly also foretold that the Great Plague would spread throughout Europe in 1665. American astrologer Louis de Wohl predicted the successful invasion of North Africa, Sicily and Italy for Army officials in the Pentagon six months before it took place during World War II. But in natal astrology no sincere astrologer predicts a specific thing will necessarily happen to an individual on a given day. Certain trends can be timed with great precision; knowing in advance that a particular influence will prevail, one is in a position to take advantage of one situation or to avoid another.

This is a conservative description of astrology, what a horoscope is and how it may be used in the business of living. Although unofficially endorsed by the American Federation of Astrologers, it lacks the philosophical impact of the following statement from *Saturday Review* by Franz Hartman, M.D.:

"Man is the quintessence of all the elements, and a son of the universe or a copy in miniature of its soul, and everything that exists or takes place in the universe, exists and may take place in the constitution of man. The congeries of forces and essences making up the constitution of what we call Man is the same as the congeries of forces and powers that on an infinitely larger scale is called the Universe, and everything in the Universe reflects itself in Man, and may come to his consciousness; and this circumstance enables a man to know himself, to know the Universe, and to perceive not only that which exists invisibly in the Universe, but to foresee and prophesy future events."

It is extremely difficult for people living in a space-age technocracy to realize that the majority of the world's greatest scientists and philosophers of the past were in fact astrologers. Only a few scientists today are studying the influence of the stars and planets on human character and destiny. Yet this field was taken very seriously by the great thinkers of the past. Astrology, "the science of the stars," and astronomy, "the order of the stars," were two sides of the same coin. With the gradual acceptance of the Copernican system (which, incidentally, was powerfully resisted by scientists and astronomers of the time), the schism between astrology and astronomy grew wider, then became complete. Despite the current popularity of astrology, it has failed to enchant most modern academic or scientific communities.

Despite Hazelrigg's and McCormack's efforts, astrology is defined in *Webster's Collegiate Dictionary* (G. & C. Merriam Co., Springfield, Mass., Fifth ed.) as:

"The pseudo or (fraudulent) science which treats of the influence of the stars upon human affairs and of foretelling terrestrial events by their positions and aspects."

It is generally (though erroneously) believed that the Copernican system dealt the death blow to astrology because astrologers still use the geocentric [Earth-centered] system of horoscopy. Even near-illiterates today know that the Sun, not the Earth, is the center of our planetary system. Some astrologers who use the heliocentric system though, have had no better luck in gaining acceptance of astrology's basic tenets than those who still use the old Earth-centered system. Moreover, the latter have a more sensible stance: "If we lived on the Sun, we'd use heliocentric charts, but the fact is that we live on the Earth. . . ."

However it may be approached, astrology is usually treated as the pariah of all sciences. Some of the hatred directed toward the idea is surprisingly irrational. Here's what the *New Modern Encyclopedia* (published by Wm. H. Wise & C., N.Y.C.) has to say:

Astrology—The ancient art of divining future events, especially the fate of human beings, from the position of the stars. Among the Greeks and Romans the word was synonymous with astronomy, and it was not until the 16th Century that a clear distinction began to be made. Astrology owes its origin to the ancient belief that the Earth was the center of the Universe to which all else was tributary. The Chinese, Egyptians, Chaldeans, Romans and most other ancient peoples were implicit believers in astrology. Even some of the great astronomers who must have known they were perpetrating a fraud, received large fees for "casting horoscopes." During the Middle Ages the ordinary method of casting horoscopes was to divide a planisphere or glove into twelve sections by cucles running from pole to pole like those which mark the meridians of longitude. Each of the twelve sections was called a "house of heaven"; each house symbolized an advantage or disadvantage, and each was ruled by one of the heavenly bodies. As the Sun, Moon and stars all pass once in 24 hours through the heavens represented by the twelve houses, the important matter was to ascertain what house and what star were in the ascendancy at the time of the person's birth, because *all persons born in the same part of the world at the same time were supposed to have the same future.**

*Author's italics.

This idea vanished among civilized people when it was learned that the Earth itself is one of the heavenly bodies— but astrology still flourishes in Asia and Africa, and is practiced by charlatans in other parts of the world.

It is difficult to imagine how, if the idea of astrology is basically fraudulent and erroneous, it was *independently* discovered by the Incas of Peru, the Hebrews, Persians, Chinese, Indians, Europeans and Polynesian peoples. Either the whole world went insane in exactly the same way about an identical set of facts—or there is something of reality and truth in astrology.

Disregarding little gems such as the fact that Mark Twain swore by astrology all his life (he was born under Halley's comet and accurately predicted his own death by its return), it is staggering to think that the five men who are responsible for creating what is now known as the New Cosmology were all astrologers: Copernicus, Kepler, Galileo, Tycho Brahe and Sir Isaac Newton.

Even today, although officially without status, serious astrological research is under way in places as interesting as the Earth and Planetary Sciences, Division of the U.S. Naval Ordinance Depot at China Lake, California. Meteorologists at the National Center for Atmospheric Research and the High Altitude Observatory in Boulder, Colorado are also checking it out. The former director of NCAR and the High Altitude Observatory once even confessed that he knew how to cast and interpret horoscopes!

Essentially, the horoscope is a map of the heavens for a given moment in time from a specific location on the Earth. The patterns made by the planets and the aspects between them at the time of birth enable almost anyone who has studied the subject to deliver some remarkable interpretations of your character, personality, individuality. In many cases an astrologer will be able to forewarn you of an accident prone period, or to advise you that when, say, jupiter enters your house of money, it will be a good financial period, one in which you could make successful investments.

The horoscope blank is a wheel divided into twelve equidistant segments of 30° each. The lines dividing these segments are called "cusps" while the segments themselves are called "houses." Each house signifies a definite sphere of life activity. The houses are counted in a counterclockwise direction, beginning with the first house (or Ascendant) at "9 o'clock."

Not only is the influence of a planet modified by the sign it is in, it is further modified by the *mundane* house in which it happens to fall. If Mars, for example, falls in the first house, the Ascendant, its influence manifests itself physically, and you will probably have a prominent mark or scar on your face or head—unless there are good aspects from Venus, Jupiter, the Sun or Moon.

The twelve houses are roughly analogous to the twelve Signs, and in their chronological order. The first house equates to Aries, the second to Taurus, the third to Gemini, etc. Here are the twelve houses and the life activities with which they compare:

First house: Physical body, self-centered
   interests.                        ARIES
Second house: Money, possessions and
   security.                         TAURUS
Third house: Communications, relationship
   to environment.               GEMINI
Fourth house: Home, parent, beginnings
   and endings.                    CANCER
Fifth house: Children, amusements, recreation and display.              LEO
Sixth house: Health, service, efficiency.   VIRGO
Seventh house: Partner(s), unity with other(s) on a personal level.       LIBRA
Eighth house: Sex expression, self-sacrifice. SCORPIO
Ninth house: Travel (abroad), self projection to new horizons.     SAGITTARIUS
Tenth house: Career, material responsibility, social status.        CAPRICORN
Eleventh house: Friends, hopes and wishes;
   identification with group objectives.   AQUARIUS
Twelfth house: Self-undoing, escapism, confinement, self-sacrifice.     PISCES

In your horoscope, Jupiter acts as the principle of expansion, good will, good fortune, successful financial dealings and foreign affairs; you can easily anticipate the result when this great planet moves into the second (money) house of your chart.

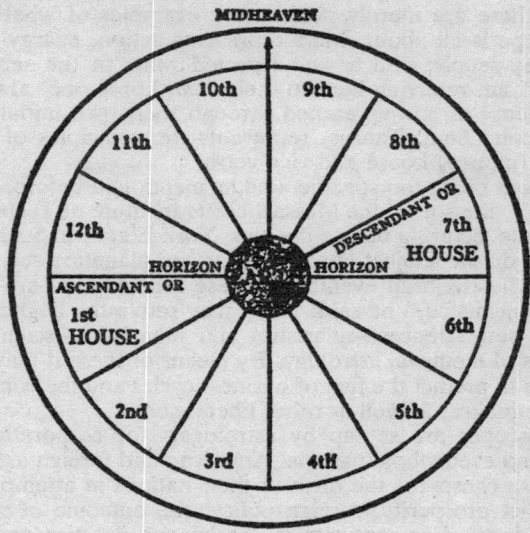

Without giving a complete description of *all* the planetary influences at the moment: the character of Saturn is almost the opposite of Jupiter; its influence is reflected in your life when this ringed planet moves into your second house of personal finances. Over periods of thousands of years during which billions of horoscopes were examined and compared, this planet has been shown to make people serious, profound and cautious, and to inspire excellent abilities to organize and execute plans for action. When transiting your *second* (financial) house, Saturn indicates a constricting or withholding of money, and means you must work even harder for what little you are able to come by.

People who have Saturn in the fifth house (of children, pleasure and amusement) at birth tend to be deprived of these things in their life. With *Jupiter* in the fifth at birth, there tends to be an *abundance* of the things represented by that department of life. This gets to be very complicated; for example, if someone has Jupiter (abundance) in the fifth house (children) and Saturn (constriction) in the second house (finances)—or vice versa, at birth.

Yet these are merely perfunctory examples of what the horoscope is all about. Mars represents action, energy and courage; people with a well-aspected Mars in the second house (I am referring here to their *natal* horoscope) always have plenty of money earned through their own initiative. The second Sign, Taurus, represents the principles of the second (money) house and vice versa.

Without being too specific, and as mentioned before, Dr. Harlan T. Stetson of the Massachusetts Institute of Technology, while lecturing before the New York Electrical Society, touched on the subject of solar, lunar and planetary correlations with terrestrial events: "If these relationships are not pure coincidence," he said, "they may prove the beginning of two new sciences—solaristics and lunaristics—scientific versions of medieval astrology. By means of these it may be possible to predict the flux of business cycles and the coming of earthquakes, as well as other phenomena."

Horoscopes are set up by astrologers for corporations, states and even whole nations. American and foreign astrologers use charts for the birth of their nations in attempting to predict prosperity, foreign policy, the outcome of wars and so forth. For centuries it has been a practice among Mundane or State astrologers (who predict events for nations, continents and cities) to calculate a horoscope for the exact moment a new ship is launched into the water. Using these charts, many astrologers have made remarkable predictions about the fates of certain ships. A comparatively recent case in point was the launching of the nuclear submarine *Thresher*. Soon after the *Thresher* slid from the stocks, a New York astrologer set up a horoscope for the launch and predicted to her class that disaster would overtake the huge submarine, with the possible loss of all lives aboard. The *Thresher* eventually broke up and sank, as predicted, with the loss of 129 men.

It seems totally and absolutely irrational to believe that cosmic forces could have anything to do with the fate or destiny of non-living things such as a ship or a space vessel. Yet astrologers seem to do this with confidence—and often with great success.

What special qualities or properties does a horoscope have? According to the *New International Encyclopedia*: "It is well to point out that the predictions of the better class of astrologers are not haphazard guesses, as is frequently supposed, but are based upon rigid scientific determinations from observed phenomena, according to rigid rules of interpretation . . . also that astrology lays no claims to absolute prediction of future events, undertaking merely to point out the direction which affairs are likely to take, other things being equal."

When you have finished this book, and I suspect you'll want to skip mostly to the meanings of the planets in the Signs at the time and from the place of your own birth, you should know enough about yourself to make some fairly accurate predictions, especially if you relate the configurations of the stars at your birth to the upcoming (or transiting) configurations.

**3**

# Three Power Points
# in Your Chart

Writer Hal Boyle once observed: "Whenever I see a young girl or an old lady reading an astrology book on the subway, I have the feeling that 5,000 years of civilization have gone down the drain of time."

Although his is a bigoted stance, I can understand how he feels. One difference between us, to me, is that I have concrete reasons for seeing *his* viewpoint. Boyle, on the other hand, knows little of a subject he publicly condemns. Never having done any hard research in the lives of people who share identical horoscopes, he cannot possibly know whether such people lead parallel existences or not. There is far more evidence in favor of this than either science or sociology currently acknowledges openly.

It's unfortunate that some young girls and old ladies credulously accept everything they read in astrology magazines. It is equally unfortunate that Hal Boyle earnestly condemns a subject he knows nothing about. Astrology isn't some sort of cult or religion. True, it isn't really a complete science, either—at least not in the accepted sense. But as long as you can go into it without taking astrology or yourself *too* seriously, it can be a lot of fun. It can also be an eye-opening adventure into the unknown. With astrology, you *are* able to determine the personality and basic character of almost everyone you meet. You can gain insight into the way others think, feel and behave.

Essentially, this tends to make other people and life itself more interesting. And it makes you more tolerant and kindly toward characteristic and personality differences. The ancient, basic rules of astrology do indeed work—just as they are supposed to.

There are some fundamentals. The position of the Sun is the single most important element in your chart. A man born with the Sun in Gemini, for example, is not as easy-going (or stubborn) as someone with the sun in Taurus. On the other hand, a Taurus Sun isn't usually as communicative, spontaneous or changeable as a Geminian.

Taking things in their proper order, the focal points of your horoscope are the *Sun's* Sign, the *Moon's* Sign and the Sign on the *Ascendant* of your chart. The Ascendant is covered in Chapter 6, and is determined by the exact hour and minute of your birth. If you don't have this information, it becomes more difficult to determine your correct Ascending Sign.

Keep in mind that the Earth (in fact the entire solar system) is totally surrounded by millions of stars—even whole constellations or groupings of stars. Along the belt of the ecliptic, i.e., the apparent path of the sun through the Zodiac, are the twelve main constellations (or Signs) with which we're concerned here, from Aries through Pisces. Just as the Earth orbits the Sun once each year, making it seem as though our local star were moving through each constellation, the Earth is also turning on its axis once every 24 hours. If you were born in N.Y.C. at 6 P.M. on September 3, 1942, the sky looked very different then than it did for a person born this minute in Los Angeles.

At night when you look at the stars or Moon over a period of time they seem to be sliding across the sky from East to West. The seeming motion of the cosmos causes the 12 constellations to rise or ascend daily from below the Eastern horizon and to set about 12 hours later in the West, depending on the latitude. Thus, if you were born on April 5 at 1:30 A.M. near the 40th degree of North Latitude, the *Sign* ascending would be Capricorn. Two hours later it would be Aquarius; in another two hours it would be Pisces, etc. Twelve Signs, each requiring two hours to "rise," complete the diurnal cycle or Earth day of 24 hours.

Sooner or later you're going to hear the argument that even if those stars *could* influence human life, they're not only too distant, but *they also are no longer there!* The light from some stars takes hundreds or even thousands of years to reach the Earth. What you're seeing is the light from a star that *used to be there*, but due to cosmic motion is, at *this* moment of time, someplace else.

This is a true statement of fact.

But astrologers use *Signs*, not the actual constellations for which the Signs were originally named. Because of what is called the Precession of the Equinoxes, i.e., the slow backward movement of the sun's apparent position with regard to the constellations, astrologers say the Sun *is* (for their purposes) in Taurus on April 29. And this method has been borne out enough times to establish it as valid. Astronomers, however, say it is in Gemini.

Astrologers who know astronomy have concluded that the stars and constellations are meant to be used as celestial *markers* for certain times of year on Earth. These positions, educated astrologers now believe, imply that a different geomagnetic condition exists at the equator than at the poles, say, and that there is variety from different longitudes and latitudes as well. (Coordinates such as right ascension and declination are extended into space in order for navigators and astronomers to locate quickly any celestial body.)

For example, the great planet Jupiter, when situated at the Vernal Equinox (the extended plane of the Earth's equator), has a completely different effect on the geomagnetic field than it has when transiting the Winter Solstice. Any astrologer who has ever seriously investigated this phenomenon has deduced that the *angles* formed among the planets as they looked when we were born are the cause of varying conditions in our lives. The Signs and constellations are merely points of reference whose real influence, if any, has never been scientifically determined.

Astrological Signs are 30-degree areas of space through which the planets move as they orbit the sun. The Signs of the Zodiac which comprise the constellations with which astrology is concerned are symbolized as follows:

| | | | |
|---|---|---|---|
| 1. | Aries | ♈ | Horns of a ram |
| 2. | Taurus | ♉ | Horns and head of a bull |
| 3. | Gemini | ♊ | A pair of twins, ideally Castor and Pollux |
| 4. | Cancer | ♋ | Stylized claws of a crab |
| 5. | Leo | ♌ | Capital lambda; first letter of Leo |
| 6. | Virgo | ♍ | ΠAP, first three letters of Parthenos, the Virgin, stylized |

| 7. | Libra | ♎ | A pictograph of a balance or scale |
| 8. | Scorpio | ♏ | A stylized scorpian |
| 9. | Sagittarius | ♐ | Arrow, symbol of the Centaur-archer |
| 10. | Capricornus | ♑ | Stylized version of a half-fish, half-goat |
| 11. | Aquarius | ♒ | Sumerian-Egyptian Symbol for water (the water bearer) |
| 12. | Pisces | ♓ | Stylized drawing of two joined fishes |

One result of NASA space probes is that increasing numbers of intelligent, unbiased people in all professions now realize that, basically, astrology has true merit. American Presidents Woodrow Wilson and Franklin D. Roosevelt, as well as some space scientists, have stated their conviction that man is indeed influenced by surrounding celestial forces. Photographer David Duncan, during a recent television interview, talked about his prize-winning pictures—photographs that have taken him all over the world, through several wars, and into the lives of great men.

"I was very interested in those astrologers who were guests here a few weeks ago," Duncan said. "I'm an Aquarian and I think there's a certain fate or destiny working in my life. I've always wanted to photograph beautiful things, but usually wound up taking pictures of violence and death. It seems to be inescapable."

This is the kind of clue by which any astrologer could deduce that photographer Duncan has a powerfully aspected Mars in his chart—or that the Signs of Scorpio and/or Aries are focal points in his horoscope, even though his Sun Sign is Aquarius. Scorpio and Aries are militant Signs closely associated with violence, war, and the military—and physical courage. His Sun Sign, taken by itself, is a powerful, but general indication of his character, and is strongly modified by other factors in his chart.

In your horoscope, the Sun represents the deepest part of your individuality. Wherever the sun happened to be at your birth, that Sign is usually the most powerful, overriding factor in considering your chart. This is why people are referred to as, say, Sagittarians, Aquarians or Taureans. They might *also* have the Moon in Capricorn, Aries, Leo—or *any* of the twelve Signs. And an Ascendant elsewhere. Another example: Someone with the Sun in Virgo might have the Moon in Cancer with Pisces Ascendant, yet they are still referred to as being a "Virgo."

In casting the horoscope, Mercury, Venus, Mars, Jupiter, Saturn, Uranus, Neptune and Pluto can be scattered around the Zodiac in any number of patterns. An astrologer will often find someone with the sun in Libra and five or six planets in Scorpio. In cases like *this*, the relatively weak Libran Sun may easily be completely overpowered by the "stellium" of planets in the strongest of all the Signs—Scorpio. This is a rare situation, however. The norm is that those who are born when the Sun is in any of the twelve Signs are called "natives" of that Sign because of the Sun's enormously powerful influence.

This could confuse people who know a little about the Egyptian, Greek, Roman and British versions of the twelve Signs. The stated physical characteristics of these Signs in turn do not seem to apply, say, to the Chinese, yet all Oriental peoples had developed a sophisticated version of astrology and astronomy before anything of its kind appeared in Europe. This also applies to the Incas of Peru and to what we prefer to call the ancient "Central American" nations.

It boils down, we must confess, to the fact that human *physical* characteristics (despite what some astrology books claim) are *mainly* influenced by genetics—only minusculely controlled by cosmic forces. By the same token, the most powerful and influential celestial body in our scheme of things is *not*, finally, the great blazing Sun, but our own planet Earth, on which we live and depend for our existence. An entirely new and probably more accurate kind of astrology will be introduced when Earth's exact influence is finally determined and included in the casting of horoscopes. This is not done today. Whether man actually originated on this planet or another world, as some scientists now propose, he has successfully adapted to *terrestrial* conditions, and is essentially a *Terran*.

(Almost all of Africa south of the Tropic of Cancer, by the way, is devoid of any original knowledge of the cosmos. In fact, no culture south of the equator has ever independently developed astronomy, mathematics *or even written a language of its own!* This is one reason why astrology addresses itself so largely to the Northern Hemisphere.)

All advanced cultures north of the equator seem to have independently discovered astrology, astronomy and mathematics, however. Every one of these nations agrees on the nature of the influence of the planets, the Sun and the Moon, the Signs of the Zodiac, and the existence and meaning of the four "elements," Fire, Air, Earth and Water.

It helps to realize that each of these "elements" (i.e., psychological conditions) relates to three of the twelve Signs. The first Sign, Aries, is called a fiery Sign (indicating zeal and enthusiasm) and is harmonious (by reason of its 120° or *trine* angle) with Leo and Sagittarius, also fiery Signs.

Taurus, the second Sign, is earthy (practical and constructive) and is in harmonious angle (120°) with Virgo and Capricorn, each of which are earth Signs.

Gemini, the third Sign, is airy (changeable and communicative) and is in trine aspect (or 120° from) the other Air Signs, Libra and Aquarius. (A popular misconception about Aquarius is that it is a Water Sign because its symbol is that of a Water Bearer, yet it is an *Air* Sign.)

Cancer, the fourth Sign is watery (emotional) and harmo-

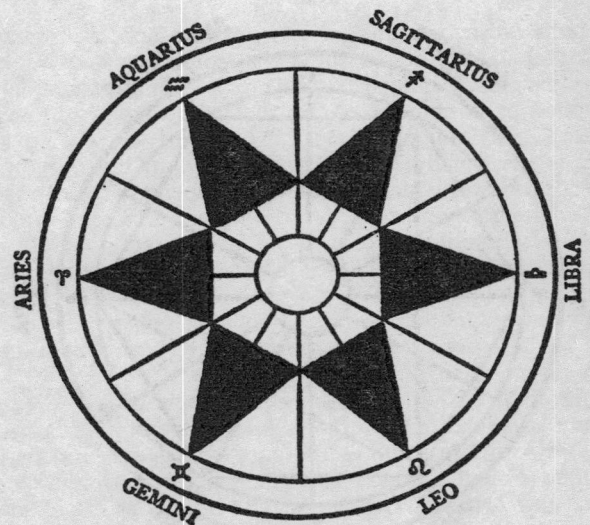

nizes with Scorpio and Pisces, also water Signs in "trine" or 120° aspect from each other.

Not only is the trine a fortunate and happy aspect among the Signs and planets, but even 60° or half this measure operates harmoniously. As a general rule of thumb, people born two months before or *after* your birthday (i.e. 60 days apart) are harmonious for you. Three months apart are harmonious. But 4 months, or about 120 days, is ideal. It makes sense if you consider that fire and water Signs do *not* mix well and that earth and water Signs instinctively tend to understand how the others think and feel. And it also works with the fire and air Signs. In the second instance, Scorpio (water) and Virgo (earth) are likely to be harmoniously related because of the 60° or sextile aspect existing between them.

With Leo (fire) and Libra (air), there is another sextile relationship, based on mutual or complementary views.

None of the foregoing implies, however, that people born with the Sun in Scorpio (water) and those born with the Sun

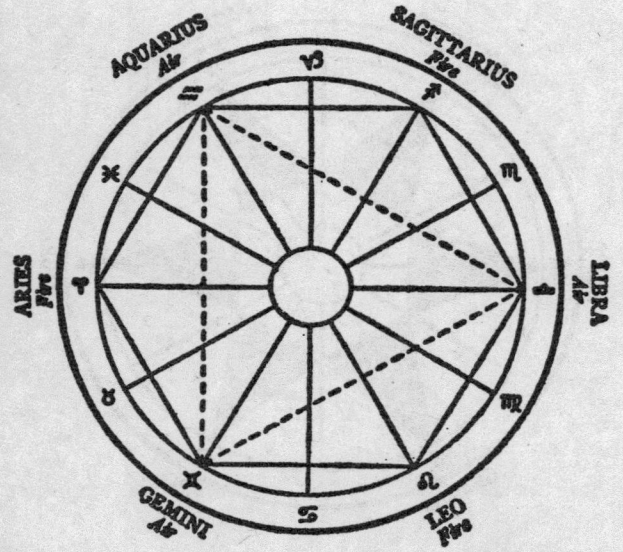

in Leo (fire), for example, can*not* get along harmoniously. Each horoscope (unless identical) is a different arrangement or pattern of planets, as we've said, and the Leo "native" may have a Scorpio Moon or Ascendant, thus giving an affinity for a Sign that would not otherwise attract.

Generally, this is how astrology works—the fundamentals painted in broad strokes. These rules can be quickly grasped and easily used by almost anyone. I'm going to avoid all possible technicalities here and acquaint you instead if I may with basic astrological data that you can easily check by only casual observation. It doesn't take long, and it's fun to see people thinking and acting in ways they're "supposed to"— according to their Sun Sign.

We've covered the twelve Signs and the four elements (which are repeated three times around the Zodiac). These

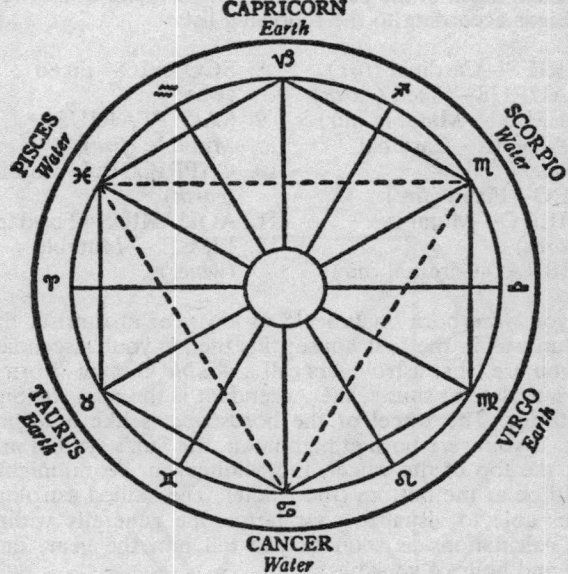

*The harmonious relationship (60° or Sextile) between water and earth Signs*

can be further refined to constitute *Cardinal*, *Fixed* and *Mutable* qualities. Consider the harmoniously *trined* fiery Signs, for example: although Aries, Leo and Sagittarius share the same basic fiery temperament, each expresses it in an entirely different and interesting way.

Aries is *Cardinal*, Leo is *Fixed* and Sagittarius is *Mutable*; yet all are fire Signs. These three adjectives apply to each of the four elements, and are therefore repeated four times around the Zodiacal wheel. Cardinal Signs (Aries, Cancer, Libra and Capricorn) are fast-acting, spontaneous. The fixed Signs (Taurus, Leo, Scorpio and Aquarius) are deliberate, difficult to move. Mutable Signs (Gemini, Virgo, Sagittarius and Pisces) are changeable, sometimes combine the characteristics of fixity and cardinality.

Beginning with the first Sign, Aries, you can quickly determine much of the personality and character of all twelve Sun Signs according to the following list:

1. ARIES—Cardinal (*fire*)
2. TAURUS—Fixed (*earth*)
3. GEMINI—Mutable (*air*)
4. CANCER—Cardinal (*water*)
5. LEO—Fixed (*fire*)
6. VIRGO—Mutable (*earth*)
7. LIBRA—Cardinal (*air*)
8. SCORPIO—Fixed (*water*)
9. SAGITTARIUS—Mutable (*fire*)
10. CAPRICORN—Cardinal (*earth*)
11. AQUARIUS—Fixed (*air*)
12. PISCES—Mutable (*water*)

If you were born on June 15 of any year at sunrise, then the Sun was in the first house; this then is your Ascendant, and you are what astrologers call a *double* Gemini. Born on the same date at sun*set*, the Ascendant is the *opposite* Sign, Sagittarius. The wheel of the horoscope is like a 24-hour clock. If you were born at high noon, the Sun's symbol must be at the top of the wheel, the Midheaven. At midnight it should be at the bottom (the Nadir). The skilled astrologer is thus able to visualize your horoscope generally without *exact* calculations as soon as you tell him the year, date, place and hour of your birth.

Every planet in your horoscope is characterized by and relates to one of the four "elements," and the Cardinal, Fixed and Mutable Signs. Your horoscope and all others (*except those of people born at the same time and place*) have different arrangements or patterns which can identify you almost as certainly as your fingerprints. It is physically impossible *even for twins* to share precisely *identical* horoscopes. Some twins, in fact, are born *hours* apart. This creates major differences in the Ascending Signs as well as in the position of the fastest moving of all celestial bodies, the Moon. In a comparatively short period of time, Mercury and Venus, also fast-moving planets, can orbit from one Sign to the next, either in different or retrograde motion (about which more later).

An important thing to remember is that, fundamentally,

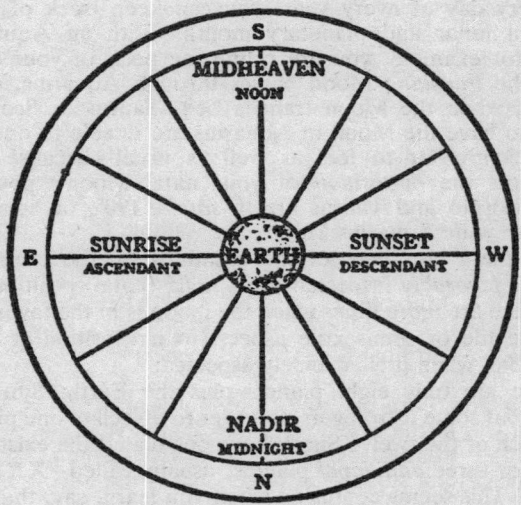

*In most temperate latitudes it takes roughly two hours for each Sign to "rise" as the Earth turns. If you were born at high noon anywhere, the symbol for the Sun (⊙) must be at the top of the chart. If you were born at midnight, the Sun's symbol must be at the bottom; at sunrise—in the east; at sunset—in the west. The horoscope is exactly opposite from a geographical map because you are looking upward at the heavens.*

the air and fire Signs are harmoniously aspected to each other, though *adversely* aspected to the earth and water Signs—and vice versa. (This is symbolized in Solomon's seal, or the Star of David, which was composed of two equilateral triangles, an upright one imposed upon an inverted one. It still survives as the religious symbol for world Jewry, yet most people seem to have little or no knowledge of the astrological wisdom it has represented since ancient times.)

The Sign of the Moon at your birth triggers certain events in your life each month as our natural satellite completes another orbit of the Earth. Let's say *your* Moon was in Aquarius when you were born. When you consult the listing of the planets' positions (in chapters Four through Thirteen) for every day of every year, you can keep track of your personal lunar and planetary month. With an Aquarian Moon for example, you are riding the peak of your cycle when the *transiting* Moon passes through Aquarius. Conversely, when the Moon transits Leo, Taurus or Scorpio, you who have the Moon in Aquarius are unable to operate as efficiently—or to feel as well as usual—because Leo represents the *opposition* of your natal Moon's position while Scorpio and Taurus are in *square* (90°, or adverse) aspect to your Aquarius Moon.

And there are times of the month when the transiting Moon is *favorably* inspected to its *radix* (natal) position. In fact, there are *more* times when the moon is in the favorable trine, sextile or semisextile aspect (to its position at your birth) than when it is adversely aspected.

There are only eight planets plus the Earth, Sun and Moon, but some astrologers, in order to associate one planet with each of the twelve Signs, have postulated the existence of two or three *additional* planets, usually called "X," "Y" or "Z." This seems confusing when you learn, say, that the Moon is the ruler of Cancer and the sun is the ruler of Leo. Neither of these celestial bodies are "planets." The ruler of a sign is that celestial body whose characteristics are most like the sign. Leo (Sun) people are dramatic, bold, regal. Cancer (Moon) people are sensitive and impressionable. Still, there's some kind of harmonious vibration between each heavenly body and the signs of the Zodiac. Every Sign has a planetary "ruler," but Mercury, Venus and Mars have traditionally been assigned as the rulers of *two* Signs each.

Mars is ascribed as the ruler of the first Sign, Aries, and also the eighth Sign, Scorpio.

Venus rules the second Sign, Taurus, and the seventh Sign, Libra.

Mercury rules the third Sign, Gemini, and the sixth Sign, Virgo.

The Moon rules the fourth Sign, Cancer.

The Sun rules the fifth Sign, Leo.

Jupiter rules the ninth Sign, Sagittarius.

Saturn rules the tenth Sign, Capricorn.

Uranus rules the eleventh Sign, Aquarius.

Neptune rules the twelfth Sign, Pisces.

The anomaly that has arisen since the discovery of Pluto in 1931 has been the assigning of this outermost planet to the Sign Scorpio, leaving Mars as the ruler only of Aries.

The Sun, Moon and Ascendant in most horoscopes are usually in three different Signs. There will be times, as we've noted, when a native will be born at sunrise, so his Sun Sign and Ascendant will be the same. If that Sign happens to be Virgo, he is called "a double Virgo." with the Sun *and Moon* in the rising Sign (or Ascendant) he's a double Virgo with the Moon on the Ascendant. Although it is rare, there are some gifted people born during a New Moon or eclipse who also have a whole stellium or grouping of planets in the ascending Sign.

A classic example of this happened on February 4th and 5th 1962. This was the date (depending on which side of the International Date Line you lived) on which the rarest astronomical phenomena in thousands of years took place. All five of the ancient planets: Mercury, Venus, Mars, Jupiter and Saturn, *plus* the Sun and Moon orbited into near-perfect alignment in the scientific-humanitarian Sign of Aquarius. Five planets in one sign is rare enough, but this occurred at the exact time that a total solar eclipse took place.

The astrological community knew about it many years in advance, and had been predicting great scientific and socio-logical upheavals. Moreover, those children born at (or close to) the Great Conjunction-Eclipse, they reasoned, would eventually become the nucleus of the greatest advancement mankind has thus far achieved. The astrological press throbbed with warnings of things to come as a result of this extraordinary celestial event. Unfortunately, a mere handful of Indian zealots, who use a different system of astrology from that of the Western hemisphere, were preparing for the end of the world—and received almost all the press coverage.

(According to the most ancient Hindu predictions, whenever the Sun, Moon and planets line up in *Capricorn*, all civilization will be destroyed and a new World Age will begin. The present Hindu system of astrology is one Sign (30°) different from the Western "Tropical" Zodiac. While American and European astrologers anticipated immense social and technological changes because the conjunction-eclipse would occur in *Aquarius*, the Hindus clung to their old systems, expecting it to take place in Capricorn.)

A single blood-chilling fact emerged from comparisons of the horoscopes of world leaders to the charts of the conjunction-eclipse. Saturn has always been considered a "malefic" planet, representing serious obstacles, and eclipses indicate radical change, often by violence and death. Six months before the great celestial event, astrologers noted that the rare eclipse would take place at the exact degree of President John F. Kennedy's natal Saturn, which at fourteen degrees of Aquarius was in the house of his career. Combining this evidence with other astrological factors, it was universally dreaded that President Kennedy would be assassinated. One of the most outstanding astrological predictions ever made was that his assassin would *also* be assassinated! (*American Astrology*, November, 1963)

The Midheaven, or President Kennedy's tenth house, was a focal, Cardinal point in his chart. With Saturn at that point in his horoscope, many astrologers who diligently searched for future planetary transits foresaw that tragedy would strike when the eclipse triggered that fatal degree of his chart.

Would anyone, knowing that such high political office might cost his life, turn it down? It hardly seems likely, but we'll explore the possibility of fate and free will in the final chapter.

*Horoscope blanks*

Horoscope blank; locate your Ascendant or rising Sign on pages 156–159, place the symbol at the "9 o'clock" position, then fill in the succeeding symbols in a *counter-clockwise* direction. At the end of each chapter outlining the influences of the planets, find the Zodiacal Sign each planet was in on your birthdate, then insert the symbol for that planet between the proper "spokes" of the horoscope wheel. Page 162 shows the symbols for the planets and Signs.

*Horoscope blanks*

*Horoscope blanks*

THREE

*Horoscope blanks*

*Horoscope blanks*

*Horoscope blanks*

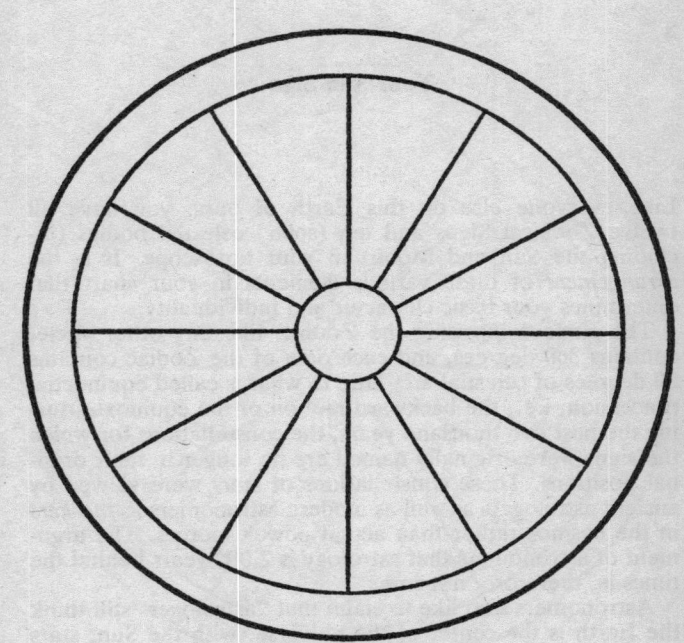

*Horoscope blanks*

**4**

# Your Sun Sign

Like everyone else on this Earth of ours, you have all twelve Zodiacal Signs and ten (solar) celestial bodies (including the Sun and Moon) in your horoscope. It is the *arrangement* of these various elements in your chart that determines your basic character and individuality.

The circle comprising the Zodiac, like any other circle, contains 360 degrees, and each *Sign* of the Zodiac contains 30 degrees of celestial arc. Due to what is called equinoctial precession, i.e., the backward motion of the equinoxes during the past two thousand years, the constellations for which the signs were originally named are no longer in their original positions. These constellations of stars were viewed by ancient astrologers as well as modern astronomers as *markers* in the cosmos rather than actual power sources. The argument of astronomers that astrology is 2,000 years behind the times is, therefore, not true.

Astronomers also like to claim that "astrologers still think the Earth is the center of the universe, with the Sun, stars and planets all revolving around it." Astrologers do realize that the sun is the center of our solar system, of course, but they also recognize that we live on the Earth (*not* the Sun) and are more interested in what happens to us on *this* planet.

If you were born with the Sun in the Sign of Cancer, Scorpio or Pisces (the Water Signs), the first *decanate* (ten days, or ten degrees) is different from the second and third decanates.

In addition to the *Water* Signs, there are three *Air* Signs, three *Fire* Signs and three *Earth* Signs, as I have indicated. And their decanates vary as well. Water in astrology indicates *emotion*.

The Air (*mental*) Signs are: Gemini, Libra and Aquarius.

The Fire (*enthusiasm*) Signs are: Aries, Leo and Sagittarius.

The Earth (*practical*) Signs are: Taurus, Virgo and Capricorn.

You have *all* these Signs in your horoscope; everyone does. But there are different degrees of the various Signs on the Ascendant (the rising Sign), in the Midheaven and on other parts of the chart. In part, this is what makes each of us interesting and different.

At this point we are dealing solely with the position of the Sun—the single most important and powerful element in your horoscope. In astrological language the sun is dry, masculine and life-giving. Our local star rules your individuality. (In this chapter on medical astrology, you will learn how the Sun rules the heart, the right eye of the male and the left eye of the female.) Its position in your chart also determines your individual success and social progress—your position in life.

The dates for the Sun's entry into each Sign are given here, but there are some years when this happens a day earlier or later than the times shown. If you were born well within the mentioned dates, you can be certain you belong to that group. If you were born at the change of Signs (called the cusp), then you are a combination of both and should read both.

Dates for the position of the Sun are given *before* each Sign is delineated. For the Moon and planets, the dates are given at the *end* of each chapter.

SUN IN ARIES: first Sign. Cardinal, fiery and masculine.

$$\odot \quad \aries$$

*(Between March 20 and April 20)*

Born when the sun is in Aries, you are pioneering, headstrong and impulsive. Full of ambition, you love new ideas and enterprises. You have tremendous enthusiasm, persistence and will power, but need to exercise discretion in personal dealings. You are inclined to go right to the point, even if it means being blunt. Indignation and anger come too easily, and your remarks can be cutting. Nobody bosses you around; you'd much rather be at the head of your own organization or at least leading the field in some new endeavor. You are self-assertive, impulsive and restless—always giving the impression of urgency. Although you probably have a fiery temper, you don't hold a grudge for long. You have a great love of justice, freedom and individual determination. The Aries man is usually frank and direct, a freedom-loving go-getter. The female of this interesting, zealous Sign is capable and ardent. Born between March 20 and March 30, the first decanate of Aries, you are inclined to be more pioneering and adventurous than usual. If you were born between March 30 and April 10, read the paragraph for LEO to gain further insight into your generous, proud and dramatic nature. If born in the SAGITTARIUS decanate of Aries (April 10 to April 20), read how the open, ingenious, sports-loving influence of Sagittarius affects you.

SUN IN TAURUS: second Sign. Fixed, earthy and feminine.

☉ ♉

*(Between April 20 and May 21)*

You like to take your time about things. You are extremely patient and probably have a pleasant, melodious voice. Your symbol is the bull—gentle and yielding when things are going smoothly, but if provoked you become angry, even furious, and difficult to appease. You are constructive, methodical and deliberate, but not very original. You'd rather follow the accepted and reliable paths worn by others. In a negative sense there are times when your natural caution and prudence degenerate into obstinacy and stubbornness. This is when you are too heavy and possibly something of a bore. The Sun in Taurus makes you stable, firm, self-reliant and persistent. You are willing and able to wait a long time for your plans to jell. You have an inordinate love of comfort and ease; the physical pleasures hold a great deal of interest for you. Venus, your ruling planet, gives you a love of peace and beauty in nature. You love amusements, good books, music and art. You have excellent powers of endurance, a sound sense of material values. Despite what is said about your love of leisure and contentment, you can be a hard, methodical worker as long as there are no sudden changes and if security is the ultimate goal. You are possessive, affectionate and sensual, completely aware of the powers of your body. If you were born between April 20 and April 30, you are more reliable, practical and steadfast than most other Taureans; you *must* have security. Born between April 30 and May 10, the VIRGO decanate of Taurus, see that Sign for its intelligent, discriminatory influence. If you were born in the CAPRICORN decanate of Taurus, between May 10 and May 20, you have high ambitions, are extremely practical, secretive and reserved; see Sun in CAPRICORN.

SUN IN GEMINI: third Sign. Mutable, airy and masculine.
☉ ♊
*(Between May 21 and June 21)*

You are the *communicator* of the Zodiac, easily recognizable for your active mind, quick wit and conversational ability. Many people born in this Sign (Mercury, "messenger of the gods" is your planetary ruler) are found in occupations where correspondence, writing, transmission or the exchange of ideas play a large part. You are excitable and mentally agile, very hard to pin down. You insist on doing things your own way, which could be very difficult for others unless they unquestioningly accept your duality. You are ingenious for figuring out ways of transmitting things from one place to another. You are ambidexterous, versatile and alert, but can be restless, inquisitive and a waster of your own energies. One of Gemini's chief faults is a tendency to be too changeable and unreliable. You are easily influenced by kindness. Apt to be a good, quick reasoner, you love logic—or at least your version of it. With the Sun in Gemini, you often seem superficial, but like Virgo, you enjoy experimentation and proof, or at least strong evidence. For this reason you'd make a good investigator, with your flair for the spoken or written word. Whatever you learn is quickly imparted to others; it is difficult for you to be secretive. You are interested in the sciences, you like to read and can easily undertake two or more occupations at once. Your active imagination can work for or against you, but you are usually able to arrive quickly at conclusions not easily reached by others. Generally, you have a kindhearted, sympathetic disposition but your sensitivities are myriad. You are idealistic and guided by a strong intuitive faculty. You like being busy and almost never lose your ambitious streak. Most of the obstacles and setbacks you experience are caused by your love of diversity and variety. Born in the first decanate, between May 21 and May 20, you are very strongly ruled by GEMINI. Between May 30 and June 10, read LIBRA for the influence of this peace-loving Sign of artistic and musical appreciation. If you were born between June 11 and June 21, read AQUARIUS to learn how this idealistic, inventive, humanitarian Sign influences the third decanate of Gemini.

SUN IN CANCER: fourth Sign. Cardinal, watery and feminine. ☉ ♋
*(Between June 21 and July 23)*

The Moon, fastest moving of all celestial bodies, is the ruler of Cancer. Born when the Sun was in Cancer, you are sensitive, versatile, and shy. Still . . . you love publicity and the limelight. Whether you show it or not, you are inordinately sensitive and influenced by kindness, consideration sympathy; you fear criticism or ridicule. You are moody, sentimental, imaginative and sympathetic. While outwardly giving the impression of self-assurance, you need security. Like your symbol, the crab, you have a self-protective, hard outer shell to hide your sensitive, soft interior. You are attracted to the mysterious and occult and probably like astrology, strange adventure and the mysteries of nature, particularly on and in the sea. Your sensitivities are not confined to people; emotional receptivity makes you vastly influenced by your surroundings. You probably have a nice comfortable home, a womblike shelter where you can withdraw to restore your self-confidence. One of your idiosyncrasies is having something to eat and drink nearby, whether you are at home or traveling. Cancer rules the stomach and emotions. You are changeable and therefore have experienced the vicissitudes of life, with many changes in occupation. You are extremely frugal, prudent and industrious. You are conscientious in your work and usually manage to squirrel away a fair portion of your earnings. Since Cancer has the most retentive memory, you never forget a cut or a kindness. You love your country, your home and family. You revere your ancestors and might have the family coat of arms hidden away somewhere. Some of the best patriots and founders of fortunes are born in this defensive, protective sign. If your birthdate is between June 21 and June 30, you are in the CANCER decanate of this sign. If born between July 1 and July 12, read SCORPIO for an insight into this shrewd, powerful, secretive decanate of your Sign. If you were born between July 13 and July 23, read PISCES for the psychic, mediumistic qualities of this Sign in your decanate.

SUN IN LEO: fifth Sign, Fixed, fiery and masculine.

☉ ♌

*(Between July 23 and August 23)*

The blazing Sun is the ruler if Leo, whose symbol is the kingly lion. You are frank, open hearted, generous and philanthropic, with a marked dramatic flair. There is a basic conflict in your nature caused by the static quality of a *fixed* Sign with the highly active fire element. You hate being bogged down in details and prefer doing things in a big way. Leo rules the heart and affections. You are a sincere affectionate lover; you thrive on it and are sincere in your desire to bring happiness into your loved one's life. You are a natural leader who feels instinctively that your place in life is one of authority and organization. You are rarely small or mean in your desire to lead and rule, but there is a chance that your great sense of pride might seem overbearing or dominating to others. You are sincere, ardent and highly appreciative of affection freely given—and you generously return it. With your philosophical, active mind and warm disposition, you have many friends who admire your independent, determined, ambitious nature. You have a strong, forceful personality and are quick to anger; like Aries and Sagittarius, however, you are equally quick to forgive. You tend to carry yourself with a kind of regal bearing and are powerful and forthright in your expression. You like the fact that your kind of physical magnetism doesn't go unnoticed. You also love drama, a high position in life—and children. Leo is an inventive, intuitive sign, industrious, honest and fond of sports. Your active mind, candid nature, generosity and sincerity are an enormous help up the ladder of success. You express an impressive urge for authority. Born between July 23 and August 2, you are in the LEO decanate of Leo, self-expressive, intense and spontaneous. Between August 3 and August 12, read SAGITTARIUS to learn how this outgoing, sportsmanlike sign influences the second decanate of LEO. If you were born between August 13 and August 23, you are an impetuous, interesting combination of Leo and the ARIES decanate of this sign. Read Aries.

SUN IN VIRGO: sixth Sign. Mutable, earthy and feminine.

⊙  ♍

*(Between August 23 and September 23)*

Although you have a mercurial disposition and may be quick to anger, you'd rather negotiate your differences than face possibly ruinous combat. Virgo, like Gemini, of which Mercury is co-ruler, is a sign of mental activity. You are good with the written and spoken word and are a good, logical reasoner; this gives you the ability to learn quickly and you have a vast store of knowledge of which few are aware because of your naturally reticent disposition. You are serious, thoughtful, modest and hard-working. In fact, a lot of your time is spent in service to others, one way or another. Your chief desire is to acquire knowledge and achieve mental refinement. Although inclined to worry too much about small details that escape most people, you are not easily discouraged. Mentally, you are a detailer, practical and cautious, with good foresight. High on your list of interests are diet and hygiene. You are critical, dicriminating and practical. You seek to evaluate life by the analysis of facts and logic. You are active and interested in many things, but these interests often change. You are reserved, conscientious and precise, a lover of art, literature and orderliness in everything. You desire the material blessings of life but cannot easily acquire them. People born with the Sun in Virgo seldom show their true age; it is one of the long-lived Signs. If you were born between August 23 and September 2, the first decanate, the foregoing tendencies of VIRGO are intensified. Born between September 3 and September 13, the CAPRICORN decanate of Virgo, read CAPRICORN to learn how this ambitious, enduring, persevering Sign influences you. Read the influence of TAURUS if you were born in the third decanate of Virgo—September 13 to September 23; this gives you the constructive, beauty-loving wealth-attracting talents of TAURUS.

### SUN IN LIBRA: seventh Sign. Cardinal, airy and masculine. ☉ ♎
*(Between September 23 and October 23)*

You love peace, beauty and harmony in your life. Chances are you either have married—or will marry—comparatively early in life. With Venus as the planetary ruler of your Sign, you dislike drudgery or any kind of dirty work. You are modest, artistically inclined, neat and particular. You love the arts and all cultural pleasures and amusements. You make the most agreeable and pleasant sort of friend, and are a natural peacemaker. At heart you are a perfectionist and are completely unhappy when placed in an environment of conflict or discord. With the Sun in Libra, you desire peace, justice and harmony in all things. You are sensitive to the conditions of friends and associates; this is particularly so in regard to your marriage or business partner. Libra is a sign that bestows a sure sense of equilibrium; you are usually known to be charming, kind, easy-going, courteous and agreeable. You may be artistically or musically inclined or trained. You can usually be found wherever there are gay social activities. You enjoy social success through your pleasant disposition and cheerful outlook. If you were born between September 23 and October 2, the influence of LIBRA will be more pronounced than at any other birthtime in October. If born between October 3 and October 13, read AQUARIUS to learn how you are influenced by this detached, scientific, humanitarian Sign. Born between October 13 and October 23, Libra blends with the GEMINI decanate to produce an interesting combination of changeable mental activity with the diplomatic characteristics of Libra.

### SUN IN SCORPIO: eighth Sign. Fixed, watery and feminine. ☉ ♏
*(Between October 23 and November 22)*

Scorpio is the most occult, secretive and powerful segment of the Zodiac. You who are born when the Sun was in this Sign are suspicious, skeptical, critical, reserved and calculating. Unless other factors modify these basic characteristics you are forceful, blunt and sarcastic. In competitive professions such as politics and law you can be extremely aggressive. At best, the Scorpio influence makes you courageous, creative and scientific, capable of boldness and daring. Most of your success in life stems from originality and shrewdness. You tend to mind your own personal business and expect others to do the same. It may be a different story in your profession or career, however. The chances are that you cause trouble for others. There is an intensity of thinking and feeling in you, a certain inflexible strength of will, the power and passion of deep inner conviction. You have tremendous reserve energy and recuperative ability. No other Sign ranges so widely between good and evil. Scorpio is the only Sign with three symbols: the lowly, deadly scorpion; the serpent, symbolizing wisdom, and the high-soaring eagle, symbolizing spiritual attainment. You have a deep love of the elemental powers of nature and are strongly conservationist. You find the sea and all activities connected with it a source of never-ending interest. You are cagey and economical on one hand and fond of luxuries on the other. There is also a kind of basic Spartanism about you, a certain willingness to rough it, or to tear everything down and begin all over again. You have shrewd, keen judgment and the ability to size up situations and people at a glance. Your emotions run deep and strong; few people know what you are thinking, except that you have strong likes and dislikes. If you were born between October 23 and November 2, the SCORPIO decanate of this Sign, you exhibit the strongest characteristics of this powerful Sign. If born between November 2 and November 12, read PISCES to learn how this psychic Sign influences the second decanate of Scorpio. Between November 12 and November 22, read the characteristics of CANCER to learn how this defensive, possessive Sign influences the third decanate of Scorpio.

SUN IN SAGITTARIUS: ninth Sign. Mutable, fiery and
masculine.  ☉  ♐
*(Between November 22 and December 22)*

More than any other Sign you love your liberty, freedom, independence. You hate bosses and dictatorial attitudes, and tend to view attacks on the weak or helpless as a personal affront. You are self-reliant, candid in your opinions, frank and outspoken in your judgments. You are ambitious, honest and possess a great store of friendliness and good will toward others—until they prove to be unworthy of it. Your symbol is the archer, half man, half horse; your remarks usually fly like arrows, directly to their mark. You have a love of outdoor sports, a respect for science, philosophy and religion. Since you are frank, honest and outspoken, you need to develop diplomacy; Sagittarians can be blunt, penetrating or cutting in their remarks. Generally, however, the sun in Sagittarius makes you generous, bright, hopeful and jovial. You have a charitable, ambitious and active nature, are not easily discouraged. You are able to make fast calculations and have a great deal of foresight that verges on the prophetic. You can often foresee the outcome of world political movements long before they become apparent to others; this also applies to business enterprises or personal developments. With your earnest, generous and charitable nature, there are times when others try to impose upon you. Fortunately, your ability to size up an individual or a situation makes these attempts transparently clear. Few people can fool you for very long. if you were born between November 22 and December 1 the SAGITTARIUS decanate of this jovial Sign, the foregoing applies doubly to you. If you were born between December 1 and December 11, the ARIES decanate of Sagittarius, read the characteristics of this fiery, pioneering Sign to learn how it modifies your basic nature. Read the influence of LEO if you were born between December 11 and December 21, because this proud, noble Sign has left its indelible imprint on your basic character.

SUN IN CAPRICORN: tenth Sign. Cardinal, earthy and feminine. ⊙ ♑
*(Between December 22 and January 19)*

The symbol of the tenth Sign of the Zodiac is the climbing, persevering mountain goat. Like this tough little animal, you find many obstacles in your path as you struggle toward your goals. By sheer persistence, patience and concentration you are eventually able to overcome all obstacles in the way of success. You are often disappointed but never entirely discouraged. With the Sun in Capricorn you act with dignity and a good sense of your own values. You have a good mind and solid reasoning ability. Usually thoughtful, quiet and serious, you make a natural executive. There may be a tendency to have trouble with your knees or to experience hyperacidity of the digestive tract. This is often brought about by worry or the suppression of emotions. You tend to be somewhat too conventional, too severe in your judgments, and rather cool and calculating in your affections. You are practical, economical and a good investigator. Being cautious and frugal, you make the most of opportunities that come your way. Saturn, the planet of constriction and discipline, rules Capricorn, and strongly affects those born when the Sun transits this patient, persistent sign. With concentrated effort you can triumph over circumstances that would discourage anyone with less willpower and determination. If you were born between December 22 and January 1, the first decanate of Capricorn, you conform almost rigidly to accepted standards of disciplined behavior. If you were born between January 1 and January 10, read the section on TAURUS to learn how this fixed, earthy Sign influences you. Read VIRGO if you were born between January 10 and January 20; this third decanate makes you highly particular and discriminating.

SUN IN AQUARIUS: eleventh Sign. Fixed, airy and masculine. ☉ ♒
(Between January 20 and February 19)

The Sun in the sign of Aquarius gives you an idealistic nature, with strong likes and dislikes. You won't be bullied or driven by anyone; you cherish your freedom and independence almost as much as a Sagittarian. You are a progressive thinker and a humanitarian with a good streak of originality. You are usually determined, quiet, patient and easy to meet. Even so, you are cautious, probably quite intelligent, thoughtful, studious and philosophical. You tend to view the world with a detached attitude and an unconventional air. However, you always identify yourself with any progressive movement and firmly believe in the brotherhood of man. Although you have excellent reasoning abilities, you are also intuitive. Others see you as refined, pleasant and generous, with many friends among the opposite sex. You have very advanced, sometimes radical new ideas. In expounding some of these views you might be looked upon as eccentric. You are inclined to be scientific, unpredictable, and a lover of the curious and unusual. You are honest, sincere and usually cheerful, which makes you slow to anger but difficult to appease. You are most influenced by kindness. As a lover, your dispassionate, independent nature creates the appearance of complete emotional detachment from the loved one. The Sun in Aquarius gives you fertile mental qualities that suit you best for group work of a reformative nature rather than endeavors involving personal factors. If you were born between January 20 and January 30, the AQUARIUS characteristics are crystallized. Between January 30 and February 9th, however, you will be influenced by the changeable, communicative nature of the GEMINI decanate. Between February 9th and February 19, the LIBRA decanate makes you more sociable, artistically or musically inclined.

SUN IN PISCES: the last Sign. Mutable, watery and
feminine. ☉ ♓
*(Between February 19 and March 20)*

In many ways Pisces is the most mystical and occult Sign of all. Compassionate to a fault, the Pisces-born cannot stand to see others suffer. You are kind and sympathetic to animals, children and people in distress. You tolerate much adversity in your life and tend to suffer inwardly. You are easily moved to tears by the sight or knowledge of someone else suffering. You are usually modest, possibly timid and lacking in self-confidence, but you have a certain faith in the unknown. In you there is a desire to care for the sick and needy, to overcome the illusion for religious and social barriers of conformity and to share the feelings of others. Being born under such a sensitive water Sign, Pisceans often have a characteristic weakness for alcohol and a love for the sea. You are the most "unworldly" of all the twelve Signs. It is nearly impossible to force your fluid nature into a regimented pattern of behavior. You have a creative imagination, and are intuitive, impressionable and receptive to what goes on around you. You are intensely emotional and submissive, just as likely to delude yourself about realty as to be fooled by the unscrupulous. You have a tendency to become despondent or over-emotional; this creates a hard-to-overcome negativism and a lack of that vital spark of life and energy. Pisceans should try to cultivate a more positive attitude, a less subjective emotional outlook. Chances are you may be too gullible, temperamental and indecisive for your own good. You are uncertain and changeable, and perhaps too reserved or secretive. If you were born between February 19 and March 1, the full influence of this PISCES decanate makes you even more psychic and impressionable. If you were born in the CANCER decanate, between March 1 and March 10, read the characteristics of this tenacious Sign. If you were born between March 10 and March 20, you belong to the SCORPIO decanate of Pisces and will have some of the intensity of thought, feeling and expression of this powerful sign.

**5**

# Your Moon Sign

One of the most important factors in selecting a favorable time to invest, marry, travel, etc., is the position of the transiting Moon at the time in relation to your own natal horoscope. For instance, if the Sun at your birth was located at 10 degrees of Gemini in its orbit, then, no matter in which Sign your *natal* Moon was located, you will experience events corresponding to this Sign each month when the Moon transits ten degrees of Gemini.

If you were born at the time of a New Moon (called a "lunation" in astrology), the Sun and Moon were in the same position of the heavens. Astrologers loosely call this a "conjunction," although a true conjunction of the two luminaries, strictly speaking, must result in a total solar eclipse. Not many people are born at the exact time of an eclipse, but those few are remarkable in one way or another, depending on the degree and Sign of the eclipse and its location in the horoscope.

The most important eclipse of modern times occurred on February 4, 1962. Children born during that total eclipse have not only the Sun and Moon located at 15 degrees of Aquarius (the altruistic, scientific, humanitarian Sign) they also have Mercury, Venus, Mars, Jupiter and Saturn closely aligned. This small group (which to a lesser degree includes all children born a couple of days before and after the eclipse) are destined for great new accomplishments during the next several decades.

Whenever an eclipse occurs in the present in the same Sign and same degree as your natal Sun, Moon or any other planet in your horoscope, something of an unusual nature will take place in your life—a change that corresponds exactly with the symbolic conditions that appear in your horoscope. A valuable piece of astrological information is that the New Moon, Full Moon and eclipses invariably bring about changes (*if* they occur where planets are located in your natal horoscope). An eclipse on your *birthday* is the simplest example of this because it occurs in conjunction with your natal Sun.

The Moon is also an important arbiter in all other terrestrial events. Military commanders of both ancient and modern times have noticed the tendency for mass troop movements to follow each eclipse. Some of these troop movements actually followed the line of the eclipse's path.

Immediately following a solar eclipse in 1945, the American First army was ordered to cross the Rhine. General Omar Bradley followed General Eisenhower's orders (which, incidentally, had been given to him by Franklin Delano Roosevelt) and withdrew his forces (behind the eclipse's path, as it happened). Russian troops were thus permitted to roll in and occupy East German territory, which is Communist-dominated to this day.

Another example of the "coincidence" of troops massing along the line of an eclipse occurred on November 2, 878 A.D. The path of this eclipse covered what is now known as Old Wapping road, which runs from Chester to London. In 878, however, there was no such road in existence. In a most remarkable battle, King Alfred, who was fighting the invading Vikings, managed to stop the enemy dead in his tracks all along the path of that ancient eclipse. Britons occupied one side and Vikings the other. This is exactly how the nation was divided.

The Moon has been shown to be a functional factor in dozens of modern scientific studies, many of them originating from large universities and medical centers. Dr. Frank Brown of Northwestern University, Evanston, Illinois, for example, has experimented in this area. Dr. Robert O. Becker of the V.A. Hospital in Syracuse, New York's Upstate Medical Center, and Dr. Igho Kornblueh of the American Institute of Medical Climatology, have given reports of their studies that favored the idea of lunar influence in our lives.

Dr. Brown took some oysters from Long Island sound at

New Haven, Connecticut and flew them to his laboratory in Evanston, Illinois where he kept them alive and nourished in a tank of salt water of even temperature under a steady, dim light. Oysters open and close their shells at 12-hour intervals (in exact phase with the tides which are caused by the Moon). The oysters continued this behavior as though they were still in New Haven—but only for a couple of weeks. At about the time Dr. Brown concluded that their activity was inherited, the mollusks "clammed" up tightly when they should have been open. It happened that a Full Moon was then directly overhead at Evanston, Illinois!

By the time the Moon had set below the horizon the oysters had "readjusted' their rhythm *exactly* as though they were in a tidal basin in Evanston. Yet they were completely divorced from temperature changes, night and day, or high and low tides. Dr. Brown, who has conducted myriad experiments of this nature, stated that some completely undetectable "force" from the Moon is responsible for virtually all monthly cycles on Earth.

As a result of practical, first-hand experiments and the knowledge he gained from them, Dr. Brown, who is Morrison Professor of Biology at Northwestern University, admitted to Chicago astrologer Katherine de Jersey that astrology must gradually be recognized as the basis of a true science.

Dr. Robert O. Becker and his colleagues in Syracuse, New York, mapped out the human bio-magnetic field and proved beyond doubt that it is powerfully influenced by the Earth's own magnetic-field. In turn, the geomagnetic field fluctuates in perfect phase with the positions of the Sun, Moon and planets.

In-depth studies have also revealed the further refinement of basic personality differences among people born during a waning Moon as compared to those born when the Moon was waxing. When the Moon is decreasing in light (waning), it tends to cause introversion. Conversely, extroverts are usually born after the New Moon, when the lunar crescent is increasing (waxing) in apparent light.

The late Llewellyn George, an erudite astrologer, teacher, writer and publisher, said: "Some New Moons are very important, depending on whether the luminaries at their conjunction form any important aspects in the individual's nativity. When the lunation occurs in a favorable place in the horoscope and in good aspect to some of the radical planets it betokens that the month, summed up in a general way, will be fortunate especially if no strongly malign aspects testify otherwise, but even then such lunation will tend to mitigate the evil."

(The ancient Oriental Yin-Yang symbol—reflected in the flag of the Republic of Korea—signifies an anciently known astrological principle: The sun is ruler of the day and the Moon of the night. The Incas of ancient Peru, who mined gold and silver in prodigious amounts, were Sun and Moon worshipers, as were virtually all civilized people at one time or another in their histories. *We* call the Incas "pagans," but the entire European economy was based on the billions of dollars' worth of gold and silver plundered from their cities and temples and shipped home by the Christian Spaniards.)

The Moon is next in importance to the Earth and the Sun. Its influence has been studied for millennia and generally concluded by astrological scholars to be "cold, moist, phlegmatic and feminine. She is fruitful and convertible in nature, being fortunate or unfortunate, according to her position by house in a chart, and her aspects and location in the Zodiac (by Sign) at that time." (William Lilly *An Introduction to Astrology*, pub. By Geo. Bell & Sons, London, 1647)

In astrology the Sun represents the positive life-giving principle, while the Moon symbolizes the receptive or passive side. So much speculation and far-out, unscientific writing has been done about the Moon that it is easy to understand how its influence corresponds to the romantic and fanciful side of human nature. Astrologically, the Moon rules the *personality*, the sun rules the basic *individuality*, and the Ascendant governs the way we walk and talk, our gestures and outer mannerisms— generally, the physical body.

A classic example of the (often weird) kind of thinking inspired by the Moon is H. P. Blavatsky's passage in *The Secret Doctrine*. ". . . then the Moon (our satellite) pouring forth into the lowest glove of our planetary ring, our Earth . . . all its life, energy and powers; and having transformed them to a new centre becoming virtually a dead planet, in which rotation has almost ceased since the birth of our globe. . . ."

It is one of the misfortunes of astrology that this kind of negativism characterized much of what passed for the science of the stars during the 19th century.

Since the Sun correlates to the character and the Moon to

the personality, it is a general rule that if the Moon is closer to the Midheaven (on top of the horoscope) at the time of your birth than the Sun, it makes the *personality* stronger than the character. This is just one of the myriad indicators astrologers use to gauge the whole man. If the sun is more highly elevated than the Moon, the *individuality* dominates the personality. According to their horoscope, some people tend to express their Moon Sign most, even though the vast majority largely manifest their Sun Signs.

From what follows, you should be able to determine the influence of the Moon on your *personality*. This is *fairly general*, and refers only to where the Moon was at the time of your birth.

*A list of the Moon's positions from 1890 to 1970 will be found at the end of this chapter.*

## MOON IN ARIES ☽ ♈

This being the first Sign of the Zodiac, the Moon here means you're liable to be impulsive and enthusiastic. Your personality is often militantly aggressive and you may be given to periods of irritation and anger. Your self-reliance and independence are highly pronounced. You want to have your own way in almost everything and will not be ordered around by anyone. The only discipline you will permit is that which is self-imposed. You tend to be impulsive and unconventional, yet these are the traits which will bring you either great popularity or notoriety. You most like being in a position of authority, and will in all likelihood eventually wind up in an executive capacity or some position of leadership. You set your own pace and choose your own life's work, regardless of the advice of friends and relatives. There is some kind of estrangement or lack of sympathy between you and your parents. Whatever you do is usually viewed as sudden or totally unexpected by conservative observers. The Moon in Aries is good for original schemes, ventures, independent operations and military life. Nevertheless, you probably have an attraction for occultism or some other form of mysticism. This tendency can also manifest itself in secrecy in some of your dealings.

## MOON IN TAURUS ☽ ♉

You are basically rather conservative, a person who tends to resist anything threatening the status quo. You love all that is beautiful and harmonious; unlike Aries, you are not impulsive. You have a deep desire to become successful, and to this end you will conservatively, positively and ambitiously work. Those with the Moon in Taurus attract good friends and usually acquire money, houses and/or land. Anything that is old, established, weighty and conservative is appealing to one with this position of the Moon. Regardless of what kind of work you do or what business you are engaged in, you will ultimately earn your share of financial remuneration. It may be that the kind of work you do is not considered worthy of your abilities or standing in the community. There may even be something mysterious or secretive about it. You can also make money through wholesale associations, trading societies, co-operative companies, etc. You have a generally kindly and sociable personality, and a good disposition, but you tend to be a little too materialistic and are probably quite sensual. You like a pleasant social life, and probably have a good speaking or singing voice, as well as a love for the theater, for making friends and joining groups or societies.

## MOON IN GEMINI ☽ ♊

You are very active, both physically and mentally. If you are not reading, studying or communicating, you are visiting other people, walking, riding and making short trips. You may have more than one house and are likely to change your residence frequently. This position of the Moon is good for the intellect; you like books, scientific and literary subjects. You are liable to live by your wits in one way or another, and could earn your livelihood as an intellectual—a writer, teacher, journalist, salesman, designer or speaker. You probably change occupations as frequently as you change your residence, or you might have more than one profession. You are probably quite skillful with your hands, or may even be ambidextrous, able to do two things at once. All things being equal, you are inclined to be involved in some occupation involving mental ability. You may lack perseverence or be somewhat less than honest in your dealings with others. Gemini is a subtle Sign. When a chart with the Sun or Moon in Gemini is adversely aspected at birth, it often results in scheming or dishonesty. Worst of all (as far as your friends and associates are concerned), you can do this with great charm and wit.

## MOON IN CANCER ☽ ♋

You are as much a lover of ease and comfort as one born with the Moon in Taurus. Yet you lack either the stubbornness or the stability of Taurus, unless the Sun or Ascendant is in this fixed, earthy Sign. You are changeable, versatile and keenly emotional. Yet when you are surrounded by home comforts, good food and drink, you are friendly, sociable, imaginative and generous. Your environment plays a large part in your attitude and outlook. In fact, you are acutely sensitive to exogenous influences, and tend to adopt a kind of protective coloring from the people and places with which you associate. You are conservative and domestic by nature, and love your home, family and ancestry. You may have been strongly attached to your mother and you may bear a strong resemblance to her. You are often luckiest when you listen to or take the advice of other people to carry out someone else's plans—unless the Sun was in Leo, Aries or Sagittarius when you were born. Each of these Signs is noted for being positive and independent. You may have an inherent talent for expressing how other people think and feel, and might be a good actor or mimic. There is a strong attraction for water in your psychology; you enjoy living or vacationing by large bodies of water or traveling by ship. You are sensitive, intuitive—perhaps able to display psychic abilities.

## MOON IN LEO ☽ ♌

You are proud, ambitious and have no hesitation about assuming heavy responsibility or appearing prominently in the public eye. You have a natural affinity for roles of authority. Your innate pride makes you rather prone to love affairs; in fact you probably enjoy great popularity with the opposite sex because of your susceptibility and sincerity in love. You attract the admiration of superiors and will eventually enjoy the favor of people in higher brackets. Where money is concerned, you are generous to a fault. You are equally generous with your affections, as well as being generally honest, straightforward and idealistic. The Moon in Leo often tends to be associated with high intelligence, a love of the arts and the theater, music, painting and literature. On the other hand, you may display an inordinate love of luxuries for their own sake—jewelry and extravagant clothing, say. You have a lively, persevering spirit, a good mind and good organizational ability.


## MOON IN VIRGO ☽ ♍

You have an excellent mind and a good memory, and are best suited for work of an intellectual nature. You could easily become highly successful in the position of an agent, manager, dealer in health foods, doctor, dietitian or druggist. Your ambitions are generally minimal, but you are a good, trustworthy employee as well as a reasonable and considerate employer. You probably lead a simple, unpretentious life, quiet and easygoing. You do best while in the employ of some sort of association, company or corporation. The general tendency of those with the Moon in Virgo is to take numerous trips and to have a lot of friends, particularly if you are a woman. Even so, there could be some secret problem concerning your own marriage. You like to investigate things and, in one way or another, you'll probably earn your living through your mental abilities. You are discriminating, highly selective and judicious. Because of these traits, you are attracted to scientific and occult subjects, and could possess great intuitive abilities or, to some degree, clairvoyance.


## MOON IN LIBRA ☽ ♎

You make friends easily and are attracted to refined and harmonious people and circumstances. The Moon in Libra usually inclines toward partnership in love, business or marriage. You are generally popular and well liked for your kindness, good will and affectionate nature. A great deal of your destiny in life stems from your association with other people, usually one person of a powerful persuasion. You are generally easily influenced and your judgment can be swayed by others; this is because of your love of company, friends and society in general. Your attraction for music, painting and the fine arts generally may stem from your own untapped artistic or musical abilities. You like good clothes and probably have a nice wardrobe. Your approach to life is harmonious, with a well-balanced outlook; these are key words for you with the Moon in Libra. Partnership indeed plays a large part in your life. Although you are not necessarily inconstant, almost everything you do in life depends to a large extent on someone else. In fact, you accomplish much more when you are working in association with another person.

## MOON IN SCORPIO ☽ ♏

You are a battler by nature and temperament. Every problem you face in life is usually faced alone, with assurance, confidence in your abilities and self-reliance. You often bring about the thing you are trying to avoid. You are outspoken, blunt, energetic, positive and hard working. You are something of a puzzle, even to yourself. While on the surface you might seem to be agreeable and amenable to change, the fact is that your motivations run a lot deeper than they appear. You are basically conservative and averse to any changes, particularly if they are forced on you by other people or circumstances. When you do switch allegiance to an idea, you are fully capable of supporting or engineering great revolutionary changes. Scorpio is probably the most misunderstood of all the signs. With the Moon placed here, you probably know why others don't understand you. You are inclined to irritation, anger and revenge; there are some people who think you lack a strong moral code or that you drink too much. Yet you have great willpower, energy, determination, a love of pleasure and the desire to satisfy your tastes. This position of the Moon is associated closely with some work in connection with death; for example, you might be an insurance claims adjustor, policeman, fireman or soldier. You have a powerful attraction toward the opposite sex, and vice versa—a condition that can cause considerable difficulty in your life, and may indicate more than one marriage.

## MOON IN SAGITTARIUS ☽ ♐

You love the great outdoors, your freedom and independence. You are jovial (derived from Jove or Jupiter, the ruling planet of Sagittarius), active, fond of travel and sports. You appear to be restless and unsettled, either physically or mentally. Even though your religious beliefs may be unorthodox, you are sincere, candid and cordial toward others. There is a tendency to be blunt, to state whatever occurs to you at the moment and to think about it afterward, if at all. You say whatever you think, an admirable quality but not always a diplomatic one. You could easily have two vocations, or frequently change your job. You are generally good-natured, kind and honest, with a high-minded regard for the welfare of others; in fact, an injustice to someone else amounts almost to a personal injury to you. You are quick to anger, but have a forgiving nature and do not usually hold a grudge. You are a natural teacher, something of a minor prophet, able to foresee the outcome of events from a long distance. You have an active intuition, with accurate dreams that often come true. You dislike being tied to one place and will often change your residence.

## MOON IN CAPRICORN ☽ ♑

You are a born administrator or executive, with enough generalship to achieve a certain degree of celebrity. Depending on the rest of your horoscope, this could work out either beneficially or adversely; it might mean fame or notoriety. Chances are your ambition, dedication, practicality and hard work will eventually bring you to public attention as a prominent and respected individual. Some of the drawbacks of this position of the Moon are that it tends to make you rather cold and calculating; too often you are careless of the feelings of others. If your Sun or Ascendant is in one of the Cardinal signs: Aries, Cancer, Libra or Capricorn, your future success is almost assured. But whatever fame or influence you gain, it is almost certain that some kind of enemy will appear, either secretly or openly, to try to ruin your reputation, whether you deserve it or not. Fortunately, this enemy will probably fail. You know how to influence others, and can put on a good show when the situation seems to call for it. You share with a person whose Moon is in Scorpio a good deal of creative energy, trouble through or with the opposite sex and (in a badly aspected chart) a lack of control in certain important areas of your life. Despite all else, you are one of the prime movers who knows how to get things done and will work tirelessly toward any goal you have set.

## MOON IN AQUARIUS ☽ ♒

You have great intuitive powers and imagination, and enjoy the good opinion of friends and colleagues. You are sympathetic, sociable, outgoing and yet can often display a highly unorthodox, independent and unconventional attitude. Unimaginative people might consider you to be slightly eccentric because of your off-beat interests or hobbies. Whatever is intellectually or socially stimulating, original or unusual will attract you. You may have a strong inclination for educational, political, scientific or social work. At heart you are something of a humanitarian, highly idealistic (though not always practical). Large movements supporting great causes gain your support, or you may belong to a mystical or secret society, brotherhood or association. You are inventive, original and scientifically inclined. With Moon in Aquarius, you are probably gifted with an inclination toward occult subjects; astrology or clairvoyance, say. You are extremely humane and broadly sympathetic, a true liberal in the best sense of the word. You get along famously with people who are congenial and think as you do. In all probability you may belong to a society, club, association or group who think and believe as you do.

## MOON IN PISCES ☽ ♓

You are attracted to whatever appeals to your emotions and feelings—in music, literature or poetry. Emotion is a major factor in all your activities. You are generally changeable, sometimes undependable, too easily discouraged when you are confronted with trouble, opposition and obstacles. You love variety and are apt to change your mind about things frequently. Yet you are rather easygoing, somewhat shy and retiring in many contacts. The Moon in Pisces has often been cited by astrologers as an unfavorable position causing glandular disorders and overweight. Although you are probably outwardly gay and hopeful, with a seemingly good sense of humor, you are prone to become easily depressed and could even lack a common sense of humor. It has been frequently observed that this position of the Moon is likely to lead to periods of intemperance, dissipation and even dishonesty, but this must be considered with the total aspects in anyone's horoscope before any flat conclusion can be drawn. The fact is that Moon in Pisces *can* be one of the most appealing, entertaining and humorous of all the positions. At one time or another, hospitals, prisons or institutions of some kind will play an important role in your life. You may have a flair for music, composing or writing. Whatever you do, it is emotional and romantic; your creative output is fluid, prodigious and imaginative.

The following tables will enable you to locate the position of the Moon by Sign at the time of your birth. Each day given is the one on which the Moon *changed* Signs. If you were born, say, on December 7, 1941, you will see that the symbol next to the date indicates that the Moon moved into Leo, but does not indicate the exact time this took place. So (depending on the time) the Moon might still have been in the *preceding* Sign). As with the ascending Sign, you simply read the characteristics bestowed by the Moon in *both* signs and insert the lunar crescent in the Sign that 'feels" most natural to you. The Moon in Leo gives an entirely different characteristic temperament than when in its own Sign, Cancer, for example. This applies to each succeeding Sign, thus making it a simple matter of choosing one or the other. This little exercise in judgment will not only sharpen your insight, it will also strengthen your intuitive ability to determine the Sun Signs, Moon Signs and Ascendants of other people.

## 1900

| JAN. | FEB. | MAR. | APR. | MAY | JUNE | JULY | AUG. | SEPT. | OCT. | NOV. | DEC. |
|---|---|---|---|---|---|---|---|---|---|---|---|
| 2 ♒ | 1 ♓ | 2 ♈ | 1 ♉ | 2 ♋ | 1 ♌ | 1 ♍ | 2 ♏ | 1 ♐ | 1 ♑ | 1 ♓ | 1 ♈ |
| 4 ♓ | 3 ♈ | 4 ♉ | 3 ♊ | 5 ♌ | 4 ♍ | 3 ♎ | 5 ♐ | 3 ♑ | 3 ♒ | 4 ♈ | 3 ♉ |
| 6 ♈ | 5 ♉ | 6 ♊ | 5 ♋ | 7 ♍ | 6 ♎ | 6 ♏ | 7 ♑ | 6 ♒ | 5 ♓ | 6 ♉ | 5 ♊ |
| 9 ♉ | 7 ♊ | 8 ♋ | 7 ♌ | 10 ♎ | 9 ♏ | 8 ♐ | 9 ♒ | 8 ♓ | 7 ♈ | 8 ♊ | 7 ♋ |
| 11 ♊ | 9 ♋ | 11 ♌ | 10 ♍ | 12 ♏ | 11 ♐ | 11 ♑ | 11 ♓ | 10 ♈ | 9 ♉ | 10 ♋ | 9 ♌ |
| 13 ♋ | 12 ♌ | 14 ♍ | 12 ♎ | 15 ♐ | 13 ♑ | 13 ♒ | 13 ♈ | 12 ♉ | 11 ♊ | 12 ♌ | 12 ♍ |
| 16 ♌ | 14 ♍ | 16 ♎ | 15 ♏ | 17 ♑ | 15 ♒ | 15 ♓ | 15 ♉ | 14 ♊ | 13 ♋ | 14 ♍ | 14 ♎ |
| 18 ♍ | 17 ♎ | 19 ♏ | 17 ♐ | 19 ♒ | 18 ♓ | 17 ♈ | 17 ♊ | 16 ♋ | 16 ♌ | 17 ♎ | 17 ♏ |
| 21 ♎ | 19 ♏ | 21 ♐ | 20 ♑ | 21 ♓ | 20 ♈ | 19 ♉ | 20 ♋ | 18 ♌ | 18 ♍ | 19 ♏ | 19 ♐ |
| 23 ♏ | 22 ♐ | 23 ♑ | 22 ♒ | 23 ♈ | 22 ♉ | 21 ♊ | 22 ♌ | 21 ♍ | 21 ♎ | 22 ♐ | 22 ♑ |
| 26 ♐ | 24 ♑ | 26 ♒ | 24 ♓ | 26 ♉ | 24 ♊ | 23 ♋ | 25 ♍ | 23 ♎ | 23 ♏ | 24 ♑ | 24 ♒ |
| 28 ♑ | 26 ♒ | 28 ♓ | 26 ♈ | 28 ♊ | 26 ♋ | 26 ♌ | 27 ♎ | 26 ♏ | 26 ♐ | 27 ♒ | 26 ♓ |
| 30 ♒ | 28 ♓ | 30 ♈ | 28 ♉ | 30 ♋ | 29 ♌ | 28 ♍ | 30 ♏ | 28 ♐ | 28 ♑ | 29 ♓ | 28 ♈ |
|  |  |  | 30 ♊ |  |  | 31 ♎ |  |  | 30 ♒ |  | 30 ♉ |

## 1901

| JAN. | FEB. | MAR. | APR. | MAY | JUNE | JULY | AUG. | SEPT. | OCT. | NOV. | DEC. |
|---|---|---|---|---|---|---|---|---|---|---|---|
| 1 ♊ | 2 ♌ | 1 ♌ | 2 ♎ | 2 ♏ | 1 ♐ | 1 ♑ | 2 ♓ | 2 ♉ | 1 ♊ | 2 ♌ | 2 ♍ |
| 3 ♋ | 4 ♍ | 4 ♍ | 5 ♏ | 5 ♐ | 3 ♑ | 3 ♒ | 4 ♈ | 4 ♊ | 4 ♋ | 4 ♍ | 4 ♎ |
| 6 ♌ | 7 ♎ | 6 ♎ | 7 ♐ | 7 ♑ | 6 ♒ | 5 ♓ | 6 ♉ | 6 ♋ | 6 ♌ | 7 ♎ | 7 ♏ |
| 8 ♍ | 9 ♏ | 9 ♏ | 10 ♑ | 10 ♒ | 8 ♓ | 7 ♈ | 8 ♊ | 9 ♌ | 8 ♍ | 9 ♏ | 9 ♐ |
| 11 ♎ | 12 ♐ | 11 ♐ | 12 ♒ | 12 ♓ | 10 ♈ | 10 ♉ | 10 ♋ | 11 ♍ | 11 ♎ | 12 ♐ | 12 ♑ |
| 13 ♏ | 14 ♑ | 14 ♑ | 14 ♓ | 14 ♈ | 12 ♉ | 12 ♊ | 12 ♌ | 13 ♎ | 13 ♏ | 14 ♑ | 14 ♒ |
| 16 ♐ | 17 ♒ | 16 ♒ | 17 ♈ | 16 ♉ | 14 ♊ | 14 ♋ | 15 ♍ | 16 ♏ | 16 ♐ | 17 ♒ | 16 ♓ |
| 18 ♑ | 19 ♓ | 18 ♓ | 19 ♉ | 18 ♊ | 16 ♋ | 16 ♌ | 17 ♎ | 18 ♐ | 19 ♑ | 19 ♓ | 19 ♈ |
| 20 ♒ | 21 ♈ | 20 ♈ | 21 ♊ | 20 ♋ | 19 ♌ | 18 ♍ | 19 ♏ | 21 ♑ | 21 ♒ | 21 ♈ | 21 ♉ |
| 22 ♓ | 23 ♉ | 22 ♉ | 23 ♋ | 22 ♌ | 21 ♍ | 21 ♎ | 22 ♐ | 23 ♒ | 23 ♓ | 23 ♉ | 23 ♊ |
| 24 ♈ | 25 ♊ | 24 ♊ | 25 ♌ | 24 ♍ | 23 ♎ | 23 ♏ | 24 ♑ | 25 ♓ | 25 ♈ | 25 ♊ | 25 ♋ |
| 26 ♉ | 27 ♋ | 26 ♋ | 27 ♍ | 27 ♎ | 26 ♏ | 26 ♐ | 27 ♒ | 27 ♈ | 27 ♉ | 27 ♋ | 27 ♌ |
| 29 ♊ |  | 29 ♌ | 30 ♎ | 29 ♏ | 28 ♐ | 28 ♑ | 29 ♓ | 29 ♉ | 29 ♊ | 29 ♌ | 29 ♍ |
| 31 ♋ |  | 31 ♍ |  |  |  | 30 ♒ | 31 ♈ |  | 31 ♋ |  | 31 ♎ |

| Libra | Scorpio | Sagittarius | Capricorn | Aquarius | Pisces |
|---|---|---|---|---|---|
| ♎ | ♏ | ♐ | ♑ | ♒ | ♓ |

## 1902

| JAN. | FEB. | MAR. | APR. | MAY | JUNE | JULY | AUG. | SEPT. | OCT. | NOV. | DEC. |
|---|---|---|---|---|---|---|---|---|---|---|---|
| 3 ♏ | 2 ♐ | 1 ♐ | 2 ♒ | 2 ♓ | 1 ♈ | 2 ♊ | 1 ♋ | 1 ♍ | 1 ♎ | 2 ♐ | 2 ♑ |
| 5 ♐ | 4 ♑ | 4 ♑ | 5 ♓ | 4 ♈ | 3 ♉ | 4 ♋ | 3 ♌ | 3 ♎ | 3 ♏ | 4 ♑ | 4 ♒ |
| 8 ♑ | 7 ♒ | 6 ♒ | 7 ♈ | 6 ♉ | 5 ♊ | 6 ♌ | 5 ♍ | 6 ♏ | 5 ♐ | 7 ♒ | 7 ♓ |
| 10 ♒ | 9 ♓ | 8 ♓ | 9 ♉ | 8 ♊ | 7 ♋ | 9 ♍ | 7 ♎ | 8 ♐ | 8 ♑ | 9 ♓ | 9 ♈ |
| 13 ♓ | 11 ♈ | 10 ♈ | 11 ♊ | 10 ♋ | 9 ♌ | 11 ♎ | 9 ♏ | 11 ♑ | 10 ♒ | 12 ♈ | 11 ♉ |
| 15 ♈ | 13 ♉ | 13 ♉ | 13 ♋ | 12 ♌ | 11 ♍ | 13 ♏ | 14 ♐ | 13 ♒ | 13 ♓ | 14 ♉ | 13 ♊ |
| 17 ♉ | 15 ♊ | 15 ♊ | 15 ♌ | 15 ♍ | 13 ♎ | 15 ♐ | 17 ♑ | 15 ♓ | 15 ♈ | 16 ♊ | 15 ♋ |
| 19 ♊ | 18 ♋ | 17 ♋ | 17 ♍ | 17 ♎ | 16 ♏ | 18 ♑ | 19 ♒ | 18 ♈ | 17 ♉ | 18 ♋ | 17 ♌ |
| 21 ♋ | 20 ♌ | 19 ♌ | 20 ♎ | 19 ♏ | 18 ♐ | 20 ♒ | 22 ♓ | 20 ♉ | 19 ♊ | 20 ♌ | 19 ♍ |
| 23 ♌ | 22 ♍ | 21 ♍ | 22 ♏ | 22 ♐ | 21 ♑ | 23 ♓ | 24 ♈ | 22 ♊ | 21 ♋ | 22 ♍ | 21 ♎ |
| 25 ♍ | 22 ♎ | 23 ♎ | 25 ♐ | 23 ♑ | 23 ♒ | 25 ♈ | 26 ♉ | 24 ♋ | 23 ♌ | 24 ♎ | 24 ♏ |
| 28 ♎ | 27 ♏ | 26 ♏ | 27 ♑ | 26 ♒ | 26 ♓ | 27 ♉ | 28 ♊ | 26 ♌ | 26 ♍ | 27 ♏ | 26 ♐ |
| 30 ♏ | | 28 ♐ | 30 ♒ | 28 ♓ | 28 ♈ | 30 ♊ | 30 ♋ | 28 ♍ | 30 ♎ | 29 ♐ | 29 ♑ |
| | | 31 ♑ | | 30 ♉ | 30 ♉ | | | | | | 31 ♒ |

## 1903

| JAN. | FEB. | MAR. | APR. | MAY | JUNE | JULY | AUG. | SEPT. | OCT. | NOV. | DEC. |
|---|---|---|---|---|---|---|---|---|---|---|---|
| 3 ♓ | 1 ♈ | 1 ♈ | 1 ♊ | 1 ♋ | 1 ♍ | 1 ♎ | 2 ♐ | 3 ♒ | 3 ♓ | 2 ♈ | 1 ♉ |
| 5 ♈ | 4 ♉ | 3 ♉ | 4 ♋ | 3 ♌ | 3 ♎ | 3 ♏ | 4 ♑ | 5 ♓ | 5 ♈ | 4 ♉ | 3 ♊ |
| 8 ♉ | 6 ♊ | 5 ♊ | 6 ♌ | 5 ♍ | 6 ♏ | 5 ♐ | 7 ♒ | 8 ♈ | 8 ♉ | 6 ♊ | 6 ♋ |
| 10 ♊ | 8 ♋ | 7 ♋ | 8 ♍ | 7 ♎ | 8 ♐ | 9 ♑ | 9 ♓ | 10 ♉ | 10 ♊ | 8 ♋ | 8 ♌ |
| 12 ♋ | 10 ♌ | 9 ♌ | 10 ♎ | 10 ♏ | 11 ♑ | 10 ♒ | 12 ♈ | 13 ♊ | 12 ♋ | 10 ♌ | 10 ♍ |
| 14 ♌ | 12 ♍ | 11 ♍ | 12 ♏ | 12 ♐ | 13 ♒ | 13 ♓ | 14 ♉ | 15 ♋ | 14 ♌ | 12 ♍ | 12 ♎ |
| 16 ♍ | 14 ♎ | 14 ♎ | 15 ♐ | 14 ♑ | 16 ♓ | 15 ♈ | 16 ♊ | 17 ♌ | 16 ♍ | 15 ♎ | 14 ♏ |
| 18 ♎ | 16 ♏ | 16 ♏ | 17 ♑ | 17 ♒ | 18 ♈ | 18 ♉ | 18 ♋ | 19 ♍ | 18 ♎ | 17 ♏ | 16 ♐ |
| 20 ♏ | 19 ♐ | 18 ♐ | 20 ♒ | 19 ♓ | 20 ♉ | 20 ♊ | 20 ♌ | 21 ♎ | 20 ♏ | 19 ♐ | 19 ♑ |
| 23 ♐ | 21 ♑ | 21 ♑ | 22 ♓ | 22 ♈ | 23 ♊ | 22 ♋ | 22 ♍ | 23 ♏ | 23 ♐ | 21 ♑ | 21 ♒ |
| 25 ♑ | 24 ♒ | 23 ♒ | 24 ♈ | 24 ♉ | 25 ♋ | 24 ♌ | 24 ♎ | 25 ♐ | 25 ♑ | 24 ♒ | 24 ♓ |
| 28 ♒ | 26 ♓ | 26 ♓ | 27 ♉ | 26 ♊ | 27 ♌ | 26 ♍ | 27 ♏ | 28 ♑ | 28 ♒ | 26 ♓ | 26 ♈ |
| 30 ♓ | | 28 ♈ | 29 ♊ | 28 ♋ | 29 ♍ | 28 ♎ | 29 ♐ | 30 ♓ | 30 ♓ | 29 ♈ | 29 ♉ |
| | | 30 ♉ | | 30 ♌ | | 30 ♏ | 31 ♑ | | | | 31 ♊ |

*Key:*  Aries  Taurus  Gemini  Cancer  Leo  Virgo

♈    ♉    ♊    ♋    ♌    ♍

## 1904

| JAN. | FEB. | MAR. | APR. | MAY | JUNE | JULY | AUG. | SEPT. | OCT. | NOV. | DEC. |
|---|---|---|---|---|---|---|---|---|---|---|---|
| 2 ♋ | 2 ♍ | 1 ♍ | 1 ♏ | 1 ♐ | 2 ♒ | 2 ♓ | 1 ♈ | 2 ♊ | 1 ♋ | 2 ♍ | 1 ♎ |
| 4 ♌ | 4 ♎ | 3 ♎ | 4 ♐ | 3 ♑ | 4 ♓ | 4 ♈ | 3 ♉ | 4 ♋ | 4 ♌ | 4 ♎ | 4 ♏ |
| 6 ♍ | 7 ♏ | 5 ♏ | 6 ♑ | 6 ♒ | 7 ♈ | 7 ♉ | 6 ♊ | 6 ♌ | 6 ♍ | 6 ♏ | 6 ♐ |
| 8 ♎ | 9 ♐ | 8 ♐ | 8 ♒ | 8 ♓ | 9 ♉ | 9 ♊ | 8 ♋ | 8 ♍ | 8 ♎ | 8 ♐ | 8 ♑ |
| 10 ♏ | 11 ♑ | 10 ♑ | 11 ♓ | 11 ♈ | 12 ♊ | 11 ♋ | 10 ♌ | 10 ♎ | 10 ♏ | 10 ♑ | 10 ♒ |
| 13 ♐ | 14 ♒ | 12 ♒ | 13 ♈ | 13 ♉ | 14 ♋ | 13 ♌ | 12 ♍ | 12 ♏ | 12 ♐ | 13 ♒ | 13 ♓ |
| 15 ♑ | 16 ♓ | 15 ♓ | 16 ♉ | 15 ♊ | 16 ♌ | 15 ♍ | 14 ♎ | 14 ♐ | 14 ♑ | 15 ♓ | 15 ♈ |
| 17 ♒ | 19 ♈ | 17 ♈ | 18 ♊ | 18 ♋ | 18 ♍ | 17 ♎ | 16 ♏ | 17 ♑ | 16 ♒ | 18 ♈ | 18 ♉ |
| 20 ♓ | 21 ♉ | 20 ♉ | 20 ♋ | 20 ♌ | 20 ♎ | 20 ♏ | 18 ♐ | 19 ♒ | 19 ♓ | 20 ♉ | 20 ♊ |
| 23 ♈ | 24 ♊ | 22 ♊ | 23 ♌ | 22 ♍ | 22 ♏ | 22 ♐ | 20 ♑ | 22 ♓ | 21 ♈ | 23 ♊ | 22 ♋ |
| 25 ♉ | 26 ♋ | 24 ♋ | 25 ♍ | 24 ♎ | 25 ♐ | 24 ♑ | 23 ♒ | 24 ♈ | 24 ♉ | 25 ♋ | 24 ♌ |
| 27 ♊ | 28 ♌ | 26 ♌ | 27 ♎ | 26 ♏ | 27 ♑ | 27 ♒ | 25 ♓ | 27 ♉ | 26 ♊ | 27 ♌ | 26 ♍ |
| 29 ♋ | | 28 ♍ | 29 ♏ | 28 ♐ | 29 ♒ | 29 ♓ | 28 ♈ | 29 ♊ | 29 ♋ | 29 ♍ | 29 ♎ |
| 31 ♌ | | 30 ♎ | | 31 ♑ | | | 31 ♉ | | 31 ♌ | | 31 ♏ |

## 1905

| JAN. | FEB. | MAR. | APR. | MAY | JUNE | JULY | AUG. | SEPT. | OCT. | NOV. | DEC. |
|---|---|---|---|---|---|---|---|---|---|---|---|
| 2 ♐ | 3 ♒ | 2 ♒ | 1 ♓ | 1 ♈ | 2 ♊ | 1 ♋ | 2 ♍ | 1 ♎ | 2 ♐ | 1 ♑ | 2 ♓ |
| 4 ♑ | 5 ♓ | 4 ♓ | 3 ♈ | 3 ♉ | 4 ♋ | 4 ♌ | 4 ♎ | 3 ♏ | 4 ♑ | 3 ♒ | 5 ♈ |
| 6 ♒ | 8 ♈ | 7 ♈ | 6 ♉ | 6 ♊ | 6 ♌ | 6 ♍ | 6 ♏ | 5 ♐ | 6 ♒ | 5 ♓ | 7 ♉ |
| 9 ♓ | 10 ♉ | 9 ♉ | 8 ♊ | 8 ♋ | 9 ♍ | 8 ♎ | 9 ♐ | 7 ♑ | 9 ♓ | 8 ♈ | 10 ♊ |
| 11 ♈ | 13 ♊ | 12 ♊ | 11 ♋ | 10 ♌ | 11 ♎ | 10 ♏ | 11 ♑ | 9 ♒ | 11 ♈ | 10 ♉ | 12 ♋ |
| 14 ♉ | 15 ♋ | 14 ♋ | 13 ♌ | 12 ♍ | 13 ♏ | 12 ♐ | 13 ♒ | 11 ♓ | 14 ♉ | 13 ♊ | 15 ♌ |
| 16 ♊ | 17 ♌ | 17 ♌ | 15 ♍ | 15 ♎ | 15 ♐ | 14 ♑ | 15 ♓ | 14 ♈ | 16 ♊ | 15 ♋ | 17 ♍ |
| 19 ♋ | 19 ♍ | 19 ♍ | 17 ♎ | 17 ♏ | 17 ♑ | 17 ♒ | 18 ♈ | 16 ♉ | 19 ♋ | 17 ♌ | 19 ♎ |
| 21 ♌ | 21 ♎ | 21 ♎ | 19 ♏ | 19 ♐ | 19 ♒ | 19 ♓ | 20 ♉ | 19 ♊ | 21 ♌ | 20 ♍ | 21 ♏ |
| 23 ♍ | 23 ♏ | 23 ♏ | 21 ♐ | 21 ♑ | 22 ♓ | 21 ♈ | 23 ♊ | 21 ♋ | 23 ♍ | 22 ♎ | 23 ♐ |
| 25 ♎ | 25 ♐ | 25 ♐ | 23 ♑ | 23 ♒ | 24 ♈ | 24 ♉ | 25 ♋ | 23 ♌ | 26 ♎ | 24 ♏ | 25 ♑ |
| 27 ♏ | 28 ♑ | 27 ♑ | 26 ♒ | 25 ♓ | 27 ♉ | 26 ♊ | 27 ♌ | 26 ♍ | 28 ♏ | 26 ♐ | 28 ♒ |
| 29 ♐ | | 29 ♒ | 28 ♓ | 28 ♈ | 29 ♊ | 29 ♋ | 30 ♍ | 28 ♎ | 29 ♐ | 28 ♑ | 30 ♓ |
| 31 ♑ | | | 30 ♈ | 30 ♉ | | 31 ♌ | | 30 ♏ | | 30 ♒ | |

| Libra | Scorpio | Sagittarius | Capricorn | Aquarius | Pisces |
|---|---|---|---|---|---|
| ♎ | ♏ | ♐ | ♑ | ♒ | ♓ |

## 1906

| JAN. | FEB. | MAR. | APR. | MAY | JUNE | JULY | AUG. | SEPT. | OCT. | NOV. | DEC. |
|---|---|---|---|---|---|---|---|---|---|---|---|
| 1 ♈ | 3 ♊ | 2 ♊ | 1 ♋ | 3 ♍ | 1 ♎ | 1 ♏ | 1 ♑ | 2 ♓ | 1 ♈ | 3 ♊ | 2 ♋ |
| 4 ♉ | 5 ♋ | 4 ♋ | 3 ♌ | 5 ♎ | 3 ♏ | 3 ♐ | 3 ♒ | 4 ♈ | 4 ♉ | 5 ♋ | 5 ♌ |
| 6 ♊ | 7 ♌ | 7 ♌ | 5 ♍ | 7 ♏ | 5 ♐ | 5 ♑ | 5 ♓ | 6 ♉ | 6 ♊ | 8 ♌ | 7 ♍ |
| 9 ♋ | 10 ♍ | 9 ♍ | 8 ♎ | 9 ♐ | 7 ♑ | 7 ♒ | 8 ♈ | 9 ♊ | 8 ♋ | 10 ♍ | 10 ♎ |
| 11 ♌ | 12 ♎ | 11 ♎ | 10 ♏ | 11 ♑ | 9 ♒ | 9 ♓ | 10 ♉ | 11 ♋ | 11 ♌ | 12 ♎ | 12 ♏ |
| 13 ♍ | 14 ♏ | 13 ♏ | 12 ♐ | 13 ♒ | 12 ♓ | 11 ♈ | 13 ♊ | 14 ♌ | 14 ♍ | 14 ♏ | 14 ♐ |
| 15 ♎ | 16 ♐ | 15 ♐ | 14 ♑ | 15 ♓ | 14 ♈ | 14 ♉ | 15 ♋ | 16 ♍ | 16 ♎ | 16 ♐ | 16 ♑ |
| 18 ♏ | 18 ♑ | 17 ♑ | 16 ♒ | 18 ♈ | 16 ♉ | 16 ♊ | 18 ♌ | 18 ♎ | 18 ♏ | 18 ♑ | 18 ♒ |
| 20 ♐ | 20 ♒ | 20 ♒ | 18 ♓ | 20 ♉ | 19 ♊ | 19 ♋ | 20 ♍ | 20 ♏ | 20 ♐ | 20 ♒ | 20 ♓ |
| 22 ♑ | 23 ♓ | 22 ♓ | 20 ♈ | 23 ♊ | 21 ♋ | 21 ♌ | 22 ♎ | 23 ♐ | 22 ♑ | 23 ♓ | 22 ♈ |
| 24 ♒ | 25 ♈ | 24 ♈ | 23 ♉ | 25 ♋ | 24 ♌ | 24 ♍ | 24 ♏ | 25 ♑ | 24 ♒ | 25 ♈ | 25 ♉ |
| 26 ♓ | 27 ♉ | 27 ♉ | 25 ♊ | 28 ♌ | 26 ♍ | 26 ♎ | 26 ♐ | 27 ♒ | 26 ♓ | 27 ♉ | 27 ♊ |
| 29 ♈ | | 29 ♊ | 28 ♋ | 30 ♍ | 29 ♎ | 28 ♏ | 28 ♑ | 29 ♓ | 29 ♈ | 30 ♊ | 30 ♋ |
| 31 ♉ | | | 30 ♌ | | | 30 ♐ | 31 ♒ | | 31 ♉ | | |

## 1907

| JAN. | FEB. | MAR. | APR. | MAY | JUNE | JULY | AUG. | SEPT. | OCT. | NOV. | DEC. |
|---|---|---|---|---|---|---|---|---|---|---|---|
| 1 ♌ | 2 ♎ | 1 ♎ | 2 ♐ | 1 ♑ | 2 ♓ | 1 ♈ | 2 ♊ | 1 ♋ | 1 ♌ | 2 ♎ | 2 ♏ |
| 4 ♍ | 4 ♏ | 4 ♏ | 4 ♑ | 3 ♒ | 4 ♈ | 4 ♉ | 5 ♋ | 4 ♌ | 4 ♍ | 5 ♏ | 4 ♐ |
| 6 ♎ | 7 ♐ | 6 ♐ | 6 ♒ | 5 ♓ | 6 ♉ | 6 ♊ | 7 ♌ | 6 ♍ | 6 ♎ | 7 ♐ | 6 ♑ |
| 8 ♏ | 9 ♑ | 8 ♑ | 8 ♓ | 8 ♈ | 9 ♊ | 8 ♋ | 10 ♍ | 8 ♎ | 8 ♏ | 9 ♑ | 8 ♒ |
| 10 ♐ | 11 ♒ | 10 ♒ | 11 ♈ | 10 ♉ | 11 ♋ | 11 ♌ | 12 ♎ | 11 ♏ | 10 ♐ | 11 ♒ | 10 ♓ |
| 12 ♑ | 13 ♓ | 12 ♓ | 13 ♉ | 13 ♊ | 14 ♌ | 14 ♍ | 15 ♏ | 13 ♐ | 13 ♑ | 13 ♓ | 12 ♈ |
| 14 ♒ | 15 ♈ | 14 ♈ | 15 ♊ | 15 ♋ | 16 ♍ | 16 ♎ | 17 ♐ | 15 ♑ | 15 ♒ | 15 ♈ | 15 ♉ |
| 16 ♓ | 17 ♉ | 17 ♉ | 18 ♋ | 18 ♌ | 19 ♎ | 18 ♏ | 19 ♑ | 17 ♒ | 17 ♓ | 17 ♉ | 17 ♊ |
| 18 ♈ | 20 ♊ | 19 ♊ | 20 ♌ | 20 ♍ | 21 ♏ | 21 ♐ | 21 ♒ | 19 ♓ | 19 ♈ | 19 ♊ | 20 ♋ |
| 21 ♉ | 22 ♋ | 22 ♋ | 23 ♍ | 23 ♎ | 23 ♐ | 23 ♑ | 23 ♓ | 22 ♈ | 21 ♉ | 22 ♋ | 22 ♌ |
| 23 ♊ | 25 ♌ | 24 ♌ | 25 ♎ | 25 ♏ | 25 ♑ | 25 ♒ | 25 ♈ | 24 ♉ | 23 ♊ | 25 ♌ | 25 ♍ |
| 26 ♋ | 27 ♍ | 26 ♍ | 27 ♏ | 27 ♐ | 27 ♒ | 27 ♓ | 27 ♉ | 26 ♊ | 26 ♋ | 27 ♍ | 27 ♎ |
| 28 ♌ | | 29 ♎ | 29 ♐ | 29 ♑ | 29 ♓ | 29 ♈ | 30 ♊ | 29 ♋ | 28 ♌ | 30 ♎ | 29 ♏ |
| 31 ♍ | | 31 ♏ | | 31 ♒ | | 31 ♉ | | | 31 ♍ | | |

*Key:*  Aries   Taurus   Gemini   Cancer   Leo   Virgo

         ♈        ♉          ♊           ♋         ♌        ♍

## 1908

| JAN. | FEB. | MAR. | APR. | MAY | JUNE | JULY | AUG. | SEPT. | OCT. | NOV. | DEC. |
|---|---|---|---|---|---|---|---|---|---|---|---|
| 1 ♐ | 1 ♒ | 2 ♓ | 2 ♉ | 2 ♊ | 3 ♌ | 3 ♍ | 1 ♎ | 3 ♐ | 2 ♑ | 3 ♓ | 2 ♈ |
| 3 ♑ | 3 ♓ | 4 ♈ | 4 ♊ | 4 ♋ | 5 ♍ | 5 ♎ | 4 ♏ | 5 ♑ | 4 ♒ | 5 ♈ | 4 ♉ |
| 5 ♒ | 5 ♈ | 6 ♉ | 7 ♋ | 7 ♌ | 7 ♎ | 8 ♏ | 6 ♐ | 7 ♒ | 6 ♓ | 7 ♉ | 6 ♊ |
| 7 ♓ | 7 ♉ | 8 ♊ | 9 ♌ | 9 ♍ | 10 ♏ | 10 ♐ | 8 ♑ | 9 ♓ | 8 ♈ | 9 ♊ | 8 ♋ |
| 9 ♈ | 10 ♊ | 10 ♋ | 12 ♍ | 11 ♎ | 12 ♐ | 12 ♑ | 10 ♒ | 11 ♈ | 10 ♉ | 11 ♋ | 11 ♌ |
| 11 ♉ | 12 ♋ | 13 ♌ | 14 ♎ | 14 ♏ | 15 ♑ | 14 ♒ | 12 ♓ | 13 ♉ | 12 ♊ | 14 ♌ | 13 ♍ |
| 13 ♊ | 15 ♌ | 15 ♍ | 16 ♏ | 16 ♐ | 17 ♒ | 16 ♓ | 14 ♈ | 15 ♊ | 15 ♋ | 16 ♍ | 16 ♎ |
| 16 ♋ | 17 ♍ | 18 ♎ | 19 ♐ | 18 ♑ | 19 ♓ | 18 ♈ | 16 ♉ | 17 ♋ | 17 ♌ | 19 ♎ | 18 ♏ |
| 18 ♌ | 20 ♎ | 20 ♏ | 21 ♑ | 20 ♒ | 21 ♈ | 20 ♉ | 19 ♊ | 20 ♌ | 20 ♍ | 21 ♏ | 21 ♐ |
| 21 ♍ | 22 ♏ | 22 ♐ | 23 ♒ | 22 ♓ | 24 ♉ | 22 ♊ | 21 ♋ | 22 ♍ | 22 ♎ | 23 ♐ | 23 ♑ |
| 23 ♎ | 24 ♐ | 25 ♑ | 25 ♓ | 25 ♈ | 26 ♊ | 25 ♋ | 24 ♌ | 25 ♎ | 25 ♏ | 26 ♑ | 25 ♒ |
| 26 ♏ | 26 ♑ | 27 ♒ | 27 ♈ | 27 ♉ | 28 ♋ | 27 ♌ | 26 ♍ | 27 ♏ | 27 ♐ | 28 ♒ | 27 ♓ |
| 28 ♐ | 29 ♒ | 29 ♓ | 29 ♉ | 29 ♊ | 30 ♌ | 30 ♍ | 29 ♎ | 30 ♐ | 29 ♑ | 30 ♓ | 29 ♈ |
| 30 ♑ |  | 31 ♈ |  | 31 ♋ |  |  | 31 ♏ |  | 31 ♒ |  | 31 ♉ |

## 1909

| JAN. | FEB. | MAR. | APR. | MAY | JUNE | JULY | AUG. | SEPT. | OCT. | NOV. | DEC. |
|---|---|---|---|---|---|---|---|---|---|---|---|
| 3 ♊ | 1 ♋ | 3 ♌ | 2 ♍ | 1 ♎ | 3 ♐ | 2 ♑ | 1 ♒ | 1 ♈ | 1 ♉ | 1 ♋ | 1 ♌ |
| 5 ♋ | 4 ♌ | 5 ♍ | 4 ♎ | 4 ♏ | 5 ♑ | 4 ♒ | 3 ♓ | 3 ♉ | 3 ♊ | 3 ♌ | 3 ♍ |
| 7 ♌ | 6 ♍ | 8 ♎ | 7 ♏ | 6 ♐ | 7 ♒ | 6 ♓ | 5 ♈ | 5 ♊ | 5 ♋ | 6 ♍ | 6 ♎ |
| 10 ♍ | 9 ♎ | 10 ♏ | 9 ♐ | 9 ♑ | 9 ♓ | 9 ♈ | 7 ♉ | 8 ♋ | 7 ♌ | 8 ♎ | 8 ♏ |
| 12 ♎ | 11 ♏ | 13 ♐ | 11 ♑ | 11 ♒ | 11 ♈ | 11 ♉ | 9 ♊ | 10 ♌ | 10 ♍ | 11 ♏ | 11 ♐ |
| 15 ♏ | 13 ♐ | 15 ♑ | 14 ♒ | 13 ♓ | 13 ♉ | 13 ♊ | 11 ♋ | 12 ♍ | 12 ♎ | 13 ♐ | 13 ♑ |
| 17 ♐ | 16 ♑ | 17 ♒ | 16 ♓ | 15 ♈ | 16 ♊ | 15 ♋ | 14 ♌ | 15 ♎ | 16 ♏ | 16 ♑ | 15 ♒ |
| 19 ♑ | 18 ♒ | 19 ♓ | 18 ♈ | 17 ♉ | 18 ♋ | 17 ♌ | 16 ♍ | 17 ♏ | 18 ♐ | 18 ♒ | 18 ♓ |
| 21 ♒ | 20 ♓ | 21 ♈ | 20 ♉ | 19 ♊ | 20 ♌ | 20 ♍ | 19 ♎ | 20 ♐ | 20 ♑ | 20 ♓ | 20 ♈ |
| 23 ♓ | 22 ♈ | 23 ♉ | 22 ♊ | 21 ♋ | 22 ♍ | 22 ♎ | 21 ♏ | 22 ♑ | 22 ♒ | 23 ♈ | 22 ♉ |
| 25 ♈ | 24 ♉ | 25 ♊ | 24 ♋ | 24 ♌ | 25 ♎ | 24 ♏ | 24 ♐ | 25 ♒ | 24 ♓ | 25 ♉ | 24 ♊ |
| 28 ♉ | 26 ♊ | 28 ♋ | 26 ♌ | 26 ♍ | 27 ♏ | 27 ♐ | 26 ♑ | 27 ♓ | 26 ♈ | 27 ♊ | 26 ♋ |
| 30 ♊ | 28 ♋ | 30 ♌ | 29 ♍ | 29 ♎ | 30 ♐ | 30 ♑ | 28 ♒ | 29 ♈ | 28 ♉ | 29 ♋ | 28 ♌ |
|  |  |  |  | 31 ♏ |  |  | 30 ♓ |  | 30 ♊ |  | 31 ♍ |

| Libra | Scorpio | Sagittarius | Capricorn | Aquarius | Pisces |
|---|---|---|---|---|---|
| ♎ | ♏ | ♐ | ♑ | ♒ | ♓ |

## 1910

| JAN. | FEB. | MAR. | APR. | MAY | JUNE | JULY | AUG. | SEPT. | OCT. | NOV. | DEC. |
|---|---|---|---|---|---|---|---|---|---|---|---|
| 2 ♎ | 1 ♏ | 3 ♐ | 2 ♑ | 1 ♒ | 2 ♈ | 1 ♉ | 2 ♋ | 2 ♍ | 2 ♎ | 1 ♏ | 1 ♐ |
| 5 ♏ | 3 ♐ | 5 ♑ | 4 ♒ | 3 ♓ | 4 ♉ | 3 ♊ | 4 ♌ | 5 ♎ | 5 ♏ | 3 ♐ | 3 ♑ |
| 7 ♐ | 6 ♑ | 8 ♒ | 6 ♓ | 6 ♈ | 6 ♊ | 5 ♋ | 6 ♍ | 7 ♏ | 7 ♐ | 6 ♑ | 6 ♒ |
| 9 ♑ | 8 ♒ | 10 ♓ | 8 ♈ | 8 ♉ | 8 ♋ | 8 ♌ | 8 ♎ | 10 ♐ | 10 ♑ | 8 ♒ | 8 ♓ |
| 12 ♒ | 10 ♓ | 12 ♈ | 10 ♉ | 10 ♊ | 10 ♌ | 10 ♍ | 11 ♏ | 12 ♑ | 12 ♒ | 11 ♓ | 10 ♈ |
| 14 ♓ | 12 ♈ | 14 ♉ | 12 ♊ | 12 ♋ | 12 ♍ | 12 ♎ | 13 ♐ | 15 ♒ | 14 ♓ | 13 ♈ | 12 ♉ |
| 16 ♈ | 14 ♉ | 16 ♊ | 14 ♋ | 14 ♌ | 15 ♎ | 15 ♏ | 16 ♑ | 17 ♓ | 16 ♈ | 15 ♉ | 14 ♊ |
| 18 ♉ | 16 ♊ | 18 ♋ | 16 ♌ | 16 ♍ | 17 ♏ | 17 ♐ | 18 ♒ | 19 ♈ | 18 ♉ | 17 ♊ | 16 ♋ |
| 20 ♊ | 19 ♋ | 20 ♌ | 19 ♍ | 18 ♎ | 20 ♐ | 20 ♑ | 21 ♓ | 21 ♉ | 20 ♊ | 19 ♋ | 18 ♌ |
| 22 ♋ | 21 ♌ | 23 ♍ | 21 ♎ | 20 ♏ | 22 ♑ | 22 ♒ | 23 ♈ | 23 ♊ | 23 ♋ | 21 ♌ | 21 ♍ |
| 25 ♌ | 23 ♍ | 25 ♎ | 24 ♏ | 24 ♐ | 25 ♒ | 24 ♓ | 25 ♉ | 25 ♋ | 25 ♌ | 23 ♍ | 23 ♎ |
| 27 ♍ | 26 ♎ | 28 ♏ | 26 ♐ | 26 ♑ | 27 ♓ | 26 ♈ | 27 ♊ | 27 ♌ | 27 ♍ | 26 ♎ | 25 ♏ |
| 29 ♎ | 28 ♏ | 30 ♐ | 29 ♑ | 28 ♒ | 29 ♈ | 29 ♉ | 29 ♋ | 30 ♍ | 29 ♎ | 28 ♏ | 28 ♐ |
|  |  |  |  | 31 ♓ |  | 31 ♊ | 31 ♌ |  |  |  | 30 ♑ |

## 1911

| JAN. | FEB. | MAR. | APR. | MAY | JUNE | JULY | AUG. | SEPT. | OCT. | NOV. | DEC. |
|---|---|---|---|---|---|---|---|---|---|---|---|
| 2 ♒ | 3 ♈ | 2 ♈ | 1 ♉ | 2 ♋ | 3 ♍ | 2 ♎ | 1 ♏ | 2 ♑ | 2 ♒ | 1 ♓ | 3 ♉ |
| 4 ♓ | 5 ♉ | 4 ♉ | 3 ♊ | 4 ♌ | 5 ♎ | 4 ♏ | 3 ♐ | 5 ♒ | 4 ♓ | 3 ♈ | 5 ♊ |
| 6 ♈ | 7 ♊ | 6 ♊ | 5 ♋ | 6 ♍ | 7 ♏ | 6 ♐ | 6 ♑ | 7 ♓ | 7 ♈ | 5 ♉ | 7 ♋ |
| 9 ♉ | 9 ♋ | 8 ♋ | 7 ♌ | 9 ♎ | 10 ♐ | 9 ♑ | 8 ♒ | 9 ♈ | 9 ♉ | 7 ♊ | 9 ♌ |
| 11 ♊ | 11 ♌ | 11 ♌ | 9 ♍ | 11 ♏ | 12 ♑ | 11 ♒ | 11 ♓ | 11 ♉ | 11 ♊ | 9 ♋ | 11 ♍ |
| 13 ♋ | 13 ♍ | 13 ♍ | 11 ♎ | 13 ♐ | 14 ♒ | 14 ♓ | 13 ♈ | 14 ♊ | 13 ♋ | 11 ♌ | 13 ♎ |
| 15 ♌ | 16 ♎ | 15 ♎ | 14 ♏ | 16 ♑ | 17 ♓ | 17 ♈ | 15 ♉ | 16 ♋ | 15 ♌ | 14 ♍ | 15 ♏ |
| 17 ♍ | 18 ♏ | 17 ♏ | 16 ♐ | 18 ♒ | 19 ♈ | 19 ♉ | 17 ♊ | 18 ♌ | 17 ♍ | 16 ♎ | 18 ♐ |
| 19 ♎ | 21 ♐ | 20 ♐ | 19 ♑ | 21 ♓ | 22 ♉ | 21 ♊ | 20 ♋ | 20 ♍ | 20 ♎ | 18 ♏ | 20 ♑ |
| 22 ♏ | 23° | 22 ♑ | 21 ♒ | 23 ♈ | 24 ♊ | 23 ♋ | 22 ♌ | 22 ♎ | 22 ♏ | 21 ♐ | 23 ♒ |
| 24 ♐ | 25 ♒ | 25 ♒ | 24 ♓ | 25 ♉ | 26 ♋ | 25 ♌ | 24 ♍ | 25 ♏ | 24 ♐ | 23 ♑ | 25 ♓ |
| 27 ♑ | 28 ♓ | 27 ♓ | 26 ♈ | 27 ♊ | 28 ♌ | 27 ♍ | 26 ♎ | 27 ♐ | 27 ♑ | 26 ♒ | 28 ♈ |
| 29 ♒ |  | 29 ♈ | 28 ♉ | 29 ♋ | 30 ♍ | 29 ♎ | 28 ♏ | 29 ♑ | 29 ♒ | 28 ♓ | 30 ♉ |
| 31 ♓ |  |  | 30 ♊ | 31 ♌ |  | 31 ♏ | 31 ♐ |  | 31 ♓ | 30 ♈ |  |

| *Key:* | Aries | Taurus | Gemini | Cancer | Leo | Virgo |
|---|---|---|---|---|---|---|
|  | ♈ | ♉ | ♊ | ♋ | ♌ | ♍ |

## 1912

| JAN. | FEB. | MAR. | APR. | MAY | JUNE | JULY | AUG. | SEPT. | OCT. | NOV. | DEC. |
|---|---|---|---|---|---|---|---|---|---|---|---|
| 1 ♊ | 2 ♌ | 2 ♍ | 1 ♎ | 2 ♐ | 1 ♑ | 1 ♒ | 2 ♈ | 1 ♉ | 3 ♋ | 1 ♌ | 2 ♎ |
| 3 ♋ | 4 ♍ | 4 ♎ | 3 ♏ | 5 ♑ | 4 ♒ | 3 ♓ | 5 ♉ | 3 ♊ | 5 ♌ | 3 ♍ | 5 ♏ |
| 5 ♌ | 6 ♎ | 6 ♏ | 5 ♐ | 7 ♒ | 6 ♓ | 6 ♈ | 7 ♊ | 5 ♋ | 7 ♍ | 5 ♎ | 7 ♐ |
| 7 ♍ | 8 ♏ | 9 ♐ | 8 ♑ | 10 ♓ | 9 ♈ | 8 ♉ | 9 ♋ | 7 ♌ | 9 ♎ | 7 ♏ | 9 ♑ |
| 9 ♎ | 10 ♐ | 11 ♑ | 10 ♒ | 12 ♈ | 11 ♉ | 11 ♊ | 11 ♌ | 9 ♍ | 11 ♏ | 10 ♐ | 12 ♒ |
| 12 ♏ | 13 ♑ | 14 ♒ | 13 ♓ | 15 ♉ | 13 ♊ | 13 ♋ | 13 ♍ | 11 ♎ | 13 ♐ | 12 ♑ | 14 ♓ |
| 14 ♐ | 15 ♒ | 16 ♓ | 15 ♈ | 17 ♊ | 15 ♋ | 15 ♌ | 15 ♎ | 14 ♏ | 16 ♑ | 14 ♒ | 17 ♈ |
| 17 ♑ | 18 ♓ | 19 ♈ | 17 ♉ | 19 ♋ | 17 ♌ | 17 ♍ | 17 ♏ | 16 ♐ | 18 ♒ | 17 ♓ | 19 ♉ |
| 19 ♒ | 20 ♈ | 21 ♉ | 19 ♊ | 21 ♌ | 19 ♍ | 19 ♎ | 19 ♐ | 18 ♑ | 21 ♓ | 19 ♈ | 21 ♊ |
| 22 ♓ | 23 ♉ | 23 ♊ | 21 ♋ | 23 ♍ | 21 ♎ | 21 ♏ | 22 ♑ | 21 ♒ | 23 ♈ | 22 ♉ | 24 ♋ |
| 24 ♈ | 25 ♊ | 25 ♋ | 24 ♌ | 25 ♎ | 24 ♏ | 23 ♐ | 24 ♒ | 23 ♓ | 25 ♉ | 24 ♊ | 26 ♌ |
| 26 ♉ | 27 ♋ | 27 ♌ | 26 ♍ | 27 ♏ | 26 ♐ | 26 ♑ | 27 ♓ | 26 ♈ | 28 ♊ | 26 ♋ | 28 ♍ |
| 29 ♊ | 29 ♌ | 29 ♍ | 28 ♎ | 30 ♐ | 28 ♑ | 28 ♒ | 29 ♈ | 28 ♉ | 30 ♋ | 28 ♌ | 30 ♎ |
| 31 ♋ |  |  | 30 ♏ |  |  | 31 ♓ |  | 30 ♊ |  | 30 ♍ |  |

## 1913

| JAN. | FEB. | MAR. | APR. | MAY | JUNE | JULY | AUG. | SEPT. | OCT. | NOV. | DEC. |
|---|---|---|---|---|---|---|---|---|---|---|---|
| 1 ♏ | 2 ♑ | 1 ♑ | 2 ♓ | 2 ♈ | 1 ♉ | 1 ♊ | 1 ♌ | 2 ♎ | 1 ♏ | 2 ♑ | 2 ♒ |
| 3 ♐ | 4 ♒ | 4 ♒ | 5 ♈ | 5 ♉ | 3 ♊ | 3 ♋ | 3 ♍ | 4 ♏ | 3 ♐ | 4 ♒ | 4 ♓ |
| 6 ♑ | 7 ♓ | 6 ♓ | 7 ♉ | 8 ♊ | 5 ♋ | 5 ♌ | 5 ♎ | 6 ♐ | 6 ♑ | 7 ♓ | 7 ♈ |
| 8 ♒ | 9 ♈ | 9 ♈ | 10 ♊ | 10 ♋ | 7 ♌ | 7 ♍ | 8 ♏ | 8 ♑ | 8 ♒ | 9 ♈ | 9 ♉ |
| 11 ♓ | 12 ♉ | 11 ♉ | 12 ♋ | 12 ♌ | 9 ♍ | 9 ♎ | 10 ♐ | 11 ♒ | 10 ♓ | 12 ♉ | 12 ♊ |
| 13 ♈ | 14 ♊ | 13 ♊ | 14 ♌ | 14 ♍ | 12 ♎ | 11 ♏ | 12 ♑ | 13 ♓ | 13 ♈ | 14 ♊ | 14 ♋ |
| 16 ♉ | 16 ♋ | 16 ♋ | 16 ♍ | 16 ♎ | 14 ♏ | 13 ♐ | 14 ♒ | 15 ♈ | 15 ♉ | 17 ♋ | 16 ♌ |
| 18 ♊ | 18 ♌ | 18 ♌ | 18 ♎ | 18 ♏ | 16 ♐ | 16 ♑ | 17 ♓ | 18 ♉ | 18 ♊ | 19 ♌ | 18 ♍ |
| 20 ♋ | 20 ♍ | 20 ♍ | 20 ♏ | 20 ♐ | 18 ♑ | 18 ♒ | 19 ♈ | 21 ♊ | 20 ♋ | 21 ♍ | 20 ♎ |
| 22 ♌ | 22 ♎ | 22 ♎ | 23 ♐ | 22 ♑ | 21 ♒ | 21 ♓ | 22 ♉ | 23 ♋ | 23 ♌ | 23 ♎ | 22 ♏ |
| 24 ♍ | 25 ♏ | 24 ♏ | 25 ♑ | 24 ♒ | 23 ♓ | 23 ♈ | 24 ♊ | 25 ♌ | 25 ♍ | 25 ♏ | 25 ♐ |
| 26 ♎ | 27 ♐ | 26 ♐ | 27 ♒ | 27 ♓ | 26 ♈ | 26 ♉ | 26 ♋ | 27 ♍ | 27 ♎ | 27 ♐ | 27 ♑ |
| 28 ♏ |  | 28 ♑ | 30 ♓ | 30 ♈ | 28 ♉ | 28 ♊ | 28 ♌ | 29 ♎ | 29 ♏ | 29 ♑ | 29 ♒ |
| 30 ♐ |  | 31 ♒ |  |  | 30 ♊ | 30 ♋ | 31 ♍ |  | 31 ♐ |  | 31 ♓ |

| Libra | Scorpio | Sagittarius | Capricorn | Aquarius | Pisces |
|---|---|---|---|---|---|
| ♎ | ♏ | ♐ | ♑ | ♒ | ♓ |

## 1914

| JAN. | FEB. | MAR. | APR. | MAY | JUNE | JULY | AUG. | SEPT. | OCT. | NOV. | DEC. |
|---|---|---|---|---|---|---|---|---|---|---|---|
| 3 ♈ | 2 ♉ | 1 ♉ | 2 ♋ | 2 ♌ | 2 ♎ | 2 ♏ | 2 ♑ | 1 ♒ | 3 ♈ | 2 ♉ | 1 ♊ |
| 5 ♉ | 4 ♊ | 4 ♊ | 5 ♌ | 4 ♍ | 5 ♏ | 4 ♐ | 5 ♒ | 3 ♓ | 5 ♉ | 4 ♊ | 4 ♋ |
| 8 ♊ | 7 ♋ | 6 ♋ | 7 ♍ | 6 ♎ | 7 ♐ | 6 ♑ | 7 ♓ | 6 ♈ | 8 ♊ | 7 ♋ | 6 ♌ |
| 10 ♋ | 9 ♌ | 8 ♌ | 9 ♎ | 8 ♏ | 9 ♑ | 8 ♒ | 9 ♈ | 8 ♉ | 10 ♋ | 9 ♌ | 9 ♍ |
| 12 ♌ | 11 ♍ | 10 ♍ | 11 ♏ | 11 ♐ | 11 ♒ | 11 ♓ | 12 ♉ | 11 ♊ | 13 ♌ | 11 ♍ | 11 ♎ |
| 14 ♍ | 13 ♎ | 12 ♎ | 13 ♐ | 13 ♑ | 13 ♓ | 13 ♈ | 14 ♊ | 13 ♋ | 15 ♍ | 14 ♎ | 13 ♏ |
| 17 ♎ | 15 ♏ | 14 ♏ | 15 ♑ | 15 ♒ | 16 ♈ | 15 ♉ | 17 ♋ | 15 ♌ | 17 ♎ | 16 ♏ | 15 ♐ |
| 19 ♏ | 17 ♐ | 16 ♐ | 17 ♒ | 18 ♓ | 18 ♉ | 17 ♊ | 19 ♌ | 18 ♍ | 20 ♏ | 18 ♐ | 17 ♑ |
| 21 ♐ | 19 ♑ | 19 ♑ | 20 ♓ | 20 ♈ | 20 ♊ | 20 ♋ | 21 ♍ | 20 ♎ | 22 ♐ | 20 ♑ | 19 ♒ |
| 23 ♑ | 22 ♒ | 21 ♒ | 22 ♈ | 22 ♉ | 23 ♋ | 22 ♌ | 23 ♎ | 22 ♏ | 24 ♑ | 22 ♒ | 21 ♓ |
| 25 ♒ | 24 ♓ | 23 ♓ | 25 ♉ | 24 ♊ | 25 ♌ | 25 ♍ | 25 ♏ | 24 ♐ | 26 ♒ | 24 ♓ | 24 ♈ |
| 28 ♓ | 27 ♈ | 26 ♈ | 27 ♊ | 26 ♋ | 28 ♍ | 27 ♎ | 27 ♐ | 26 ♑ | 28 ♓ | 26 ♈ | 26 ♉ |
| 30 ♈ | | 28 ♉ | 30 ♋ | 29 ♌ | 30 ♎ | 29 ♏ | 30 ♑ | 28 ♒ | 30 ♈ | 29 ♉ | 29 ♊ |
| | | 31 ♊ | | 31 ♍ | | 31 ♐ | | 30 ♓ | | | 31 ♋ |

## 1915

| JAN. | FEB. | MAR. | APR. | MAY | JUNE | JULY | AUG. | SEPT. | OCT. | NOV. | DEC. |
|---|---|---|---|---|---|---|---|---|---|---|---|
| 3 ♌ | 1 ♍ | 1 ♍ | 1 ♏ | 1 ♐ | 1 ♒ | 1 ♓ | 2 ♉ | 3 ♋ | 3 ♌ | 2 ♍ | 1 ♎ |
| 5 ♍ | 3 ♎ | 3 ♎ | 3 ♐ | 3 ♑ | 3 ♓ | 3 ♈ | 4 ♊ | 5 ♌ | 5 ♍ | 4 ♎ | 3 ♏ |
| 7 ♎ | 5 ♏ | 5 ♏ | 5 ♑ | 5 ♒ | 5 ♈ | 5 ♉ | 7 ♋ | 8 ♍ | 7 ♎ | 6 ♏ | 5 ♐ |
| 9 ♏ | 8 ♐ | 7 ♐ | 7 ♒ | 7 ♓ | 8 ♉ | 8 ♊ | 9 ♌ | 10 ♎ | 9 ♏ | 8 ♐ | 7 ♑ |
| 11 ♐ | 10 ♑ | 9 ♑ | 10 ♓ | 9 ♈ | 10 ♊ | 10 ♋ | 11 ♍ | 12 ♏ | 11 ♐ | 10 ♑ | 9 ♒ |
| 13 ♑ | 12 ♒ | 11 ♒ | 12 ♈ | 11 ♉ | 12 ♋ | 13 ♌ | 14 ♎ | 14 ♐ | 14 ♑ | 12 ♒ | 11 ♓ |
| 16 ♒ | 14 ♓ | 13 ♓ | 15 ♉ | 14 ♊ | 15 ♌ | 15 ♍ | 16 ♏ | 16 ♑ | 16 ♒ | 14 ♓ | 14 ♈ |
| 18 ♓ | 16 ♈ | 16 ♈ | 17 ♊ | 16 ♋ | 17 ♍ | 17 ♎ | 18 ♐ | 18 ♒ | 18 ♓ | 16 ♈ | 16 ♉ |
| 20 ♈ | 18 ♉ | 18 ♉ | 20 ♋ | 18 ♌ | 19 ♎ | 20 ♏ | 20 ♑ | 21 ♓ | 20 ♈ | 19 ♉ | 19 ♊ |
| 23 ♉ | 21 ♊ | 21 ♊ | 22 ♌ | 20 ♍ | 22 ♏ | 22 ♐ | 22 ♒ | 23 ♈ | 23 ♉ | 21 ♊ | 21 ♋ |
| 25 ♊ | 24 ♋ | 23 ♋ | 24 ♍ | 22 ♎ | 24 ♐ | 24 ♑ | 24 ♓ | 25 ♉ | 25 ♊ | 24 ♋ | 23 ♌ |
| 28 ♋ | 26 ♌ | 26 ♌ | 27 ♎ | 24 ♏ | 26 ♑ | 26 ♒ | 27 ♈ | 28 ♊ | 28 ♋ | 26 ♌ | 26 ♍ |
| 30 ♌ | | 28 ♍ | 29 ♏ | 26 ♐ | 28 ♒ | 28 ♓ | 29 ♉ | 30 ♋ | 30 ♌ | 29 ♍ | 29 ♎ |
| | | 30 ♎ | | 28 ♑ | | 30 ♈ | 31 ♊ | | | | 31 ♏ |

*Key:*  Aries   Taurus   Gemini   Cancer   Leo   Virgo

♈        ♉          ♊          ♋         ♌      ♍

## 1916

| JAN. | FEB. | MAR. | APR. | MAY | JUNE | JULY | AUG. | SEPT. | OCT. | NOV. | DEC. |
|---|---|---|---|---|---|---|---|---|---|---|---|
| 2 ♐ | 2 ♒ | 1 ♒ | 1 ♈ | 1 ♉ | 2 ♋ | 2 ♌ | 1 ♍ | 2 ♏ | 1 ♐ | 2 ♒ | 1 ♓ |
| 4 ♑ | 4 ♓ | 3 ♓ | 4 ♉ | 3 ♊ | 5 ♌ | 3 ♎ | 3 ♎ | 4 ♐ | 3 ♑ | 4 ♓ | 3 ♈ |
| 6 ♒ | 6 ♈ | 5 ♈ | 6 ♊ | 6 ♋ | 7 ♍ | 5 ♏ | 5 ♏ | 6 ♑ | 5 ♒ | 6 ♈ | 5 ♉ |
| 8 ♓ | 9 ♉ | 7 ♉ | 8 ♋ | 8 ♌ | 9 ♎ | 9 ♏ | 8 ♐ | 8 ♒ | 7 ♓ | 8 ♉ | 8 ♊ |
| 10 ♈ | 11 ♊ | 10 ♊ | 11 ♌ | 11 ♍ | 12 ♏ | 11 ♐ | 10 ♑ | 10 ♒ | 10 ♈ | 10 ♊ | 10 ♋ |
| 12 ♉ | 14 ♋ | 12 ♋ | 13 ♍ | 13 ♎ | 14 ♐ | 13 ♑ | 12 ♒ | 12 ♓ | 12 ♉ | 13 ♋ | 13 ♌ |
| 15 ♊ | 16 ♌ | 15 ♌ | 16 ♎ | 15 ♏ | 16 ♑ | 15 ♒ | 14 ♓ | 14 ♉ | 14 ♊ | 15 ♌ | 15 ♍ |
| 17 ♋ | 19 ♍ | 17 ♍ | 18 ♏ | 17 ♐ | 18 ♒ | 17 ♓ | 16 ♈ | 17 ♊ | 16 ♋ | 18 ♍ | 18 ♎ |
| 20 ♌ | 21 ♎ | 19 ♎ | 20 ♐ | 19 ♑ | 20 ♓ | 19 ♈ | 18 ♉ | 19 ♋ | 19 ♌ | 20 ♎ | 20 ♏ |
| 22 ♍ | 23 ♏ | 22 ♏ | 22 ♑ | 21 ♒ | 22 ♈ | 22 ♉ | 20 ♊ | 22 ♌ | 21 ♍ | 23 ♏ | 22 ♐ |
| 25 ♎ | 25 ♐ | 24 ♐ | 24 ♒ | 24 ♓ | 24 ♉ | 24 ♊ | 22 ♋ | 24 ♍ | 25 ♎ | 25 ♐ | 24 ♑ |
| 27 ♏ | 28 ♑ | 26 ♑ | 26 ♓ | 26 ♈ | 26 ♋ | 26 ♋ | 25 ♌ | 27 ♎ | 26 ♏ | 27 ♑ | 26 ♒ |
| 29 ♐ | | 28 ♒ | 29 ♈ | 28 ♉ | 29 ♋ | 29 ♌ | 28 ♍ | 29 ♏ | 28 ♐ | 29 ♒ | 28 ♓ |
| 31 ♑ | | 30 ♓ | | 30 ♊ | | | 30 ♎ | | 30 ♑ | | 30 ♈ |

## 1917

| JAN. | FEB. | MAR. | APR. | MAY | JUNE | JULY | AUG. | SEPT. | OCT. | NOV. | DEC. |
|---|---|---|---|---|---|---|---|---|---|---|---|
| 2 ♉ | 3 ♋ | 2 ♋ | 1 ♌ | 1 ♍ | 2 ♏ | 1 ♐ | 2 ♒ | 2 ♈ | 2 ♉ | 3 ♋ | 2 ♌ |
| 4 ♊ | 5 ♌ | 4 ♌ | 3 ♍ | 3 ♎ | 4 ♐ | 4 ♑ | 4 ♓ | 4 ♉ | 4 ♊ | 5 ♌ | 5 ♍ |
| 6 ♋ | 8 ♍ | 7 ♍ | 6 ♎ | 5 ♏ | 6 ♑ | 6 ♒ | 6 ♈ | 7 ♊ | 6 ♋ | 8 ♍ | 7 ♎ |
| 9 ♌ | 10 ♎ | 9 ♎ | 8 ♏ | 8 ♐ | 8 ♒ | 8 ♓ | 8 ♉ | 9 ♋ | 9 ♌ | 10 ♎ | 10 ♏ |
| 11 ♍ | 13 ♏ | 12 ♏ | 10 ♐ | 10 ♑ | 10 ♓ | 10 ♈ | 10 ♊ | 11 ♌ | 11 ♍ | 13 ♏ | 12 ♐ |
| 14 ♎ | 15 ♐ | 14 ♐ | 13 ♑ | 12 ♒ | 12 ♈ | 12 ♉ | 13 ♋ | 14 ♍ | 14 ♎ | 15 ♐ | 14 ♑ |
| 16 ♏ | 17 ♑ | 16 ♑ | 15 ♒ | 14 ♓ | 15 ♉ | 14 ♊ | 15 ♌ | 17 ♎ | 16 ♏ | 17 ♑ | 17 ♒ |
| 19 ♐ | 19 ♒ | 18 ♒ | 17 ♓ | 16 ♈ | 17 ♊ | 16 ♋ | 18 ♍ | 19 ♏ | 19 ♐ | 19 ♒ | 19 ♓ |
| 21 ♑ | 21 ♓ | 21 ♓ | 19 ♈ | 18 ♉ | 19 ♋ | 19 ♌ | 20 ♎ | 21 ♐ | 21 ♑ | 22 ♓ | 21 ♈ |
| 23 ♒ | 23 ♈ | 23 ♈ | 21 ♉ | 21 ♊ | 22 ♌ | 21 ♍ | 23 ♏ | 24 ♑ | 23 ♒ | 24 ♈ | 23 ♉ |
| 25 ♓ | 25 ♉ | 25 ♉ | 23 ♊ | 23 ♋ | 24 ♍ | 26 ♏ | 25 ♐ | 28 ♓ | 25 ♈ | 26 ♉ | 25 ♊ |
| 27 ♈ | 27 ♊ | 27 ♊ | 26 ♋ | 25 ♌ | 27 ♎ | 27 ♑ | 28 ♓ | 30 ♈ | 27 ♈ | 28 ♊ | 27 ♋ |
| 29 ♉ | | 29 ♋ | 28 ♌ | 28 ♍ | 29 ♏ | 29 ♒ | 29 ♒ | | 29 ♉ | 30 ♋ | 30 ♌ |
| 31 ♊ | | 30 ♎ | | | | 31 ♓ | 31 ♓ | | 31 ♊ | | |

| Libra | Scorpio | Sagittarius | Capricorn | Aquarius | Pisces |
|---|---|---|---|---|---|
| ♎ | ♏ | ♐ | ♑ | ♒ | ♓ |

## 1918

| JAN. | FEB. | MAR. | APR. | MAY | JUNE | JULY | AUG. | SEPT. | OCT. | NOV. | DEC. |
|---|---|---|---|---|---|---|---|---|---|---|---|
| 1 ♍ | 3 ♏ | 2 ♏ | 1 ♐ | 3 ♒ | 1 ♓ | 2 ♉ | 1 ♊ | 2 ♌ | 1 ♍ | 2 ♏ | 2 ♐ |
| 4 ♎ | 5 ♐ | 4 ♐ | 3 ♑ | 5 ♓ | 3 ♈ | 5 ♊ | 3 ♋ | 4 ♍ | 4 ♎ | 5 ♐ | 5 ♑ |
| 6 ♏ | 7 ♑ | 7 ♑ | 5 ♒ | 7 ♈ | 5 ♉ | 7 ♋ | 5 ♌ | 6 ♎ | 6 ♏ | 7 ♑ | 7 ♒ |
| 9 ♐ | 9 ♒ | 9 ♒ | 7 ♓ | 9 ♉ | 7 ♊ | 9 ♌ | 8 ♍ | 9 ♏ | 9 ♐ | 10 ♒ | 9 ♓ |
| 11 ♑ | 11 ♓ | 11 ♓ | 9 ♈ | 11 ♊ | 9 ♋ | 11 ♍ | 10 ♎ | 11 ♐ | 11 ♑ | 12 ♓ | 11 ♈ |
| 13 ♒ | 13 ♈ | 13 ♈ | 11 ♉ | 13 ♋ | 12 ♌ | 14 ♎ | 13 ♏ | 14 ♑ | 14 ♒ | 14 ♈ | 14 ♉ |
| 15 ♓ | 15 ♉ | 15 ♉ | 13 ♊ | 15 ♌ | 14 ♍ | 16 ♏ | 15 ♐ | 16 ♒ | 16 ♓ | 16 ♉ | 16 ♊ |
| 17 ♈ | 18 ♊ | 17 ♊ | 16 ♋ | 18 ♍ | 17 ♎ | 19 ♐ | 18 ♑ | 18 ♓ | 18 ♈ | 18 ♊ | 18 ♋ |
| 19 ♉ | 20 ♋ | 19 ♋ | 18 ♌ | 20 ♎ | 19 ♏ | 21 ♑ | 20 ♒ | 20 ♈ | 20 ♉ | 20 ♋ | 20 ♌ |
| 21 ♊ | 22 ♌ | 22 ♌ | 20 ♍ | 23 ♏ | 21 ♐ | 23 ♒ | 22 ♓ | 22 ♉ | 22 ♊ | 22 ♌ | 22 ♍ |
| 24 ♋ | 25 ♍ | 24 ♍ | 23 ♎ | 25 ♐ | 24 ♑ | 25 ♓ | 24 ♈ | 24 ♊ | 24 ♋ | 25 ♍ | 25 ♎ |
| 26 ♌ | 27 ♎ | 27 ♎ | 25 ♏ | 27 ♑ | 26 ♒ | 27 ♈ | 26 ♉ | 26 ♋ | 26 ♌ | 27 ♎ | 27 ♏ |
| 29 ♍ | | 29 ♏ | 28 ♐ | 30 ♒ | 28 ♓ | 30 ♉ | 28 ♊ | 29 ♌ | 28 ♍ | 30 ♏ | 30 ♐ |
| 31 ♎ | | | 30 ♑ | | 30 ♈ | | 30 ♋ | | 31 ♎ | | |

## 1919

| JAN. | FEB. | MAR. | APR. | MAY | JUNE | JULY | AUG. | SEPT. | OCT. | NOV. | DEC. |
|---|---|---|---|---|---|---|---|---|---|---|---|
| 1 ♑ | 2 ♓ | 1 ♓ | 2 ♉ | 1 ♊ | 2 ♌ | 1 ♍ | 2 ♏ | 1 ♐ | 1 ♑ | 2 ♓ | 2 ♈ |
| 3 ♒ | 4 ♈ | 3 ♈ | 4 ♊ | 3 ♋ | 4 ♍ | 4 ♎ | 5 ♐ | 4 ♑ | 4 ♒ | 4 ♈ | 4 ♉ |
| 6 ♓ | 6 ♉ | 5 ♉ | 6 ♋ | 5 ♌ | 6 ♎ | 6 ♏ | 7 ♑ | 6 ♒ | 6 ♓ | 7 ♉ | 6 ♊ |
| 8 ♈ | 8 ♊ | 7 ♊ | 8 ♌ | 8 ♍ | 9 ♏ | 9 ♐ | 10 ♒ | 8 ♓ | 8 ♈ | 9 ♊ | 8 ♋ |
| 10 ♉ | 10 ♋ | 10 ♋ | 10 ♍ | 10 ♎ | 11 ♐ | 11 ♑ | 12 ♓ | 11 ♈ | 10 ♉ | 11 ♋ | 10 ♌ |
| 12 ♊ | 13 ♌ | 12 ♌ | 13 ♎ | 13 ♏ | 14 ♑ | 14 ♒ | 14 ♈ | 13 ♉ | 12 ♊ | 13 ♌ | 12 ♍ |
| 14 ♋ | 15 ♍ | 14 ♍ | 15 ♏ | 15 ♐ | 16 ♒ | 16 ♓ | 16 ♉ | 15 ♊ | 14 ♋ | 15 ♍ | 14 ♎ |
| 16 ♌ | 17 ♎ | 17 ♎ | 18 ♐ | 18 ♑ | 19 ♓ | 18 ♈ | 18 ♊ | 17 ♋ | 16 ♌ | 17 ♎ | 17 ♏ |
| 18 ♍ | 20 ♏ | 19 ♏ | 20 ♑ | 20 ♒ | 21 ♈ | 20 ♉ | 21 ♋ | 19 ♌ | 19 ♍ | 20 ♏ | 19 ♐ |
| 21 ♎ | 22 ♐ | 22 ♐ | 23 ♒ | 22 ♓ | 23 ♉ | 22 ♊ | 23 ♌ | 21 ♍ | 21 ♎ | 22 ♐ | 22 ♑ |
| 23 ♏ | 25 ♑ | 24 ♑ | 25 ♓ | 25 ♈ | 25 ♊ | 25 ♋ | 25 ♍ | 24 ♎ | 24 ♏ | 25 ♑ | 24 ♒ |
| 26 ♐ | 27 ♒ | 26 ♒ | 27 ♈ | 27 ♉ | 27 ♋ | 27 ♌ | 27 ♎ | 26 ♏ | 26 ♐ | 27 ♒ | 27 ♓ |
| 28 ♑ | | 29 ♓ | 29 ♉ | 29 ♊ | 29 ♌ | 29 ♍ | 29 ♏ | 28 ♐ | 28 ♑ | 30 ♓ | 29 ♈ |
| 31 ♒ | | 31 ♈ | | 31 ♋ | | 31 ♎ | | | 31 ♒ | | 31 ♉ |

*Key:*  Aries   Taurus   Gemini   Cancer   Leo   Virgo

♈       ♉       ♊       ♋       ♌     ♍

## 1920

| JAN. | FEB. | MAR. | APR. | MAY | JUNE | JULY | AUG. | SEPT. | OCT. | NOV. | DEC. |
|---|---|---|---|---|---|---|---|---|---|---|---|
| 2 ♊ | 1 ♋ | 1 ♌ | 2 ♎ | 2 ♏ | 3 ♑ | 3 ♒ | 1 ♓ | 2 ♉ | 2 ♊ | 2 ♌ | 1 ♍ |
| 4 ♋ | 3 ♌ | 3 ♍ | 4 ♏ | 4 ♐ | 5 ♒ | 5 ♓ | 4 ♈ | 4 ♊ | 4 ♋ | 4 ♍ | 4 ♎ |
| 6 ♌ | 5 ♍ | 6 ♎ | 7 ♐ | 7 ♑ | 8 ♓ | 7 ♈ | 6 ♉ | 6 ♋ | 6 ♌ | 6 ♎ | 6 ♏ |
| 9 ♍ | 7 ♎ | 8 ♏ | 9 ♑ | 9 ♒ | 10 ♈ | 10 ♉ | 8 ♊ | 9 ♌ | 8 ♍ | 9 ♏ | 8 ♐ |
| 11 ♎ | 10 ♏ | 10 ♐ | 12 ♒ | 12 ♓ | 12 ♉ | 12 ♊ | 10 ♋ | 11 ♍ | 10 ♎ | 11 ♐ | 11 ♑ |
| 13 ♏ | 12 ♐ | 13 ♑ | 14 ♓ | 14 ♈ | 14 ♊ | 14 ♋ | 12 ♌ | 13 ♎ | 12 ♏ | 14 ♑ | 13 ♒ |
| 16 ♐ | 15 ♑ | 15 ♒ | 16 ♈ | 16 ♉ | 16 ♋ | 16 ♌ | 14 ♍ | 15 ♏ | 15 ♐ | 16 ♒ | 15 ♓ |
| 18 ♑ | 17 ♒ | 18 ♓ | 19 ♉ | 18 ♊ | 18 ♌ | 18 ♍ | 16 ♎ | 17 ♐ | 17 ♑ | 19 ♓ | 18 ♈ |
| 21 ♒ | 19 ♓ | 20 ♈ | 21 ♊ | 20 ♋ | 20 ♍ | 20 ♎ | 19 ♏ | 20 ♑ | 20 ♒ | 21 ♈ | 21 ♉ |
| 23 ♓ | 22 ♈ | 22 ♉ | 23 ♋ | 22 ♌ | 23 ♎ | 22 ♏ | 21 ♐ | 22 ♒ | 22 ♓ | 23 ♉ | 23 ♊ |
| 25 ♈ | 24 ♉ | 24 ♊ | 25 ♌ | 24 ♍ | 25 ♏ | 25 ♐ | 24 ♑ | 25 ♓ | 25 ♈ | 25 ♊ | 25 ♋ |
| 28 ♉ | 26 ♊ | 26 ♋ | 27 ♍ | 26 ♎ | 28 ♐ | 27 ♑ | 26 ♒ | 27 ♈ | 27 ♉ | 27 ♋ | 27 ♌ |
| 30 ♊ | 28 ♋ | 28 ♌ | 29 ♎ | 29 ♏ | 30 ♑ | 30 ♒ | 29 ♓ | 29 ♉ | 29 ♊ | 29 ♌ | 29 ♍ |
|  |  | 31 ♍ |  | 31 ♐ |  |  | 31 ♈ |  | 31 ♋ |  | 31 ♎ |

## 1921

| JAN. | FEB. | MAR. | APR. | MAY | JUNE | JULY | AUG. | SEPT. | OCT. | NOV. | DEC. |
|---|---|---|---|---|---|---|---|---|---|---|---|
| 2 ♏ | 1 ♐ | 3 ♑ | 2 ♒ | 1 ♓ | 3 ♉ | 2 ♊ | 1 ♋ | 1 ♌ | 3 ♏ | 1 ♐ | 1 ♑ |
| 5 ♐ | 3 ♑ | 5 ♒ | 4 ♓ | 4 ♈ | 5 ♊ | 4 ♋ | 3 ♌ | 3 ♍ | 5 ♐ | 3 ♑ | 3 ♒ |
| 7 ♑ | 6 ♒ | 8 ♓ | 6 ♈ | 6 ♉ | 7 ♋ | 6 ♌ | 5 ♍ | 5 ♎ | 7 ♑ | 6 ♒ | 6 ♓ |
| 10 ♒ | 8 ♓ | 10 ♈ | 9 ♉ | 8 ♊ | 9 ♌ | 8 ♍ | 7 ♎ | 7 ♏ | 10 ♒ | 8 ♓ | 8 ♈ |
| 12 ♓ | 11 ♈ | 13 ♉ | 11 ♊ | 10 ♋ | 11 ♍ | 10 ♎ | 9 ♏ | 10 ♐ | 12 ♓ | 11 ♈ | 11 ♉ |
| 15 ♈ | 13 ♉ | 15 ♊ | 13 ♋ | 13 ♌ | 13 ♎ | 12 ♏ | 11 ♐ | 12 ♑ | 15 ♈ | 13 ♉ | 13 ♊ |
| 17 ♉ | 16 ♊ | 17 ♋ | 15 ♌ | 15 ♍ | 15 ♏ | 15 ♐ | 14 ♑ | 15 ♒ | 17 ♉ | 16 ♊ | 15 ♋ |
| 19 ♊ | 18 ♋ | 19 ♌ | 17 ♍ | 17 ♎ | 18 ♐ | 17 ♑ | 16 ♒ | 17 ♓ | 19 ♊ | 18 ♋ | 17 ♌ |
| 21 ♋ | 20 ♌ | 21 ♍ | 20 ♎ | 19 ♏ | 20 ♑ | 20 ♒ | 19 ♓ | 19 ♈ | 22 ♋ | 20 ♌ | 19 ♍ |
| 23 ♌ | 22 ♍ | 23 ♎ | 22 ♏ | 21 ♐ | 23 ♒ | 22 ♓ | 21 ♈ | 22 ♉ | 24 ♌ | 22 ♍ | 21 ♎ |
| 25 ♍ | 24 ♎ | 25 ♏ | 24 ♐ | 24 ♑ | 25 ♓ | 25 ♈ | 24 ♉ | 24 ♊ | 26 ♍ | 24 ♎ | 24 ♏ |
| 27 ♎ | 26 ♏ | 28 ♐ | 26 ♑ | 26 ♒ | 28 ♈ | 27 ♉ | 26 ♊ | 26 ♋ | 28 ♎ | 26 ♏ | 26 ♐ |
| 30 ♏ | 28 ♐ | 30 ♑ | 29 ♒ | 28 ♓ | 30 ♉ | 30 ♊ | 28 ♋ | 28 ♌ | 30 ♏ | 29 ♐ | 28 ♑ |
|  |  |  |  | 31 ♈ |  |  | 30 ♌ | 30 ♍ |  |  | 31 ♒ |

| Libra | Scorpio | Sagittarius | Capricorn | Aquarius | Pisces |
|---|---|---|---|---|---|
| ♎ | ♏ | ♐ | ♑ | ♒ | ♓ |

## 1922

| JAN. | FEB. | MAR. | APR. | MAY | JUNE | JULY | AUG. | SEPT. | OCT. | NOV. | DEC. |
|---|---|---|---|---|---|---|---|---|---|---|---|
| 2 ♓ | 1 ♈ | 3 ♉ | 1 ♊ | 1 ♋ | 1 ♍ | 1 ♎ | 1 ♐ | 2 ♒ | 2 ♓ | 1 ♈ | 1 ♉ |
| 5 ♈ | 3 ♉ | 5 ♊ | 4 ♋ | 3 ♌ | 4 ♎ | 3 ♏ | 4 ♑ | 5 ♓ | 5 ♈ | 3 ♉ | 3 ♊ |
| 7 ♉ | 6 ♊ | 7 ♋ | 6 ♌ | 5 ♍ | 6 ♏ | 6 ♐ | 6 ♒ | 7 ♈ | 7 ♉ | 6 ♊ | 5 ♋ |
| 9 ♊ | 8 ♋ | 10 ♌ | 8 ♍ | 7 ♎ | 8 ♐ | 8 ♑ | 8 ♓ | 10 ♉ | 10 ♊ | 8 ♋ | 8 ♌ |
| 12 ♋ | 10 ♌ | 12 ♍ | 10 ♎ | 9 ♏ | 10 ♑ | 10 ♒ | 11 ♈ | 12 ♊ | 12 ♋ | 10 ♌ | 10 ♍ |
| 14 ♌ | 12 ♍ | 13 ♎ | 12 ♏ | 11 ♐ | 12 ♒ | 12 ♓ | 14 ♉ | 15 ♋ | 14 ♌ | 13 ♍ | 12 ♎ |
| 16 ♍ | 14 ♏ | 14 ♏ | 14 ♐ | 14 ♑ | 15 ♓ | 15 ♈ | 16 ♊ | 17 ♌ | 16 ♍ | 15 ♎ | 14 ♏ |
| 18 ♎ | 16 ♏ | 18 ♐ | 16 ♑ | 16 ♒ | 17 ♈ | 17 ♉ | 18 ♋ | 19 ♍ | 18 ♎ | 17 ♏ | 16 ♐ |
| 20 ♏ | 18 ♐ | 20 ♑ | 19 ♒ | 19 ♓ | 20 ♉ | 20 ♊ | 20 ♌ | 21 ♎ | 20 ♏ | 19 ♐ | 18 ♑ |
| 22 ♐ | 21 ♑ | 22 ♒ | 21 ♓ | 21 ♈ | 22 ♊ | 22 ♋ | 22 ♍ | 23 ♏ | 22 ♐ | 21 ♑ | 21 ♒ |
| 24 ♑ | 23 ♒ | 25 ♓ | 24 ♈ | 24 ♉ | 24 ♋ | 24 ♌ | 24 ♎ | 25 ♐ | 24 ♑ | 23 ♒ | 23 ♓ |
| 27 ♒ | 26 ♓ | 27 ♈ | 26 ♉ | 26 ♊ | 27 ♌ | 26 ♍ | 26 ♏ | 27 ♑ | 27 ♒ | 26 ♓ | 25 ♈ |
| 29 ♓ | 28 ♈ | 30 ♉ | 28 ♊ | 28 ♋ | 29 ♍ | 28 ♎ | 29 ♐ | 30 ♒ | 29 ♓ | 28 ♈ | 28 ♉ |
|  |  |  |  | 30 ♌ |  | 30 ♏ | 31 ♑ |  |  |  | 30 ♊ |

## 1923

| JAN. | FEB. | MAR. | APR. | MAY | JUNE | JULY | AUG. | SEPT. | OCT. | NOV. | DEC. |
|---|---|---|---|---|---|---|---|---|---|---|---|
| 2 ♋ | 2 ♍ | 2 ♍ | 2 ♏ | 2 ♐ | 2 ♒ | 2 ♓ | 1 ♉ | 2 ♊ | 2 ♋ | 1 ♌ | 3 ♎ |
| 4 ♌ | 4 ♎ | 4 ♎ | 4 ♐ | 4 ♑ | 4 ♓ | 4 ♈ | 3 ♊ | 5 ♋ | 5 ♌ | 3 ♍ | 5 ♏ |
| 6 ♍ | 7 ♏ | 6 ♏ | 6 ♑ | 6 ♒ | 7 ♈ | 7 ♉ | 6 ♋ | 7 ♌ | 7 ♍ | 5 ♎ | 7 ♐ |
| 8 ♎ | 9 ♐ | 8 ♐ | 9 ♒ | 8 ♓ | 10 ♉ | 10 ♊ | 8 ♌ | 9 ♍ | 9 ♎ | 7 ♏ | 9 ♑ |
| 10 ♏ | 11 ♑ | 10 ♑ | 11 ♓ | 11 ♈ | 12 ♊ | 12 ♋ | 11 ♍ | 11 ♎ | 11 ♏ | 9 ♐ | 11 ♒ |
| 12 ♐ | 13 ♒ | 12 ♒ | 14 ♈ | 13 ♉ | 15 ♋ | 14 ♌ | 13 ♎ | 13 ♏ | 13 ♐ | 11 ♑ | 13 ♓ |
| 15 ♑ | 15 ♓ | 14 ♓ | 16 ♉ | 16 ♊ | 17 ♌ | 16 ♍ | 15 ♏ | 15 ♐ | 15 ♑ | 13 ♒ | 15 ♈ |
| 17 ♒ | 18 ♈ | 17 ♈ | 19 ♊ | 18 ♋ | 19 ♍ | 19 ♎ | 17 ♐ | 17 ♑ | 17 ♒ | 16 ♓ | 18 ♉ |
| 19 ♓ | 21 ♉ | 20 ♉ | 21 ♋ | 21 ♌ | 21 ♎ | 21 ♏ | 19 ♑ | 20 ♒ | 19 ♓ | 18 ♈ | 20 ♊ |
| 22 ♈ | 23 ♊ | 22 ♊ | 23 ♌ | 23 ♍ | 24 ♏ | 23 ♐ | 21 ♒ | 22 ♓ | 22 ♈ | 20 ♉ | 23 ♋ |
| 24 ♉ | 26 ♋ | 25 ♋ | 26 ♍ | 25 ♎ | 26 ♐ | 25 ♑ | 23 ♓ | 24 ♈ | 24 ♉ | 23 ♊ | 25 ♌ |
| 27 ♊ | 28 ♌ | 27 ♌ | 28 ♎ | 27 ♏ | 28 ♑ | 27 ♒ | 26 ♈ | 27 ♉ | 27 ♊ | 26 ♋ | 28 ♍ |
| 29 ♋ |  | 29 ♍ | 30 ♏ | 29 ♐ | 30 ♒ | 29 ♓ | 28 ♉ | 30 ♊ | 29 ♋ | 28 ♌ | 30 ♎ |
| 31 ♌ |  | 31 ♎ |  | 31 ♑ |  |  | 31 ♊ |  |  | 30 ♍ |  |

| Key: | Aries | Taurus | Gemini | Cancer | Leo | Virgo |
|---|---|---|---|---|---|---|
|  | ♈ | ♉ | ♊ | ♋ | ♌ | ♍ |

## 1924

| JAN. | FEB. | MAR. | APR. | MAY | JUNE | JULY | AUG. | SEPT. | OCT. | NOV. | DEC. |
|---|---|---|---|---|---|---|---|---|---|---|---|
| 1 ♏ | 1 ♑ | 2 ♒ | 3 ♈ | 2 ♉ | 1 ♊ | 1 ♋ | 2 ♍ | 1 ♎ | 2 ♐ | 1 ♑ | 2 ♓ |
| 3 ♐ | 3 ♒ | 4 ♓ | 5 ♉ | 5 ♊ | 4 ♋ | 3 ♌ | 4 ♎ | 3 ♏ | 4 ♑ | 3 ♒ | 4 ♈ |
| 5 ♑ | 6 ♓ | 6 ♈ | 8 ♊ | 7 ♋ | 6 ♌ | 6 ♍ | 7 ♏ | 5 ♐ | 6 ♒ | 5 ♓ | 7 ♉ |
| 7 ♒ | 8 ♈ | 9 ♉ | 10 ♋ | 10 ♌ | 9 ♍ | 8 ♎ | 9 ♐ | 7 ♑ | 9 ♓ | 7 ♈ | 9 ♊ |
| 9 ♓ | 10 ♉ | 11 ♊ | 13 ♌ | 12 ♍ | 11 ♎ | 10 ♏ | 11 ♑ | 9 ♒ | 11 ♈ | 9 ♉ | 12 ♋ |
| 12 ♈ | 13 ♊ | 14 ♋ | 15 ♍ | 15 ♎ | 13 ♏ | 12 ♐ | 13 ♒ | 11 ♓ | 13 ♉ | 12 ♊ | 14 ♌ |
| 14 ♉ | 15 ♋ | 16 ♌ | 17 ♎ | 17 ♏ | 15 ♐ | 14 ♑ | 15 ♓ | 14 ♈ | 16 ♊ | 14 ♋ | 17 ♍ |
| 17 ♊ | 18 ♌ | 19 ♍ | 19 ♏ | 19 ♐ | 17 ♑ | 16 ♒ | 17 ♈ | 16 ♉ | 18 ♋ | 17 ♌ | 19 ♎ |
| 19 ♋ | 20 ♍ | 21 ♎ | 21 ♐ | 21 ♑ | 19 ♒ | 19 ♓ | 19 ♉ | 18 ♊ | 21 ♌ | 19 ♍ | 21 ♏ |
| 21 ♌ | 22 ♎ | 23 ♏ | 23 ♑ | 23 ♒ | 21 ♓ | 21 ♈ | 22 ♊ | 21 ♋ | 23 ♍ | 22 ♎ | 23 ♐ |
| 24 ♍ | 24 ♏ | 25 ♐ | 25 ♒ | 25 ♓ | 23 ♈ | 23 ♉ | 24 ♋ | 23 ♌ | 25 ♎ | 24 ♏ | 25 ♑ |
| 26 ♎ | 27 ♐ | 27 ♑ | 28 ♓ | 27 ♈ | 26 ♉ | 26 ♊ | 27 ♌ | 26 ♍ | 27 ♏ | 26 ♐ | 27 ♒ |
| 28 ♏ | 29 ♑ | 29 ♒ | 30 ♈ | 30 ♉ | 28 ♊ | 28 ♋ | 29 ♍ | 28 ♎ | 30 ♐ | 28 ♑ | 29 ♓ |
| 30 ♐ | | 31 ♓ | | | | 31 ♌ | | 30 ♏ | | 30 ♒ | |

## 1925

| JAN. | FEB. | MAR. | APR. | MAY | JUNE | JULY | AUG. | SEPT. | OCT. | NOV. | DEC. |
|---|---|---|---|---|---|---|---|---|---|---|---|
| 1 ♈ | 2 ♊ | 1 ♊ | 2 ♌ | 2 ♍ | 1 ♎ | 1 ♏ | 1 ♑ | 2 ♓ | 1 ♈ | 2 ♊ | 2 ♋ |
| 3 ♉ | 4 ♋ | 4 ♋ | 5 ♍ | 5 ♎ | 3 ♏ | 3 ♐ | 3 ♒ | 4 ♈ | 3 ♉ | 4 ♋ | 4 ♌ |
| 5 ♊ | 7 ♌ | 6 ♌ | 7 ♎ | 7 ♏ | 5 ♐ | 5 ♑ | 5 ♓ | 6 ♉ | 6 ♊ | 7 ♌ | 7 ♍ |
| 8 ♋ | 9 ♍ | 9 ♍ | 9 ♏ | 9 ♐ | 7 ♑ | 7 ♒ | 7 ♈ | 8 ♊ | 8 ♋ | 9 ♍ | 9 ♎ |
| 11 ♌ | 12 ♎ | 11 ♎ | 12 ♐ | 11 ♑ | 9 ♒ | 9 ♓ | 9 ♉ | 11 ♋ | 10 ♌ | 12 ♎ | 12 ♏ |
| 13 ♍ | 14 ♏ | 13 ♏ | 14 ♑ | 13 ♒ | 11 ♓ | 11 ♈ | 12 ♊ | 13 ♌ | 13 ♍ | 14 ♏ | 14 ♐ |
| 15 ♎ | 16 ♐ | 15 ♐ | 16 ♒ | 15 ♓ | 14 ♈ | 13 ♉ | 14 ♋ | 16 ♍ | 15 ♎ | 16 ♐ | 16 ♑ |
| 18 ♏ | 18 ♑ | 17 ♑ | 18 ♓ | 16 ♈ | 16 ♉ | 16 ♊ | 16 ♌ | 18 ♎ | 18 ♏ | 18 ♑ | 18 ♒ |
| 20 ♐ | 20 ♒ | 20 ♒ | 20 ♈ | 18 ♉ | 18 ♊ | 18 ♋ | 19 ♍ | 20 ♏ | 20 ♐ | 20 ♒ | 20 ♓ |
| 22 ♑ | 22 ♓ | 22 ♓ | 22 ♉ | 20 ♊ | 21 ♋ | 21 ♌ | 22 ♎ | 22 ♐ | 22 ♑ | 23 ♓ | 22 ♈ |
| 24 ♒ | 24 ♈ | 24 ♈ | 25 ♊ | 23 ♋ | 23 ♌ | 23 ♍ | 24 ♏ | 24 ♑ | 24 ♒ | 25 ♈ | 24 ♉ |
| 26 ♓ | 27 ♉ | 26 ♉ | 27 ♋ | 26 ♌ | 26 ♍ | 26 ♎ | 26 ♐ | 27 ♒ | 26 ♓ | 27 ♉ | 27 ♊ |
| 28 ♈ | | 28 ♊ | 30 ♌ | 28 ♍ | 28 ♎ | 28 ♏ | 29 ♑ | 28 ♓ | 28 ♈ | 29 ♊ | 29 ♋ |
| 30 ♉ | | 31 ♋ | | 30 ♎ | | 30 ♐ | 31 ♒ | | 31 ♉ | | 31 ♌ |

| Libra | Scorpio | Sagittarius | Capricorn | Aquarius | Pisces |
|---|---|---|---|---|---|
| ♎ | ♏ | ♐ | ♑ | ♒ | ♓ |

## 1926

| JAN. | FEB. | MAR. | APR. | MAY | JUNE | JULY | AUG. | SEPT. | OCT. | NOV. | DEC. |
|---|---|---|---|---|---|---|---|---|---|---|---|
| 3 ♍ | 2 ♎ | 1 ♎ | 2 ♐ | 1 ♑ | 2 ♓ | 1 ♈ | 2 ♊ | 1 ♋ | 3 ♍ | 2 ♎ | 1 ♏ |
| 5 ♎ | 4 ♏ | 3 ♏ | 4 ♑ | 4 ♒ | 4 ♈ | 3 ♉ | 4 ♋ | 3 ♌ | 5 ♎ | 4 ♏ | 4 ♐ |
| 8 ♏ | 7 ♐ | 6 ♐ | 6 ♒ | 6 ♓ | 6 ♉ | 6 ♊ | 7 ♌ | 6 ♍ | 8 ♏ | 6 ♐ | 6 ♑ |
| 10 ♐ | 9 ♑ | 8 ♑ | 9 ♓ | 8 ♈ | 8 ♊ | 8 ♋ | 9 ♍ | 8 ♎ | 10 ♐ | 8 ♑ | 8 ♒ |
| 12 ♑ | 11 ♒ | 10 ♒ | 11 ♈ | 10 ♉ | 11 ♋ | 11 ♌ | 12 ♎ | 11 ♏ | 13 ♑ | 11 ♒ | 10 ♓ |
| 14 ♒ | 13 ♓ | 12 ♓ | 13 ♉ | 12 ♊ | 13 ♌ | 13 ♍ | 14 ♏ | 13 ♐ | 15 ♒ | 13 ♓ | 13 ♈ |
| 16 ♓ | 15 ♈ | 14 ♈ | 15 ♊ | 14 ♋ | 16 ♍ | 16 ♎ | 17 ♐ | 15 ♑ | 17 ♓ | 15 ♈ | 15 ♉ |
| 18 ♈ | 17 ♉ | 16 ♉ | 17 ♋ | 17 ♌ | 18 ♎ | 18 ♏ | 19 ♑ | 17 ♒ | 19 ♈ | 17 ♉ | 17 ♊ |
| 20 ♉ | 19 ♊ | 18 ♊ | 20 ♌ | 19 ♍ | 21 ♏ | 20 ♐ | 21 ♒ | 19 ♓ | 21 ♉ | 19 ♊ | 19 ♋ |
| 23 ♊ | 21 ♋ | 21 ♋ | 22 ♍ | 22 ♎ | 23 ♐ | 23 ♑ | 23 ♓ | 21 ♈ | 23 ♊ | 22 ♋ | 21 ♌ |
| 25 ♋ | 24 ♌ | 23 ♌ | 25 ♎ | 24 ♏ | 25 ♑ | 25 ♒ | 25 ♈ | 23 ♉ | 25 ♋ | 24 ♌ | 24 ♍ |
| 28 ♌ | 26 ♍ | 26 ♍ | 27 ♏ | 27 ♐ | 27 ♒ | 27 ♓ | 27 ♉ | 26 ♊ | 28 ♌ | 26 ♍ | 26 ♎ |
| 30 ♍ |  | 28 ♎ | 29 ♐ | 29 ♑ | 29 ♓ | 29 ♈ | 29 ♊ | 28 ♋ | 30 ♍ | 29 ♎ | 29 ♏ |
|  |  | 31 ♏ |  | 31 ♒ |  | 31 ♉ |  | 30 ♌ |  |  | 31 ♐ |

## 1927

| JAN. | FEB. | MAR. | APR. | MAY | JUNE | JULY | AUG. | SEPT. | OCT. | NOV. | DEC. |
|---|---|---|---|---|---|---|---|---|---|---|---|
| 2 ♑ | 1 ♒ | 3 ♓ | 1 ♈ | 2 ♊ | 1 ♋ | 1 ♌ | 2 ♎ | 1 ♏ | 3 ♑ | 1 ♒ | 1 ♓ |
| 5 ♒ | 3 ♓ | 4 ♈ | 3 ♉ | 4 ♋ | 3 ♌ | 3 ♍ | 4 ♏ | 3 ♐ | 5 ♒ | 4 ♓ | 3 ♈ |
| 7 ♓ | 5 ♈ | 6 ♉ | 5 ♊ | 6 ♌ | 5 ♍ | 5 ♎ | 7 ♐ | 5 ♑ | 7 ♓ | 6 ♈ | 5 ♉ |
| 9 ♈ | 7 ♉ | 9 ♊ | 7 ♋ | 8 ♍ | 8 ♎ | 7 ♏ | 9 ♑ | 8 ♒ | 9 ♈ | 8 ♉ | 7 ♊ |
| 11 ♉ | 9 ♊ | 11 ♋ | 9 ♌ | 12 ♎ | 10 ♏ | 10 ♐ | 11 ♒ | 10 ♓ | 11 ♉ | 10 ♊ | 9 ♋ |
| 13 ♊ | 12 ♋ | 13 ♌ | 12 ♍ | 14 ♏ | 13 ♐ | 13 ♑ | 13 ♓ | 12 ♈ | 13 ♊ | 12 ♋ | 11 ♌ |
| 15 ♋ | 14 ♌ | 16 ♍ | 14 ♎ | 17 ♐ | 15 ♑ | 15 ♒ | 15 ♈ | 14 ♉ | 15 ♋ | 14 ♌ | 14 ♍ |
| 18 ♌ | 16 ♍ | 18 ♎ | 17 ♏ | 19 ♑ | 18 ♒ | 17 ♓ | 18 ♉ | 16 ♊ | 18 ♌ | 16 ♍ | 16 ♎ |
| 20 ♍ | 19 ♎ | 21 ♏ | 19 ♐ | 21 ♒ | 20 ♓ | 19 ♈ | 20 ♊ | 18 ♋ | 20 ♍ | 19 ♎ | 19 ♏ |
| 23 ♎ | 21 ♏ | 23 ♐ | 22 ♑ | 24 ♓ | 22 ♈ | 21 ♉ | 22 ♋ | 20 ♌ | 23 ♎ | 21 ♏ | 21 ♐ |
| 25 ♏ | 24 ♐ | 26 ♑ | 24 ♒ | 26 ♈ | 24 ♉ | 23 ♊ | 24 ♌ | 23 ♍ | 25 ♏ | 24 ♐ | 24 ♑ |
| 28 ♐ | 26 ♑ | 28 ♒ | 26 ♓ | 28 ♉ | 26 ♊ | 26 ♋ | 27 ♍ | 25 ♎ | 28 ♐ | 26 ♑ | 26 ♒ |
| 30 ♑ | 28 ♒ | 30 ♓ | 28 ♈ | 30 ♊ | 28 ♋ | 28 ♌ | 29 ♎ | 28 ♏ | 30 ♑ | 29 ♒ | 28 ♓ |
|  |  |  | 30 ♉ |  |  | 30 ♍ |  | 30 ♐ |  |  | 30 ♈ |

*Key:*  **Aries   Taurus   Gemini   Cancer   Leo   Virgo**

♈   ♉   ♊   ♋   ♌   ♍

## 1928

| JAN. | FEB. | MAR. | APR. | MAY | JUNE | JULY | AUG. | SEPT. | OCT. | NOV. | DEC. |
|---|---|---|---|---|---|---|---|---|---|---|---|
| 1 ♉ | 2 ♋ | 2 ♌ | 1 ♍ | 1 ♎ | 2 ♐ | 2 ♑ | 3 ♓ | 1 ♈ | 1 ♉ | 1 ♋ | 1 ♌ |
| 4 ♊ | 4 ♌ | 5 ♍ | 3 ♎ | 3 ♏ | 4 ♑ | 4 ♒ | 5 ♈ | 3 ♉ | 3 ♊ | 2 ♌ | 3 ♍ |
| 6 ♋ | 6 ♍ | 7 ♎ | 6 ♏ | 6 ♐ | 7 ♒ | 6 ♓ | 7 ♉ | 5 ♊ | 5 ♋ | 5 ♍ | 5 ♎ |
| 8 ♌ | 9 ♎ | 10 ♏ | 8 ♐ | 8 ♑ | 9 ♓ | 9 ♈ | 9 ♊ | 8 ♋ | 7 ♌ | 8 ♎ | 7 ♏ |
| 10 ♍ | 11 ♏ | 12 ♐ | 11 ♑ | 11 ♒ | 11 ♈ | 11 ♉ | 11 ♋ | 10 ♌ | 9 ♍ | 10 ♏ | 10 ♐ |
| 12 ♎ | 14 ♐ | 15 ♑ | 13 ♒ | 13 ♓ | 14 ♉ | 13 ♊ | 13 ♌ | 12 ♍ | 12 ♎ | 13 ♐ | 13 ♑ |
| 15 ♏ | 16 ♑ | 17 ♒ | 16 ♓ | 15 ♈ | 16 ♊ | 15 ♋ | 16 ♍ | 14 ♎ | 14 ♏ | 15 ♑ | 15 ♒ |
| 17 ♐ | 19 ♒ | 19 ♓ | 18 ♈ | 17 ♉ | 18 ♋ | 17 ♌ | 18 ♎ | 17 ♏ | 16 ♐ | 18 ♒ | 17 ♓ |
| 20 ♑ | 21 ♓ | 21 ♈ | 20 ♉ | 19 ♊ | 20 ♌ | 19 ♍ | 20 ♏ | 19 ♐ | 19 ♑ | 20 ♓ | 20 ♈ |
| 22 ♒ | 23 ♈ | 23 ♉ | 22 ♊ | 21 ♋ | 22 ♍ | 22 ♎ | 23 ♐ | 22 ♑ | 22 ♒ | 22 ♈ | 22 ♉ |
| 24 ♓ | 25 ♉ | 25 ♊ | 24 ♋ | 23 ♌ | 24 ♎ | 24 ♏ | 25 ♑ | 24 ♒ | 24 ♓ | 25 ♉ | 24 ♊ |
| 27 ♈ | 27 ♊ | 27 ♋ | 26 ♌ | 26 ♍ | 27 ♏ | 27 ♐ | 28 ♒ | 26 ♓ | 26 ♈ | 27 ♊ | 26 ♋ |
| 29 ♉ | 29 ♋ | 30 ♌ | 28 ♍ | 28 ♎ | 29 ♐ | 29 ♑ | 30 ♓ | 29 ♈ | 28 ♉ | 29 ♋ | 28 ♌ |
| 31 ♊ | | | | 30 ♏ | | 31 ♒ | | | 30 ♊ | | 30 ♍ |

## 1929

| JAN. | FEB. | MAR. | APR. | MAY | JUNE | JULY | AUG. | SEPT. | OCT. | NOV. | DEC. |
|---|---|---|---|---|---|---|---|---|---|---|---|
| 1 ♎ | 3 ♐ | 2 ♐ | 1 ♑ | 1 ♒ | 2 ♈ | 1 ♉ | 2 ♋ | 2 ♍ | 2 ♎ | 3 ♐ | 2 ♑ |
| 4 ♏ | 5 ♑ | 4 ♑ | 3 ♒ | 3 ♓ | 4 ♉ | 3 ♊ | 4 ♌ | 4 ♎ | 4 ♏ | 5 ♑ | 5 ♒ |
| 6 ♐ | 8 ♒ | 7 ♒ | 6 ♓ | 5 ♈ | 6 ♊ | 5 ♋ | 6 ♍ | 7 ♏ | 6 ♐ | 8 ♒ | 8 ♓ |
| 9 ♑ | 10 ♓ | 9 ♓ | 8 ♈ | 8 ♉ | 8 ♋ | 6 ♌ | 7 ♎ | 9 ♐ | 9 ♑ | 10 ♓ | 10 ♈ |
| 11 ♒ | 12 ♈ | 12 ♈ | 10 ♉ | 10 ♊ | 10 ♌ | 9 ♍ | 11 ♏ | 11 ♑ | 11 ♒ | 13 ♈ | 12 ♉ |
| 14 ♓ | 15 ♉ | 14 ♉ | 12 ♊ | 12 ♋ | 12 ♍ | 11 ♎ | 13 ♐ | 14 ♒ | 14 ♓ | 15 ♉ | 14 ♊ |
| 16 ♈ | 17 ♊ | 16 ♊ | 14 ♋ | 14 ♌ | 14 ♎ | 14 ♏ | 15 ♑ | 16 ♓ | 16 ♈ | 17 ♊ | 16 ♋ |
| 18 ♉ | 19 ♋ | 18 ♋ | 16 ♌ | 16 ♍ | 17 ♏ | 16 ♐ | 18 ♒ | 19 ♈ | 18 ♉ | 19 ♋ | 18 ♌ |
| 20 ♊ | 21 ♌ | 20 ♌ | 19 ♍ | 18 ♎ | 19 ♐ | 19 ♑ | 20 ♓ | 21 ♉ | 21 ♊ | 21 ♌ | 20 ♍ |
| 22 ♋ | 23 ♍ | 22 ♍ | 21 ♎ | 20 ♏ | 22 ♑ | 21 ♒ | 23 ♈ | 23 ♊ | 23 ♋ | 23 ♍ | 22 ♎ |
| 24 ♌ | 25 ♎ | 25 ♎ | 23 ♏ | 23 ♐ | 24 ♒ | 24 ♓ | 25 ♉ | 25 ♋ | 25 ♌ | 25 ♎ | 25 ♏ |
| 27 ♍ | 27 ♏ | 27 ♏ | 26 ♐ | 25 ♑ | 27 ♓ | 26 ♈ | 28 ♊ | 27 ♍ | 27 ♍ | 28 ♏ | 27 ♐ |
| 29 ♎ | | 29 ♐ | 28 ♑ | 28 ♒ | 29 ♈ | 29 ♉ | 30 ♋ | 29 ♎ | 29 ♎ | 30 ♐ | 30 ♑ |
| 31 ♏ | | | | 30 ♓ | | 31 ♊ | 31 ♌ | | 31 ♏ | | |

| Libra | Scorpio | Sagittarius | Capricorn | Aquarius | Pisces |
|---|---|---|---|---|---|
| ♎ | ♏ | ♐ | ♑ | ♒ | ♓ |

## 1930

| JAN. | FEB. | MAR. | APR. | MAY | JUNE | JULY | AUG. | SEPT. | OCT. | NOV. | DEC. |
|---|---|---|---|---|---|---|---|---|---|---|---|
| 1 ♒ | 3 ♈ | 2 ♈ | 3 ♊ | 2 ♋ | 3 ♍ | 2 ♎ | 3 ♐ | 1 ♑ | 1 ♒ | 2 ♈ | 2 ♉ |
| 4 ♓ | 5 ♉ | 4 ♉ | 5 ♋ | 4 ♌ | 5 ♎ | 4 ♏ | 5 ♑ | 4 ♒ | 4 ♓ | 5 ♉ | 5 ♊ |
| 6 ♈ | 7 ♊ | 6 ♊ | 7 ♌ | 6 ♍ | 7 ♏ | 6 ♐ | 7 ♒ | 6 ♓ | 6 ♈ | 7 ♊ | 7 ♋ |
| 9 ♉ | 9 ♋ | 9 ♋ | 9 ♍ | 8 ♎ | 9 ♐ | 8 ♑ | 9 ♓ | 9 ♈ | 9 ♉ | 10 ♋ | 9 ♌ |
| 11 ♊ | 11 ♌ | 11 ♌ | 11 ♎ | 11 ♏ | 11 ♑ | 11 ♒ | 11 ♈ | 11 ♉ | 11 ♊ | 12 ♌ | 11 ♍ |
| 13 ♋ | 13 ♍ | 13 ♍ | 13 ♏ | 13 ♐ | 14 ♒ | 13 ♓ | 13 ♉ | 13 ♊ | 13 ♋ | 14 ♍ | 13 ♎ |
| 15 ♌ | 15 ♎ | 15 ♎ | 16 ♐ | 15 ♑ | 16 ♓ | 16 ♈ | 15 ♊ | 16 ♋ | 15 ♌ | 16 ♎ | 15 ♏ |
| 17 ♍ | 17 ♏ | 17 ♏ | 18 ♑ | 18 ♒ | 19 ♈ | 18 ♉ | 17 ♋ | 18 ♌ | 18 ♍ | 18 ♏ | 17 ♐ |
| 19 ♎ | 20 ♐ | 19 ♐ | 20 ♒ | 20 ♓ | 21 ♉ | 20 ♊ | 20 ♌ | 20 ♍ | 20 ♎ | 20 ♐ | 20 ♑ |
| 21 ♏ | 22 ♑ | 22 ♑ | 23 ♓ | 23 ♈ | 23 ♊ | 22 ♋ | 22 ♍ | 22 ♎ | 22 ♏ | 22 ♑ | 22 ♒ |
| 23 ♐ | 25 ♒ | 24 ♒ | 25 ♈ | 26 ♉ | 25 ♋ | 24 ♌ | 24 ♎ | 24 ♏ | 24 ♐ | 24 ♒ | 25 ♓ |
| 26 ♑ | 27 ♓ | 27 ♓ | 28 ♉ | 28 ♊ | 27 ♌ | 26 ♍ | 26 ♏ | 26 ♐ | 26 ♑ | 27 ♓ | 27 ♈ |
| 29 ♒ | | 29 ♈ | 30 ♊ | 29 ♋ | 30 ♍ | 29 ♎ | 29 ♐ | 29 ♑ | 28 ♒ | 30 ♈ | 30 ♉ |
| 31 ♒ | | 31 ♒ | | 31 ♌ | | 31 ♏ | | | 31 ♓ | | |

## 1931

| JAN. | FEB. | MAR. | APR. | MAY | JUNE | JULY | AUG. | SEPT. | OCT. | NOV. | DEC. |
|---|---|---|---|---|---|---|---|---|---|---|---|
| 1 ♊ | 2 ♌ | 1 ♌ | 2 ♎ | 1 ♏ | 2 ♑ | 1 ♒ | 3 ♈ | 1 ♉ | 1 ♊ | 2 ♌ | 2 ♍ |
| 3 ♋ | 4 ♍ | 3 ♍ | 4 ♏ | 3 ♐ | 4 ♒ | 4 ♓ | 5 ♉ | 4 ♊ | 4 ♋ | 4 ♍ | 4 ♎ |
| 5 ♌ | 6 ♎ | 5 ♎ | 6 ♐ | 5 ♑ | 6 ♓ | 6 ♈ | 8 ♊ | 6 ♋ | 6 ♌ | 6 ♎ | 6 ♏ |
| 7 ♍ | 8 ♏ | 7 ♏ | 8 ♑ | 7 ♒ | 9 ♈ | 9 ♉ | 10 ♋ | 8 ♌ | 8 ♍ | 8 ♏ | 8 ♐ |
| 9 ♎ | 10 ♐ | 9 ♐ | 10 ♒ | 9 ♓ | 11 ♉ | 11 ♊ | 12 ♌ | 10 ♍ | 10 ♎ | 10 ♐ | 10 ♑ |
| 11 ♏ | 12 ♑ | 12 ♑ | 13 ♓ | 11 ♈ | 14 ♊ | 13 ♋ | 14 ♍ | 12 ♎ | 12 ♏ | 12 ♑ | 12 ♒ |
| 14 ♐ | 15 ♒ | 14 ♒ | 15 ♈ | 14 ♉ | 16 ♋ | 16 ♌ | 16 ♎ | 14 ♏ | 14 ♐ | 15 ♒ | 14 ♓ |
| 16 ♑ | 17 ♓ | 16 ♓ | 18 ♉ | 16 ♊ | 18 ♌ | 18 ♍ | 18 ♏ | 17 ♐ | 17 ♑ | 17 ♓ | 17 ♈ |
| 18 ♒ | 20 ♈ | 19 ♈ | 20 ♊ | 18 ♋ | 20 ♍ | 20 ♎ | 20 ♐ | 19 ♑ | 19 ♒ | 20 ♈ | 19 ♉ |
| 21 ♓ | 22 ♉ | 22 ♉ | 23 ♋ | 20 ♌ | 22 ♎ | 22 ♏ | 22 ♑ | 21 ♒ | 21 ♓ | 22 ♉ | 22 ♊ |
| 23 ♈ | 25 ♊ | 24 ♊ | 25 ♌ | 22 ♍ | 24 ♏ | 24 ♐ | 25 ♒ | 24 ♓ | 23 ♈ | 25 ♊ | 24 ♋ |
| 26 ♉ | 27 ♋ | 26 ♋ | 27 ♍ | 24 ♎ | 27 ♐ | 26 ♑ | 27 ♓ | 26 ♈ | 26 ♉ | 27 ♋ | 27 ♌ |
| 28 ♊ | | 28 ♌ | 29 ♎ | 26 ♏ | 29 ♑ | 29 ♒ | 30 ♈ | 29 ♉ | 28 ♊ | 29 ♌ | 29 ♍ |
| 31 ♋ | | 31 ♍ | | 29 ♐ | | 31 ♓ | | | 31 ♋ | | 31 ♎ |

*Key:*  Aries  Taurus  Gemini  Cancer  Leo  Virgo

♈  ♉  ♊  ♋  ♌  ♍

## 1932

| JAN. | FEB. | MAR. | APR. | MAY | JUNE | JULY | AUG. | SEPT. | OCT. | NOV. | DEC. |
|---|---|---|---|---|---|---|---|---|---|---|---|
| 2 ♏ | 3 ♑ | 1 ♑ | 2 ♓ | 1 ♈ | 3 ♊ | 3 ♋ | 1 ♌ | 2 ♎ | 1 ♏ | 2 ♑ | 1 ♒ |
| 4 ♐ | 5 ♒ | 3 ♒ | 4 ♈ | 4 ♉ | 5 ♋ | 5 ♌ | 3 ♍ | 4 ♏ | 3 ♐ | 4 ♒ | 3 ♓ |
| 6 ♑ | 7 ♓ | 5 ♓ | 7 ♉ | 7 ♊ | 8 ♌ | 7 ♍ | 6 ♎ | 6 ♐ | 5 ♑ | 6 ♓ | 6 ♈ |
| 8 ♒ | 10 ♈ | 7 ♈ | 9 ♊ | 9 ♋ | 10 ♍ | 9 ♎ | 8 ♏ | 8 ♑ | 8 ♒ | 9 ♈ | 8 ♉ |
| 11 ♓ | 12 ♉ | 10 ♉ | 12 ♋ | 11 ♌ | 12 ♎ | 11 ♏ | 10 ♐ | 10 ♒ | 10 ♓ | 11 ♉ | 11 ♊ |
| 13 ♈ | 15 ♊ | 13 ♊ | 14 ♌ | 14 ♍ | 14 ♏ | 14 ♐ | 12 ♑ | 13 ♓ | 12 ♈ | 14 ♊ | 13 ♋ |
| 16 ♉ | 17 ♋ | 15 ♋ | 16 ♍ | 16 ♎ | 16 ♐ | 16 ♑ | 14 ♒ | 15 ♈ | 14 ♉ | 16 ♋ | 16 ♌ |
| 18 ♊ | 19 ♌ | 18 ♌ | 18 ♎ | 18 ♏ | 18 ♑ | 18 ♒ | 16 ♓ | 18 ♉ | 17 ♊ | 19 ♌ | 18 ♍ |
| 21 ♋ | 21 ♍ | 20 ♍ | 20 ♏ | 20 ♐ | 20 ♒ | 20 ♓ | 19 ♈ | 20 ♊ | 20 ♋ | 21 ♍ | 20 ♎ |
| 23 ♌ | 23 ♎ | 22 ♎ | 22 ♐ | 22 ♑ | 23 ♓ | 22 ♈ | 21 ♉ | 23 ♋ | 22 ♌ | 23 ♎ | 23 ♏ |
| 25 ♍ | 26 ♏ | 24 ♏ | 24 ♑ | 24 ♒ | 25 ♈ | 25 ♉ | 24 ♊ | 25 ♌ | 25 ♍ | 25 ♏ | 25 ♐ |
| 27 ♎ | 28 ♐ | 26 ♐ | 27 ♒ | 26 ♓ | 28 ♉ | 27 ♊ | 26 ♋ | 27 ♍ | 27 ♎ | 27 ♐ | 27 ♑ |
| 29 ♏ |  | 28 ♑ | 29 ♓ | 28 ♈ | 30 ♊ | 30 ♋ | 29 ♌ | 29 ♎ | 29 ♏ | 29 ♑ | 29 ♒ |
| 31 ♐ |  | 30 ♒ |  | 31 ♉ |  |  | 31 ♍ |  | 31 ♐ |  | 31 ♓ |

## 1933

| JAN. | FEB. | MAR. | APR. | MAY | JUNE | JULY | AUG. | SEPT. | OCT. | NOV. | DEC. |
|---|---|---|---|---|---|---|---|---|---|---|---|
| 2 ♈ | 1 ♉ | 3 ♊ | 2 ♋ | 1 ♌ | 2 ♎ | 2 ♏ | 2 ♑ | 1 ♒ | 2 ♈ | 1 ♉ | 1 ♊ |
| 5 ♉ | 3 ♊ | 5 ♋ | 4 ♌ | 4 ♍ | 5 ♏ | 4 ♐ | 4 ♒ | 3 ♓ | 5 ♉ | 4 ♊ | 3 ♋ |
| 7 ♊ | 6 ♋ | 8 ♌ | 6 ♍ | 6 ♎ | 7 ♐ | 6 ♑ | 7 ♓ | 5 ♈ | 7 ♊ | 6 ♋ | 6 ♌ |
| 10 ♋ | 8 ♌ | 10 ♍ | 9 ♎ | 8 ♏ | 9 ♑ | 8 ♒ | 9 ♈ | 7 ♉ | 10 ♋ | 9 ♌ | 8 ♍ |
| 12 ♌ | 11 ♍ | 12 ♎ | 11 ♏ | 10 ♐ | 11 ♒ | 10 ♓ | 11 ♉ | 10 ♊ | 12 ♌ | 11 ♍ | 11 ♎ |
| 14 ♍ | 13 ♎ | 14 ♏ | 13 ♐ | 12 ♑ | 13 ♓ | 12 ♈ | 13 ♊ | 12 ♋ | 15 ♍ | 13 ♎ | 13 ♏ |
| 17 ♎ | 15 ♏ | 16 ♐ | 15 ♑ | 14 ♒ | 15 ♈ | 15 ♉ | 16 ♋ | 15 ♌ | 17 ♎ | 15 ♏ | 15 ♐ |
| 19 ♏ | 17 ♐ | 19 ♑ | 17 ♒ | 16 ♓ | 17 ♉ | 17 ♊ | 18 ♌ | 17 ♍ | 19 ♏ | 18 ♐ | 17 ♑ |
| 21 ♐ | 19 ♑ | 21 ♒ | 19 ♓ | 19 ♈ | 20 ♊ | 20 ♋ | 21 ♍ | 20 ♎ | 21 ♐ | 20 ♑ | 19 ♒ |
| 23 ♑ | 21 ♒ | 23 ♓ | 22 ♈ | 21 ♉ | 22 ♋ | 22 ♌ | 23 ♎ | 22 ♏ | 23 ♑ | 22 ♒ | 21 ♓ |
| 25 ♒ | 24 ♓ | 25 ♈ | 24 ♉ | 24 ♊ | 25 ♌ | 25 ♍ | 25 ♏ | 24 ♐ | 25 ♒ | 24 ♓ | 23 ♈ |
| 27 ♓ | 26 ♈ | 28 ♉ | 26 ♊ | 26 ♋ | 27 ♍ | 27 ♎ | 28 ♐ | 26 ♑ | 27 ♓ | 26 ♈ | 26 ♉ |
| 30 ♈ | 28 ♉ | 30 ♊ | 29 ♋ | 29 ♌ | 30 ♎ | 29 ♏ | 30 ♑ | 28 ♒ | 30 ♈ | 28 ♉ | 28 ♊ |
|  |  |  |  | 31 ♍ |  | 31 ♐ |  | 30 ♓ |  |  | 31 ♋ |

| Libra | Scorpio | Sagittarius | Capricorn | Aquarius | Pisces |
|---|---|---|---|---|---|
| ♎ | ♏ | ♐ | ♑ | ♒ | ♓ |

## 1934

| JAN. | FEB. | MAR. | APR. | MAY | JUNE | JULY | AUG. | SEPT. | OCT. | NOV. | DEC. |
|---|---|---|---|---|---|---|---|---|---|---|---|
| 2 ♌ | 1 ♍ | 3 ♎ | 1 ♏ | 1 ♐ | 1 ♒ | 3 ♈ | 1 ♉ | 2 ♋ | 2 ♌ | 1 ♍ | 1 ♎ |
| 5 ♍ | 3 ♎ | 5 ♏ | 3 ♐ | 3 ♑ | 3 ♓ | 5 ♉ | 3 ♊ | 5 ♌ | 5 ♍ | 3 ♎ | 3 ♏ |
| 7 ♎ | 6 ♏ | 7 ♐ | 5 ♑ | 5 ♒ | 5 ♈ | 7 ♊ | 6 ♋ | 7 ♍ | 7 ♎ | 6 ♏ | 5 ♐ |
| 9 ♏ | 8 ♐ | 9 ♑ | 7 ♒ | 7 ♓ | 7 ♉ | 10 ♋ | 8 ♌ | 10 ♎ | 9 ♏ | 8 ♐ | 7 ♑ |
| 11 ♐ | 10 ♑ | 11 ♒ | 10 ♓ | 9 ♈ | 10 ♊ | 12 ♌ | 11 ♍ | 12 ♏ | 12 ♐ | 10 ♑ | 9 ♒ |
| 13 ♑ | 12 ♒ | 13 ♓ | 12 ♈ | 11 ♉ | 12 ♋ | 15 ♍ | 13 ♎ | 14 ♐ | 14 ♑ | 12 ♒ | 11 ♓ |
| 15 ♒ | 14 ♓ | 15 ♈ | 14 ♉ | 14 ♊ | 15 ♌ | 17 ♎ | 16 ♏ | 17 ♑ | 16 ♒ | 14 ♓ | 14 ♈ |
| 17 ♓ | 16 ♈ | 18 ♉ | 16 ♊ | 16 ♋ | 17 ♍ | 20 ♏ | 18 ♐ | 19 ♒ | 18 ♓ | 16 ♈ | 16 ♉ |
| 20 ♈ | 18 ♉ | 20 ♊ | 19 ♋ | 19 ♌ | 20 ♎ | 22 ♐ | 20 ♑ | 21 ♓ | 20 ♈ | 19 ♉ | 18 ♊ |
| 22 ♉ | 21 ♊ | 22 ♋ | 21 ♌ | 21 ♍ | 22 ♏ | 24 ♑ | 22 ♒ | 23 ♈ | 22 ♉ | 21 ♊ | 21 ♋ |
| 24 ♊ | 23 ♋ | 25 ♌ | 24 ♍ | 24 ♎ | 24 ♐ | 26 ♒ | 24 ♓ | 25 ♉ | 24 ♊ | 23 ♋ | 23 ♌ |
| 27 ♋ | 26 ♌ | 27 ♍ | 26 ♎ | 26 ♏ | 26 ♑ | 28 ♓ | 26 ♈ | 27 ♊ | 27 ♋ | 26 ♌ | 26 ♍ |
| 29 ♌ | 28 ♍ | 30 ♎ | 28 ♏ | 28 ♐ | 28 ♒ | 30 ♈ | 28 ♉ | 29 ♋ | 29 ♌ | 28 ♍ | 28 ♎ |
|  |  |  |  | 30 ♑ | 30 ♓ |  | 31 ♊ |  |  |  | 30 ♏ |

## 1935

| JAN. | FEB. | MAR. | APR. | MAY | JUNE | JULY | AUG. | SEPT. | OCT. | NOV. | DEC. |
|---|---|---|---|---|---|---|---|---|---|---|---|
| 2 ♐ | 2 ♒ | 2 ♒ | 2 ♈ | 2 ♉ | 2 ♋ | 2 ♌ | 1 ♍ | 2 ♏ | 2 ♐ | 3 ♒ | 2 ♓ |
| 4 ♑ | 4 ♓ | 4 ♓ | 4 ♉ | 4 ♊ | 5 ♌ | 5 ♍ | 3 ♎ | 5 ♐ | 4 ♑ | 5 ♓ | 4 ♈ |
| 6 ♒ | 6 ♈ | 6 ♈ | 6 ♊ | 6 ♋ | 7 ♍ | 7 ♎ | 6 ♏ | 7 ♑ | 6 ♒ | 7 ♈ | 6 ♉ |
| 8 ♓ | 8 ♉ | 8 ♉ | 9 ♋ | 8 ♌ | 10 ♎ | 10 ♏ | 8 ♐ | 9 ♒ | 9 ♓ | 9 ♉ | 8 ♊ |
| 10 ♈ | 11 ♊ | 10 ♊ | 11 ♌ | 11 ♍ | 12 ♏ | 12 ♐ | 11 ♑ | 11 ♓ | 11 ♈ | 11 ♊ | 11 ♋ |
| 12 ♉ | 13 ♋ | 12 ♋ | 14 ♍ | 13 ♎ | 15 ♐ | 14 ♑ | 13 ♒ | 13 ♈ | 13 ♉ | 13 ♋ | 13 ♌ |
| 14 ♊ | 16 ♌ | 15 ♌ | 16 ♎ | 16 ♏ | 17 ♑ | 16 ♒ | 15 ♓ | 15 ♉ | 15 ♊ | 15 ♌ | 15 ♍ |
| 17 ♋ | 18 ♍ | 17 ♍ | 19 ♏ | 18 ♐ | 19 ♒ | 19 ♓ | 17 ♈ | 17 ♊ | 17 ♋ | 18 ♍ | 18 ♎ |
| 19 ♌ | 21 ♎ | 20 ♎ | 21 ♐ | 20 ♑ | 21 ♓ | 21 ♈ | 19 ♉ | 19 ♋ | 20 ♌ | 20 ♎ | 20 ♏ |
| 22 ♍ | 23 ♏ | 22 ♏ | 23 ♑ | 23 ♒ | 23 ♈ | 23 ♉ | 21 ♊ | 22 ♌ | 22 ♍ | 23 ♏ | 23 ♐ |
| 24 ♎ | 25 ♐ | 25 ♐ | 25 ♒ | 25 ♓ | 25 ♉ | 25 ♊ | 23 ♋ | 24 ♍ | 24 ♎ | 25 ♐ | 25 ♑ |
| 27 ♏ | 28 ♑ | 27 ♑ | 27 ♓ | 27 ♈ | 27 ♊ | 27 ♋ | 26 ♌ | 27 ♎ | 27 ♏ | 28 ♑ | 27 ♒ |
| 29 ♐ |  | 29 ♒ | 30 ♈ | 29 ♉ | 30 ♋ | 29 ♌ | 28 ♍ | 29 ♏ | 29 ♐ | 30 ♒ | 29 ♓ |
| 31 ♑ |  | 31 ♓ |  | 31 ♊ |  |  | 31 ♎ |  | 31 ♑ |  | 31 ♈ |

*Key:*  Aries   Taurus   Gemini   Cancer   Leo   Virgo

♈       ♉        ♊        ♋        ♌       ♍

## 1936

| JAN. | FEB. | MAR. | APR. | MAY | JUNE | JULY | AUG. | SEPT. | OCT. | NOV. | DEC. |
|---|---|---|---|---|---|---|---|---|---|---|---|
| 3 ♉ | 1 ♊ | 1 ♋ | 3 ♍ | 2 ♎ | 1 ♏ | 1 ♐ | 2 ♒ | 2 ♈ | 2 ♉ | 2 ♋ | 2 ♌ |
| 5 ♊ | 3 ♋ | 4 ♌ | 5 ♎ | 5 ♏ | 4 ♐ | 3 ♑ | 4 ♓ | 4 ♉ | 4 ♊ | 5 ♌ | 4 ♍ |
| 7 ♋ | 6 ♌ | 6 ♍ | 8 ♏ | 7 ♐ | 6 ♑ | 6 ♒ | 6 ♈ | 7 ♊ | 6 ♋ | 7 ♍ | 7 ♎ |
| 9 ♌ | 8 ♍ | 9 ♎ | 10 ♐ | 10 ♑ | 8 ♒ | 8 ♓ | 8 ♉ | 9 ♋ | 8 ♌ | 9 ♎ | 9 ♏ |
| 12 ♍ | 10 ♎ | 11 ♏ | 12 ♑ | 12 ♒ | 10 ♓ | 10 ♈ | 10 ♊ | 11 ♌ | 11 ♍ | 12 ♏ | 12 ♐ |
| 14 ♎ | 13 ♏ | 14 ♐ | 15 ♒ | 14 ♓ | 13 ♈ | 12 ♉ | 12 ♋ | 13 ♍ | 13 ♎ | 14 ♐ | 14 ♑ |
| 17 ♏ | 15 ♐ | 16 ♑ | 17 ♓ | 16 ♈ | 15 ♉ | 14 ♊ | 15 ♌ | 16 ♎ | 16 ♏ | 17 ♑ | 17 ♒ |
| 19 ♐ | 18 ♑ | 18 ♒ | 19 ♈ | 18 ♉ | 17 ♊ | 16 ♋ | 17 ♍ | 18 ♏ | 18 ♐ | 19 ♒ | 19 ♓ |
| 21 ♑ | 20 ♒ | 21 ♓ | 21 ♉ | 20 ♊ | 19 ♋ | 18 ♌ | 20 ♎ | 21 ♐ | 21 ♑ | 22 ♓ | 21 ♈ |
| 24 ♒ | 22 ♓ | 23 ♈ | 23 ♊ | 22 ♋ | 21 ♌ | 21 ♍ | 22 ♏ | 23 ♑ | 23 ♒ | 24 ♈ | 23 ♉ |
| 26 ♓ | 24 ♈ | 24 ♉ | 25 ♋ | 25 ♌ | 23 ♍ | 23 ♎ | 25 ♐ | 26 ♒ | 25 ♓ | 26 ♉ | 25 ♊ |
| 28 ♈ | 26 ♉ | 27 ♊ | 27 ♌ | 27 ♍ | 26 ♎ | 26 ♏ | 27 ♑ | 28 ♓ | 27 ♈ | 28 ♊ | 27 ♋ |
| 30 ♉ | 8 ♊ | 29 ♋ | 30 ♍ | 30 ♎ | 28 ♏ | 28 ♐ | 29 ♒ | 30 ♈ | 29 ♉ | 30 ♋ | 29 ♌ |
|  |  | 31 ♌ |  |  |  | 31 ♑ | 31 ♓ |  | 31 ♊ |  |  |

## 1937

| JAN. | FEB. | MAR. | APR. | MAY | JUNE | JULY | AUG. | SEPT. | OCT. | NOV. | DEC. |
|---|---|---|---|---|---|---|---|---|---|---|---|
| 1 ♍ | 2 ♏ | 1 ♏ | 3 ♑ | 2 ♒ | 1 ♓ | 3 ♉ | 1 ♊ | 1 ♌ | 1 ♍ | 2 ♏ | 2 ♐ |
| 3 ♎ | 4 ♐ | 4 ♐ | 5 ♒ | 5 ♓ | 3 ♈ | 5 ♊ | 3 ♋ | 4 ♍ | 3 ♎ | 4 ♐ | 4 ♑ |
| 5 ♏ | 7 ♑ | 6 ♑ | 7 ♓ | 7 ♈ | 5 ♉ | 7 ♋ | 5 ♌ | 6 ♎ | 6 ♏ | 7 ♑ | 7 ♒ |
| 8 ♐ | 9 ♒ | 9 ♒ | 9 ♈ | 9 ♉ | 7 ♊ | 9 ♌ | 7 ♍ | 8 ♏ | 8 ♐ | 9 ♒ | 9 ♓ |
| 10 ♑ | 11 ♓ | 11 ♓ | 11 ♉ | 11 ♊ | 9 ♋ | 11 ♍ | 9 ♎ | 11 ♐ | 11 ♑ | 12 ♓ | 11 ♈ |
| 13 ♒ | 14 ♈ | 13 ♈ | 13 ♊ | 13 ♋ | 11 ♌ | 13 ♎ | 12 ♏ | 13 ♑ | 13 ♒ | 14 ♈ | 14 ♉ |
| 15 ♓ | 16 ♉ | 15 ♉ | 15 ♋ | 15 ♌ | 13 ♍ | 16 ♏ | 14 ♐ | 16 ♒ | 15 ♓ | 16 ♉ | 16 ♊ |
| 17 ♈ | 18 ♊ | 17 ♊ | 18 ♌ | 17 ♍ | 16 ♎ | 18 ♐ | 17 ♑ | 18 ♓ | 18 ♈ | 18 ♊ | 18 ♋ |
| 19 ♉ | 20 ♋ | 19 ♋ | 20 ♍ | 19 ♎ | 18 ♏ | 21 ♑ | 19 ♒ | 20 ♈ | 20 ♉ | 20 ♋ | 20 ♌ |
| 21 ♊ | 22 ♌ | 21 ♌ | 22 ♎ | 21 ♏ | 21 ♐ | 23 ♒ | 22 ♓ | 22 ♉ | 22 ♊ | 22 ♌ | 22 ♍ |
| 24 ♋ | 24 ♍ | 24 ♍ | 25 ♏ | 23 ♐ | 23 ♑ | 25 ♓ | 24 ♈ | 24 ♊ | 24 ♋ | 24 ♍ | 24 ♎ |
| 26 ♌ | 27 ♎ | 26 ♎ | 27 ♐ | 26 ♑ | 26 ♒ | 28 ♈ | 26 ♉ | 26 ♋ | 26 ♌ | 27 ♎ | 26 ♏ |
| 28 ♍ |  | 28 ♏ | 30 ♑ | 28 ♒ | 28 ♓ | 30 ♉ | 28 ♊ | 28 ♍ | 28 ♎ | 29 ♏ | 29 ♐ |
| 30 ♎ |  | 31 ♐ |  | 30 ♈ |  |  | 30 ♋ |  | 30 ♎ |  | 31 ♑ |

| Libra | Scorpio | Sagittarius | Capricorn | Aquarius | Pisces |
|---|---|---|---|---|---|
| ♎ | ♏ | ♐ | ♑ | ♒ | ♓ |

## 1938

| JAN. | FEB. | MAR. | APR. | MAY | JUNE | JULY | AUG. | SEPT. | OCT. | NOV. | DEC. |
|---|---|---|---|---|---|---|---|---|---|---|---|
| 3 ♒ | 2 ♓ | 1 ♓ | 2 ♉ | 1 ♊ | 2 ♌ | 1 ♍ | 2 ♏ | 1 ♐ | 3 ♒ | 2 ♓ | 1 ♈ |
| 5 ♓ | 4 ♈ | 3 ♈ | 4 ♊ | 3 ♋ | 4 ♍ | 3 ♎ | 4 ♐ | 3 ♑ | 5 ♓ | 4 ♈ | 4 ♉ |
| 8 ♈ | 6 ♉ | 5 ♉ | 6 ♋ | 5 ♌ | 6 ♎ | 5 ♏ | 7 ♑ | 6 ♒ | 8 ♈ | 6 ♉ | 6 ♊ |
| 10 ♉ | 8 ♊ | 8 ♊ | 8 ♌ | 7 ♍ | 8 ♏ | 7 ♐ | 9 ♒ | 8 ♓ | 10 ♉ | 9 ♊ | 8 ♋ |
| 12 ♊ | 10 ♋ | 10 ♋ | 10 ♍ | 10 ♎ | 11 ♐ | 9 ♑ | 12 ♓ | 10 ♈ | 12 ♊ | 11 ♋ | 10 ♌ |
| 14 ♋ | 12 ♌ | 12 ♌ | 12 ♎ | 12 ♏ | 13 ♑ | 11 ♒ | 14 ♈ | 13 ♉ | 14 ♋ | 13 ♌ | 12 ♍ |
| 16 ♌ | 15 ♍ | 14 ♍ | 15 ♏ | 14 ♐ | 16 ♒ | 14 ♓ | 16 ♉ | 15 ♊ | 16 ♌ | 15 ♍ | 14 ♎ |
| 18 ♍ | 17 ♎ | 16 ♎ | 17 ♐ | 17 ♑ | 18 ♓ | 16 ♈ | 19 ♊ | 17 ♋ | 19 ♍ | 17 ♎ | 16 ♏ |
| 20 ♎ | 19 ♏ | 18 ♏ | 20 ♑ | 19 ♒ | 21 ♈ | 18 ♉ | 21 ♋ | 19 ♌ | 21 ♎ | 19 ♏ | 19 ♐ |
| 23 ♏ | 21 ♐ | 21 ♐ | 22 ♒ | 22 ♓ | 23 ♉ | 20 ♊ | 23 ♌ | 21 ♍ | 23 ♏ | 22 ♐ | 21 ♑ |
| 25 ♐ | 24 ♑ | 23 ♑ | 25 ♓ | 24 ♈ | 25 ♊ | 22 ♋ | 25 ♍ | 23 ♎ | 25 ♐ | 24 ♑ | 24 ♒ |
| 28 ♑ | 26 ♒ | 26 ♒ | 27 ♈ | 27 ♉ | 27 ♋ | 24 ♌ | 27 ♎ | 26 ♏ | 28 ♑ | 27 ♒ | 26 ♓ |
| 30 ♒ |  | 28 ♓ | 29 ♉ | 29 ♊ | 29 ♌ | 26 ♍ | 29 ♏ | 28 ♐ | 30 ♒ | 29 ♓ | 29 ♈ |
|  |  | 31 ♈ |  | 31 ♋ |  | 28 ♎ |  | 30 ♑ |  |  | 31 ♉ |
|  |  |  |  |  |  | 31 ♏ |  |  |  |  |  |

## 1939

| JAN. | FEB. | MAR. | APR. | MAY | JUNE | JULY | AUG. | SEPT. | OCT. | NOV. | DEC. |
|---|---|---|---|---|---|---|---|---|---|---|---|
| 2 ♊ | 1 ♋ | 2 ♌ | 1 ♍ | 2 ♏ | 1 ♐ | 3 ♒ | 2 ♓ | 3 ♈ | 3 ♊ | 1 ♋ | 3 ♍ |
| 4 ♋ | 3 ♌ | 4 ♍ | 3 ♎ | 4 ♐ | 3 ♑ | 5 ♓ | 4 ♈ | 5 ♉ | 5 ♋ | 3 ♌ | 5 ♎ |
| 6 ♌ | 5 ♍ | 6 ♎ | 5 ♏ | 7 ♑ | 6 ♒ | 8 ♈ | 6 ♉ | 7 ♊ | 7 ♌ | 5 ♍ | 7 ♏ |
| 8 ♍ | 7 ♎ | 8 ♏ | 7 ♐ | 9 ♒ | 8 ♓ | 10 ♉ | 8 ♊ | 9 ♋ | 9 ♍ | 7 ♎ | 9 ♐ |
| 10 ♎ | 9 ♏ | 11 ♐ | 9 ♑ | 12 ♓ | 11 ♈ | 13 ♊ | 11 ♋ | 12 ♌ | 11 ♎ | 10 ♏ | 11 ♑ |
| 13 ♏ | 11 ♐ | 13 ♑ | 12 ♒ | 14 ♈ | 13 ♉ | 15 ♋ | 13 ♌ | 14 ♍ | 13 ♏ | 12 ♐ | 14 ♒ |
| 15 ♐ | 14 ♑ | 16 ♒ | 14 ♓ | 17 ♉ | 15 ♊ | 17 ♌ | 15 ♍ | 16 ♎ | 15 ♐ | 14 ♑ | 16 ♓ |
| 18 ♑ | 16 ♒ | 18 ♓ | 17 ♈ | 19 ♊ | 17 ♋ | 19 ♍ | 17 ♎ | 18 ♏ | 18 ♑ | 16 ♒ | 19 ♈ |
| 20 ♒ | 19 ♓ | 20 ♈ | 19 ♉ | 21 ♋ | 19 ♌ | 21 ♎ | 19 ♏ | 20 ♐ | 20 ♒ | 19 ♓ | 21 ♉ |
| 23 ♓ | 21 ♈ | 23 ♉ | 21 ♊ | 23 ♌ | 21 ♍ | 23 ♏ | 22 ♐ | 23 ♑ | 23 ♓ | 21 ♈ | 24 ♊ |
| 25 ♈ | 24 ♉ | 25 ♊ | 23 ♋ | 25 ♍ | 23 ♎ | 25 ♐ | 24 ♑ | 25 ♒ | 25 ♈ | 24 ♉ | 26 ♋ |
| 28 ♉ | 26 ♊ | 28 ♋ | 26 ♌ | 27 ♎ | 25 ♏ | 28 ♑ | 26 ♒ | 27 ♓ | 27 ♉ | 26 ♊ | 28 ♌ |
| 30 ♊ | 28 ♋ | 30 ♌ | 28 ♍ | 30 ♏ | 28 ♐ | 30 ♒ | 28 ♓ | 30 ♈ | 30 ♊ | 28 ♋ | 30 ♍ |
|  |  |  | 30 ♎ |  | 30 ♑ |  | 31 ♈ |  |  | 30 ♌ |  |

*Key:*  Aries   Taurus   Gemini   Cancer   Leo   Virgo

♈        ♉         ♊          ♋           ♌       ♍

## 1940

| JAN. | FEB. | MAR. | APR. | MAY | JUNE | JULY | AUG. | SEPT. | OCT. | NOV. | DEC. |
|---|---|---|---|---|---|---|---|---|---|---|---|
| 1 ♎ | 2 ♐ | 2 ♑ | 1 ♒ | 1 ♓ | 2 ♉ | 2 ♊ | 3 ♌ | 1 ♍ | 2 ♏ | 1 ♐ | 3 ♒ |
| 3 ♏ | 4 ♑ | 5 ♒ | 3 ♓ | 3 ♈ | 4 ♊ | 4 ♋ | 5 ♍ | 3 ♎ | 4 ♐ | 3 ♑ | 5 ♓ |
| 5 ♐ | 6 ♒ | 7 ♓ | 6 ♈ | 6 ♉ | 7 ♋ | 6 ♌ | 7 ♎ | 5 ♏ | 7 ♑ | 5 ♒ | 7 ♈ |
| 8 ♑ | 9 ♓ | 10 ♈ | 8 ♉ | 8 ♊ | 9 ♌ | 8 ♍ | 9 ♏ | 7 ♐ | 9 ♒ | 8 ♓ | 10 ♉ |
| 10 ♒ | 11 ♈ | 12 ♉ | 11 ♊ | 10 ♋ | 11 ♍ | 10 ♎ | 11 ♐ | 9 ♑ | 11 ♓ | 10 ♈ | 13 ♊ |
| 13 ♓ | 14 ♉ | 15 ♊ | 13 ♋ | 13 ♌ | 13 ♎ | 13 ♏ | 13 ♑ | 12 ♒ | 14 ♈ | 13 ♉ | 15 ♋ |
| 15 ♈ | 16 ♊ | 17 ♋ | 15 ♌ | 15 ♍ | 15 ♏ | 15 ♐ | 15 ♒ | 14 ♈ | 16 ♉ | 15 ♊ | 17 ♌ |
| 18 ♉ | 19 ♋ | 19 ♌ | 18 ♍ | 17 ♎ | 17 ♐ | 17 ♑ | 18 ♓ | 17 ♉ | 19 ♊ | 18 ♋ | 19 ♍ |
| 20 ♊ | 21 ♌ | 21 ♍ | 20 ♎ | 19 ♏ | 20 ♑ | 19 ♒ | 20 ♈ | 19 ♊ | 21 ♋ | 20 ♌ | 22 ♎ |
| 22 ♋ | 23 ♍ | 23 ♎ | 22 ♏ | 21 ♐ | 22 ♒ | 22 ♓ | 22 ♉ | 21 ♋ | 23 ♌ | 22 ♍ | 24 ♏ |
| 24 ♌ | 25 ♎ | 25 ♏ | 24 ♐ | 23 ♑ | 24 ♓ | 24 ♈ | 25 ♊ | 24 ♌ | 26 ♍ | 24 ♎ | 26 ♐ |
| 26 ♍ | 27 ♏ | 27 ♐ | 26 ♑ | 25 ♒ | 27 ♈ | 27 ♉ | 28 ♋ | 26 ♍ | 28 ♎ | 26 ♏ | 28 ♑ |
| 28 ♎ | 29 ♐ | 29 ♑ | 28 ♒ | 28 ♓ | 29 ♉ | 29 ♊ | 30 ♌ | 28 ♍ | 30 ♏ | 28 ♐ | 30 ♒ |
| 30 ♏ | | | | 30 ♈ | | 31 ♋ | | 30 ♎ | | 30 ♑ | |

## 1941

| JAN. | FEB. | MAR. | APR. | MAY | JUNE | JULY | AUG. | SEPT. | OCT. | NOV. | DEC. |
|---|---|---|---|---|---|---|---|---|---|---|---|
| 1 ♓ | 3 ♉ | 2 ♉ | 1 ♊ | 1 ♋ | 2 ♍ | 1 ♎ | 1 ♐ | 2 ♒ | 2 ♓ | 3 ♉ | 2 ♊ |
| 4 ♈ | 5 ♊ | 5 ♊ | 3 ♋ | 3 ♌ | 4 ♎ | 3 ♏ | 4 ♑ | 4 ♓ | 4 ♈ | 5 ♊ | 5 ♋ |
| 6 ♉ | 8 ♋ | 7 ♋ | 6 ♌ | 5 ♍ | 6 ♏ | 5 ♐ | 6 ♒ | 7 ♈ | 6 ♉ | 8 ♋ | 7 ♌ |
| 9 ♊ | 10 ♌ | 9 ♌ | 8 ♍ | 7 ♎ | 8 ♐ | 7 ♑ | 8 ♓ | 9 ♉ | 9 ♊ | 10 ♌ | 10 ♍ |
| 11 ♋ | 12 ♍ | 11 ♍ | 10 ♎ | 9 ♏ | 10 ♑ | 9 ♒ | 10 ♈ | 12 ♊ | 11 ♋ | 13 ♍ | 12 ♎ |
| 13 ♌ | 14 ♎ | 13 ♎ | 12 ♏ | 11 ♐ | 12 ♒ | 12 ♓ | 12 ♉ | 14 ♋ | 13 ♌ | 15 ♎ | 14 ♏ |
| 16 ♍ | 16 ♏ | 16 ♏ | 14 ♐ | 13 ♑ | 14 ♓ | 14 ♈ | 15 ♊ | 16 ♌ | 15 ♍ | 17 ♏ | 16 ♐ |
| 18 ♎ | 18 ♐ | 18 ♐ | 16 ♑ | 16 ♒ | 17 ♈ | 16 ♉ | 18 ♋ | 18 ♍ | 17 ♎ | 19 ♐ | 18 ♑ |
| 20 ♏ | 20 ♑ | 20 ♑ | 18 ♒ | 18 ♓ | 19 ♉ | 19 ♊ | 20 ♌ | 21 ♎ | 19 ♏ | 21 ♑ | 20 ♒ |
| 22 ♐ | 23 ♒ | 22 ♒ | 21 ♓ | 20 ♈ | 22 ♊ | 21 ♋ | 22 ♍ | 23 ♏ | 22 ♐ | 23 ♒ | 22 ♓ |
| 24 ♑ | 25 ♓ | 24 ♓ | 23 ♈ | 22 ♉ | 24 ♋ | 24 ♌ | 24 ♎ | 25 ♐ | 24 ♑ | 25 ♓ | 25 ♈ |
| 26 ♒ | 27 ♈ | 27 ♈ | 25 ♉ | 24 ♊ | 26 ♌ | 26 ♍ | 27 ♏ | 27 ♑ | 26 ♒ | 27 ♈ | 27 ♉ |
| 29 ♓ | | 29 ♉ | 28 ♊ | 28 ♋ | 29 ♍ | 28 ♎ | 29 ♐ | 29 ♒ | 29 ♓ | 30 ♉ | 30 ♊ |
| 31 ♈ | | | | 30 ♌ | | 30 ♏ | | | 31 ♈ | | |

| | Libra | Scorpio | Sagittarius | Capricorn | Aquarius | Pisces |
|---|---|---|---|---|---|---|
| | ♎ | ♏ | ♐ | ♑ | ♒ | ♓ |

## 1942

| JAN. | FEB. | MAR. | APR. | MAY | JUNE | JULY | AUG. | SEPT. | OCT. | NOV. | DEC. |
|---|---|---|---|---|---|---|---|---|---|---|---|
| 1 ♋ | 2 ♍ | 2 ♍ | 2 ♏ | 2 ♐ | 2 ♒ | 2 ♓ | 3 ♈ | 1 ♊ | 1 ♋ | 3 ♍ | 2 ♎ |
| 4 ♌ | 5 ♎ | 4 ♎ | 4 ♐ | 4 ♑ | 4 ♓ | 4 ♈ | 5 ♊ | 4 ♋ | 4 ♌ | 5 ♎ | 4 ♏ |
| 6 ♍ | 7 ♏ | 6 ♏ | 6 ♑ | 6 ♒ | 7 ♈ | 6 ♉ | 8 ♋ | 6 ♌ | 6 ♍ | 7 ♏ | 7 ♐ |
| 8 ♎ | 9 ♐ | 8 ♐ | 9 ♒ | 8 ♓ | 9 ♉ | 9 ♊ | 10 ♌ | 9 ♍ | 8 ♎ | 9 ♐ | 9 ♑ |
| 11 ♏ | 11 ♑ | 10 ♑ | 11 ♓ | 10 ♈ | 12 ♊ | 11 ♋ | 13 ♍ | 11 ♎ | 11 ♏ | 11 ♑ | 11 ♒ |
| 13 ♐ | 13 ♒ | 12 ♒ | 13 ♈ | 13 ♉ | 14 ♋ | 14 ♌ | 15 ♎ | 13 ♏ | 13 ♐ | 13 ♒ | 13 ♓ |
| 15 ♑ | 15 ♓ | 15 ♓ | 16 ♉ | 15 ♊ | 17 ♌ | 16 ♍ | 17 ♏ | 15 ♐ | 15 ♑ | 15 ♓ | 15 ♈ |
| 17 ♒ | 17 ♈ | 17 ♈ | 18 ♊ | 18 ♋ | 19 ♍ | 19 ♎ | 19 ♐ | 18 ♑ | 17 ♒ | 18 ♈ | 17 ♉ |
| 19 ♓ | 20 ♉ | 19 ♉ | 21 ♋ | 20 ♌ | 21 ♎ | 21 ♏ | 21 ♑ | 20 ♒ | 19 ♓ | 20 ♉ | 20 ♊ |
| 21 ♈ | 22 ♊ | 21 ♊ | 23 ♌ | 23 ♍ | 24 ♏ | 23 ♐ | 23 ♒ | 22 ♓ | 21 ♈ | 22 ♊ | 22 ♋ |
| 23 ♉ | 25 ♋ | 24 ♋ | 25 ♍ | 25 ♎ | 26 ♐ | 25 ♑ | 25 ♓ | 24 ♈ | 24 ♉ | 25 ♋ | 25 ♌ |
| 26 ♊ | 27 ♌ | 27 ♌ | 28 ♎ | 27 ♏ | 28 ♑ | 27 ♒ | 28 ♈ | 26 ♉ | 26 ♊ | 27 ♌ | 27 ♍ |
| 29 ♋ |  | 29 ♍ | 30 ♏ | 29 ♐ | 30 ♒ | 29 ♓ | 30 ♉ | 29 ♊ | 29 ♋ | 30 ♍ | 30 ♎ |
| 31 ♌ |  | 31 ♎ |  | 31 ♑ |  | 31 ♈ |  |  | 31 ♌ |  |  |

## 1943

| JAN. | FEB. | MAR. | APR. | MAY | JUNE | JULY | AUG. | SEPT. | OCT. | NOV. | DEC. |
|---|---|---|---|---|---|---|---|---|---|---|---|
| 1 ♏ | 1 ♑ | 1 ♑ | 1 ♓ | 1 ♈ | 2 ♊ | 1 ♋ | 3 ♍ | 1 ♎ | 1 ♏ | 2 ♑ | 1 ♒ |
| 3 ♐ | 3 ♒ | 3 ♒ | 3 ♈ | 3 ♉ | 4 ♋ | 4 ♌ | 5 ♎ | 4 ♏ | 3 ♐ | 4 ♒ | 3 ♓ |
| 5 ♑ | 5 ♓ | 5 ♓ | 6 ♉ | 5 ♊ | 6 ♌ | 6 ♍ | 8 ♏ | 5 ♑ | 5 ♑ | 6 ♓ | 5 ♈ |
| 7 ♒ | 8 ♈ | 7 ♈ | 8 ♊ | 8 ♋ | 9 ♍ | 9 ♎ | 10 ♐ | 8 ♒ | 8 ♒ | 8 ♈ | 7 ♉ |
| 9 ♓ | 10 ♉ | 9 ♉ | 10 ♋ | 10 ♌ | 11 ♎ | 11 ♏ | 12 ♑ | 10 ♓ | 10 ♓ | 10 ♉ | 10 ♊ |
| 11 ♈ | 12 ♊ | 11 ♊ | 13 ♌ | 13 ♍ | 14 ♏ | 13 ♐ | 14 ♒ | 12 ♈ | 12 ♈ | 12 ♊ | 12 ♋ |
| 13 ♉ | 15 ♋ | 14 ♋ | 15 ♍ | 15 ♎ | 16 ♐ | 15 ♑ | 16 ♓ | 14 ♈ | 14 ♉ | 15 ♋ | 15 ♌ |
| 16 ♊ | 17 ♌ | 16 ♌ | 18 ♎ | 17 ♏ | 18 ♑ | 17 ♒ | 18 ♈ | 16 ♉ | 16 ♊ | 17 ♌ | 17 ♍ |
| 18 ♋ | 20 ♍ | 19 ♍ | 20 ♏ | 20 ♐ | 20 ♒ | 19 ♓ | 20 ♉ | 19 ♊ | 18 ♋ | 20 ♍ | 20 ♎ |
| 21 ♌ | 22 ♎ | 21 ♎ | 22 ♐ | 22 ♑ | 22 ♓ | 21 ♈ | 22 ♊ | 21 ♋ | 21 ♌ | 22 ♎ | 22 ♐ |
| 23 ♍ | 24 ♏ | 24 ♏ | 24 ♑ | 24 ♒ | 24 ♈ | 24 ♉ | 25 ♋ | 24 ♌ | 23 ♍ | 25 ♏ | 24 ♐ |
| 26 ♎ | 27 ♐ | 26 ♐ | 26 ♒ | 26 ♓ | 26 ♉ | 26 ♊ | 27 ♌ | 26 ♍ | 26 ♎ | 27 ♐ | 26 ♑ |
| 28 ♏ |  | 28 ♑ | 29 ♓ | 28 ♈ | 29 ♊ | 28 ♋ | 30 ♍ | 29 ♎ | 28 ♏ | 29 ♑ | 28 ♒ |
| 30 ♐ |  | 30 ♒ |  | 30 ♉ |  | 31 ♌ |  |  | 30 ♐ |  | 30 ♓ |

| *Key:* | Aries | Taurus | Gemini | Cancer | Leo | Virgo |
|---|---|---|---|---|---|---|
|  | ♈ | ♉ | ♊ | ♋ | ♌ | ♍ |

## 1944

| JAN. | FEB. | MAR. | APR. | MAY | JUNE | JULY | AUG. | SEPT. | OCT. | NOV. | DEC. |
|---|---|---|---|---|---|---|---|---|---|---|---|
| 2 ♈ | 2 ♊ | 1 ♊ | 2 ♌ | 1 ♍ | 3 ♏ | 2 ♐ | 1 ♑ | 2 ♓ | 1 ♈ | 2 ♊ | 1 ♋ |
| 4 ♉ | 5 ♋ | 3 ♋ | 4 ♍ | 4 ♎ | 5 ♐ | 5 ♑ | 3 ♒ | 4 ♈ | 3 ♉ | 4 ♋ | 3 ♌ |
| 6 ♊ | 7 ♌ | 5 ♌ | 7 ♎ | 6 ♏ | 7 ♑ | 7 ♒ | 5 ♓ | 6 ♉ | 5 ♊ | 6 ♌ | 6 ♍ |
| 8 ♋ | 10 ♍ | 8 ♍ | 9 ♏ | 9 ♐ | 9 ♒ | 9 ♓ | 7 ♈ | 8 ♊ | 7 ♋ | 9 ♍ | 8 ♎ |
| 11 ♌ | 12 ♎ | 10 ♎ | 11 ♐ | 11 ♑ | 12 ♓ | 11 ♈ | 9 ♉ | 10 ♋ | 10 ♌ | 11 ♎ | 11 ♏ |
| 13 ♍ | 15 ♏ | 13 ♏ | 14 ♑ | 13 ♒ | 14 ♈ | 13 ♉ | 11 ♊ | 12 ♌ | 12 ♍ | 14 ♏ | 13 ♐ |
| 16 ♎ | 17 ♐ | 15 ♐ | 16 ♒ | 15 ♓ | 16 ♉ | 15 ♊ | 14 ♋ | 15 ♍ | 14 ♎ | 16 ♐ | 16 ♑ |
| 18 ♏ | 19 ♑ | 18 ♑ | 18 ♓ | 17 ♈ | 18 ♊ | 18 ♋ | 16 ♌ | 17 ♎ | 17 ♏ | 18 ♑ | 18 ♒ |
| 21 ♐ | 21 ♒ | 20 ♒ | 20 ♈ | 20 ♉ | 20 ♋ | 20 ♌ | 19 ♍ | 20 ♏ | 19 ♐ | 21 ♒ | 20 ♓ |
| 23 ♑ | 23 ♓ | 22 ♓ | 22 ♉ | 22 ♊ | 23 ♌ | 22 ♍ | 21 ♎ | 22 ♐ | 22 ♑ | 23 ♓ | 22 ♈ |
| 25 ♒ | 25 ♈ | 24 ♈ | 24 ♊ | 24 ♋ | 25 ♍ | 25 ♎ | 24 ♏ | 25 ♑ | 24 ♒ | 25 ♈ | 24 ♉ |
| 27 ♓ | 27 ♉ | 26 ♉ | 27 ♋ | 26 ♌ | 28 ♎ | 27 ♏ | 26 ♐ | 27 ♒ | 26 ♓ | 27 ♉ | 26 ♊ |
| 29 ♈ |  | 28 ♊ | 29 ♌ | 28 ♍ | 30 ♏ | 30 ♐ | 29 ♑ | 29 ♓ | 29 ♈ | 29 ♊ | 29 ♋ |
| 31 ♉ |  | 30 ♋ |  | 31 ♎ |  |  | 31 ♒ |  | 31 ♉ |  | 31 ♌ |

## 1945

| JAN. | FEB. | MAR. | APR. | MAY | JUNE | JULY | AUG. | SEPT. | OCT. | NOV. | DEC. |
|---|---|---|---|---|---|---|---|---|---|---|---|
| 2 ♍ | 1 ♎ | 3 ♏ | 2 ♐ | 1 ♑ | 2 ♓ | 2 ♈ | 2 ♊ | 3 ♌ | 2 ♍ | 1 ♎ | 1 ♏ |
| 5 ♎ | 4 ♏ | 5 ♐ | 4 ♑ | 4 ♒ | 4 ♈ | 4 ♉ | 4 ♋ | 5 ♍ | 5 ♎ | 3 ♏ | 3 ♐ |
| 7 ♏ | 6 ♐ | 8 ♑ | 6 ♒ | 6 ♓ | 6 ♉ | 6 ♊ | 6 ♌ | 7 ♎ | 7 ♏ | 6 ♐ | 6 ♑ |
| 10 ♐ | 8 ♑ | 10 ♒ | 9 ♓ | 8 ♈ | 8 ♊ | 8 ♋ | 9 ♍ | 10 ♏ | 10 ♐ | 8 ♑ | 8 ♒ |
| 12 ♑ | 11 ♒ | 12 ♓ | 11 ♈ | 10 ♉ | 10 ♋ | 10 ♌ | 11 ♎ | 12 ♐ | 12 ♑ | 11 ♒ | 10 ♓ |
| 14 ♒ | 13 ♓ | 14 ♈ | 13 ♉ | 12 ♊ | 13 ♌ | 12 ♍ | 14 ♏ | 15 ♑ | 15 ♒ | 13 ♓ | 13 ♈ |
| 16 ♓ | 15 ♈ | 16 ♉ | 15 ♊ | 14 ♋ | 15 ♍ | 15 ♎ | 16 ♐ | 17 ♒ | 17 ♓ | 15 ♈ | 15 ♉ |
| 18 ♈ | 17 ♉ | 18 ♊ | 17 ♋ | 16 ♌ | 17 ♎ | 17 ♏ | 19 ♑ | 19 ♓ | 19 ♈ | 17 ♉ | 17 ♊ |
| 20 ♉ | 19 ♊ | 20 ♋ | 19 ♌ | 19 ♍ | 20 ♏ | 20 ♐ | 21 ♒ | 21 ♈ | 21 ♉ | 19 ♊ | 19 ♋ |
| 23 ♊ | 21 ♋ | 23 ♌ | 21 ♍ | 21 ♎ | 22 ♐ | 22 ♑ | 23 ♓ | 23 ♉ | 23 ♊ | 21 ♋ | 21 ♌ |
| 25 ♋ | 23 ♌ | 25 ♍ | 24 ♎ | 24 ♏ | 25 ♑ | 24 ♒ | 25 ♈ | 25 ♊ | 25 ♋ | 23 ♌ | 23 ♍ |
| 27 ♌ | 26 ♍ | 28 ♎ | 26 ♏ | 26 ♐ | 27 ♒ | 27 ♓ | 27 ♉ | 28 ♋ | 28 ♌ | 26 ♍ | 25 ♎ |
| 30 ♍ | 28 ♎ | 30 ♏ | 29 ♐ | 29 ♑ | 29 ♓ | 29 ♈ | 29 ♊ | 30 ♌ | 29 ♍ | 28 ♎ | 28 ♏ |
|  |  |  |  | 31 ♒ |  | 31 ♉ | 31 ♋ |  |  |  | 31 ♐ |

| Libra | Scorpio | Sagittarius | Capricorn | Aquarius | Pisces |
|---|---|---|---|---|---|
| ♎ | ♏ | ♐ | ♑ | ♒ | ♓ |

## 1946

| JAN. | FEB. | MAR. | APR. | MAY | JUNE | JULY | AUG. | SEPT. | OCT. | NOV. | DEC. |
|---|---|---|---|---|---|---|---|---|---|---|---|
| 2 ♑ | 1 ♒ | 2 ♓ | 1 ♈ | 2 ♊ | 1 ♋ | 2 ♍ | 1 ♎ | 2 ♐ | 2 ♑ | 1 ♒ | 1 ♓ |
| 4 ♒ | 3 ♓ | 4 ♈ | 3 ♉ | 4 ♋ | 3 ♌ | 5 ♎ | 3 ♏ | 5 ♑ | 5 ♒ | 3 ♓ | 3 ♈ |
| 7 ♓ | 5 ♈ | 7 ♉ | 5 ♊ | 6 ♌ | 5 ♍ | 7 ♏ | 6 ♐ | 7 ♒ | 7 ♓ | 6 ♈ | 5 ♉ |
| 9 ♈ | 7 ♉ | 9 ♊ | 7 ♋ | 8 ♍ | 7 ♎ | 10 ♐ | 8 ♑ | 10 ♓ | 9 ♈ | 8 ♉ | 7 ♊ |
| 11 ♉ | 9 ♊ | 11 ♋ | 9 ♌ | 11 ♎ | 10 ♏ | 12 ♑ | 11 ♒ | 12 ♈ | 11 ♉ | 10 ♊ | 9 ♋ |
| 13 ♊ | 12 ♋ | 13 ♌ | 11 ♍ | 14 ♏ | 12 ♐ | 15 ♒ | 13 ♓ | 14 ♉ | 13 ♊ | 12 ♋ | 11 ♌ |
| 15 ♋ | 14 ♌ | 15 ♍ | 14 ♎ | 16 ♐ | 15 ♑ | 17 ♓ | 15 ♈ | 16 ♊ | 15 ♋ | 14 ♌ | 13 ♍ |
| 17 ♌ | 16 ♍ | 18 ♎ | 16 ♏ | 19 ♑ | 17 ♒ | 19 ♈ | 18 ♉ | 18 ♋ | 18 ♌ | 16 ♍ | 16 ♎ |
| 20 ♍ | 18 ♎ | 20 ♏ | 19 ♐ | 21 ♒ | 20 ♓ | 21 ♉ | 20 ♊ | 20 ♌ | 20 ♍ | 18 ♎ | 18 ♏ |
| 22 ♎ | 21 ♏ | 23 ♐ | 21 ♑ | 23 ♓ | 22 ♈ | 24 ♊ | 22 ♋ | 23 ♍ | 22 ♎ | 21 ♏ | 20 ♐ |
| 24 ♏ | 23 ♐ | 25 ♑ | 24 ♒ | 26 ♈ | 24 ♉ | 26 ♋ | 24 ♌ | 25 ♎ | 24 ♏ | 23 ♐ | 23 ♑ |
| 27 ♐ | 26 ♑ | 27 ♒ | 26 ♓ | 28 ♉ | 26 ♊ | 28 ♌ | 26 ♍ | 27 ♏ | 27 ♐ | 26 ♑ | 25 ♒ |
| 29 ♑ | 28 ♒ | 30 ♓ | 28 ♈ | 30 ♊ | 28 ♋ | 30 ♍ | 28 ♎ | 30 ♐ | 29 ♑ | 28 ♒ | 28 ♓ |
|  |  |  | 30 ♉ |  | 30 ♌ |  | 31 ♏ |  |  |  | 30 ♈ |

## 1947

| JAN. | FEB. | MAR. | APR. | MAY | JUNE | JULY | AUG. | SEPT. | OCT. | NOV. | DEC. |
|---|---|---|---|---|---|---|---|---|---|---|---|
| 2 ♉ | 2 ♋ | 1 ♋ | 2 ♍ | 1 ♎ | 2 ♐ | 2 ♑ | 1 ♓ | 2 ♉ | 1 ♊ | 2 ♌ | 2 ♍ |
| 4 ♊ | 4 ♌ | 3 ♌ | 4 ♎ | 4 ♏ | 5 ♑ | 5 ♒ | 3 ♈ | 4 ♊ | 4 ♋ | 4 ♍ | 4 ♎ |
| 6 ♋ | 6 ♍ | 5 ♍ | 6 ♏ | 6 ♐ | 7 ♒ | 7 ♓ | 5 ♉ | 6 ♋ | 6 ♌ | 6 ♎ | 6 ♏ |
| 8 ♌ | 8 ♎ | 8 ♎ | 9 ♐ | 9 ♑ | 10 ♓ | 9 ♈ | 8 ♊ | 9 ♌ | 8 ♍ | 8 ♏ | 8 ♐ |
| 10 ♍ | 11 ♏ | 10 ♏ | 11 ♑ | 11 ♒ | 12 ♈ | 12 ♉ | 10 ♋ | 11 ♍ | 10 ♎ | 11 ♐ | 10 ♑ |
| 12 ♎ | 13 ♐ | 12 ♐ | 14 ♒ | 14 ♓ | 14 ♉ | 14 ♊ | 13 ♌ | 13 ♎ | 12 ♏ | 13 ♑ | 12 ♒ |
| 14 ♏ | 16 ♑ | 15 ♑ | 16 ♓ | 16 ♈ | 16 ♊ | 16 ♋ | 15 ♍ | 15 ♏ | 15 ♐ | 16 ♒ | 15 ♓ |
| 17 ♐ | 18 ♒ | 17 ♒ | 18 ♈ | 18 ♉ | 19 ♋ | 18 ♌ | 17 ♎ | 17 ♐ | 17 ♑ | 18 ♓ | 17 ♈ |
| 19 ♑ | 20 ♓ | 20 ♓ | 21 ♉ | 20 ♊ | 21 ♌ | 20 ♍ | 19 ♏ | 19 ♑ | 19 ♒ | 21 ♈ | 20 ♉ |
| 22 ♒ | 23 ♈ | 22 ♈ | 23 ♊ | 22 ♋ | 23 ♍ | 22 ♎ | 21 ♐ | 22 ♒ | 22 ♓ | 23 ♉ | 22 ♊ |
| 24 ♓ | 25 ♉ | 24 ♉ | 25 ♋ | 24 ♌ | 25 ♎ | 24 ♏ | 23 ♑ | 24 ♓ | 24 ♈ | 25 ♊ | 25 ♋ |
| 27 ♈ | 27 ♊ | 26 ♊ | 27 ♌ | 26 ♍ | 27 ♏ | 27 ♐ | 26 ♒ | 27 ♈ | 27 ♉ | 28 ♋ | 27 ♌ |
| 29 ♉ |  | 29 ♋ | 29 ♍ | 29 ♎ | 30 ♐ | 29 ♑ | 28 ♓ | 29 ♉ | 29 ♊ | 30 ♌ | 29 ♍ |
| 31 ♊ |  | 31 ♌ |  | 31 ♏ |  | 31 ♒ | 31 ♈ |  | 31 ♋ |  | 31 ♎ |

| *Key:* | Aries | Taurus | Gemini | Cancer | Leo | Virgo |
|---|---|---|---|---|---|---|
|  | ♈ | ♉ | ♊ | ♋ | ♌ | ♍ |

## 1948

| JAN. | FEB. | MAR. | APR. | MAY | JUNE | JULY | AUG. | SEPT. | OCT. | NOV. | DEC. |
|---|---|---|---|---|---|---|---|---|---|---|---|
| 2 ♎ | 1 ♏ | 1 ♐ | 2 ♒ | 2 ♓ | 1 ♈ | 1 ♉ | 2 ♋ | 2 ♍ | 2 ♎ | 2 ♐ | 2 ♑ |
| 4 ♏ | 3 ♐ | 4 ♑ | 5 ♓ | 5 ♈ | 3 ♉ | 3 ♊ | 4 ♌ | 4 ♎ | 4 ♏ | 4 ♑ | 4 ♒ |
| 7 ♐ | 5 ♑ | 6 ♒ | 7 ♈ | 7 ♉ | 6 ♊ | 5 ♋ | 6 ♍ | 6 ♏ | 6 ♐ | 7 ♒ | 7 ♓ |
| 9 ♑ | 8 ♒ | 9 ♓ | 10 ♉ | 9 ♊ | 8 ♋ | 7 ♌ | 8 ♎ | 8 ♐ | 8 ♑ | 9 ♓ | 9 ♈ |
| 12 ♒ | 10 ♓ | 11 ♈ | 12 ♊ | 12 ♋ | 10 ♌ | 9 ♍ | 10 ♏ | 11 ♑ | 11 ♒ | 12 ♈ | 12 ♉ |
| 14 ♓ | 13 ♈ | 14 ♉ | 14 ♋ | 14 ♌ | 12 ♍ | 11 ♎ | 12 ♐ | 13 ♒ | 13 ♓ | 14 ♉ | 14 ♊ |
| 17 ♈ | 15 ♉ | 16 ♊ | 17 ♌ | 16 ♍ | 14 ♎ | 14 ♏ | 15 ♑ | 16 ♓ | 16 ♈ | 17 ♊ | 16 ♋ |
| 19 ♉ | 18 ♊ | 18 ♋ | 19 ♍ | 18 ♎ | 16 ♏ | 16 ♐ | 17 ♒ | 18 ♈ | 18 ♉ | 19 ♋ | 18 ♌ |
| 21 ♊ | 20 ♋ | 20 ♌ | 21 ♎ | 20 ♏ | 19 ♐ | 18 ♑ | 20 ♓ | 21 ♉ | 20 ♊ | 21 ♌ | 21 ♍ |
| 23 ♋ | 22 ♌ | 22 ♍ | 23 ♏ | 22 ♐ | 21 ♑ | 20 ♒ | 22 ♈ | 23 ♊ | 23 ♋ | 23 ♍ | 23 ♎ |
| 25 ♌ | 24 ♍ | 24 ♎ | 25 ♐ | 25 ♑ | 23 ♒ | 23 ♓ | 24 ♉ | 25 ♋ | 25 ♌ | 25 ♎ | 25 ♏ |
| 27 ♍ | 26 ♎ | 26 ♏ | 27 ♑ | 27 ♒ | 26 ♓ | 25 ♈ | 26 ♊ | 28 ♌ | 27 ♍ | 28 ♏ | 27 ♐ |
| 29 ♎ | 28 ♏ | 29 ♐ | 30 ♒ | 30 ♓ | 28 ♈ | 27 ♉ | 29 ♋ | 30 ♍ | 29 ♎ | 30 ♐ | 29 ♑ |
|  |  | 31 ♑ |  |  |  | 31 ♊ | 31 ♌ |  | 31 ♏ |  |  |

## 1949

| JAN. | FEB. | MAR. | APR. | MAY | JUNE | JULY | AUG. | SEPT. | OCT. | NOV. | DEC. |
|---|---|---|---|---|---|---|---|---|---|---|---|
| 1 ♒ | 2 ♈ | 1 ♈ | 2 ♊ | 2 ♋ | 1 ♌ | 2 ♎ | 3 ♐ | 1 ♑ | 1 ♒ | 2 ♈ | 2 ♉ |
| 3 ♓ | 4 ♉ | 4 ♉ | 5 ♋ | 4 ♌ | 3 ♍ | 4 ♏ | 5 ♑ | 3 ♒ | 3 ♓ | 4 ♉ | 4 ♊ |
| 6 ♈ | 7 ♊ | 6 ♊ | 7 ♌ | 7 ♍ | 5 ♎ | 6 ♐ | 7 ♒ | 6 ♓ | 5 ♈ | 7 ♊ | 6 ♋ |
| 8 ♉ | 9 ♋ | 8 ♋ | 9 ♍ | 9 ♎ | 7 ♏ | 9 ♑ | 9 ♓ | 8 ♈ | 8 ♉ | 9 ♋ | 9 ♌ |
| 10 ♊ | 11 ♌ | 11 ♌ | 11 ♎ | 11 ♏ | 9 ♐ | 11 ♒ | 12 ♈ | 11 ♉ | 11 ♊ | 12 ♌ | 11 ♍ |
| 13 ♋ | 13 ♍ | 13 ♍ | 13 ♏ | 13 ♐ | 11 ♑ | 13 ♓ | 14 ♉ | 13 ♊ | 13 ♋ | 14 ♍ | 13 ♎ |
| 15 ♌ | 15 ♎ | 15 ♎ | 15 ♐ | 15 ♑ | 13 ♒ | 16 ♈ | 17 ♊ | 16 ♋ | 15 ♌ | 16 ♎ | 15 ♏ |
| 17 ♍ | 17 ♏ | 17 ♏ | 17 ♑ | 18 ♒ | 15 ♓ | 18 ♉ | 19 ♋ | 18 ♌ | 18 ♍ | 18 ♏ | 17 ♐ |
| 19 ♎ | 19 ♐ | 19 ♐ | 20 ♒ | 20 ♓ | 18 ♈ | 21 ♊ | 22 ♌ | 20 ♍ | 20 ♎ | 20 ♐ | 19 ♑ |
| 21 ♏ | 22 ♑ | 21 ♑ | 22 ♓ | 22 ♈ | 21 ♉ | 23 ♋ | 24 ♍ | 22 ♎ | 22 ♏ | 22 ♑ | 22 ♒ |
| 23 ♐ | 24 ♒ | 23 ♒ | 25 ♈ | 24 ♉ | 23 ♊ | 25 ♌ | 26 ♎ | 24 ♏ | 24 ♐ | 24 ♒ | 24 ♓ |
| 26 ♑ | 27 ♓ | 26 ♓ | 27 ♉ | 26 ♊ | 25 ♋ | 27 ♍ | 28 ♏ | 26 ♐ | 26 ♑ | 27 ♓ | 26 ♈ |
| 28 ♒ |  | 28 ♈ | 30 ♊ | 28 ♋ | 27 ♌ | 29 ♎ | 30 ♐ | 28 ♑ | 28 ♒ | 29 ♈ | 29 ♉ |
| 30 ♓ |  | 31 ♉ |  | 30 ♌ | 30 ♍ | 31 ♏ |  | 30 ♒ | 30 ♓ |  | 31 ♊ |

| Libra | Scorpio | Sagittarius | Capricorn | Aquarius | Pisces |
|---|---|---|---|---|---|
| ♎ | ♏ | ♐ | ♑ | ♒ | ♓ |

## 1950

| JAN. | FEB. | MAR. | APR. | MAY | JUNE | JULY | AUG. | SEPT. | OCT. | NOV. | DEC. |
|---|---|---|---|---|---|---|---|---|---|---|---|
| 3 ♋ | 1 ♌ | 1 ♌ | 2 ♎ | 1 ♏ | 1 ♑ | 1 ♒ | 2 ♈ | 1 ♉ | 3 ♋ | 2 ♌ | 1 ♍ |
| 5 ♌ | 4 ♍ | 3 ♍ | 4 ♏ | 3 ♐ | 3 ♒ | 3 ♓ | 4 ♉ | 3 ♊ | 5 ♌ | 4 ♍ | 4 ♎ |
| 7 ♍ | 6 ♎ | 5 ♎ | 6 ♐ | 5 ♑ | 6 ♓ | 5 ♈ | 7 ♊ | 6 ♋ | 8 ♍ | 6 ♎ | 6 ♏ |
| 9 ♎ | 8 ♏ | 7 ♏ | 8 ♑ | 7 ♒ | 8 ♈ | 8 ♉ | 9 ♋ | 8 ♌ | 10 ♎ | 8 ♏ | 8 ♐ |
| 12 ♏ | 10 ♐ | 9 ♐ | 10 ♒ | 9 ♓ | 11 ♉ | 10 ♊ | 12 ♌ | 10 ♍ | 12 ♏ | 10 ♐ | 10 ♑ |
| 14 ♐ | 12 ♑ | 11 ♑ | 12 ♓ | 12 ♈ | 13 ♊ | 13 ♋ | 14 ♍ | 12 ♎ | 14 ♐ | 12 ♑ | 12 ♒ |
| 16 ♑ | 14 ♒ | 14 ♒ | 15 ♈ | 14 ♉ | 16 ♋ | 15 ♌ | 16 ♎ | 15 ♏ | 16 ♑ | 14 ♒ | 14 ♓ |
| 18 ♒ | 17 ♓ | 16 ♓ | 17 ♉ | 17 ♊ | 18 ♌ | 18 ♍ | 18 ♏ | 17 ♐ | 18 ♒ | 17 ♓ | 16 ♈ |
| 20 ♓ | 19 ♈ | 18 ♈ | 20 ♊ | 19 ♋ | 20 ♍ | 20 ♎ | 20 ♐ | 19 ♑ | 20 ♓ | 19 ♈ | 19 ♉ |
| 23 ♈ | 22 ♉ | 21 ♉ | 22 ♋ | 22 ♌ | 22 ♎ | 22 ♏ | 22 ♑ | 21 ♒ | 23 ♈ | 21 ♉ | 21 ♊ |
| 25 ♉ | 24 ♊ | 23 ♊ | 25 ♌ | 24 ♍ | 25 ♏ | 24 ♐ | 25 ♒ | 23 ♓ | 25 ♉ | 24 ♊ | 24 ♋ |
| 28 ♊ | 27 ♋ | 26 ♋ | 27 ♍ | 26 ♎ | 27 ♐ | 26 ♑ | 27 ♓ | 25 ♈ | 28 ♊ | 27 ♋ | 26 ♌ |
| 30 ♋ | | 28 ♌ | 29 ♎ | 28 ♏ | 29 ♑ | 28 ♒ | 29 ♈ | 28 ♉ | 30 ♋ | 29 ♌ | 29 ♍ |
| | | 30 ♍ | | 30 ♐ | | 30 ♓ | | 30 ♊ | | | 31 ♎ |

## 1951

| JAN. | FEB. | MAR. | APR. | MAY | JUNE | JULY | AUG. | SEPT. | OCT. | NOV. | DEC. |
|---|---|---|---|---|---|---|---|---|---|---|---|
| 2 ♏ | 1 ♐ | 2 ♑ | 2 ♓ | 2 ♈ | 1 ♉ | 3 ♋ | 2 ♌ | 3 ♎ | 2 ♏ | 1 ♐ | 2 ♒ |
| 4 ♐ | 3 ♑ | 4 ♒ | 5 ♈ | 4 ♉ | 3 ♊ | 5 ♌ | 4 ♍ | 5 ♏ | 4 ♐ | 3 ♑ | 4 ♓ |
| 6 ♑ | 5 ♒ | 6 ♓ | 7 ♉ | 7 ♊ | 6 ♋ | 8 ♍ | 6 ♎ | 7 ♐ | 7 ♑ | 5 ♒ | 6 ♈ |
| 8 ♒ | 7 ♓ | 8 ♈ | 10 ♊ | 9 ♋ | 8 ♌ | 10 ♎ | 8 ♏ | 9 ♑ | 9 ♒ | 7 ♓ | 9 ♉ |
| 10 ♓ | 9 ♈ | 11 ♉ | 12 ♋ | 12 ♌ | 10 ♍ | 13 ♏ | 11 ♐ | 11 ♒ | 11 ♓ | 9 ♈ | 11 ♊ |
| 13 ♈ | 11 ♉ | 13 ♊ | 15 ♌ | 14 ♍ | 13 ♎ | 15 ♐ | 13 ♑ | 13 ♓ | 13 ♈ | 12 ♉ | 14 ♋ |
| 15 ♉ | 14 ♊ | 16 ♋ | 17 ♍ | 17 ♎ | 15 ♏ | 17 ♑ | 15 ♒ | 16 ♈ | 15 ♉ | 14 ♊ | 16 ♌ |
| 18 ♊ | 16 ♋ | 18 ♌ | 19 ♎ | 19 ♏ | 17 ♐ | 19 ♒ | 17 ♓ | 18 ♉ | 18 ♊ | 16 ♋ | 19 ♍ |
| 20 ♋ | 19 ♌ | 21 ♍ | 21 ♏ | 21 ♐ | 19 ♑ | 21 ♓ | 19 ♈ | 20 ♊ | 20 ♋ | 19 ♌ | 21 ♎ |
| 23 ♌ | 21 ♍ | 23 ♎ | 23 ♐ | 23 ♑ | 21 ♒ | 23 ♈ | 21 ♉ | 23 ♋ | 23 ♌ | 21 ♍ | 23 ♏ |
| 25 ♍ | 23 ♎ | 25 ♏ | 25 ♑ | 25 ♒ | 23 ♓ | 25 ♉ | 24 ♊ | 25 ♌ | 25 ♍ | 23 ♎ | 26 ♐ |
| 27 ♎ | 26 ♏ | 27 ♐ | 27 ♒ | 27 ♓ | 25 ♈ | 28 ♊ | 26 ♋ | 27 ♍ | 27 ♎ | 26 ♏ | 28 ♑ |
| 29 ♏ | 28 ♐ | 29 ♑ | 30 ♓ | 30 ♈ | 28 ♉ | 30 ♋ | 29 ♌ | 30 ♎ | 30 ♏ | 28 ♐ | 30 ♒ |
| | | 31 ♒ | | | 30 ♊ | | 31 ♍ | | | 30 ♑ | |

*Key:*  Aries   Taurus   Gemini   Cancer   Leo   Virgo
       ♈     ♉     ♊     ♋     ♌   ♍

## 1952

| JAN. | FEB. | MAR. | APR. | MAY | JUNE | JULY | AUG. | SEPT. | OCT. | NOV. | DEC. |
|---|---|---|---|---|---|---|---|---|---|---|---|
| 1 ♓ | 1 ♉ | 2 ♊ | 1 ♋ | 1 ♌ | 2 ♎ | 2 ♏ | 2 ♑ | 1 ♒ | 2 ♈ | 1 ♉ | 3 ♋ |
| 3 ♈ | 4 ♊ | 5 ♋ | 3 ♌ | 3 ♍ | 4 ♏ | 4 ♐ | 4 ♒ | 3 ♓ | 4 ♉ | 3 ♊ | 5 ♌ |
| 5 ♉ | 6 ♋ | 7 ♌ | 6 ♍ | 6 ♎ | 7 ♐ | 6 ♑ | 6 ♓ | 5 ♈ | 7 ♊ | 5 ♋ | 8 ♍ |
| 7 ♊ | 9 ♌ | 10 ♍ | 8 ♎ | 8 ♏ | 9 ♑ | 8 ♒ | 8 ♈ | 7 ♉ | 9 ♋ | 8 ♌ | 10 ♎ |
| 10 ♋ | 11 ♍ | 12 ♎ | 11 ♏ | 10 ♐ | 11 ♒ | 10 ♓ | 11 ♉ | 10 ♊ | 11 ♌ | 10 ♍ | 13 ♏ |
| 12 ♌ | 14 ♎ | 14 ♏ | 13 ♐ | 12 ♑ | 13 ♓ | 12 ♈ | 13 ♊ | 12 ♋ | 14 ♍ | 13 ♎ | 15 ♐ |
| 15 ♍ | 16 ♏ | 17 ♐ | 15 ♑ | 14 ♒ | 15 ♈ | 14 ♉ | 15 ♋ | 14 ♌ | 16 ♎ | 15 ♏ | 17 ♑ |
| 17 ♎ | 18 ♐ | 19 ♑ | 17 ♒ | 16 ♓ | 17 ♉ | 17 ♊ | 18 ♌ | 17 ♍ | 19 ♏ | 17 ♐ | 19 ♒ |
| 20 ♏ | 20 ♑ | 21 ♒ | 19 ♓ | 19 ♈ | 19 ♊ | 19 ♋ | 20 ♍ | 19 ♎ | 21 ♐ | 19 ♑ | 21 ♓ |
| 22 ♐ | 22 ♒ | 23 ♓ | 21 ♈ | 21 ♉ | 22 ♋ | 22 ♌ | 23 ♎ | 21 ♏ | 23 ♑ | 21 ♒ | 23 ♈ |
| 24 ♑ | 24 ♓ | 25 ♈ | 24 ♉ | 23 ♊ | 24 ♌ | 24 ♍ | 25 ♏ | 23 ♐ | 26 ♒ | 24 ♓ | 25 ♉ |
| 26 ♒ | 27 ♈ | 27 ♉ | 26 ♊ | 26 ♋ | 27 ♍ | 27 ♎ | 28 ♐ | 26 ♑ | 28 ♓ | 26 ♈ | 28 ♊ |
| 28 ♓ | 29 ♉ | 29 ♊ | 28 ♋ | 28 ♌ | 29 ♎ | 29 ♏ | 30 ♑ | 28 ♒ | 30 ♈ | 28 ♉ | 30 ♋ |
| 30 ♈ | | | | 31 ♍ | | 31 ♐ | | 30 ♓ | | 30 ♊ | |

## 1953

| JAN. | FEB. | MAR. | APR. | MAY | JUNE | JULY | AUG. | SEPT. | OCT. | NOV. | DEC. |
|---|---|---|---|---|---|---|---|---|---|---|---|
| 1 ♌ | 3 ♎ | 2 ♎ | 1 ♏ | 3 ♑ | 1 ♒ | 1 ♓ | 1 ♉ | 2 ♋ | 1 ♌ | 3 ♎ | 2 ♏ |
| 4 ♍ | 5 ♏ | 4 ♏ | 3 ♐ | 5 ♒ | 3 ♓ | 3 ♈ | 3 ♊ | 4 ♌ | 4 ♍ | 5 ♏ | 5 ♐ |
| 6 ♎ | 8 ♐ | 7 ♐ | 5 ♑ | 7 ♓ | 5 ♈ | 5 ♉ | 5 ♋ | 6 ♍ | 6 ♎ | 8 ♐ | 7 ♑ |
| 9 ♏ | 10 ♑ | 9 ♑ | 8 ♒ | 9 ♈ | 7 ♉ | 7 ♊ | 8 ♌ | 9 ♎ | 9 ♏ | 10 ♑ | 9 ♒ |
| 11 ♐ | 12 ♒ | 11 ♒ | 10 ♓ | 11 ♉ | 10 ♊ | 9 ♋ | 10 ♍ | 12 ♏ | 11 ♐ | 12 ♒ | 12 ♓ |
| 13 ♑ | 14 ♓ | 13 ♓ | 12 ♈ | 13 ♊ | 12 ♋ | 12 ♌ | 13 ♎ | 14 ♐ | 14 ♑ | 14 ♓ | 14 ♈ |
| 15 ♒ | 16 ♈ | 15 ♈ | 14 ♉ | 15 ♋ | 14 ♌ | 14 ♍ | 15 ♏ | 16 ♑ | 16 ♒ | 17 ♈ | 16 ♉ |
| 17 ♓ | 18 ♉ | 17 ♉ | 16 ♊ | 18 ♌ | 16 ♍ | 16 ♎ | 18 ♐ | 18 ♒ | 18 ♓ | 19 ♉ | 18 ♊ |
| 19 ♈ | 20 ♊ | 19 ♊ | 18 ♋ | 20 ♍ | 19 ♎ | 19 ♏ | 20 ♑ | 21 ♓ | 20 ♈ | 21 ♊ | 20 ♋ |
| 22 ♉ | 22 ♋ | 22 ♋ | 20 ♌ | 23 ♎ | 21 ♏ | 21 ♐ | 22 ♒ | 23 ♈ | 22 ♉ | 23 ♋ | 22 ♌ |
| 24 ♊ | 25 ♌ | 24 ♌ | 23 ♍ | 25 ♏ | 24 ♐ | 24 ♑ | 24 ♓ | 25 ♉ | 24 ♊ | 25 ♌ | 25 ♍ |
| 26 ♋ | 27 ♍ | 27 ♍ | 26 ♎ | 28 ♐ | 26 ♑ | 26 ♒ | 26 ♈ | 27 ♊ | 26 ♋ | 27 ♍ | 27 ♎ |
| 29 ♌ | | 29 ♎ | 28 ♏ | 30 ♑ | 28 ♒ | 28 ♓ | 28 ♉ | 29 ♋ | 29 ♌ | 30 ♎ | 30 ♏ |
| 31 ♍ | | | 30 ♐ | | | 30 ♈ | 30 ♊ | | 31 ♍ | | |

| Libra | Scorpio | Sagittarius | Capricorn | Aquarius | Pisces |
|---|---|---|---|---|---|
| ♎ | ♏ | ♐ | ♑ | ♒ | ♓ |

## 1954

| JAN. | FEB. | MAR. | APR. | MAY | JUNE | JULY | AUG. | SEPT. | OCT. | NOV. | DEC. |
|---|---|---|---|---|---|---|---|---|---|---|---|
| 1♐ | 2♒ | 2♒ | 2♈ | 2♉ | 2♋ | 2♌ | 3♎ | 1♏ | 1♐ | 2♒ | 2♓ |
| 4♑ | 4♓ | 4♓ | 4♉ | 4♊ | 4♌ | 4♍ | 5♏ | 4♐ | 4♑ | 5♓ | 4♈ |
| 6♒ | 6♈ | 6♈ | 6♊ | 6♋ | 6♍ | 6♎ | 8♐ | 6♑ | 6♒ | 7♈ | 6♉ |
| 8♓ | 8♉ | 8♉ | 8♋ | 8♌ | 9♎ | 9♏ | 10♑ | 9♒ | 8♓ | 9♉ | 8♊ |
| 10♈ | 11♊ | 10♊ | 11♌ | 10♍ | 12♏ | 11♐ | 12♒ | 11♓ | 11♈ | 11♊ | 10♋ |
| 12♉ | 13♋ | 12♋ | 13♍ | 13♎ | 14♐ | 14♑ | 15♓ | 13♈ | 13♉ | 13♋ | 12♌ |
| 14♊ | 15♌ | 14♌ | 15♎ | 15♏ | 16♑ | 16♒ | 17♈ | 15♉ | 14♊ | 15♋ | 14♍ |
| 16♋ | 17♍ | 17♍ | 18♏ | 18♐ | 19♒ | 18♓ | 19♉ | 17♊ | 16♋ | 17♍ | 17♎ |
| 19♌ | 20♎ | 19♎ | 20♐ | 20♑ | 21♓ | 21♈ | 21♊ | 19♋ | 19♌ | 20♎ | 20♏ |
| 21♍ | 22♏ | 22♏ | 23♑ | 23♒ | 23♈ | 23♉ | 23♋ | 22♌ | 21♍ | 22♏ | 22♐ |
| 24♎ | 25♐ | 24♐ | 25♒ | 25♓ | 25♉ | 25♊ | 25♌ | 24♍ | 24♎ | 25♐ | 25♑ |
| 26♏ | 27♑ | 27♑ | 28♓ | 27♈ | 27♊ | 27♋ | 28♍ | 26♎ | 26♏ | 27♑ | 27♒ |
| 29♐ |  | 29♒ | 30♈ | 29♉ | 29♋ | 29♌ | 30♎ | 29♐ | 29♒ |  | 29♓ |
| 31♑ |  | 31♓ |  | 31♊ |  | 31♍ |  |  | 31♑ |  |  |

## 1955

| JAN. | FEB. | MAR. | APR. | MAY | JUNE | JULY | AUG. | SEPT. | OCT. | NOV. | DEC. |
|---|---|---|---|---|---|---|---|---|---|---|---|
| 1♈ | 1♊ | 2♋ | 1♌ | 3♎ | 1♏ | 1♐ | 2♒ | 1♓ | 1♈ | 1♊ | 1♋ |
| 3♉ | 3♋ | 5♌ | 3♍ | 5♏ | 4♐ | 4♑ | 5♓ | 3♈ | 3♉ | 3♋ | 3♌ |
| 5♊ | 5♌ | 7♍ | 5♎ | 8♐ | 6♑ | 7♒ | 7♈ | 5♉ | 5♊ | 5♌ | 5♍ |
| 7♋ | 7♍ | 9♎ | 8♏ | 10♑ | 9♒ | 9♓ | 9♉ | 7♊ | 7♋ | 8♍ | 7♎ |
| 9♌ | 10♎ | 12♏ | 10♐ | 13♒ | 11♓ | 11♈ | 11♊ | 9♋ | 9♌ | 10♎ | 10♏ |
| 11♍ | 12♏ | 14♐ | 13♑ | 15♓ | 14♈ | 13♉ | 14♋ | 12♌ | 11♍ | 12♏ | 12♐ |
| 13♎ | 15♐ | 17♑ | 15♒ | 17♈ | 16♉ | 15♊ | 16♌ | 14♍ | 13♎ | 15♐ | 15♑ |
| 16♏ | 17♑ | 19♒ | 17♓ | 19♉ | 18♊ | 18♋ | 18♍ | 16♎ | 16♏ | 17♑ | 17♒ |
| 18♐ | 20♒ | 21♓ | 20♈ | 21♊ | 20♋ | 19♌ | 20♎ | 18♐ | 18♐ | 20♒ | 20♓ |
| 21♑ | 22♓ | 23♈ | 22♉ | 23♋ | 22♌ | 21♍ | 22♏ | 21♑ | 21♑ | 22♓ | 22♈ |
| 23♒ | 24♈ | 26♉ | 24♊ | 25♌ | 24♍ | 24♎ | 25♐ | 23♒ | 23♒ | 25♈ | 24♉ |
| 26♓ | 26♉ | 28♊ | 26♋ | 28♍ | 26♎ | 26♏ | 27♑ | 26♓ | 26♓ | 27♉ | 26♊ |
| 28♈ | 28♊ | 30♋ | 28♌ | 30♎ | 29♏ | 28♐ | 30♒ | 28♈ | 28♈ | 29♊ | 28♋ |
| 30♉ |  |  | 30♍ |  |  | 31♑ |  |  | 30♉ |  | 30♌ |

*Key:*  **Aries  Taurus  Gemini  Cancer  Leo  Virgo**

♈　　♉　　♊　　♋　　♌　　♍

## 1956

| JAN. | FEB. | MAR. | APR. | MAY | JUNE | JULY | AUG. | SEPT. | OCT. | NOV. | DEC. |
|---|---|---|---|---|---|---|---|---|---|---|---|
| 1 ♍ | 2 ♏ | 3 ♐ | 2 ♑ | 2 ♒ | 3 ♈ | 2 ♉ | 1 ♊ | 1 ♌ | 1 ♍ | 1 ♏ | 1 ♐ |
| 3 ♎ | 5 ♐ | 5 ♑ | 4 ♒ | 4 ♓ | 5 ♉ | 5 ♊ | 3 ♋ | 3 ♍ | 3 ♎ | 4 ♐ | 3 ♑ |
| 6 ♏ | 7 ♑ | 8 ♒ | 7 ♓ | 6 ♈ | 7 ♊ | 7 ♋ | 5 ♌ | 6 ♎ | 5 ♏ | 6 ♑ | 6 ♒ |
| 8 ♐ | 10 ♒ | 10 ♓ | 9 ♈ | 9 ♉ | 9 ♋ | 9 ♌ | 7 ♍ | 8 ♏ | 7 ♐ | 9 ♒ | 8 ♓ |
| 11 ♑ | 12 ♓ | 13 ♈ | 11 ♉ | 11 ♊ | 11 ♌ | 11 ♍ | 9 ♎ | 10 ♐ | 10 ♑ | 11 ♓ | 11 ♈ |
| 13 ♒ | 14 ♈ | 15 ♉ | 13 ♊ | 13 ♋ | 13 ♍ | 13 ♎ | 11 ♏ | 12 ♑ | 12 ♒ | 14 ♈ | 13 ♉ |
| 16 ♓ | 17 ♉ | 17 ♊ | 16 ♋ | 15 ♌ | 15 ♎ | 15 ♏ | 14 ♐ | 15 ♒ | 15 ♓ | 16 ♉ | 16 ♊ |
| 18 ♈ | 19 ♊ | 19 ♋ | 18 ♌ | 17 ♍ | 18 ♏ | 17 ♐ | 16 ♑ | 17 ♓ | 17 ♈ | 18 ♊ | 18 ♋ |
| 20 ♉ | 21 ♋ | 21 ♌ | 20 ♍ | 19 ♎ | 20 ♐ | 20 ♑ | 19 ♒ | 20 ♈ | 20 ♉ | 20 ♋ | 20 ♌ |
| 23 ♊ | 23 ♌ | 23 ♍ | 22 ♎ | 21 ♏ | 23 ♑ | 22 ♒ | 21 ♓ | 22 ♉ | 22 ♊ | 22 ♌ | 22 ♍ |
| 25 ♋ | 25 ♍ | 26 ♎ | 24 ♏ | 24 ♐ | 25 ♒ | 25 ♓ | 24 ♈ | 24 ♊ | 24 ♋ | 24 ♍ | 24 ♎ |
| 27 ♌ | 27 ♎ | 28 ♏ | 27 ♐ | 26 ♑ | 28 ♓ | 27 ♈ | 26 ♉ | 27 ♋ | 26 ♌ | 27 ♎ | 26 ♏ |
| 29 ♍ | 29 ♏ | 30 ♐ | 29 ♑ | 28 ♒ | 30 ♈ | 30 ♉ | 28 ♊ | 29 ♌ | 28 ♍ | 29 ♏ | 28 ♐ |
| 31 ♎ | | | | 31 ♓ | | | 30 ♋ | | 30 ♎ | | 31 ♑ |

## 1957

| JAN. | FEB. | MAR. | APR. | MAY | JUNE | JULY | AUG. | SEPT. | OCT. | NOV. | DEC. |
|---|---|---|---|---|---|---|---|---|---|---|---|
| 2 ♒ | 1 ♓ | 3 ♈ | 1 ♉ | 1 ♊ | 2 ♌ | 1 ♍ | 2 ♏ | 2 ♐ | 2 ♑ | 1 ♓ | 1 ♈ |
| 5 ♓ | 4 ♈ | 5 ♉ | 4 ♊ | 3 ♋ | 4 ♍ | 3 ♎ | 4 ♐ | 5 ♑ | 5 ♒ | 3 ♈ | 3 ♉ |
| 7 ♈ | 6 ♉ | 8 ♊ | 6 ♋ | 5 ♌ | 6 ♎ | 5 ♏ | 6 ♑ | 7 ♒ | 7 ♓ | 6 ♉ | 6 ♊ |
| 10 ♉ | 8 ♊ | 10 ♋ | 8 ♌ | 8 ♍ | 8 ♏ | 8 ♐ | 9 ♒ | 10 ♓ | 10 ♈ | 8 ♊ | 8 ♋ |
| 12 ♊ | 10 ♋ | 12 ♌ | 10 ♍ | 10 ♎ | 11 ♐ | 10 ♑ | 11 ♓ | 12 ♈ | 12 ♉ | 11 ♋ | 10 ♌ |
| 14 ♋ | 12 ♌ | 14 ♍ | 12 ♎ | 12 ♏ | 13 ♑ | 12 ♒ | 14 ♈ | 15 ♉ | 14 ♊ | 13 ♌ | 12 ♍ |
| 16 ♌ | 14 ♍ | 16 ♎ | 14 ♏ | 14 ♐ | 15 ♒ | 15 ♓ | 16 ♉ | 17 ♊ | 16 ♋ | 15 ♍ | 14 ♎ |
| 18 ♍ | 16 ♎ | 18 ♏ | 17 ♐ | 16 ♑ | 18 ♓ | 17 ♈ | 19 ♊ | 19 ♋ | 18 ♌ | 17 ♎ | 16 ♏ |
| 20 ♎ | 18 ♏ | 20 ♐ | 19 ♑ | 19 ♒ | 20 ♈ | 19 ♉ | 21 ♋ | 21 ♌ | 21 ♍ | 19 ♏ | 19 ♐ |
| 22 ♏ | 21 ♐ | 23 ♑ | 21 ♒ | 21 ♓ | 22 ♉ | 21 ♊ | 23 ♌ | 23 ♍ | 23 ♎ | 21 ♐ | 21 ♑ |
| 25 ♐ | 23 ♑ | 25 ♒ | 24 ♓ | 24 ♈ | 25 ♊ | 24 ♋ | 25 ♍ | 25 ♎ | 25 ♏ | 23 ♑ | 23 ♒ |
| 27 ♑ | 26 ♒ | 28 ♓ | 26 ♈ | 26 ♉ | 27 ♋ | 26 ♌ | 27 ♎ | 27 ♏ | 27 ♐ | 26 ♒ | 26 ♓ |
| 29 ♒ | 28 ♓ | 30 ♈ | 29 ♉ | 28 ♊ | 29 ♌ | 28 ♍ | 29 ♏ | 30 ♐ | 29 ♑ | 28 ♓ | 28 ♈ |
| | | | | 31 ♋ | | 30 ♎ | 31 ♐ | | 31 ♒ | | 31 ♉ |

| Libra | Scorpio | Sagittarius | Capricorn | Aquarius | Pisces |
|---|---|---|---|---|---|
| ♎ | ♏ | ♐ | ♑ | ♒ | ♓ |

## 1958

| JAN. | FEB. | MAR. | APR. | MAY | JUNE | JULY | AUG. | SEPT. | OCT. | NOV. | DEC. |
|---|---|---|---|---|---|---|---|---|---|---|---|
| 2 ♊ | 1 ♋ | 2 ♌ | 1 ♍ | 2 ♏ | 1 ♐ | 2 ♒ | 1 ♓ | 2 ♉ | 2 ♊ | 1 ♋ | 3 ♍ |
| 4 ♋ | 3 ♌ | 4 ♍ | 3 ♎ | 4 ♐ | 3 ♑ | 5 ♓ | 3 ♈ | 5 ♊ | 5 ♋ | 3 ♌ | 5 ♎ |
| 6 ♌ | 5 ♍ | 6 ♎ | 5 ♏ | 6 ♑ | 5 ♒ | 7 ♈ | 5 ♉ | 7 ♋ | 7 ♌ | 5 ♍ | 7 ♏ |
| 8 ♍ | 7 ♎ | 8 ♏ | 7 ♐ | 9 ♒ | 7 ♓ | 9 ♉ | 7 ♊ | 9 ♌ | 9 ♍ | 7 ♎ | 9 ♐ |
| 11 ♎ | 9 ♏ | 10 ♐ | 9 ♑ | 11 ♓ | 10 ♈ | 12 ♊ | 9 ♋ | 12 ♍ | 11 ♎ | 10 ♏ | 11 ♑ |
| 13 ♏ | 11 ♐ | 13 ♑ | 11 ♒ | 14 ♈ | 12 ♉ | 15 ♋ | 11 ♌ | 14 ♎ | 13 ♏ | 12 ♐ | 13 ♒ |
| 15 ♐ | 13 ♑ | 15 ♒ | 14 ♓ | 16 ♉ | 15 ♊ | 17 ♌ | 13 ♍ | 16 ♏ | 15 ♐ | 14 ♑ | 15 ♓ |
| 17 ♑ | 16 ♒ | 17 ♓ | 16 ♈ | 18 ♊ | 17 ♋ | 19 ♍ | 16 ♎ | 18 ♐ | 17 ♑ | 16 ♒ | 18 ♈ |
| 19 ♒ | 18 ♓ | 20 ♈ | 19 ♉ | 21 ♋ | 19 ♌ | 21 ♎ | 18 ♏ | 20 ♑ | 19 ♒ | 18 ♓ | 20 ♉ |
| 22 ♓ | 21 ♈ | 23 ♉ | 21 ♊ | 23 ♌ | 22 ♍ | 23 ♏ | 21 ♐ | 23 ♒ | 22 ♓ | 21 ♈ | 23 ♊ |
| 24 ♈ | 23 ♉ | 25 ♊ | 24 ♋ | 25 ♍ | 24 ♎ | 25 ♐ | 24 ♑ | 25 ♓ | 24 ♈ | 23 ♉ | 25 ♋ |
| 27 ♉ | 26 ♊ | 27 ♋ | 26 ♌ | 28 ♎ | 26 ♏ | 27 ♑ | 26 ♒ | 27 ♈ | 27 ♉ | 26 ♊ | 28 ♌ |
| 29 ♊ | 28 ♋ | 30 ♌ | 28 ♍ | 30 ♏ | 28 ♐ | 30 ♒ | 28 ♓ | 30 ♉ | 29 ♊ | 28 ♋ | 30 ♍ |
|  |  |  | 30 ♎ |  | 30 ♑ |  | 31 ♈ |  |  |  |  |

## 1959

| JAN. | FEB. | MAR. | APR. | MAY | JUNE | JULY | AUG. | SEPT. | OCT. | NOV. | DEC. |
|---|---|---|---|---|---|---|---|---|---|---|---|
| 1 ♎ | 2 ♐ | 1 ♐ | 1 ♒ | 1 ♓ | 2 ♉ | 2 ♊ | 1 ♋ | 2 ♍ | 1 ♎ | 2 ♐ | 1 ♑ |
| 3 ♏ | 4 ♑ | 3 ♑ | 4 ♓ | 3 ♈ | 5 ♊ | 5 ♋ | 3 ♌ | 4 ♎ | 3 ♏ | 4 ♑ | 3 ♒ |
| 5 ♐ | 6 ♒ | 5 ♒ | 6 ♈ | 6 ♉ | 7 ♋ | 7 ♌ | 6 ♍ | 6 ♏ | 6 ♐ | 6 ♒ | 6 ♓ |
| 7 ♑ | 8 ♓ | 7 ♓ | 9 ♉ | 8 ♊ | 10 ♌ | 9 ♍ | 8 ♎ | 8 ♐ | 8 ♑ | 8 ♓ | 8 ♈ |
| 10 ♒ | 11 ♈ | 10 ♈ | 11 ♊ | 11 ♋ | 12 ♍ | 12 ♎ | 10 ♏ | 10 ♑ | 10 ♒ | 11 ♈ | 11 ♉ |
| 12 ♓ | 13 ♉ | 12 ♉ | 14 ♋ | 13 ♌ | 14 ♎ | 14 ♏ | 12 ♐ | 13 ♒ | 12 ♓ | 13 ♉ | 13 ♊ |
| 14 ♈ | 16 ♊ | 15 ♊ | 16 ♌ | 16 ♍ | 16 ♏ | 16 ♐ | 14 ♑ | 15 ♓ | 14 ♈ | 16 ♊ | 15 ♋ |
| 17 ♉ | 18 ♋ | 17 ♋ | 18 ♍ | 18 ♎ | 18 ♐ | 18 ♑ | 16 ♒ | 17 ♈ | 17 ♉ | 18 ♋ | 18 ♌ |
| 19 ♊ | 20 ♌ | 20 ♌ | 21 ♎ | 20 ♏ | 20 ♑ | 20 ♒ | 18 ♓ | 19 ♉ | 19 ♊ | 21 ♌ | 20 ♍ |
| 22 ♋ | 23 ♍ | 22 ♍ | 23 ♏ | 22 ♐ | 22 ♒ | 22 ♓ | 21 ♈ | 22 ♊ | 21 ♋ | 23 ♍ | 23 ♎ |
| 24 ♌ | 25 ♎ | 24 ♎ | 25 ♐ | 25 ♑ | 25 ♓ | 24 ♈ | 23 ♉ | 24 ♋ | 24 ♌ | 25 ♎ | 25 ♏ |
| 26 ♍ | 27 ♏ | 26 ♏ | 27 ♑ | 28 ♒ | 27 ♈ | 27 ♉ | 26 ♊ | 27 ♌ | 27 ♍ | 27 ♏ | 27 ♐ |
| 28 ♎ |  | 28 ♐ | 29 ♒ | 31 ♈ | 29 ♉ | 29 ♊ | 28 ♋ | 29 ♍ | 29 ♎ | 29 ♐ | 29 ♑ |
| 31 ♏ |  | 30 ♑ |  |  |  |  | 31 ♌ |  | 31 ♏ |  | 31 ♒ |

*Key:*  **Aries**  **Taurus**  **Gemini**  **Cancer**  **Leo**  **Virgo**
         ♈         ♉          ♊          ♋          ♌        ♍

## 1960

| JAN. | FEB. | MAR. | APR. | MAY | JUNE | JULY | AUG. | SEPT. | OCT. | NOV. | DEC. |
|---|---|---|---|---|---|---|---|---|---|---|---|
| 2♓ | 1♈ | 1♉ | 3♋ | 2♌ | 1♍ | 1♎ | 2♐ | 2♒ | 1♓ | 2♉ | 2♊ |
| 4♈ | 3♉ | 4♊ | 5♌ | 5♍ | 4♎ | 3♏ | 4♑ | 4♓ | 4♈ | 4♊ | 4♋ |
| 7♉ | 5♊ | 6♋ | 8♍ | 7♎ | 6♏ | 5♐ | 6♒ | 6♈ | 6♉ | 7♋ | 7♌ |
| 9♊ | 8♋ | 9♌ | 10♎ | 9♏ | 8♐ | 7♑ | 8♓ | 8♉ | 8♊ | 9♌ | 9♍ |
| 12♋ | 10♌ | 13♍ | 14♏ | 11♐ | 10♑ | 9♒ | 10♈ | 11♊ | 11♋ | 12♍ | 12♎ |
| 14♌ | 13♍ | 16♎ | 16♐ | 13♑ | 12♒ | 11♓ | 12♉ | 13♋ | 13♌ | 14♎ | 14♏ |
| 17♍ | 15♎ | 18♏ | 18♑ | 15♒ | 14♓ | 13♈ | 14♊ | 16♌ | 16♍ | 17♏ | 16♐ |
| 19♎ | 17♏ | 20♐ | 20♒ | 18♓ | 16♈ | 15♉ | 16♋ | 18♍ | 18♎ | 19♐ | 18♑ |
| 21♏ | 19♐ | 22♑ | 23♈ | 20♈ | 18♉ | 18♊ | 19♌ | 21♎ | 20♏ | 21♑ | 20♒ |
| 23♐ | 22♑ | 24♒ | 25♉ | 22♉ | 21♊ | 21♋ | 22♍ | 23♏ | 22♐ | 23♒ | 22♓ |
| 25♑ | 24♒ | 26♈ | 27♊ | 25♊ | 23♋ | 23♌ | 24♎ | 25♐ | 24♑ | 25♓ | 24♈ |
| 27♒ | 26♓ | 29♉ | 30♋ | 27♋ | 26♌ | 26♍ | 27♏ | 27♑ | 27♒ | 27♈ | 27♉ |
| 29♓ | 28♈ | 31♊ |  | 30♌ | 28♍ | 28♎ | 29♐ | 29♒ | 29♓ | 29♉ | 29♊ |
|  |  |  |  |  |  | 30♏ | 31♑ |  | 31♈ |  |  |

## 1961

| JAN. | FEB. | MAR. | APR. | MAY | JUNE | JULY | AUG. | SEPT. | OCT. | NOV. | DEC. |
|---|---|---|---|---|---|---|---|---|---|---|---|
| 1♋ | 2♍ | 1♍ | 2♏ | 2♐ | 2♒ | 2♓ | 2♉ | 1♊ | 3♌ | 2♍ | 2♎ |
| 3♌ | 4♎ | 4♎ | 4♐ | 4♑ | 4♓ | 4♈ | 4♊ | 3♋ | 5♍ | 4♎ | 4♏ |
| 6♍ | 7♏ | 6♏ | 7♑ | 6♒ | 6♈ | 6♉ | 6♋ | 6♌ | 8♎ | 7♏ | 6♐ |
| 8♎ | 9♐ | 8♐ | 9♒ | 8♓ | 9♉ | 8♊ | 9♌ | 8♍ | 10♏ | 9♐ | 9♑ |
| 10♏ | 11♑ | 10♑ | 11♓ | 11♈ | 11♊ | 11♋ | 12♍ | 11♎ | 13♐ | 11♑ | 11♒ |
| 13♐ | 13♒ | 12♒ | 13♈ | 13♉ | 13♋ | 13♌ | 14♎ | 13♏ | 15♑ | 13♒ | 13♓ |
| 15♑ | 15♓ | 15♓ | 15♉ | 15♊ | 16♌ | 16♍ | 17♏ | 15♐ | 17♒ | 16♓ | 15♈ |
| 17♒ | 17♈ | 17♈ | 17♊ | 18♋ | 18♍ | 18♎ | 19♐ | 18♑ | 19♓ | 18♈ | 17♉ |
| 19♓ | 19♉ | 19♉ | 20♋ | 20♌ | 21♎ | 21♏ | 22♑ | 20♒ | 21♈ | 20♉ | 19♊ |
| 21♈ | 22♊ | 21♊ | 22♌ | 22♍ | 23♏ | 23♐ | 24♒ | 22♓ | 24♉ | 22♊ | 22♋ |
| 23♉ | 24♋ | 23♋ | 25♍ | 25♎ | 26♐ | 25♑ | 26♓ | 24♈ | 26♊ | 24♋ | 24♌ |
| 25♊ | 27♌ | 26♌ | 27♎ | 27♏ | 28♑ | 27♒ | 28♈ | 26♉ | 28♋ | 27♌ | 26♍ |
| 28♋ |  | 28♍ | 30♏ | 29♐ | 30♒ | 29♓ | 30♉ | 28♊ | 30♌ | 29♍ | 29♎ |
| 30♌ |  | 31♎ |  | 31♑ |  | 31♈ |  | 30♋ |  |  | 31♏ |

| Libra | Scorpio | Sagittarius | Capricorn | Aquarius | Pisces |
|---|---|---|---|---|---|
| ♎ | ♏ | ♐ | ♑ | ♒ | ♓ |

## 1962

| JAN. | FEB. | MAR. | APR. | MAY | JUNE | JULY | AUG. | SEPT. | OCT. | NOV. | DEC. |
|---|---|---|---|---|---|---|---|---|---|---|---|
| 3 ♐ | 1 ♑ | 1 ♑ | 1 ♓ | 1 ♈ | 1 ♊ | 1 ♋ | 2 ♍ | 1 ♎ | 3 ♐ | 2 ♑ | 1 ♒ |
| 5 ♑ | 3 ♒ | 3 ♒ | 3 ♈ | 3 ♉ | 3 ♋ | 3 ♌ | 4 ♎ | 3 ♏ | 5 ♑ | 4 ♒ | 3 ♓ |
| 7 ♒ | 5 ♓ | 5 ♓ | 5 ♉ | 5 ♊ | 6 ♌ | 6 ♍ | 6 ♏ | 6 ♐ | 8 ♒ | 6 ♓ | 5 ♈ |
| 9 ♓ | 7 ♈ | 7 ♈ | 7 ♊ | 7 ♋ | 8 ♍ | 8 ♎ | 9 ♐ | 8 ♑ | 10 ♓ | 8 ♈ | 8 ♉ |
| 11 ♈ | 10 ♉ | 9 ♉ | 10 ♋ | 9 ♌ | 11 ♎ | 11 ♏ | 12 ♑ | 10 ♒ | 12 ♈ | 10 ♉ | 10 ♊ |
| 13 ♉ | 12 ♊ | 11 ♊ | 12 ♌ | 12 ♍ | 13 ♏ | 13 ♐ | 14 ♒ | 12 ♓ | 14 ♉ | 12 ♊ | 12 ♋ |
| 16 ♊ | 14 ♋ | 13 ♋ | 15 ♍ | 14 ♎ | 16 ♐ | 15 ♑ | 16 ♓ | 14 ♈ | 16 ♊ | 14 ♋ | 14 ♌ |
| 18 ♋ | 17 ♌ | 16 ♌ | 17 ♎ | 17 ♏ | 18 ♑ | 17 ♒ | 18 ♈ | 16 ♉ | 18 ♋ | 17 ♌ | 16 ♍ |
| 20 ♌ | 19 ♍ | 18 ♍ | 20 ♏ | 19 ♐ | 20 ♒ | 19 ♓ | 20 ♉ | 18 ♊ | 20 ♌ | 19 ♍ | 19 ♎ |
| 23 ♍ | 22 ♎ | 21 ♎ | 22 ♐ | 22 ♑ | 22 ♓ | 22 ♈ | 23 ♊ | 21 ♋ | 23 ♍ | 21 ♎ | 21 ♏ |
| 25 ♎ | 24 ♏ | 23 ♏ | 24 ♑ | 24 ♒ | 24 ♈ | 24 ♉ | 25 ♋ | 23 ♌ | 25 ♎ | 24 ♏ | 24 ♐ |
| 28 ♏ | 26 ♐ | 26 ♐ | 27 ♒ | 26 ♓ | 26 ♉ | 26 ♊ | 27 ♌ | 25 ♍ | 28 ♏ | 26 ♐ | 26 ♑ |
| 30 ♐ |  | 28 ♑ | 29 ♓ | 28 ♈ | 29 ♊ | 28 ♋ | 29 ♍ | 28 ♎ | 30 ♐ | 29 ♑ | 28 ♒ |
|  |  | 30 ♒ |  | 30 ♉ |  | 30 ♌ |  | 30 ♏ |  |  | 31 ♓ |

## 1963

| JAN. | FEB. | MAR. | APR. | MAY | JUNE | JULY | AUG. | SEPT. | OCT. | NOV. | DEC. |
|---|---|---|---|---|---|---|---|---|---|---|---|
| 2 ♈ | 2 ♊ | 1 ♊ | 2 ♌ | 2 ♍ | 1 ♎ | 3 ♐ | 2 ♑ | 3 ♓ | 2 ♈ | 1 ♉ | 2 ♋ |
| 4 ♉ | 4 ♋ | 4 ♋ | 5 ♍ | 4 ♎ | 3 ♏ | 5 ♑ | 4 ♒ | 5 ♈ | 4 ♉ | 3 ♊ | 4 ♌ |
| 6 ♊ | 7 ♌ | 6 ♌ | 7 ♎ | 7 ♏ | 6 ♐ | 8 ♒ | 6 ♓ | 7 ♉ | 6 ♊ | 5 ♋ | 6 ♍ |
| 8 ♋ | 9 ♍ | 8 ♍ | 10 ♏ | 9 ♐ | 8 ♑ | 10 ♓ | 8 ♈ | 9 ♊ | 8 ♋ | 7 ♌ | 9 ♎ |
| 10 ♌ | 11 ♎ | 11 ♎ | 12 ♐ | 12 ♑ | 10 ♒ | 12 ♈ | 10 ♉ | 11 ♋ | 10 ♌ | 9 ♍ | 11 ♏ |
| 13 ♍ | 14 ♏ | 13 ♏ | 15 ♑ | 14 ♒ | 13 ♓ | 14 ♉ | 13 ♊ | 13 ♌ | 13 ♍ | 11 ♎ | 14 ♐ |
| 15 ♎ | 16 ♐ | 16 ♐ | 17 ♒ | 16 ♓ | 15 ♈ | 16 ♊ | 15 ♋ | 15 ♍ | 15 ♎ | 14 ♏ | 16 ♑ |
| 18 ♏ | 19 ♑ | 18 ♑ | 19 ♓ | 19 ♈ | 17 ♉ | 18 ♋ | 17 ♌ | 18 ♎ | 18 ♏ | 16 ♐ | 19 ♒ |
| 20 ♐ | 21 ♒ | 21 ♒ | 21 ♈ | 21 ♉ | 19 ♊ | 21 ♌ | 19 ♍ | 20 ♏ | 20 ♐ | 19 ♑ | 21 ♓ |
| 22 ♑ | 23 ♓ | 23 ♓ | 23 ♉ | 23 ♊ | 21 ♋ | 23 ♍ | 22 ♎ | 23 ♐ | 23 ♑ | 21 ♒ | 23 ♈ |
| 25 ♒ | 25 ♈ | 25 ♈ | 25 ♊ | 25 ♋ | 23 ♌ | 25 ♎ | 24 ♏ | 25 ♑ | 25 ♒ | 24 ♓ | 25 ♉ |
| 27 ♓ | 27 ♉ | 27 ♉ | 27 ♋ | 27 ♌ | 25 ♍ | 28 ♏ | 27 ♐ | 28 ♒ | 27 ♓ | 26 ♈ | 27 ♊ |
| 29 ♈ |  | 29 ♊ | 29 ♌ | 29 ♍ | 28 ♎ | 30 ♐ | 29 ♑ | 30 ♓ | 30 ♈ | 28 ♉ | 29 ♋ |
| 31 ♉ |  | 31 ♋ |  |  | 30 ♏ |  | 31 ♒ |  |  | 30 ♊ | 31 ♌ |

*Key:*   Aries   Taurus   Gemini   Cancer   Leo   Virgo

     ♈    ♉    ♊    ♋    ♌    ♍

## 1964

| JAN. | FEB. | MAR. | APR. | MAY | JUNE | JULY | AUG. | SEPT. | OCT. | NOV. | DEC. |
|---|---|---|---|---|---|---|---|---|---|---|---|
| 3 ♍ | 1 ♎ | 2 ♏ | 1 ♐ | 1 ♑ | 2 ♓ | 2 ♈ | 2 ♊ | 1 ♋ | 2 ♍ | 1 ♎ | 3 ♐ |
| 5 ♎ | 3 ♏ | 5 ♐ | 3 ♑ | 3 ♒ | 4 ♈ | 4 ♉ | 4 ♋ | 3 ♌ | 4 ♎ | 3 ♏ | 5 ♑ |
| 7 ♏ | 6 ♐ | 7 ♑ | 6 ♒ | 6 ♓ | 6 ♉ | 6 ♊ | 6 ♌ | 5 ♍ | 7 ♏ | 5 ♐ | 8 ♒ |
| 10 ♐ | 9 ♑ | 10 ♒ | 8 ♓ | 8 ♈ | 8 ♊ | 8 ♋ | 8 ♍ | 7 ♎ | 9 ♐ | 8 ♑ | 10 ♓ |
| 12 ♑ | 11 ♒ | 12 ♓ | 10 ♈ | 10 ♉ | 10 ♋ | 10 ♌ | 10 ♎ | 9 ♏ | 11 ♑ | 10 ♒ | 13 ♈ |
| 15 ♒ | 13 ♓ | 14 ♈ | 13 ♉ | 12 ♊ | 12 ♌ | 12 ♍ | 13 ♏ | 12 ♐ | 14 ♒ | 13 ♓ | 15 ♈ |
| 17 ♓ | 16 ♈ | 16 ♉ | 15 ♊ | 14 ♋ | 15 ♍ | 14 ♎ | 15 ♐ | 14 ♑ | 16 ♓ | 15 ♈ | 17 ♊ |
| 19 ♈ | 18 ♉ | 18 ♊ | 17 ♋ | 16 ♌ | 17 ♎ | 16 ♏ | 18 ♑ | 17 ♒ | 19 ♈ | 17 ♉ | 19 ♋ |
| 22 ♉ | 20 ♊ | 20 ♋ | 19 ♌ | 18 ♍ | 19 ♏ | 18 ♐ | 20 ♒ | 19 ♓ | 21 ♉ | 19 ♊ | 21 ♌ |
| 24 ♊ | 22 ♋ | 23 ♌ | 21 ♍ | 21 ♎ | 22 ♐ | 22 ♑ | 23 ♓ | 21 ♈ | 23 ♊ | 21 ♋ | 23 ♍ |
| 26 ♋ | 24 ♌ | 25 ♍ | 23 ♎ | 23 ♏ | 24 ♑ | 24 ♒ | 25 ♈ | 23 ♉ | 25 ♋ | 23 ♌ | 25 ♎ |
| 28 ♌ | 26 ♍ | 27 ♎ | 26 ♏ | 25 ♐ | 27 ♒ | 26 ♓ | 27 ♉ | 26 ♊ | 27 ♌ | 26 ♍ | 27 ♏ |
| 30 ♍ | 29 ♎ | 29 ♏ | 28 ♐ | 28 ♑ | 29 ♓ | 29 ♈ | 29 ♊ | 28 ♋ | 29 ♍ | 28 ♎ | 30 ♐ |
|  |  |  |  | 30 ♒ |  | 31 ♉ |  | 30 ♌ |  |  | 30 ♏ |

## 1965

| JAN. | FEB. | MAR. | APR. | MAY | JUNE | JULY | AUG. | SEPT. | OCT. | NOV. | DEC. |
|---|---|---|---|---|---|---|---|---|---|---|---|
| 1 ♑ | 3 ♓ | 2 ♓ | 1 ♈ | 2 ♊ | 1 ♋ | 2 ♍ | 1 ♎ | 2 ♐ | 1 ♑ | 3 ♓ | 2 ♈ |
| 4 ♒ | 5 ♈ | 4 ♈ | 3 ♉ | 4 ♋ | 3 ♌ | 4 ♎ | 3 ♏ | 4 ♑ | 4 ♒ | 5 ♈ | 5 ♉ |
| 6 ♓ | 7 ♉ | 7 ♉ | 5 ♊ | 7 ♌ | 5 ♍ | 7 ♏ | 5 ♐ | 6 ♒ | 6 ♓ | 7 ♉ | 7 ♊ |
| 9 ♈ | 9 ♊ | 9 ♊ | 7 ♋ | 9 ♍ | 7 ♎ | 9 ♐ | 8 ♑ | 9 ♓ | 9 ♈ | 10 ♊ | 9 ♋ |
| 11 ♉ | 12 ♋ | 11 ♋ | 9 ♌ | 11 ♎ | 9 ♏ | 11 ♑ | 10 ♒ | 11 ♈ | 11 ♉ | 12 ♋ | 11 ♌ |
| 13 ♊ | 14 ♌ | 13 ♌ | 11 ♍ | 13 ♏ | 12 ♐ | 14 ♒ | 13 ♓ | 14 ♉ | 13 ♊ | 14 ♌ | 13 ♍ |
| 15 ♋ | 16 ♍ | 15 ♍ | 14 ♎ | 15 ♐ | 14 ♑ | 16 ♓ | 15 ♈ | 16 ♊ | 16 ♌ | 16 ♍ | 15 ♎ |
| 17 ♌ | 18 ♎ | 17 ♎ | 16 ♏ | 18 ♑ | 17 ♒ | 19 ♈ | 18 ♉ | 18 ♋ | 18 ♎ | 18 ♎ | 18 ♏ |
| 19 ♍ | 20 ♏ | 19 ♏ | 18 ♐ | 20 ♒ | 19 ♓ | 21 ♉ | 20 ♊ | 20 ♌ | 20 ♏ | 20 ♐ | 20 ♐ |
| 21 ♎ | 22 ♐ | 22 ♐ | 21 ♑ | 23 ♓ | 22 ♈ | 24 ♊ | 22 ♋ | 22 ♍ | 22 ♐ | 23 ♑ | 22 ♑ |
| 24 ♏ | 25 ♑ | 24 ♑ | 23 ♒ | 25 ♈ | 24 ♉ | 26 ♋ | 24 ♌ | 25 ♎ | 24 ♑ | 25 ♒ | 25 ♒ |
| 26 ♐ | 27 ♒ | 27 ♒ | 26 ♓ | 28 ♉ | 26 ♊ | 28 ♌ | 26 ♍ | 27 ♏ | 26 ♐ | 27 ♓ | 27 ♓ |
| 29 ♑ |  | 29 ♓ | 28 ♈ | 30 ♊ | 28 ♋ | 30 ♍ | 28 ♎ | 29 ♑ | 29 ♑ | 30 ♈ | 30 ♈ |
| 31 ♒ |  |  | 30 ♉ |  | 30 ♌ |  | 30 ♏ |  | 31 ♒ |  |  |

| Libra | Scorpio | Sagittarius | Capricorn | Aquarius | Pisces |
|---|---|---|---|---|---|
| ♎ | ♏ | ♐ | ♑ | ♒ | ♓ |

## 1966

| JAN. | FEB. | MAR. | APR. | MAY | JUNE | JULY | AUG. | SEPT. | OCT. | NOV. | DEC. |
|---|---|---|---|---|---|---|---|---|---|---|---|
| 1 ♉ | 2 ♋ | 1 ♋ | 2 ♍ | 1 ♎ | 2 ♐ | 1 ♑ | 3 ♓ | 1 ♈ | 1 ♉ | 2 ♋ | 2 ♌ |
| 4 ♊ | 4 ♌ | 4 ♌ | 4 ♎ | 3 ♏ | 4 ♑ | 4 ♒ | 5 ♈ | 4 ♉ | 4 ♊ | 4 ♌ | 4 ♍ |
| 6 ♋ | 6 ♍ | 6 ♍ | 6 ♏ | 6 ♐ | 7 ♒ | 6 ♓ | 8 ♉ | 6 ♊ | 6 ♋ | 7 ♍ | 6 ♎ |
| 8 ♌ | 8 ♎ | 7 ♎ | 8 ♐ | 8 ♑ | 9 ♓ | 9 ♈ | 10 ♊ | 9 ♋ | 8 ♌ | 9 ♎ | 8 ♏ |
| 10 ♍ | 10 ♏ | 10 ♏ | 10 ♑ | 10 ♒ | 11 ♈ | 11 ♉ | 12 ♋ | 11 ♌ | 10 ♍ | 11 ♏ | 10 ♐ |
| 12 ♎ | 12 ♐ | 12 ♐ | 13 ♒ | 13 ♓ | 14 ♉ | 14 ♊ | 14 ♌ | 13 ♍ | 12 ♎ | 13 ♐ | 12 ♑ |
| 14 ♏ | 14 ♑ | 14 ♑ | 15 ♓ | 15 ♈ | 16 ♊ | 16 ♋ | 16 ♍ | 15 ♎ | 14 ♏ | 15 ♑ | 15 ♒ |
| 16 ♐ | 17 ♒ | 17 ♒ | 18 ♈ | 18 ♉ | 19 ♋ | 18 ♌ | 18 ♎ | 17 ♏ | 16 ♐ | 17 ♒ | 17 ♓ |
| 19 ♑ | 20 ♓ | 19 ♓ | 20 ♉ | 20 ♊ | 21 ♌ | 20 ♍ | 20 ♏ | 19 ♐ | 19 ♑ | 20 ♓ | 20 ♈ |
| 21 ♒ | 22 ♈ | 21 ♈ | 23 ♊ | 22 ♋ | 23 ♍ | 22 ♎ | 23 ♐ | 21 ♑ | 21 ♒ | 22 ♈ | 22 ♉ |
| 24 ♓ | 25 ♉ | 24 ♉ | 25 ♋ | 24 ♌ | 25 ♎ | 24 ♏ | 25 ♑ | 24 ♒ | 23 ♓ | 25 ♉ | 25 ♊ |
| 26 ♈ | 27 ♊ | 26 ♊ | 27 ♌ | 26 ♍ | 27 ♏ | 26 ♐ | 27 ♒ | 26 ♓ | 26 ♈ | 27 ♊ | 27 ♋ |
| 29 ♉ |  | 29 ♋ | 29 ♍ | 29 ♎ | 29 ♐ | 29 ♑ | 30 ♓ | 29 ♈ | 28 ♉ | 29 ♋ | 29 ♌ |
| 31 ♊ |  | 31 ♌ |  | 31 ♏ |  | 31 ♒ |  |  | 31 ♊ |  | 31 ♍ |

## 1967

| JAN. | FEB. | MAR. | APR. | MAY | JUNE | JULY | AUG. | SEPT. | OCT. | NOV. | DEC. |
|---|---|---|---|---|---|---|---|---|---|---|---|
| 2 ♎ | 1 ♏ | 2 ♐ | 1 ♑ | 3 ♓ | 1 ♈ | 1 ♉ | 2 ♊ | 1 ♌ | 1 ♍ | 1 ♏ | 1 ♐ |
| 4 ♏ | 3 ♐ | 4 ♑ | 3 ♒ | 5 ♈ | 4 ♉ | 4 ♊ | 5 ♋ | 3 ♍ | 3 ♎ | 3 ♐ | 3 ♑ |
| 7 ♐ | 5 ♑ | 7 ♒ | 5 ♓ | 8 ♉ | 6 ♊ | 6 ♋ | 7 ♌ | 5 ♎ | 5 ♏ | 5 ♑ | 5 ♒ |
| 9 ♑ | 7 ♒ | 9 ♓ | 8 ♈ | 10 ♊ | 9 ♋ | 8 ♌ | 9 ♍ | 7 ♏ | 7 ♐ | 7 ♒ | 7 ♓ |
| 11 ♒ | 10 ♓ | 12 ♈ | 10 ♉ | 12 ♋ | 11 ♌ | 11 ♍ | 11 ♎ | 9 ♐ | 9 ♑ | 9 ♓ | 9 ♈ |
| 13 ♓ | 12 ♈ | 14 ♉ | 12 ♊ | 15 ♌ | 13 ♍ | 13 ♎ | 13 ♏ | 12 ♑ | 11 ♒ | 12 ♈ | 12 ♉ |
| 16 ♈ | 15 ♉ | 17 ♊ | 15 ♋ | 17 ♍ | 15 ♎ | 15 ♏ | 16 ♐ | 14 ♒ | 13 ♓ | 15 ♉ | 14 ♊ |
| 18 ♉ | 17 ♊ | 19 ♋ | 18 ♌ | 19 ♎ | 18 ♏ | 17 ♐ | 18 ♑ | 16 ♓ | 16 ♈ | 17 ♊ | 17 ♋ |
| 21 ♊ | 20 ♋ | 21 ♌ | 20 ♍ | 21 ♏ | 20 ♐ | 19 ♑ | 20 ♒ | 19 ♈ | 18 ♉ | 20 ♋ | 19 ♌ |
| 23 ♋ | 22 ♌ | 23 ♍ | 22 ♎ | 23 ♐ | 22 ♑ | 21 ♒ | 22 ♓ | 21 ♉ | 21 ♊ | 22 ♌ | 22 ♍ |
| 25 ♌ | 24 ♍ | 25 ♎ | 24 ♏ | 25 ♑ | 24 ♒ | 24 ♓ | 25 ♈ | 24 ♊ | 23 ♋ | 24 ♍ | 24 ♎ |
| 27 ♍ | 26 ♎ | 27 ♏ | 26 ♐ | 27 ♒ | 26 ♓ | 26 ♈ | 27 ♉ | 26 ♋ | 26 ♌ | 27 ♎ | 26 ♏ |
| 30 ♎ | 28 ♏ | 29 ♐ | 28 ♑ | 30 ♓ | 29 ♈ | 29 ♉ | 30 ♊ | 28 ♌ | 28 ♍ | 29 ♏ | 28 ♐ |
|  |  | 30 ♑ | 30 ♒ |  |  | 31 ♊ |  | 30 ♍ | 30 ♎ |  | 30 ♑ |

| *Key:* | Aries | Taurus | Gemini | Cancer | Leo | Virgo |
|---|---|---|---|---|---|---|
|  | ♈ | ♉ | ♊ | ♋ | ♌ | ♍ |

## 1968

| JAN. | FEB. | MAR. | APR. | MAY | JUNE | JULY | AUG. | SEPT. | OCT. | NOV. | DEC. |
|---|---|---|---|---|---|---|---|---|---|---|---|
| 1 ♒ | 2 ♈ | 3 ♉ | 2 ♊ | 2 ♋ | 3 ♍ | 2 ♎ | 1 ♏ | 1 ♑ | 3 ♓ | 1 ♈ | 1 ♉ |
| 3 ♓ | 5 ♉ | 5 ♊ | 4 ♋ | 4 ♌ | 5 ♎ | 4 ♏ | 3 ♐ | 3 ♒ | 5 ♈ | 4 ♉ | 3 ♊ |
| 6 ♈ | 7 ♊ | 8 ♋ | 7 ♌ | 6 ♍ | 7 ♏ | 6 ♐ | 5 ♑ | 5 ♓ | 7 ♉ | 6 ♊ | 6 ♋ |
| 8 ♉ | 10 ♋ | 10 ♌ | 9 ♍ | 9 ♎ | 9 ♐ | 8 ♑ | 7 ♒ | 8 ♈ | 10 ♊ | 9 ♋ | 8 ♌ |
| 11 ♊ | 12 ♌ | 13 ♍ | 11 ♎ | 11 ♏ | 11 ♑ | 10 ♒ | 9 ♓ | 10 ♉ | 12 ♋ | 11 ♌ | 11 ♍ |
| 13 ♋ | 14 ♍ | 15 ♎ | 13 ♏ | 13 ♐ | 13 ♒ | 13 ♓ | 11 ♈ | 12 ♊ | 15 ♌ | 14 ♍ | 13 ♎ |
| 16 ♌ | 16 ♎ | 17 ♏ | 15 ♐ | 15 ♑ | 15 ♓ | 15 ♈ | 14 ♉ | 15 ♋ | 17 ♍ | 16 ♎ | 15 ♏ |
| 18 ♍ | 18 ♏ | 19 ♐ | 17 ♑ | 17 ♒ | 17 ♈ | 17 ♉ | 16 ♊ | 17 ♌ | 19 ♎ | 18 ♏ | 17 ♐ |
| 20 ♎ | 21 ♐ | 21 ♑ | 19 ♒ | 19 ♓ | 20 ♉ | 20 ♊ | 19 ♋ | 20 ♍ | 22 ♏ | 20 ♐ | 19 ♑ |
| 22 ♏ | 23 ♑ | 23 ♒ | 22 ♓ | 21 ♈ | 23 ♊ | 22 ♋ | 21 ♌ | 22 ♎ | 24 ♐ | 22 ♑ | 21 ♒ |
| 24 ♐ | 25 ♒ | 25 ♓ | 24 ♈ | 23 ♉ | 25 ♋ | 25 ♌ | 24 ♍ | 24 ♏ | 26 ♑ | 24 ♒ | 23 ♓ |
| 26 ♑ | 27 ♓ | 28 ♈ | 27 ♉ | 25 ♊ | 28 ♌ | 27 ♍ | 26 ♎ | 26 ♐ | 28 ♒ | 26 ♓ | 26 ♈ |
| 29 ♒ | 29 ♈ | 30 ♉ | 29 ♊ | 28 ♋ | 30 ♍ | 29 ♎ | 28 ♏ | 28 ♑ | 30 ♓ | 28 ♈ | 28 ♉ |
| 31 ♓ |  |  |  | 31 ♌ |  |  | 30 ♐ | 30 ♒ |  |  | 31 ♊ |

## 1969

| JAN. | FEB. | MAR. | APR. | MAY | JUNE | JULY | AUG. | SEPT. | OCT. | NOV. | DEC. |
|---|---|---|---|---|---|---|---|---|---|---|---|
| 2 ♋ | 1 ♌ | 3 ♍ | 1 ♎ | 1 ♏ | 1 ♑ | 1 ♒ | 1 ♈ | 2 ♊ | 2 ♋ | 1 ♌ | 1 ♍ |
| 5 ♌ | 3 ♍ | 5 ♎ | 4 ♏ | 3 ♐ | 3 ♒ | 3 ♓ | 4 ♉ | 5 ♋ | 5 ♌ | 4 ♍ | 3 ♎ |
| 7 ♍ | 6 ♎ | 7 ♏ | 6 ♐ | 5 ♑ | 5 ♓ | 5 ♈ | 6 ♊ | 7 ♌ | 7 ♍ | 6 ♎ | 6 ♏ |
| 9 ♎ | 8 ♏ | 9 ♐ | 8 ♑ | 7 ♒ | 8 ♈ | 7 ♉ | 9 ♋ | 10 ♍ | 10 ♎ | 8 ♏ | 8 ♐ |
| 12 ♏ | 10 ♐ | 11 ♑ | 10 ♒ | 9 ♓ | 10 ♉ | 10 ♊ | 11 ♌ | 12 ♎ | 12 ♏ | 10 ♐ | 10 ♑ |
| 14 ♐ | 12 ♑ | 14 ♒ | 12 ♓ | 11 ♈ | 13 ♊ | 12 ♋ | 14 ♍ | 14 ♏ | 14 ♐ | 12 ♑ | 12 ♒ |
| 16 ♑ | 14 ♒ | 16 ♓ | 14 ♈ | 14 ♉ | 15 ♋ | 15 ♌ | 16 ♎ | 17 ♐ | 16 ♑ | 14 ♒ | 14 ♓ |
| 18 ♒ | 16 ♓ | 18 ♈ | 17 ♉ | 16 ♊ | 17 ♌ | 17 ♍ | 18 ♏ | 19 ♑ | 18 ♒ | 16 ♓ | 16 ♈ |
| 20 ♓ | 18 ♈ | 20 ♉ | 19 ♊ | 19 ♋ | 20 ♍ | 20 ♎ | 20 ♐ | 21 ♒ | 20 ♓ | 19 ♈ | 18 ♉ |
| 22 ♈ | 21 ♉ | 23 ♊ | 21 ♋ | 21 ♌ | 22 ♎ | 22 ♏ | 23 ♑ | 23 ♓ | 22 ♈ | 21 ♉ | 20 ♊ |
| 24 ♉ | 23 ♊ | 25 ♋ | 24 ♌ | 24 ♍ | 25 ♏ | 24 ♐ | 25 ♒ | 25 ♈ | 25 ♉ | 23 ♊ | 23 ♋ |
| 27 ♊ | 26 ♋ | 28 ♌ | 26 ♍ | 26 ♎ | 27 ♐ | 26 ♑ | 27 ♓ | 27 ♉ | 27 ♊ | 26 ♋ | 25 ♌ |
| 29 ♋ | 28 ♌ | 30 ♍ | 29 ♎ | 28 ♏ | 29 ♑ | 28 ♒ | 29 ♈ | 30 ♊ | 30 ♋ | 28 ♌ | 28 ♍ |
|  |  |  |  | 30 ♐ |  | 30 ♓ | 31 ♉ |  |  |  | 31 ♎ |

| Libra | Scorpio | Sagittarius | Capricorn | Aquarius | Pisces |
|---|---|---|---|---|---|
| ♎ | ♏ | ♐ | ♑ | ♒ | ♓ |

## 1970

| JAN. | FEB. | MAR. | APR. | MAY | JUNE | JULY | AUG. | SEPT. | OCT. | NOV. | DEC. |
|---|---|---|---|---|---|---|---|---|---|---|---|
| 2 ♏ | 1 ♐ | 2 ♑ | 3 ♓ | 2 ♈ | 3 ♊ | 2 ♋ | 1 ♌ | 2 ♎ | 2 ♏ | 1 ♐ | 2 ♒ |
| 4 ♐ | 3 ♑ | 4 ♒ | 5 ♈ | 4 ♉ | 5 ♋ | 5 ♌ | 3 ♍ | 5 ♏ | 4 ♐ | 3 ♑ | 4 ♓ |
| 6 ♑ | 5 ♒ | 6 ♓ | 7 ♉ | 6 ♊ | 7 ♌ | 7 ♍ | 6 ♎ | 7 ♐ | 7 ♑ | 5 ♒ | 7 ♈ |
| 8 ♒ | 7 ♓ | 8 ♈ | 9 ♊ | 9 ♋ | 10 ♍ | 10 ♎ | 8 ♏ | 9 ♑ | 9 ♒ | 7 ♓ | 9 ♉ |
| 10 ♓ | 9 ♈ | 10 ♉ | 11 ♋ | 11 ♌ | 12 ♎ | 12 ♏ | 11 ♐ | 11 ♒ | 11 ♓ | 9 ♈ | 11 ♊ |
| 12 ♈ | 11 ♉ | 12 ♊ | 14 ♌ | 14 ♍ | 15 ♏ | 14 ♐ | 13 ♑ | 14 ♓ | 13 ♈ | 11 ♉ | 13 ♋ |
| 15 ♉ | 13 ♊ | 15 ♋ | 16 ♍ | 16 ♎ | 17 ♐ | 17 ♑ | 15 ♒ | 16 ♈ | 15 ♉ | 14 ♊ | 15 ♌ |
| 17 ♊ | 16 ♋ | 17 ♌ | 19 ♎ | 18 ♏ | 19 ♑ | 19 ♒ | 17 ♓ | 18 ♉ | 17 ♊ | 16 ♋ | 18 ♍ |
| 19 ♋ | 18 ♌ | 20 ♍ | 21 ♏ | 21 ♐ | 21 ♒ | 21 ♓ | 19 ♈ | 20 ♊ | 19 ♋ | 18 ♌ | 20 ♎ |
| 22 ♌ | 21 ♍ | 22 ♎ | 23 ♐ | 23 ♑ | 23 ♓ | 23 ♈ | 21 ♉ | 22 ♋ | 22 ♌ | 21 ♍ | 23 ♏ |
| 24 ♍ | 23 ♎ | 25 ♏ | 26 ♑ | 25 ♒ | 25 ♈ | 25 ♉ | 23 ♊ | 24 ♌ | 24 ♍ | 23 ♎ | 25 ♐ |
| 27 ♎ | 26 ♏ | 27 ♐ | 28 ♒ | 27 ♓ | 28 ♉ | 27 ♊ | 26 ♋ | 27 ♍ | 26 ♎ | 26 ♏ | 28 ♑ |
| 29 ♏ | 28 ♐ | 29 ♑ | 30 ♓ | 29 ♈ | 30 ♊ | 29 ♋ | 28 ♌ | 30 ♎ | 29 ♏ | 28 ♐ | 30 ♒ |
|  |  | 31 ♒ |  | 31 ♉ |  |  | 31 ♍ |  |  | 30 ♑ |  |

## 1971

| JAN. | FEB. | MAR. | APR. | MAY | JUNE | JULY | AUG. | SEPT. | OCT. | NOV. | DEC. |
|---|---|---|---|---|---|---|---|---|---|---|---|
| 1 ♒ | 1 ♈ | 1 ♉ | 1 ♊ | 1 ♋ | 1 ♍ | 1 ♎ | 1 ♏ | 1 ♑ | 1 ♒ | 1 ♈ | 1 ♊ |
| 2 ♓ | 2 ♉ | 4 ♊ | 2 ♋ | 2 ♌ | 3 ♎ | 3 ♏ | 2 ♐ | 3 ♒ | 2 ♓ | 3 ♉ | 2 ♋ |
| 4 ♈ | 4 ♊ | 6 ♋ | 5 ♌ | 4 ♍ | 6 ♏ | 5 ♐ | 4 ♑ | 5 ♓ | 4 ♈ | 5 ♊ | 4 ♌ |
| 6 ♉ | 7 ♋ | 8 ♌ | 7 ♍ | 7 ♎ | 8 ♐ | 7 ♑ | 6 ♒ | 7 ♈ | 6 ♉ | 7 ♋ | 6 ♍ |
| 8 ♊ | 9 ♌ | 11 ♍ | 9 ♎ | 9 ♏ | 10 ♑ | 10 ♒ | 8 ♓ | 9 ♉ | 8 ♊ | 9 ♌ | 9 ♎ |
| 10 ♋ | 12 ♍ | 13 ♎ | 12 ♏ | 12 ♐ | 13 ♒ | 12 ♓ | 10 ♈ | 11 ♊ | 10 ♋ | 11 ♍ | 11 ♏ |
| 13 ♌ | 14 ♎ | 16 ♏ | 15 ♐ | 14 ♑ | 15 ♓ | 14 ♈ | 13 ♉ | 13 ♋ | 13 ♌ | 14 ♎ | 14 ♐ |
| 15 ♍ | 17 ♏ | 18 ♐ | 17 ♑ | 16 ♒ | 17 ♈ | 16 ♉ | 15 ♊ | 15 ♌ | 15 ♍ | 16 ♏ | 16 ♑ |
| 18 ♎ | 19 ♐ | 21 ♑ | 19 ♒ | 19 ♓ | 19 ♉ | 18 ♊ | 17 ♋ | 18 ♍ | 17 ♎ | 19 ♐ | 19 ♒ |
| 20 ♏ | 21 ♑ | 23 ♒ | 21 ♓ | 21 ♈ | 21 ♊ | 21 ♋ | 19 ♌ | 20 ♎ | 19 ♏ | 21 ♑ | 21 ♓ |
| 23 ♐ | 23 ♒ | 25 ♓ | 23 ♈ | 23 ♉ | 23 ♋ | 23 ♌ | 22 ♍ | 23 ♏ | 21 ♐ | 24 ♒ | 23 ♈ |
| 25 ♑ | 26 ♓ | 27 ♈ | 25 ♉ | 25 ♊ | 26 ♌ | 25 ♍ | 24 ♎ | 25 ♐ | 23 ♑ | 26 ♓ | 25 ♉ |
| 27 ♒ | 27 ♈ | 29 ♉ | 27 ♊ | 27 ♋ | 28 ♍ | 28 ♎ | 27 ♏ | 28 ♑ | 25 ♒ | 28 ♈ | 27 ♊ |
| 29 ♓ |  | 31 ♊ | 30 ♋ | 29 ♌ |  | 30 ♏ | 29 ♐ | 30 ♒ | 28 ♓ | 30 ♉ | 30 ♋ |
| 31 ♈ |  |  |  |  |  |  |  |  | 30 ♈ |  |  |

*Key:*  Aries  Taurus  Gemini  Cancer  Leo  Virgo

♈      ♉      ♊      ♋      ♌     ♍

## 1972

| JAN. | FEB. | MAR. | APR. | MAY | JUNE | JULY | AUG. | SEPT. | OCT. | NOV. | DEC. |
|---|---|---|---|---|---|---|---|---|---|---|---|
| 1 ♋ | 1 ♌ | 1 ♍ | 1 ♏ | 1 ♐ | 1 ♑ | 1 ♒ | 1 ♈ | 1 ♊ | 1 ♋ | 1 ♍ | 1 ♎ |
| 3 ♌ | 2 ♍ | 2 ♎ | 4 ♐ | 3 ♑ | 2 ♒ | 2 ♓ | 2 ♉ | 3 ♋ | 2 ♌ | 3 ♎ | 3 ♏ |
| 5 ♍ | 4 ♎ | 5 ♏ | 6 ♑ | 6 ♒ | 4 ♓ | 4 ♈ | 4 ♊ | 5 ♌ | 4 ♍ | 5 ♏ | 5 ♐ |
| 8 ♎ | 6 ♏ | 7 ♐ | 8 ♒ | 8 ♓ | 7 ♈ | 6 ♉ | 6 ♋ | 7 ♍ | 7 ♎ | 8 ♐ | 8 ♑ |
| 10 ♏ | 9 ♐ | 10 ♑ | 11 ♓ | 10 ♈ | 9 ♉ | 8 ♊ | 8 ♌ | 9 ♎ | 9 ♏ | 10 ♑ | 10 ♒ |
| 13 ♐ | 11 ♑ | 12 ♒ | 13 ♈ | 12 ♉ | 11 ♊ | 10 ♋ | 11 ♍ | 12 ♏ | 12 ♐ | 13 ♒ | 13 ♓ |
| 15 ♑ | 14 ♒ | 14 ♓ | 15 ♉ | 14 ♊ | 13 ♋ | 12 ♌ | 13 ♎ | 14 ♐ | 14 ♑ | 15 ♓ | 15 ♈ |
| 17 ♒ | 16 ♓ | 16 ♈ | 17 ♊ | 16 ♋ | 15 ♌ | 14 ♍ | 16 ♏ | 17 ♑ | 17 ♒ | 18 ♈ | 17 ♉ |
| 19 ♓ | 18 ♈ | 18 ♉ | 19 ♋ | 18 ♌ | 17 ♍ | 17 ♎ | 18 ♐ | 19 ♒ | 19 ♓ | 20 ♉ | 19 ♊ |
| 22 ♈ | 20 ♉ | 20 ♊ | 21 ♌ | 22 ♍ | 19 ♎ | 19 ♏ | 21 ♑ | 21 ♓ | 21 ♈ | 22 ♊ | 21 ♋ |
| 24 ♉ | 22 ♊ | 22 ♋ | 23 ♍ | 24 ♎ | 22 ♏ | 22 ♐ | 23 ♒ | 24 ♈ | 23 ♉ | 24 ♋ | 23 ♌ |
| 26 ♊ | 24 ♋ | 25 ♌ | 26 ♎ | 26 ♏ | 24 ♐ | 24 ♑ | 25 ♓ | 26 ♉ | 25 ♊ | 26 ♌ | 25 ♍ |
| 28 ♋ | 27 ♌ | 27 ♍ | 28 ♏ | 28 ♐ | 27 ♑ | 27 ♒ | 27 ♈ | 28 ♊ | 26 ♋ | 28 ♍ | 27 ♎ |
| 30 ♌ | 29 ♍ | 30 ♎ | | 31 ♑ | 29 ♒ | 29 ♓ | 29 ♉ | 30 ♋ | 28 ♌ | 30 ♎ | 30 ♏ |
| | | | | | | 31 ♈ | 31 ♊ | | | | |

## 1973

| JAN. | FEB. | MAR. | APR. | MAY | JUNE | JULY | AUG. | SEPT. | OCT. | NOV. | DEC. |
|---|---|---|---|---|---|---|---|---|---|---|---|
| 1 ♐ | 1 ♑ | 1 ♑ | 1 ♓ | 1 ♈ | 1 ♊ | 1 ♋ | 1 ♍ | 1 ♎ | 1 ♐ | 1 ♑ | 1 ♒ |
| 4 ♑ | 3 ♒ | 2 ♒ | 3 ♈ | 3 ♉ | 3 ♋ | 3 ♌ | 3 ♎ | 2 ♏ | 4 ♑ | 3 ♒ | 3 ♓ |
| 6 ♒ | 5 ♓ | 4 ♓ | 5 ♉ | 5 ♊ | 5 ♌ | 5 ♍ | 5 ♏ | 4 ♐ | 7 ♒ | 5 ♓ | 5 ♈ |
| 9 ♓ | 7 ♈ | 7 ♈ | 7 ♊ | 7 ♋ | 7 ♍ | 7 ♎ | 8 ♐ | 7 ♑ | 9 ♓ | 8 ♈ | 7 ♉ |
| 11 ♈ | 10 ♉ | 9 ♉ | 9 ♋ | 9 ♌ | 9 ♎ | 9 ♏ | 10 ♑ | 9 ♒ | 11 ♈ | 10 ♉ | 9 ♊ |
| 13 ♉ | 12 ♊ | 11 ♊ | 11 ♌ | 11 ♍ | 12 ♏ | 12 ♐ | 13 ♒ | 11 ♓ | 13 ♉ | 12 ♊ | 11 ♋ |
| 15 ♊ | 14 ♋ | 13 ♋ | 14 ♍ | 13 ♎ | 14 ♐ | 14 ♑ | 15 ♓ | 14 ♈ | 16 ♊ | 14 ♋ | 13 ♌ |
| 17 ♋ | 16 ♌ | 15 ♌ | 16 ♎ | 16 ♏ | 17 ♑ | 17 ♒ | 18 ♈ | 16 ♉ | 18 ♋ | 16 ♌ | 15 ♍ |
| 19 ♌ | 18 ♍ | 17 ♍ | 18 ♏ | 18 ♐ | 19 ♒ | 19 ♓ | 20 ♉ | 18 ♊ | 20 ♌ | 18 ♍ | 17 ♎ |
| 22 ♍ | 20 ♎ | 20 ♎ | 21 ♐ | 21 ♑ | 22 ♓ | 22 ♈ | 22 ♊ | 20 ♋ | 22 ♍ | 20 ♎ | 20 ♏ |
| 24 ♎ | 23 ♏ | 22 ♏ | 23 ♑ | 23 ♒ | 24 ♈ | 24 ♉ | 24 ♋ | 23 ♌ | 24 ♎ | 22 ♏ | 22 ♐ |
| 26 ♏ | 25 ♐ | 24 ♐ | 26 ♒ | 26 ♓ | 26 ♉ | 26 ♊ | 26 ♌ | 25 ♍ | 26 ♏ | 25 ♐ | 25 ♑ |
| 29 ♐ | 28 ♑ | 27 ♑ | 28 ♓ | 28 ♈ | 28 ♊ | 28 ♋ | 28 ♍ | 27 ♎ | 29 ♐ | 28 ♑ | 27 ♒ |
| | | 29 ♒ | 30 ♈ | 30 ♉ | 30 ♋ | 30 ♌ | 30 ♎ | 29 ♏ | 31 ♑ | 30 ♒ | 30 ♓ |

| Libra | Scorpio | Sagittarius | Capricorn | Aquarius | Pisces |
|---|---|---|---|---|---|
| ♎ | ♏ | ♐ | ♑ | ♒ | ♓ |

## 1974

| JAN. | FEB. | MAR. | APR. | MAY | JUNE | JULY | AUG. | SEPT. | OCT. | NOV. | DEC. |
|---|---|---|---|---|---|---|---|---|---|---|---|
| 1 ♈ | 1 ♉ | 1 ♊ | 1 ♋ | 1 ♍ | 1 ♎ | 1 ♏ | 1 ♑ | 1 ♒ | 1 ♈ | 1 ♉ | 1 ♊ |
| 4 ♉ | 2 ♊ | 4 ♋ | 2 ♌ | 3 ♎ | 2 ♏ | 2 ♐ | 3 ♒ | 2 ♓ | 4 ♉ | 2 ♊ | 2 ♋ |
| 6 ♊ | 4 ♋ | 6 ♌ | 4 ♍ | 6 ♏ | 4 ♐ | 4 ♑ | 5 ♓ | 4 ♈ | 6 ♊ | 4 ♋ | 4 ♌ |
| 8 ♋ | 6 ♌ | 8 ♍ | 6 ♎ | 8 ♐ | 7 ♑ | 7 ♒ | 8 ♈ | 6 ♉ | 8 ♋ | 7 ♌ | 6 ♍ |
| 10 ♌ | 8 ♍ | 10 ♎ | 8 ♏ | 10 ♑ | 9 ♒ | 9 ♓ | 10 ♉ | 9 ♊ | 10 ♌ | 9 ♍ | 8 ♎ |
| 12 ♍ | 10 ♎ | 12 ♏ | 11 ♐ | 13 ♒ | 12 ♓ | 12 ♈ | 13 ♊ | 11 ♋ | 12 ♍ | 11 ♎ | 10 ♏ |
| 14 ♎ | 13 ♏ | 14 ♐ | 13 ♑ | 15 ♓ | 14 ♈ | 14 ♉ | 15 ♋ | 13 ♌ | 15 ♎ | 13 ♏ | 13 ♐ |
| 16 ♏ | 15 ♐ | 17 ♑ | 16 ♒ | 18 ♈ | 17 ♉ | 16 ♊ | 17 ♌ | 15 ♍ | 17 ♏ | 15 ♐ | 15 ♑ |
| 19 ♐ | 17 ♑ | 19 ♒ | 18 ♓ | 20 ♉ | 19 ♊ | 18 ♋ | 19 ♍ | 17 ♎ | 19 ♐ | 18 ♑ | 17 ♒ |
| 21 ♑ | 20 ♒ | 22 ♓ | 22 ♈ | 22 ♊ | 21 ♋ | 20 ♌ | 21 ♎ | 19 ♏ | 21 ♑ | 20 ♒ | 20 ♓ |
| 24 ♒ | 22 ♓ | 24 ♈ | 24 ♉ | 24 ♋ | 23 ♌ | 22 ♍ | 23 ♏ | 21 ♐ | 24 ♒ | 23 ♓ | 22 ♈ |
| 26 ♓ | 25 ♈ | 26 ♉ | 25 ♊ | 26 ♌ | 25 ♍ | 24 ♎ | 25 ♐ | 24 ♑ | 26 ♓ | 25 ♈ | 25 ♉ |
| 29 ♈ | 27 ♉ | 29 ♊ | 27 ♋ | 29 ♍ | 27 ♎ | 26 ♏ | 28 ♑ | 26 ♒ | 29 ♈ | 27 ♉ | 27 ♊ |
| 31 ♉ |  | 31 ♋ | 29 ♍ | 31 ♎ | 29 ♏ | 29 ♐ | 30 ♒ | 29 ♓ | 31 ♉ | 30 ♊ | 29 ♋ |
|  |  |  |  |  |  | 31 ♑ |  |  |  |  | 31 ♌ |

## 1975

| JAN. | FEB. | MAR. | APR. | MAY | JUNE | JULY | AUG. | SEPT. | OCT. | NOV. | DEC. |
|---|---|---|---|---|---|---|---|---|---|---|---|
| 1 ♌ | 1 ♎ | 1 ♎ | 1 ♐ | 1 ♑ | 1 ♒ | 1 ♈ | 1 ♉ | 1 ♋ | 1 ♌ | 1 ♎ | 1 ♏ |
| 2 ♍ | 3 ♏ | 2 ♏ | 3 ♑ | 3 ♒ | 2 ♓ | 4 ♉ | 3 ♊ | 3 ♌ | 3 ♍ | 3 ♏ | 3 ♐ |
| 4 ♎ | 5 ♐ | 4 ♐ | 5 ♒ | 5 ♓ | 4 ♈ | 6 ♊ | 5 ♋ | 5 ♍ | 5 ♎ | 5 ♐ | 5 ♑ |
| 6 ♏ | 7 ♑ | 7 ♑ | 8 ♓ | 8 ♈ | 7 ♉ | 9 ♋ | 7 ♌ | 7 ♎ | 7 ♏ | 8 ♑ | 7 ♒ |
| 9 ♐ | 10 ♒ | 9 ♒ | 10 ♈ | 10 ♉ | 9 ♊ | 11 ♌ | 9 ♍ | 9 ♏ | 9 ♐ | 10 ♒ | 10 ♓ |
| 11 ♑ | 12 ♓ | 12 ♓ | 13 ♉ | 13 ♊ | 11 ♋ | 13 ♍ | 11 ♎ | 12 ♐ | 11 ♑ | 12 ♓ | 13 ♈ |
| 14 ♒ | 15 ♈ | 14 ♈ | 15 ♊ | 15 ♋ | 13 ♌ | 15 ♎ | 13 ♏ | 14 ♑ | 14 ♒ | 15 ♈ | 15 ♉ |
| 16 ♓ | 17 ♉ | 17 ♉ | 18 ♋ | 17 ♌ | 15 ♍ | 17 ♏ | 15 ♐ | 16 ♒ | 16 ♓ | 17 ♉ | 17 ♊ |
| 19 ♈ | 19 ♊ | 19 ♊ | 20 ♌ | 19 ♍ | 17 ♎ | 19 ♐ | 18 ♑ | 19 ♓ | 19 ♈ | 20 ♊ | 20 ♋ |
| 21 ♉ | 22 ♋ | 21 ♋ | 22 ♍ | 21 ♎ | 20 ♏ | 21 ♑ | 20 ♒ | 21 ♈ | 21 ♉ | 22 ♋ | 22 ♌ |
| 23 ♊ | 24 ♌ | 24 ♌ | 24 ♎ | 23 ♏ | 22 ♐ | 23 ♒ | 23 ♓ | 23 ♉ | 23 ♊ | 24 ♌ | 24 ♍ |
| 26 ♋ | 26 ♍ | 26 ♍ | 25 ♏ | 25 ♐ | 24 ♑ | 26 ♓ | 25 ♈ | 26 ♊ | 26 ♋ | 27 ♍ | 26 ♎ |
| 28 ♌ | 28 ♎ | 28 ♎ | 28 ♐ | 28 ♑ | 26 ♒ | 29 ♈ | 28 ♉ | 29 ♋ | 28 ♌ | 29 ♎ | 28 ♏ |
| 30 ♍ |  | 30 ♏ | 30 ♑ | 30 ♒ | 29 ♓ |  | 30 ♊ |  | 30 ♍ |  | 30 ♐ |

*Key:*  Aries   Taurus   Gemini   Cancer   Leo   Virgo

      ♈     ♉     ♊     ♋     ♌     ♍

## 1976

| JAN. | FEB. | MAR. | APR. | MAY | JUNE | JULY | AUG. | SEPT. | OCT. | NOV. | DEC. |
|---|---|---|---|---|---|---|---|---|---|---|---|
| 1 ♑ | 2 ♓ | 1 ♓ | 2 ♉ | 2 ♊ | 3 ♌ | 2 ♍ | 1 ♎ | 1 ♐ | 3 ♒ | 1 ♓ | 1 ♈ |
| 4 ♒ | 5 ♈ | 3 ♈ | 4 ♊ | 4 ♋ | 5 ♍ | 4 ♎ | 3 ♏ | 3 ♑ | 5 ♓ | 4 ♈ | 3 ♉ |
| 6 ♓ | 7 ♉ | 6 ♉ | 7 ♋ | 6 ♌ | 7 ♎ | 6 ♏ | 5 ♐ | 5 ♒ | 7 ♈ | 6 ♉ | 6 ♊ |
| 8 ♈ | 10 ♊ | 8 ♊ | 9 ♌ | 9 ♍ | 9 ♏ | 9 ♐ | 7 ♑ | 8 ♓ | 10 ♉ | 9 ♊ | 8 ♋ |
| 11 ♉ | 12 ♋ | 11 ♋ | 11 ♍ | 11 ♎ | 11 ♐ | 11 ♑ | 9 ♒ | 10 ♈ | 13 ♊ | 11 ♋ | 11 ♌ |
| 13 ♊ | 14 ♌ | 13 ♌ | 13 ♎ | 13 ♏ | 13 ♑ | 13 ♒ | 11 ♓ | 13 ♉ | 15 ♋ | 14 ♌ | 13 ♍ |
| 16 ♋ | 16 ♍ | 15 ♍ | 15 ♏ | 15 ♐ | 15 ♒ | 15 ♓ | 14 ♈ | 15 ♊ | 17 ♌ | 16 ♍ | 15 ♎ |
| 18 ♌ | 18 ♎ | 17 ♎ | 17 ♐ | 17 ♑ | 18 ♓ | 17 ♈ | 16 ♉ | 18 ♋ | 19 ♍ | 18 ♎ | 18 ♏ |
| 20 ♍ | 21 ♏ | 19 ♏ | 19 ♑ | 19 ♒ | 20 ♈ | 20 ♉ | 18 ♊ | 20 ♌ | 22 ♎ | 20 ♏ | 20 ♐ |
| 22 ♎ | 23 ♐ | 21 ♐ | 22 ♒ | 21 ♓ | 23 ♉ | 23 ♊ | 21 ♋ | 22 ♍ | 24 ♏ | 22 ♐ | 22 ♑ |
| 24 ♏ | 25 ♑ | 23 ♑ | 24 ♓ | 24 ♈ | 25 ♊ | 25 ♋ | 24 ♌ | 24 ♎ | 26 ♐ | 24 ♑ | 24 ♒ |
| 26 ♐ | 27 ♒ | 25 ♒ | 27 ♈ | 26 ♉ | 28 ♋ | 27 ♌ | 26 ♍ | 26 ♏ | 28 ♑ | 26 ♒ | 26 ♓ |
| 29 ♑ | | 28 ♓ | 29 ♉ | 29 ♊ | 30 ♌ | 29 ♍ | 28 ♎ | 28 ♐ | 30 ♒ | 29 ♓ | 28 ♈ |
| 31 ♒ | | 30 ♈ | | 31 ♋ | | | 30 ♏ | 30 ♑ | | | 31 ♉ |

## 1977

| JAN. | FEB. | MAR. | APR. | MAY | JUNE | JULY | AUG. | SEPT. | OCT. | NOV. | DEC. |
|---|---|---|---|---|---|---|---|---|---|---|---|
| 2 ♊ | 1 ♋ | 1 ♋ | 2 ♍ | 1 ♎ | 2 ♐ | 1 ♑ | 2 ♓ | 3 ♉ | 2 ♊ | 1 ♋ | 1 ♌ |
| 5 ♋ | 4 ♌ | 3 ♌ | 4 ♎ | 3 ♏ | 4 ♑ | 3 ♒ | 4 ♈ | 5 ♊ | 5 ♋ | 4 ♌ | 3 ♍ |
| 7 ♌ | 6 ♍ | 5 ♍ | 6 ♏ | 5 ♐ | 6 ♒ | 5 ♓ | 6 ♉ | 8 ♋ | 8 ♌ | 6 ♍ | 6 ♎ |
| 9 ♍ | 8 ♎ | 7 ♎ | 8 ♐ | 7 ♑ | 8 ♓ | 7 ♈ | 9 ♊ | 10 ♌ | 10 ♍ | 8 ♎ | 8 ♏ |
| 12 ♎ | 10 ♏ | 9 ♏ | 10 ♑ | 9 ♒ | 10 ♈ | 10 ♉ | 11 ♋ | 12 ♍ | 12 ♎ | 11 ♏ | 10 ♐ |
| 14 ♏ | 12 ♐ | 11 ♐ | 12 ♒ | 11 ♓ | 13 ♉ | 12 ♊ | 14 ♌ | 15 ♎ | 14 ♏ | 13 ♐ | 12 ♑ |
| 16 ♐ | 14 ♑ | 14 ♑ | 14 ♓ | 14 ♈ | 15 ♊ | 15 ♋ | 16 ♍ | 17 ♏ | 16 ♐ | 15 ♑ | 14 ♒ |
| 18 ♑ | 16 ♒ | 16 ♒ | 17 ♈ | 16 ♉ | 18 ♋ | 17 ♌ | 18 ♎ | 19 ♐ | 18 ♑ | 17 ♒ | 16 ♓ |
| 20 ♒ | 19 ♓ | 18 ♓ | 19 ♉ | 19 ♊ | 20 ♌ | 20 ♍ | 20 ♏ | 21 ♑ | 20 ♒ | 19 ♓ | 18 ♈ |
| 22 ♓ | 21 ♈ | 20 ♈ | 22 ♊ | 21 ♋ | 23 ♍ | 22 ♎ | 23 ♐ | 23 ♒ | 23 ♓ | 21 ♈ | 21 ♉ |
| 25 ♈ | 23 ♉ | 23 ♉ | 24 ♋ | 24 ♌ | 25 ♎ | 24 ♏ | 25 ♑ | 25 ♓ | 25 ♈ | 23 ♉ | 23 ♊ |
| 27 ♉ | 26 ♊ | 25 ♊ | 27 ♌ | 26 ♍ | 27 ♏ | 26 ♐ | 27 ♒ | 28 ♈ | 27 ♉ | 26 ♊ | 26 ♋ |
| 30 ♊ | | 28 ♋ | 29 ♍ | 29 ♎ | 29 ♐ | 28 ♑ | 29 ♓ | 30 ♉ | 30 ♊ | 28 ♋ | 28 ♌ |
| | | 30 ♌ | | 31 ♏ | | 30 ♒ | 31 ♈ | | | | 31 ♍ |

| Libra | Scorpio | Sagittarius | Capricorn | Aquarius | Pisces |
|---|---|---|---|---|---|
| ♎ | ♏ | ♐ | ♑ | ♒ | ♓ |

## 1978

| JAN. | FEB. | MAR. | APR. | MAY | JUNE | JULY | AUG. | SEPT. | OCT. | NOV. | DEC. |
|---|---|---|---|---|---|---|---|---|---|---|---|
| 2 ♎ | 1 ♏ | 2 ♐ | 3 ♒ | 2 ♓ | 3 ♉ | 2 ♊ | 1 ⊕ | 2 ♍ | 2 ♎ | 1 ♏ | 2 ♑ |
| 4 ♏ | 3 ♐ | 4 ♑ | 5 ♓ | 4 ♈ | 5 ♊ | 5 ⊕ | 4 ♌ | 5 ♎ | 4 ♏ | 3 ♐ | 4 ♒ |
| 6 ♐ | 5 ♑ | 6 ♒ | 7 ♈ | 6 ♉ | 8 ⊕ | 7 ♌ | 6 ♍ | 7 ♏ | 7 ♐ | 5 ♑ | 6 ♓ |
| 8 ♑ | 7 ♒ | 8 ♓ | 9 ♉ | 8 ♊ | 10 ♌ | 10 ♍ | 9 ♎ | 9 ♐ | 9 ♑ | 7 ♒ | 9 ♈ |
| 10 ♒ | 9 ♓ | 10 ♈ | 11 ♊ | 11 ⊕ | 13 ♍ | 12 ♎ | 11 ♏ | 12 ♑ | 11 ♒ | 9 ♓ | 11 ♉ |
| 12 ♓ | 11 ♈ | 13 ♉ | 14 ⊕ | 14 ♌ | 17 ♎ | 15 ♏ | 13 ♐ | 14 ♒ | 13 ♓ | 11 ♈ | 13 ♊ |
| 15 ♈ | 13 ♉ | 15 ♊ | 16 ♌ | 16 ♍ | 19 ♏ | 17 ♐ | 15 ♑ | 16 ♓ | 15 ♈ | 14 ♉ | 16 ⊕ |
| 17 ♉ | 16 ♊ | 18 ⊕ | 19 ♍ | 19 ♎ | 21 ♐ | 19 ♑ | 17 ♒ | 18 ♈ | 17 ♉ | 16 ♊ | 18 ♌ |
| 19 ♊ | 18 ⊕ | 20 ♌ | 21 ♎ | 21 ♏ | 23 ♑ | 21 ♒ | 19 ♓ | 20 ♉ | 20 ♊ | 18 ⊕ | 21 ♍ |
| 22 ⊕ | 21 ♌ | 23 ♍ | 23 ♏ | 23 ♐ | 25 ♒ | 23 ♓ | 21 ♈ | 22 ♊ | 22 ⊕ | 21 ♌ | 23 ♎ |
| 25 ♌ | 23 ♍ | 25 ♎ | 26 ♐ | 25 ♑ | 28 ♓ | 25 ♈ | 24 ♉ | 25 ⊕ | 25 ♌ | 23 ♍ | 26 ♏ |
| 27 ♍ | 26 ♎ | 27 ♏ | 28 ♑ | 27 ♒ | 30 ♈ | 27 ♉ | 26 ♊ | 27 ♌ | 27 ♍ | 26 ♎ | 28 ♐ |
| 29 ♎ | 28 ♏ | 29 ♐ | 30 ♒ | 29 ♓ |  | 30 ♊ | 28 ⊕ | 30 ♍ | 29 ♎ | 28 ♏ | 30 ♑ |
|  |  | 31 ♑ |  | 31 ♈ |  |  | 31 ♌ |  |  | 30 ♐ |  |

## 1979

| JAN. | FEB. | MAR. | APR. | MAY | JUNE | JULY | AUG. | SEPT. | OCT. | NOV. | DEC. |
|---|---|---|---|---|---|---|---|---|---|---|---|
| 1 ♒ | 1 ♈ | 1 ♈ | 1 ♊ | 1 ⊕ | 2 ♍ | 2 ♎ | 1 ♏ | 2 ♑ | 1 ♒ | 2 ♈ | 2 ♉ |
| 3 ♓ | 3 ♉ | 3 ♉ | 4 ⊕ | 4 ♌ | 5 ♎ | 5 ♏ | 3 ♐ | 4 ♒ | 4 ♓ | 4 ♉ | 3 ♊ |
| 5 ♈ | 6 ♊ | 5 ♊ | 6 ♌ | 6 ♍ | 7 ♏ | 7 ♐ | 5 ♑ | 6 ♓ | 6 ♈ | 6 ♊ | 6 ⊕ |
| 7 ♉ | 8 ⊕ | 7 ⊕ | 9 ♍ | 9 ♎ | 9 ♐ | 9 ♑ | 8 ♒ | 8 ♈ | 8 ♉ | 8 ⊕ | 8 ♌ |
| 9 ♊ | 11 ♌ | 10 ♌ | 11 ♎ | 11 ♏ | 11 ♑ | 11 ♒ | 10 ♓ | 10 ♉ | 10 ♊ | 11 ♌ | 10 ♍ |
| 12 ⊕ | 13 ♍ | 12 ♍ | 14 ♏ | 13 ♐ | 14 ♒ | 13 ♓ | 12 ♈ | 12 ♊ | 12 ⊕ | 13 ♍ | 13 ♎ |
| 14 ♌ | 16 ♎ | 15 ♎ | 16 ♐ | 15 ♑ | 16 ♓ | 15 ♈ | 14 ♉ | 15 ⊕ | 14 ♌ | 16 ♎ | 15 ♏ |
| 17 ♍ | 18 ♏ | 18 ♏ | 18 ♑ | 18 ♒ | 18 ♈ | 17 ♉ | 16 ♊ | 17 ♌ | 17 ♍ | 18 ♏ | 18 ♐ |
| 19 ♎ | 20 ♐ | 20 ♐ | 20 ♒ | 20 ♓ | 20 ♉ | 20 ♊ | 18 ⊕ | 20 ♍ | 19 ♎ | 20 ♐ | 20 ♑ |
| 22 ♏ | 23 ♑ | 22 ♑ | 22 ♓ | 22 ♈ | 22 ♊ | 22 ⊕ | 20 ♌ | 22 ♎ | 22 ♏ | 23 ♑ | 22 ♒ |
| 24 ♐ | 25 ♒ | 24 ♒ | 25 ♈ | 24 ♉ | 25 ⊕ | 25 ♌ | 23 ♍ | 25 ♏ | 24 ♐ | 25 ♒ | 24 ♓ |
| 26 ♑ | 27 ♓ | 26 ♓ | 27 ♉ | 26 ♊ | 27 ♌ | 27 ♍ | 26 ♎ | 27 ♐ | 27 ♑ | 27 ♓ | 26 ♈ |
| 28 ♒ |  | 28 ♈ | 29 ♊ | 28 ⊕ | 30 ♍ | 30 ♎ | 28 ♏ | 29 ♑ | 29 ♒ | 29 ♈ | 29 ♉ |
| 30 ♓ |  | 30 ♉ |  | 31 ♌ |  |  | 31 ♐ |  | 31 ♓ |  | 31 ♊ |

*Key:*   Aries   Taurus   Gemini   Cancer   Leo   Virgo
           ♈        ♉         ♊         ⊕        ♌      ♍

## 1980

| JAN. | FEB. | MAR. | APR. | MAY | JUNE | JULY | AUG. | SEPT. | OCT. | NOV. | DEC. |
|---|---|---|---|---|---|---|---|---|---|---|---|
| 2 ♋ | 1 ♌ | 1 ♍ | 3 ♏ | 2 ♐ | 1 ♑ | 1 ♒ | 1 ♈ | 2 ♊ | 1 ♋ | 2 ♍ | 2 ♎ |
| 4 ♌ | 3 ♍ | 4 ♎ | 5 ♐ | 5 ♑ | 3 ♒ | 3 ♓ | 3 ♉ | 4 ♋ | 3 ♌ | 5 ♎ | 4 ♏ |
| 7 ♍ | 6 ♎ | 6 ♏ | 8 ♑ | 7 ♒ | 6 ♓ | 5 ♈ | 5 ♊ | 6 ♌ | 6 ♍ | 7 ♏ | 7 ♐ |
| 9 ♎ | 8 ♏ | 9 ♐ | 10 ♒ | 9 ♓ | 8 ♈ | 7 ♉ | 8 ♋ | 9 ♍ | 8 ♎ | 10 ♐ | 9 ♑ |
| 12 ♏ | 11 ♐ | 11 ♑ | 12 ♓ | 11 ♈ | 10 ♉ | 9 ♊ | 10 ♌ | 11 ♎ | 11 ♏ | 12 ♑ | 12 ♒ |
| 14 ♐ | 13 ♑ | 13 ♒ | 14 ♈ | 13 ♉ | 12 ♊ | 11 ♋ | 12 ♍ | 14 ♏ | 13 ♐ | 14 ♒ | 14 ♓ |
| 16 ♑ | 15 ♒ | 16 ♓ | 16 ♉ | 15 ♊ | 14 ♋ | 14 ♌ | 14 ♎ | 16 ♐ | 16 ♑ | 17 ♓ | 16 ♈ |
| 19 ♒ | 17 ♓ | 18 ♈ | 18 ♊ | 18 ♋ | 16 ♌ | 16 ♍ | 17 ♏ | 18 ♑ | 18 ♒ | 19 ♈ | 18 ♉ |
| 21 ♓ | 19 ♈ | 20 ♉ | 20 ♋ | 20 ♌ | 19 ♍ | 18 ♎ | 20 ♐ | 21 ♒ | 20 ♓ | 21 ♉ | 20 ♊ |
| 23 ♈ | 21 ♉ | 22 ♊ | 22 ♌ | 22 ♍ | 21 ♎ | 21 ♏ | 22 ♑ | 23 ♓ | 22 ♈ | 23 ♊ | 22 ♋ |
| 25 ♉ | 23 ♊ | 24 ♋ | 25 ♍ | 25 ♎ | 24 ♏ | 23 ♐ | 24 ♒ | 25 ♈ | 24 ♉ | 25 ♋ | 24 ♌ |
| 27 ♊ | 26 ♋ | 26 ♌ | 27 ♎ | 27 ♏ | 26 ♐ | 26 ♑ | 26 ♓ | 27 ♉ | 26 ♊ | 27 ♌ | 27 ♍ |
| 29 ♋ | 28 ♌ | 29 ♍ | 30 ♏ | 30 ♐ | 28 ♑ | 28 ♒ | 28 ♈ | 29 ♊ | 28 ♋ | 29 ♍ | 29 ♎ |
|  |  | 31 ♎ |  |  |  | 30 ♓ | 30 ♉ |  | 31 ♌ |  |  |

## 1981

| JAN. | FEB. | MAR. | APR. | MAY | JUNE | JULY | AUG. | SEPT. | OCT. | NOV. | DEC. |
|---|---|---|---|---|---|---|---|---|---|---|---|
| 1 ♏ | 2 ♑ | 1 ♑ | 2 ♓ | 1 ♈ | 2 ♊ | 2 ♋ | 2 ♍ | 1 ♎ | 1 ♏ | 2 ♑ | 2 ♒ |
| 3 ♐ | 4 ♒ | 3 ♒ | 4 ♈ | 4 ♉ | 4 ♋ | 4 ♌ | 5 ♎ | 3 ♏ | 3 ♐ | 5 ♒ | 4 ♓ |
| 6 ♑ | 6 ♓ | 5 ♓ | 6 ♉ | 6 ♊ | 6 ♌ | 6 ♍ | 7 ♏ | 6 ♐ | 6 ♑ | 7 ♓ | 6 ♈ |
| 8 ♒ | 9 ♈ | 7 ♈ | 8 ♊ | 8 ♋ | 9 ♍ | 8 ♎ | 10 ♐ | 8 ♑ | 8 ♒ | 9 ♈ | 9 ♉ |
| 10 ♓ | 11 ♉ | 9 ♉ | 10 ♋ | 10 ♌ | 11 ♎ | 11 ♏ | 12 ♑ | 11 ♒ | 11 ♓ | 11 ♉ | 11 ♊ |
| 12 ♈ | 13 ♊ | 11 ♊ | 13 ♌ | 12 ♍ | 13 ♏ | 13 ♐ | 15 ♒ | 13 ♓ | 13 ♈ | 13 ♊ | 13 ♋ |
| 14 ♉ | 15 ♋ | 14 ♋ | 15 ♍ | 15 ♎ | 16 ♐ | 16 ♑ | 17 ♓ | 15 ♈ | 15 ♉ | 15 ♋ | 15 ♌ |
| 17 ♊ | 17 ♌ | 16 ♌ | 17 ♎ | 17 ♏ | 18 ♑ | 18 ♒ | 19 ♈ | 17 ♉ | 17 ♊ | 17 ♌ | 17 ♍ |
| 19 ♋ | 19 ♍ | 18 ♍ | 20 ♏ | 20 ♐ | 21 ♒ | 20 ♓ | 21 ♉ | 19 ♊ | 19 ♋ | 19 ♍ | 19 ♎ |
| 21 ♌ | 22 ♎ | 21 ♎ | 22 ♐ | 22 ♑ | 23 ♓ | 23 ♈ | 23 ♊ | 21 ♋ | 21 ♌ | 22 ♎ | 21 ♏ |
| 23 ♍ | 24 ♏ | 24 ♏ | 25 ♑ | 25 ♒ | 25 ♈ | 25 ♉ | 25 ♋ | 24 ♌ | 23 ♍ | 24 ♏ | 24 ♐ |
| 25 ♎ | 26 ♐ | 26 ♐ | 27 ♒ | 27 ♓ | 27 ♉ | 27 ♊ | 27 ♌ | 26 ♍ | 26 ♎ | 27 ♐ | 27 ♑ |
| 28 ♏ |  | 29 ♑ | 29 ♓ | 29 ♈ | 30 ♊ | 29 ♋ | 30 ♍ | 28 ♎ | 28 ♏ | 29 ♑ | 29 ♒ |
| 31 ♐ |  | 31 ♒ |  | 31 ♉ |  | 31 ♌ |  | 30 ♏ | 30 ♐ |  | 31 ♓ |

| Libra | Scorpio | Sagittarius | Capricorn | Aquarius | Pisces |
|---|---|---|---|---|---|
| ♎ | ♏ | ♐ | ♑ | ♒ | ♓ |

## 1982

| JAN. | FEB. | MAR. | APR. | MAY | JUNE | JULY | AUG. | SEPT. | OCT. | NOV. | DEC. |
|---|---|---|---|---|---|---|---|---|---|---|---|
| 1 ♓ | 1 ♉ | 1 ♉ | 1 ♋ | 1 ♌ | 1 ♎ | 2 ♏ | 2 ♑ | 1 ♒ | 1 ♓ | 1 ♉ | 1 ♊ |
| 3 ♈ | 3 ♊ | 3 ♊ | 3 ♌ | 2 ♍ | 3 ♏ | 4 ♐ | 4 ♒ | 3 ♓ | 3 ♈ | 4 ♊ | 3 ♋ |
| 5 ♉ | 5 ♋ | 5 ♋ | 5 ♍ | 5 ♎ | 6 ♐ | 6 ♑ | 7 ♓ | 6 ♈ | 5 ♉ | 6 ♋ | 5 ♌ |
| 7 ♊ | 7 ♌ | 7 ♌ | 8 ♎ | 7 ♏ | 8 ♑ | 7 ♒ | 9 ♈ | 8 ♉ | 7 ♊ | 8 ♌ | 7 ♍ |
| 9 ♋ | 10 ♍ | 9 ♍ | 10 ♏ | 10 ♐ | 11 ♒ | 11 ♓ | 12 ♉ | 10 ♊ | 9 ♋ | 10 ♍ | 9 ♎ |
| 11 ♌ | 12 ♎ | 11 ♎ | 12 ♐ | 12 ♑ | 13 ♓ | 13 ♈ | 14 ♊ | 12 ♋ | 11 ♌ | 12 ♎ | 12 ♏ |
| 13 ♍ | 14 ♏ | 14 ♏ | 15 ♑ | 15 ♒ | 16 ♈ | 15 ♉ | 16 ♋ | 14 ♌ | 14 ♍ | 14 ♏ | 14 ♐ |
| 15 ♎ | 17 ♐ | 16 ♐ | 17 ♒ | 17 ♓ | 18 ♉ | 18 ♊ | 18 ♌ | 16 ♍ | 16 ♎ | 17 ♐ | 16 ♑ |
| 18 ♏ | 19 ♑ | 18 ♑ | 19 ♓ | 19 ♈ | 20 ♊ | 20 ♋ | 20 ♍ | 18 ♎ | 18 ♏ | 19 ♑ | 19 ♒ |
| 20 ♐ | 22 ♒ | 21 ♒ | 21 ♈ | 22 ♉ | 22 ♋ | 21 ♌ | 22 ♎ | 20 ♏ | 20 ♐ | 22 ♒ | 22 ♓ |
| 23 ♑ | 24 ♓ | 23 ♓ | 24 ♉ | 24 ♊ | 24 ♌ | 23 ♍ | 24 ♏ | 23 ♐ | 23 ♑ | 24 ♓ | 24 ♈ |
| 25 ♒ | 26 ♈ | 26 ♈ | 26 ♊ | 26 ♋ | 26 ♍ | 26 ♎ | 27 ♐ | 26 ♑ | 25 ♒ | 27 ♈ | 26 ♉ |
| 28 ♓ | 28 ♉ | 28 ♉ | 28 ♋ | 28 ♌ | 28 ♎ | 28 ♏ | 29 ♑ | 28 ♒ | 28 ♓ | 29 ♉ | 28 ♊ |
| 30 ♈ | | 30 ♊ | 30 ♌ | 30 ♍ | | 30 ♐ | | | 30 ♈ | | 30 ♋ |

## 1983

| JAN. | FEB. | MAR. | APR. | MAY | JUNE | JULY | AUG. | SEPT. | OCT. | NOV. | DEC. |
|---|---|---|---|---|---|---|---|---|---|---|---|
| 1 ♌ | 2 ♎ | 1 ♎ | 2 ♐ | 2 ♑ | 1 ♒ | 1 ♓ | 2 ♉ | 1 ♊ | 2 ♌ | 2 ♎ | 2 ♏ |
| 3 ♍ | 4 ♏ | 3 ♏ | 5 ♑ | 4 ♒ | 3 ♓ | 3 ♈ | 4 ♊ | 3 ♋ | 4 ♍ | 5 ♏ | 4 ♐ |
| 6 ♎ | 6 ♐ | 6 ♐ | 7 ♒ | 7 ♓ | 6 ♈ | 6 ♉ | 6 ♋ | 5 ♌ | 6 ♎ | 7 ♐ | 6 ♑ |
| 8 ♏ | 9 ♑ | 8 ♑ | 10 ♓ | 9 ♈ | 8 ♉ | 8 ♊ | 8 ♌ | 7 ♍ | 8 ♏ | 9 ♑ | 9 ♒ |
| 10 ♐ | 12 ♒ | 11 ♒ | 12 ♈ | 12 ♉ | 10 ♊ | 10 ♋ | 10 ♍ | 9 ♎ | 10 ♐ | 12 ♒ | 11 ♓ |
| 13 ♑ | 14 ♓ | 13 ♓ | 14 ♉ | 14 ♊ | 12 ♋ | 12 ♌ | 12 ♎ | 11 ♏ | 13 ♑ | 14 ♓ | 14 ♈ |
| 15 ♒ | 16 ♈ | 16 ♈ | 17 ♊ | 16 ♋ | 14 ♌ | 14 ♍ | 14 ♏ | 13 ♐ | 15 ♒ | 17 ♈ | 16 ♉ |
| 18 ♓ | 19 ♉ | 18 ♉ | 19 ♋ | 18 ♌ | 16 ♍ | 16 ♎ | 17 ♐ | 15 ♑ | 17 ♓ | 19 ♉ | 18 ♊ |
| 20 ♈ | 21 ♊ | 20 ♊ | 21 ♌ | 20 ♍ | 19 ♎ | 18 ♏ | 19 ♑ | 18 ♒ | 19 ♈ | 21 ♊ | 21 ♋ |
| 23 ♉ | 23 ♋ | 23 ♋ | 23 ♍ | 22 ♎ | 21 ♏ | 20 ♐ | 22 ♒ | 20 ♓ | 21 ♉ | 23 ♋ | 23 ♌ |
| 25 ♊ | 25 ♌ | 25 ♌ | 25 ♎ | 25 ♏ | 23 ♐ | 22 ♑ | 24 ♓ | 23 ♈ | 23 ♊ | 26 ♌ | 25 ♍ |
| 27 ♋ | 27 ♍ | 27 ♍ | 27 ♏ | 27 ♐ | 26 ♑ | 25 ♒ | 27 ♈ | 25 ♉ | 25 ♋ | 28 ♍ | 27 ♎ |
| 29 ♌ | | 29 ♎ | 30 ♐ | 29 ♑ | 28 ♒ | 28 ♓ | 29 ♉ | 28 ♊ | 27 ♌ | 30 ♎ | 29 ♏ |
| 31 ♍ | | 31 ♏ | | | | 30 ♈ | | 30 ♋ | 29 ♍ | | 31 ♐ |
| | | | | | | | | | 31 ♎ | | |

| Key: | Aries | Taurus | Gemini | Cancer | Leo | Virgo |
|---|---|---|---|---|---|---|
| | ♈ | ♉ | ♊ | ♋ | ♌ | ♍ |

## 1984

| JAN. | FEB. | MAR. | APR. | MAY | JUNE | JULY | AUG. | SEPT. | OCT. | NOV. | DEC. |
|---|---|---|---|---|---|---|---|---|---|---|---|
| 3 ♑ | 1 ♒ | 2 ♓ | 1 ♈ | 1 ♉ | 2 ♋ | 1 ♌ | 2 ♎ | 2 ♐ | 2 ♑ | 1 ♒ | 3 ♈ |
| 5 ♒ | 4 ♓ | 5 ♈ | 3 ♉ | 3 ♊ | 4 ♌ | 3 ♍ | 4 ♏ | 4 ♑ | 4 ♒ | 3 ♓ | 5 ♉ |
| 8 ♓ | 7 ♈ | 7 ♉ | 6 ♊ | 5 ♋ | 6 ♍ | 5 ♎ | 6 ♐ | 7 ♒ | 7 ♓ | 5 ♈ | 8 ♊ |
| 10 ♈ | 9 ♉ | 10 ♊ | 8 ♋ | 8 ♌ | 8 ♎ | 8 ♏ | 8 ♑ | 9 ♓ | 9 ♈ | 8 ♉ | 10 ♋ |
| 13 ♉ | 11 ♊ | 12 ♋ | 10 ♌ | 10 ♍ | 10 ♏ | 10 ♐ | 11 ♒ | 12 ♈ | 12 ♉ | 10 ♊ | 12 ♌ |
| 15 ♊ | 14 ♋ | 14 ♌ | 13 ♍ | 12 ♎ | 12 ♐ | 12 ♑ | 13 ♓ | 14 ♉ | 14 ♊ | 13 ♋ | 14 ♍ |
| 17 ♋ | 16 ♌ | 16 ♍ | 15 ♎ | 14 ♏ | 15 ♑ | 14 ♒ | 16 ♈ | 17 ♊ | 17 ♋ | 15 ♌ | 17 ♎ |
| 19 ♌ | 18 ♍ | 18 ♎ | 16 ♏ | 16 ♐ | 17 ♒ | 17 ♓ | 18 ♉ | 19 ♋ | 19 ♌ | 17 ♍ | 19 ♏ |
| 21 ♍ | 20 ♎ | 20 ♏ | 19 ♐ | 18 ♑ | 19 ♓ | 19 ♈ | 21 ♊ | 21 ♌ | 21 ♍ | 19 ♎ | 21 ♐ |
| 23 ♎ | 22 ♏ | 22 ♐ | 21 ♑ | 21 ♒ | 22 ♈ | 22 ♉ | 23 ♋ | 24 ♍ | 23 ♎ | 21 ♏ | 23 ♑ |
| 25 ♏ | 24 ♐ | 25 ♑ | 23 ♒ | 23 ♓ | 24 ♉ | 24 ♊ | 25 ♌ | 25 ♎ | 25 ♏ | 23 ♐ | 25 ♒ |
| 28 ♐ | 26 ♑ | 27 ♒ | 26 ♓ | 26 ♈ | 27 ♊ | 26 ♋ | 27 ♍ | 27 ♏ | 27 ♐ | 26 ♑ | 28 ♓ |
| 30 ♑ | 29 ♒ | 29 ♓ | 28 ♈ | 28 ♉ | 29 ♋ | 29 ♌ | 29 ♎ | 30 ♐ | 29 ♑ | 28 ♒ | 30 ♈ |
|  |  |  |  | 30 ♊ |  | 31 ♍ | 31 ♏ |  | 31 ♒ | 30 ♓ |  |

## 1985

| JAN. | FEB. | MAR. | APR. | MAY | JUNE | JULY | AUG. | SEPT. | OCT. | NOV. | DEC. |
|---|---|---|---|---|---|---|---|---|---|---|---|
| 2 ♉ | 1 ♊ | 2 ♋ | 1 ♌ | 2 ♎ | 1 ♏ | 2 ♑ | 1 ♒ | 2 ♈ | 2 ♉ | 1 ♊ | 1 ♋ |
| 4 ♊ | 3 ♋ | 4 ♌ | 3 ♍ | 4 ♏ | 3 ♐ | 4 ♒ | 3 ♓ | 4 ♉ | 4 ♊ | 3 ♋ | 3 ♌ |
| 6 ♋ | 5 ♌ | 6 ♍ | 5 ♎ | 6 ♐ | 5 ♑ | 7 ♓ | 5 ♈ | 6 ♊ | 7 ♋ | 5 ♌ | 5 ♍ |
| 9 ♌ | 7 ♍ | 8 ♎ | 7 ♏ | 8 ♑ | 7 ♒ | 9 ♈ | 8 ♉ | 9 ♋ | 9 ♌ | 8 ♍ | 7 ♎ |
| 11 ♍ | 9 ♎ | 10 ♏ | 9 ♐ | 11 ♒ | 9 ♓ | 12 ♉ | 10 ♊ | 11 ♌ | 11 ♍ | 10 ♎ | 9 ♏ |
| 13 ♎ | 11 ♏ | 13 ♐ | 11 ♑ | 13 ♓ | 12 ♈ | 14 ♊ | 13 ♋ | 13 ♍ | 13 ♎ | 12 ♏ | 11 ♐ |
| 15 ♏ | 13 ♐ | 15 ♑ | 13 ♒ | 15 ♈ | 14 ♉ | 17 ♋ | 15 ♌ | 16 ♎ | 15 ♏ | 14 ♐ | 13 ♑ |
| 17 ♐ | 16 ♑ | 17 ♒ | 16 ♓ | 18 ♉ | 17 ♊ | 19 ♌ | 18 ♍ | 18 ♏ | 17 ♐ | 16 ♑ | 15 ♒ |
| 19 ♑ | 18 ♒ | 19 ♓ | 18 ♈ | 21 ♊ | 19 ♋ | 21 ♍ | 20 ♎ | 20 ♐ | 19 ♑ | 18 ♒ | 17 ♓ |
| 22 ♒ | 20 ♓ | 22 ♈ | 21 ♉ | 23 ♋ | 22 ♌ | 23 ♎ | 22 ♏ | 22 ♑ | 22 ♒ | 20 ♓ | 20 ♈ |
| 24 ♓ | 23 ♈ | 24 ♉ | 23 ♊ | 25 ♌ | 24 ♍ | 25 ♏ | 24 ♐ | 24 ♒ | 24 ♓ | 23 ♈ | 22 ♉ |
| 26 ♈ | 25 ♉ | 27 ♊ | 26 ♋ | 27 ♍ | 26 ♎ | 27 ♐ | 27 ♑ | 27 ♓ | 26 ♈ | 25 ♉ | 25 ♊ |
| 29 ♉ | 28 ♊ | 29 ♋ | 28 ♌ | 30 ♎ | 28 ♏ | 30 ♑ | 28 ♒ | 29 ♈ | 29 ♉ | 28 ♊ | 27 ♋ |
| 31 ♊ |  |  | 30 ♍ |  | 30 ♐ |  | 30 ♓ |  | 31 ♊ | 30 ♋ | 30 ♌ |

| Libra | Scorpio | Sagittarius | Capricorn | Aquarius | Pisces |
|---|---|---|---|---|---|
| ♎ | ♏ | ♐ | ♑ | ♒ | ♓ |

## 1986

| JAN. | FEB. | MAR. | APR. | MAY | JUNE | JULY | AUG. | SEPT. | OCT. | NOV. | DEC. |
|---|---|---|---|---|---|---|---|---|---|---|---|
| 1 ♍ | 2 ♏ | 1 ♏ | 1 ♑ | 1 ♒ | 2 ♈ | 1 ♉ | 1 ♊ | 2 ♌ | 1 ♍ | 2 ♏ | 2 ♐ |
| 3 ♎ | 4 ♐ | 3 ♐ | 4 ♒ | 3 ♓ | 4 ♉ | 4 ♊ | 3 ♋ | 4 ♍ | 4 ♎ | 4 ♐ | 4 ♑ |
| 6 ♏ | 6 ♑ | 5 ♑ | 6 ♓ | 5 ♈ | 7 ♊ | 6 ♋ | 5 ♌ | 6 ♎ | 6 ♏ | 6 ♑ | 6 ♒ |
| 8 ♐ | 8 ♒ | 7 ♒ | 8 ♈ | 8 ♉ | 9 ♋ | 9 ♌ | 8 ♍ | 8 ♏ | 8 ♐ | 8 ♒ | 8 ♓ |
| 10 ♑ | 10 ♓ | 10 ♓ | 11 ♉ | 10 ♊ | 12 ♌ | 11 ♍ | 10 ♎ | 11 ♐ | 10 ♑ | 10 ♓ | 10 ♈ |
| 12 ♒ | 13 ♈ | 12 ♈ | 13 ♊ | 13 ♋ | 14 ♍ | 14 ♎ | 12 ♏ | 13 ♑ | 12 ♒ | 13 ♈ | 12 ♉ |
| 14 ♓ | 15 ♉ | 14 ♉ | 16 ♋ | 15 ♌ | 16 ♎ | 16 ♏ | 14 ♐ | 15 ♒ | 14 ♓ | 15 ♉ | 15 ♊ |
| 16 ♈ | 18 ♊ | 16 ♊ | 18 ♌ | 18 ♍ | 19 ♏ | 18 ♐ | 16 ♑ | 17 ♓ | 16 ♈ | 18 ♊ | 17 ♋ |
| 19 ♉ | 20 ♋ | 18 ♋ | 21 ♍ | 20 ♎ | 21 ♐ | 20 ♑ | 18 ♒ | 19 ♈ | 19 ♉ | 20 ♋ | 20 ♌ |
| 21 ♊ | 22 ♌ | 20 ♌ | 23 ♎ | 22 ♏ | 23 ♑ | 22 ♒ | 21 ♓ | 21 ♉ | 21 ♊ | 22 ♌ | 22 ♍ |
| 24 ♋ | 25 ♍ | 22 ♍ | 25 ♏ | 24 ♐ | 25 ♒ | 24 ♓ | 23 ♈ | 24 ♊ | 24 ♋ | 25 ♍ | 25 ♎ |
| 26 ♌ | 27 ♎ | 24 ♎ | 27 ♐ | 26 ♑ | 27 ♓ | 26 ♈ | 25 ♉ | 26 ♋ | 26 ♌ | 27 ♎ | 27 ♏ |
| 28 ♍ |  | 26 ♏ | 29 ♑ | 28 ♒ | 29 ♈ | 29 ♉ | 28 ♊ | 29 ♌ | 28 ♍ | 29 ♏ | 29 ♐ |
| 31 ♎ |  | 28 ♐ |  | 30 ♓ |  | 31 ♊ | 30 ♋ |  | 31 ♎ |  | 31 ♑ |
|  |  | 30 ♑ |  |  |  |  |  |  |  |  |  |

## 1987

| JAN. | FEB. | MAR. | APR. | MAY | JUNE | JULY | AUG. | SEPT. | OCT. | NOV. | DEC. |
|---|---|---|---|---|---|---|---|---|---|---|---|
| 2 ♒ | 1 ♓ | 2 ♈ | 1 ♉ | 3 ♋ | 2 ♌ | 1 ♍ | 3 ♎ | 2 ♏ | 3 ♑ | 1 ♒ | 1 ♓ |
| 4 ♓ | 3 ♈ | 4 ♉ | 3 ♊ | 5 ♌ | 4 ♍ | 4 ♎ | 5 ♏ | 4 ♐ | 5 ♒ | 3 ♓ | 3 ♈ |
| 6 ♈ | 5 ♉ | 6 ♊ | 5 ♋ | 8 ♍ | 7 ♎ | 6 ♏ | 7 ♐ | 6 ♑ | 7 ♓ | 5 ♈ | 5 ♉ |
| 9 ♉ | 7 ♊ | 9 ♋ | 8 ♌ | 10 ♎ | 9 ♏ | 8 ♐ | 9 ♑ | 8 ♒ | 9 ♈ | 7 ♉ | 7 ♊ |
| 11 ♊ | 10 ♋ | 12 ♌ | 10 ♍ | 12 ♏ | 11 ♐ | 11 ♑ | 11 ♒ | 10 ♓ | 11 ♉ | 10 ♊ | 10 ♋ |
| 14 ♋ | 12 ♌ | 14 ♍ | 12 ♎ | 15 ♐ | 13 ♑ | 13 ♒ | 13 ♓ | 12 ♈ | 14 ♊ | 12 ♋ | 12 ♌ |
| 16 ♌ | 15 ♍ | 16 ♎ | 15 ♏ | 17 ♑ | 15 ♒ | 15 ♓ | 15 ♈ | 14 ♉ | 16 ♋ | 15 ♌ | 15 ♍ |
| 19 ♍ | 17 ♎ | 19 ♏ | 17 ♐ | 19 ♒ | 17 ♓ | 17 ♈ | 17 ♉ | 17 ♊ | 18 ♌ | 17 ♍ | 17 ♎ |
| 21 ♎ | 20 ♏ | 21 ♐ | 19 ♑ | 21 ♓ | 19 ♈ | 19 ♉ | 20 ♊ | 19 ♋ | 21 ♍ | 20 ♎ | 19 ♏ |
| 23 ♏ | 22 ♐ | 23 ♑ | 21 ♒ | 23 ♈ | 22 ♉ | 21 ♊ | 22 ♋ | 21 ♌ | 23 ♎ | 22 ♏ | 21 ♐ |
| 25 ♐ | 24 ♑ | 25 ♒ | 24 ♓ | 25 ♉ | 24 ♊ | 24 ♋ | 24 ♌ | 24 ♍ | 26 ♏ | 24 ♐ | 23 ♑ |
| 27 ♑ | 26 ♒ | 27 ♓ | 26 ♈ | 28 ♊ | 26 ♋ | 26 ♌ | 27 ♍ | 26 ♎ | 28 ♐ | 26 ♑ | 25 ♒ |
| 29 ♒ | 28 ♓ | 29 ♈ | 28 ♉ | 30 ♋ | 29 ♌ | 29 ♍ | 29 ♎ | 29 ♏ | 30 ♑ | 28 ♒ | 28 ♓ |
|  |  |  | 30 ♊ |  |  |  |  | 30 ♐ |  |  | 30 ♈ |

| *Key:* | Aries | Taurus | Gemini | Cancer | Leo | Virgo |
|---|---|---|---|---|---|---|
|  | ♈ | ♉ | ♊ | ♋ | ♌ | ♍ |

## 1988

| JAN. | FEB. | MAR. | APR. | MAY | JUNE | JULY | AUG. | SEPT. | OCT. | NOV. | DEC. |
|---|---|---|---|---|---|---|---|---|---|---|---|
| 1 ♊ | 1 ♋ | 1 ♌ | 2 ♎ | 2 ♏ | 2 ♑ | 2 ♒ | 2 ♈ | 1 ♉ | 2 ♋ | 1 ♌ | 1 ♍ |
| 4 ♋ | 2 ♌ | 3 ♍ | 4 ♏ | 4 ♐ | 4 ♒ | 4 ♓ | 4 ♉ | 3 ♊ | 5 ♌ | 4 ♍ | 4 ♎ |
| 6 ♌ | 5 ♍ | 6 ♎ | 7 ♐ | 6 ♑ | 7 ♓ | 6 ♈ | 7 ♊ | 5 ♋ | 7 ♍ | 6 ♎ | 6 ♏ |
| 9 ♍ | 7 ♎ | 8 ♏ | 9 ♑ | 8 ♒ | 9 ♈ | 7 ♉ | 9 ♋ | 7 ♌ | 10 ♎ | 9 ♏ | 8 ♐ |
| 11 ♎ | 10 ♏ | 10 ♐ | 11 ♒ | 10 ♓ | 11 ♉ | 10 ♊ | 11 ♌ | 10 ♍ | 12 ♏ | 11 ♐ | 11 ♑ |
| 13 ♏ | 12 ♐ | 13 ♑ | 13 ♓ | 12 ♈ | 13 ♊ | 13 ♋ | 14 ♍ | 12 ♎ | 15 ♐ | 13 ♑ | 13 ♒ |
| 16 ♐ | 14 ♑ | 15 ♒ | 15 ♈ | 15 ♉ | 15 ♋ | 15 ♌ | 16 ♎ | 15 ♏ | 17 ♑ | 16 ♒ | 15 ♓ |
| 18 ♑ | 16 ♒ | 17 ♓ | 17 ♉ | 17 ♊ | 18 ♌ | 18 ♍ | 19 ♏ | 17 ♐ | 19 ♒ | 18 ♓ | 17 ♈ |
| 20 ♑ | 18 ♓ | 19 ♈ | 19 ♊ | 19 ♋ | 20 ♍ | 20 ♎ | 21 ♐ | 20 ♑ | 21 ♓ | 20 ♈ | 19 ♉ |
| 22 ♓ | 20 ♈ | 21 ♉ | 22 ♋ | 21 ♌ | 23 ♎ | 23 ♏ | 24 ♑ | 22 ♒ | 24 ♈ | 22 ♉ | 21 ♊ |
| 25 ♈ | 22 ♉ | 23 ♊ | 24 ♌ | 24 ♍ | 25 ♏ | 25 ♐ | 26 ♒ | 24 ♓ | 26 ♉ | 24 ♊ | 24 ♋ |
| 27 ♉ | 25 ♊ | 25 ♋ | 27 ♍ | 26 ♎ | 28 ♐ | 27 ♑ | 28 ♓ | 26 ♈ | 28 ♊ | 26 ♋ | 26 ♌ |
| 30 ♊ | 27 ♋ | 28 ♌ | 29 ♎ | 29 ♏ | 30 ♑ | 29 ♒ | 30 ♈ | 28 ♉ | 30 ♋ | 29 ♌ | 28 ♍ |
|  |  | 30 ♍ |  | 31 ♐ |  | 31 ♓ |  | 30 ♊ |  |  | 31 ♎ |

## 1989

| JAN. | FEB. | MAR. | APR. | MAY | JUNE | JULY | AUG. | SEPT. | OCT. | NOV. | DEC. |
|---|---|---|---|---|---|---|---|---|---|---|---|
| 2 ♏ | 1 ♐ | 1 ♐ | 1 ♒ | 1 ♓ | 1 ♉ | 1 ♊ | 1 ♌ | 1 ♍ | 2 ♏ | 1 ♐ | 1 ♑ |
| 5 ♐ | 3 ♑ | 3 ♑ | 4 ♓ | 3 ♈ | 3 ♊ | 3 ♋ | 4 ♍ | 3 ♎ | 5 ♐ | 4 ♑ | 3 ♒ |
| 7 ♑ | 6 ♒ | 5 ♒ | 6 ♈ | 5 ♉ | 6 ♋ | 5 ♌ | 6 ♎ | 5 ♏ | 7 ♑ | 6 ♒ | 6 ♓ |
| 9 ♒ | 8 ♓ | 7 ♓ | 8 ♉ | 7 ♊ | 8 ♌ | 7 ♍ | 9 ♏ | 8 ♐ | 10 ♒ | 8 ♓ | 8 ♈ |
| 11 ♓ | 10 ♈ | 9 ♈ | 10 ♊ | 9 ♋ | 10 ♍ | 10 ♎ | 11 ♐ | 10 ♑ | 12 ♓ | 10 ♈ | 10 ♉ |
| 13 ♈ | 12 ♉ | 11 ♉ | 12 ♋ | 11 ♌ | 13 ♎ | 12 ♏ | 14 ♑ | 12 ♒ | 14 ♈ | 12 ♉ | 12 ♊ |
| 15 ♉ | 14 ♊ | 13 ♊ | 14 ♌ | 14 ♍ | 15 ♏ | 15 ♐ | 16 ♒ | 14 ♓ | 16 ♉ | 14 ♊ | 14 ♋ |
| 18 ♊ | 16 ♋ | 15 ♋ | 16 ♍ | 16 ♎ | 18 ♐ | 17 ♑ | 18 ♓ | 16 ♈ | 18 ♊ | 16 ♋ | 16 ♌ |
| 20 ♋ | 19 ♌ | 18 ♌ | 19 ♎ | 19 ♏ | 20 ♑ | 20 ♒ | 20 ♈ | 18 ♉ | 20 ♋ | 19 ♌ | 18 ♍ |
| 22 ♌ | 21 ♍ | 20 ♍ | 22 ♏ | 21 ♐ | 22 ♒ | 22 ♓ | 22 ♉ | 20 ♊ | 22 ♌ | 21 ♍ | 21 ♎ |
| 25 ♍ | 24 ♎ | 23 ♎ | 24 ♐ | 24 ♑ | 24 ♓ | 24 ♈ | 24 ♊ | 23 ♋ | 25 ♍ | 23 ♎ | 23 ♏ |
| 27 ♎ | 26 ♏ | 25 ♏ | 26 ♑ | 26 ♒ | 27 ♈ | 26 ♉ | 26 ♋ | 25 ♌ | 27 ♎ | 26 ♏ | 26 ♐ |
| 30 ♏ |  | 28 ♐ | 29 ♒ | 28 ♓ | 29 ♉ | 28 ♊ | 29 ♌ | 27 ♍ | 30 ♏ | 28 ♐ | 28 ♑ |
|  |  | 31 ♑ |  | 30 ♈ |  | 30 ♋ |  | 30 ♎ |  |  | 30 ♒ |

| Libra | Scorpio | Sagittarius | Capricorn | Aquarius | Pisces |
|---|---|---|---|---|---|
| ♎ | ♏ | ♐ | ♑ | ♒ | ♓ |

## 1990

| JAN. | FEB. | MAR. | APR. | MAY | JUNE | JULY | AUG. | SEPT. | OCT. | NOV. | DEC. |
|---|---|---|---|---|---|---|---|---|---|---|---|
| 2 ♓ | 2 ♉ | 2 ♉ | 2 ♋ | 2 ♌ | 2 ♎ | 2 ♏ | 1 ♐ | 2 ♒ | 2 ♓ | 1 ♈ | 2 ♊ |
| 4 ♈ | 4 ♊ | 4 ♊ | 4 ♌ | 4 ♍ | 5 ♏ | 5 ♐ | 4 ♑ | 5 ♓ | 4 ♈ | 3 ♉ | 4 ♋ |
| 6 ♉ | 7 ♋ | 6 ♋ | 7 ♍ | 6 ♎ | 8 ♐ | 7 ♑ | 6 ♒ | 7 ♈ | 6 ♉ | 5 ♊ | 6 ♌ |
| 8 ♊ | 9 ♌ | 8 ♌ | 9 ♎ | 9 ♏ | 10 ♑ | 10 ♒ | 8 ♓ | 9 ♉ | 8 ♊ | 7 ♋ | 8 ♍ |
| 10 ♋ | 11 ♍ | 10 ♍ | 11 ♏ | 11 ♐ | 12 ♒ | 12 ♓ | 11 ♈ | 11 ♊ | 10 ♋ | 9 ♌ | 11 ♎ |
| 12 ♌ | 13 ♎ | 13 ♎ | 14 ♐ | 14 ♑ | 15 ♓ | 14 ♈ | 13 ♉ | 13 ♋ | 13 ♌ | 11 ♍ | 13 ♏ |
| 15 ♍ | 16 ♏ | 15 ♏ | 17 ♑ | 16 ♒ | 17 ♈ | 16 ♉ | 15 ♊ | 15 ♌ | 15 ♍ | 13 ♎ | 16 ♐ |
| 17 ♎ | 18 ♐ | 18 ♐ | 19 ♒ | 19 ♓ | 19 ♉ | 19 ♊ | 17 ♋ | 18 ♍ | 17 ♎ | 16 ♏ | 18 ♑ |
| 20 ♏ | 21 ♑ | 20 ♑ | 21 ♓ | 21 ♈ | 21 ♊ | 21 ♋ | 19 ♌ | 20 ♎ | 20 ♏ | 18 ♐ | 21 ♒ |
| 22 ♐ | 23 ♒ | 23 ♒ | 23 ♈ | 23 ♉ | 23 ♋ | 23 ♌ | 21 ♍ | 22 ♏ | 22 ♐ | 21 ♑ | 23 ♓ |
| 24 ♑ | 25 ♓ | 25 ♓ | 25 ♉ | 25 ♊ | 25 ♌ | 25 ♍ | 24 ♎ | 25 ♐ | 25 ♑ | 23 ♒ | 25 ♈ |
| 27 ♒ | 28 ♈ | 27 ♈ | 27 ♊ | 27 ♋ | 27 ♍ | 27 ♎ | 26 ♏ | 27 ♑ | 27 ♒ | 26 ♓ | 28 ♉ |
| 29 ♓ | | 29 ♉ | 29 ♋ | 29 ♌ | 30 ♎ | 30 ♏ | 28 ♐ | 30 ♒ | 29 ♓ | 28 ♈ | 30 ♊ |
| 31 ♈ | | 31 ♊ | | 31 ♍ | | | 31 ♑ | | | 30 ♉ | |

| *Key:* | Aries | Taurus | Gemini | Cancer | Leo | Virgo |
|---|---|---|---|---|---|---|
| | ♈ | ♉ | ♊ | ♋ | ♌ | ♍ |

**6**

## Your Ascendant
## or Rising Sign

Your Ascendant is the Sign rising on the horizon at the time of your birth; it is third in importance after the Sun and Moon.

One of the most absorbing facts in astrology, next to the uncanny manner in which we tend to demonstrate our Sun Signs, is the remarkable influence our *exact hour* of birth has on us. The man or woman with a Sagittarius Ascendant, for example, loves outdoor life, travel, horses and sports in general. He or she is usually outspoken, kindhearted and candid. Scorpio rising, on the other hand, is pretty much the opposite. Usually physically strong and enduring, the person with Scorpio rising is secretive, rather suspicious and determined. These are cursory examples of the differences that can exist between people born only two hours apart, so you can see how important it is to know the hour and minute of your birth.

If you were born a half hour or 45 minutes sooner or later than you believe, it *may* mean you have an entirely different rising Sun than the one indicated. All sunrise births have the same Ascendant as the Sun Sign, as we've noted before. For instance, if you were born at dawn on June 4th you are a *double* Gemini. At the end of this chapter a table will enable you quickly to find your own Ascendant. Simply check it against the delineations based on the rising Signs:

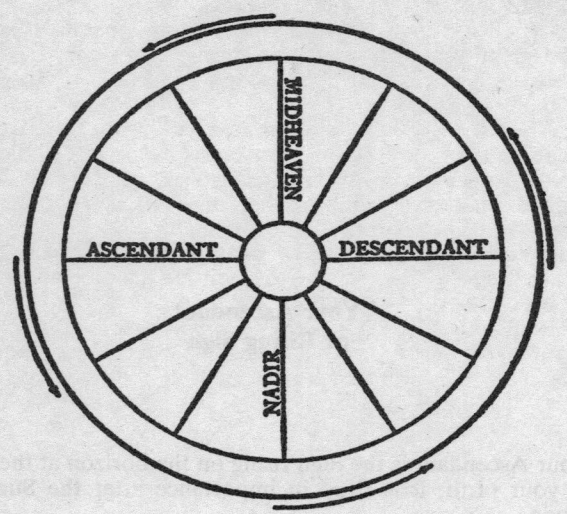

*Locate your Ascendant from Chapter 6, write the symbol of the Ascendant at the "9 o'clock" position, then simply fill in the remaining Signs on the house cusps (the spokes of the wheel) in counterclockwise fashion.*

## ARIES ♈

You have good executive ability, are apt to be something of a pioneer. You have strong likes and dislikes and are usually courageous and adventurous. Chances are you tend to have outbursts of anger or irritation, but you rarely hold a grudge for long. There is something of the iconoclast about you, a tendency to kick over existing practices and institutions, to crusade for newer and better ways—at least *your* version of such improvements! You are inclined to try to force your opinions on others rather than to use the gentle art of persuasion. You are enthusiastic and generally progressive in whatever idea you happen to be pursuing—as long as the idea lasts. Although you frequently change your viewpoint and opinions, you are extremely certain of whatever you happen to believe—at the moment. At some time in your life your ambition for high office or an executive position will tax all your willpower and courage. You are so passionately opinionated that many people regard your expressions as being violent.

Wherever you have legal trouble with money or property, there will almost certainly be women involved—particularly if you are a man. With Aries ascending, you may be an only child or may lose your brother or sister. People with this Sign rising often lose their fathers at an early age; this doesn't necessarily mean by death, but in one way or another the father leaves no provision for the care and welfare of his children.

You will travel a lot, either for business or else to avoid trouble. Chances are you'll change your residence frequently and may become successful in another country. You typify the cliche of marrying in haste and repenting in leisure. Probably you'll get a divorce. One way or another, you are a true pioneer, a climber of every kind of obstacle fate put in your path. There's a kind of martyr complex about Aries, however. When afflicted, people born under this Sign can cause injury or even death to themselves.

## TAURUS ♉

You don't, as a rule, easily become angered; but by the same token you're difficult to appease annd liable to harbor a grudge for long periods. You tend to be self-possessed, and may seem dogmatic or even stubborn. Despite your essentially egotistical attitude, you are outwardly kindly, essentially diplomatic. You are precise, patient and probably love your own ideas. Generally you are calm, somewhat obstinate and therefore strongly passionate. Taurus ascending has a deep and abiding love of physical ease and comfort—a characteristic that might be regarded as pure laziness.

This is not necessarily so. You are firm-willed and flexible, capable of making silent decisions and pursuing them with strong, steady perseverance. You hanker for recognition and are very fond of your own possessions and property. You will probably realize your ambitions. Either by your own efforts or through some unexpected good luck, you'll acquire a fair amount of wealth. Usually your father will be helpful; in all likelihood he was or is a man of some consequence in his field.

You will also realize much happiness through children, yet you may lose your first if it happens to be a boy. You are artistic; you love peace and harmony to such a degree that you may resist change and try to avoid all obstacles. This makes you so conservative that the chief cause of your unhappiness is your own stubborn opinions.

Even though your youth may be plagued by financial insecurity, you will gain materially through your adulthood and middle age, and develop a full appreciation for the physical comforts of life.

## GEMINI  ♊

You are fully capable of success in radio, television, journalism, literature or motion pictures. Although you tend to be somewhat excitable and easily upset, you are just as easily assuaged. You are original, have good ideas, are clever in legal matters, inventive, a lover of logic, science, art and literature. Generally you are well-informed, humane, flexible and easy to talk to—a born communicator.

With great subtlety you express a desire for command situations or executive position. You are one of the few who can do this with neither tyranny nor excessive pride. You come from a small to moderate-sized family which is usually well versed in music or art, although some family secrets are a cause of much unhappiness.

You have such a beautifully balanced willpower and resoluteness of purpose that few people realize your potential for real achievement. Chances are you may have a brother who holds some kind of executive office or important position.

In love there are many secrets or changes, with difficulty through or loss of children. Intrigue is your stock in trade. Gemini ascending often has two or more affairs going at once . . . either that or you may marry twice—once to a foreigner or someone from another country. This most dual of all signs frequently means the holding of two jobs or positions at once and a wide variety of friends. In fact, there is such an inordinate love of variety in your life that strife occurs as a result of the jealousy or selfishness of others.

Generally, Gemini ascending also realizes unhappiness and trouble through lawyers and clergymen, even though he may be a member of one of these groups himself. In this unfortunate situation he might easily bring about his own downfall. You will probably, though, inherit property or land and accrue a great deal of professional influence.

## CANCER ♋

Although some notoriety goes with it, you have many changes in position throughout your life. In a quiet way your disposition is rather impatient and severe, with an abrupt temper and a reserved exterior. You have an almost fantastic ability to absorb the ideas of others, and also possess a remarkable imagination—one that delights in exotic adventures in faraway places. Your unremitting compulsion for each new love, friendship or temporary attachment often propels you into yet another place and relationship—which usually ends in disillusion. This faculty has probably developed your most dramatic capabilities. You can be capricious and clever at using the ideas of other people. In extreme cases you could become a plagiarist or copier, one who is extraordinarily sensitive in perceiving the intentions of friends and associates.

Because of the rather fluid nature of the Moon's influence in your rising Sign, you are highly sensitive, changeable and nervous. Yet because of this nervous irritability you are enormously adaptable. Cancer ascending is remarkably capable, extremely independent and discreet in most things. You love public recognition, honor and wealth.

Still, inconstancy is your name. Your moods are as changeable as the tides. You can be timid in the face of physical danger and resourceful as well as courageous in your moral or intellectual attitudes. You can also be fanciful, gay and nebulous, or suddenly revert to caution, prudence—even mistrust. You lose materially through love affairs, children, relatives and speculation. This, moreover, occurs in the early part of your life. You are bound to become more prosperous and successful later on. There's a great tendency for obstacles, even danger, to crop up during your travels. Whatever your position, it is usually achieved in spite of the difficulties you experience through the jealousy of those who stoop to slander or spread false rumors about you.

Thirty-five is the median age of stabilization for you. Whatever success you achieve is a result of your own enterprising spirit.

## LEO  ♌

You have nothing but contempt for the small or petty things in life. Basically, your nature is a benevolent and noble one, manifesting great pride, generosity, and probably a lot of talent. Leo ascending is the Sign of one who aspires to the higher, more influential and powerful positions in life. You are dramatic and poetic, with a love of display which others could interpret as nothing more than pure egotism. Although you are a hard worker and your success comes through persistence and endurance, whatever fame and fortune you realize usually comes without your seeking it. Like those born under the other fixed Signs, you display a good deal of self-determination and may seem haughty. Like Aries, you can reveal a flaring temperament, but your anger is a straw fire that doesn't last long.

Somehow or other you are often associated with important and influential people. You love grandeur in nature as well as in the human soul; you are attracted to everything that is bright and large and noble. Your undertakings are done with courage, yet you have fixed opinions, dogmatic ideals and strong passions. You could never admit to being ruled by these passions.

Chances are there is some disaffection or estrangement from your father—or he was separated from you while you were still very young. You love children and could have many yourself, but there is much difficulty—even sorrow—over the health of your oldest. Those with Leo ascending frequently marry more than once and can have children by each marriage. Men with Leo rising at one time or another in their lives are forced to endure great hardship, often lacking in the basic necessities of existence, such as food and a place to live.

You are likely to come into an inheritance, and so will your children. Successful business or professional people are attracted to you and vice versa; you will prosper through these associations. In the final analysis, all the vicissitudes of life will have little effect on you; you are almost certain to emerge ahead of the game.

## VIRGO ♍

You have a finely discriminating sense of justice, humility, a good mind and a rather attractive and diplomatic demeanor. You'll rise in life through your own merit, attention to detail and hard work . . . in short, through your own achievements. Nevertheless, there's a lack of perspective or proportion in your outlook that causes you to overemphasize the importance of small, unimportant details.

Despite your pleasant and attractive public personality, you are difficult to know well. Only those whom you feel are sincerely affectionate or trustworthy can ever become your confidantes. You are definitely not the temperamental type; as a rule you are slow to anger, but by the same token, you don't find it easy to forgive people who have wronged you.

Being a mental Sign, Virgo ascending clings to its own ideas with a tenacity and esteem that seems to counter all the other influences of this earthly, mercurial Sign. Your willpower is strong, yet you are perfectly capable of being swayed by logic, reason and finesse. Generally of a quiet nature, you are nevertheless capable of eloquence and remarkable persuasiveness—when the occasion calls for it. By vocation you are probably inclined to theoretical science, health, hygiene and the more abstract areas of human knowledge. Your avocation could easily be gardening or amateur farming.

As an infant or child you probably endured poor health— possibly poverty. Even as an adult, most of what you manage to acquire is through your own hard work and is, therefore, richly deserved. You will probably realize some financial gain through inheritance and/or the property of your business or marriage partner. This could happen some distance from your place of birth—probably in another country. Whatever else you do, avoid speculation if you want to hold onto what you have earned. Chances are your father will marry twice, and that there are some family secrets you'd rather forget.

Although there are exceptions in every instance, relatives and neighbors are frequently inimical to your personal welfare. Probably there is a coldness or lack of sympathy in your relationship with brothers or sisters. Your own family will be small and your children not as keenly interested in marriage as you'd like them to be.

Solid happiness in love comes late to the person with Virgo rising. He or she often marries twice or has an extra-marital affair. Whatever difficulties you face, your achievements and ultimate success will somehow revolve around trips and voyages, possibly associated with some changes in occupation. Don't be surprised to find yourself in later years with two homes and property in two different countries.

## LIBRA ≃

This is one of the most likeable and harmonious Ascendants to have. You are sensitive and strongly influenced by your surroundings as well as existing conditions. Libra rising gives you an innate sense of fairness, makes you honest, courteous, compassionate and kind. You are optimistic, candid and have a good deal of willpower but very little perseverance. One of your chief drawbacks stems from the fact that you will weigh first one side of a question and then the other— and then perhaps wait to see what someone else will do— before making a decision of your own.

Your talents include constructive and inventive ability. Probably you have untapped genius for anything harmonious or beautiful in life: poetry, art, music or sculpture. You learn quickly and can master almost any branch of business. The difficulty lies in the fact that you may, while engrossed in any avocation, suddenly change your mind and follow an entirely different line of interest.

Social and personal pleasures are matters of great absorption for you with Libra ascending. This is the natural Sign of partnership and harmonious relationships; unfortunately, too many of these connections are more disruptive than amicable. If you haven't been born into a large family, chances are that you'll marry into one; the only trouble with this is that some of them may be so disputatious that legal action will be involved.

Somehow your father is a source of difficulty or loss. If he did not leave the scene when you were very young, he may be a source of unforeseen obstacles, argument and unnecessary restraint, due to his loss of position in life. There's some kind of duplicity in your parental allegiance; either you were adopted or your father and/or mother has remarried. On the other hand, you'll gain enormous satisisfaction and happiness from and through your children, who will be few in number but extremely fortunate.

You marriage partner is apt to be comfortably fixed, and you have a good relationship with your children. Still, you are or will be in the public eye and will probably do considerable traveling and changing of address as a result of your occupation. You'll take some long trips, but your chief source of profit and success will be in your own country—probably your home town. You will discover that your best friends are people of great professional accomplishment and standing in the world. Association with artists, writers and other creative people will eventually reveal that one of your closest friends comes from this group.

When all is said and done, and you've lived your life to the best of your abilities, your children will be your best inspiration during your waning years.


## SCORPIO ♏

By nature, inclination and temperament you are an extremist. Whatever you attempt, it is usually done with the full force of all your being. Your will is so strong you stick to a fight to the bloody end, regardless of the outcome. Scorpio rising is largely misunderstood by almost every standard. Don't overlook the fact that there are other planetary arrangements in your chart to offset what is often regarded as your Scorpio harshness, bitter critical quality and acid sarcasm. You are a born executive and like very much to operate behind the scenes. It helps to realize that Scorpio is representative of sex, death and regeneration, and that these things occupy an important area of your existence.

You share a kind of iconoclasm with Aquarius, though the latter is not the extremist you are. There's an apparently unquenchable thirst in you for finding out what makes things tick, then reassembling them to make them work better. You do this with objects, people—even institutions, if given half a chance. Very little, if anything, escapes the penetrating power of your observation. If it doesn't meet with your approval, you'll tear down any facade, any theory, any belief, to get at the truth. This makes you a natural detective. In science the intensity and keenness of your curiosity can bring you rich rewards, yet there is an Aries-like kind of martyrdom or "self-destruct" button in the mind of almost everyone with strong Scorpio aspects.

Extremism again. You have strong likes and dislikes. You hate and love with a white-hot fire, yet you are able to keep things to yourself until some plan of action is mapped out. Scorpio is exceptionally resourceful and self-reliant, and frequently malicious. You have a fertile imagination. Still . . . there are several types within the Scorpio nature, and it is difficult to know in advance just how anger will be handled. The undeveloped type, symbolized by the deadly, stinging scorpion, is capable of almost any outrage. The intermediate type is symbolized by the wily serpent, representing increased wisdom. The developed type is characterized by the high-soaring eagle, aspiring to the greatest possible heights. Here you will find scientists, orators, intensely devout evangelists and fiery debaters.

Scorpio ascending is always ambitious and usually manages to gain some sort of high office or executive position. You probably admire the military and maritime professions. You may have been close to poverty, a condition that prevails in the early part of your existence. But during the second half of your life there is more material prosperity and good fortune than you would otherwise have believed. There are excellent opportunities to travel and make money in other countries—through your marriage partner, legal dealings and/or through relatives by marriage. You are something of a lone wolf and probably have many secret love affairs. More than one marriage is indicated for those with Scorpio ascending. The first could result in the premature loss of the husband or wife through illness or accident. Eventually, despite a great series of difficulties and setbacks, you will achieve the success, good position and probably the honors you have so long desired.


## SAGITTARIUS ♐

You often display two entirely different facets of personality. One of these is rather reticent, sensitive and impressionable. The other is courageous, daring—even reckless. By any measure, you are not easy to know well. One of your chief drawbacks is the overemphasis you place on action rather than its consequences. You are basically sympathetic, and driven by your ambition for achievement to action of some kind or another. You can't tolerate injury or injustice to others—it seems almost a personal affront. People with Sagittarius rising are usually versatile and clever in several areas at once. You are able to master more than one specialty.

Constraint or restraint of any kind is unbearable. You are quick to anger, but just as quickly recover and do not often hold a grudge. You comprehend new ideas and ways of life with scarcely any effort, and are very progressive and clear-minded. Sagittarians carry an exuberant, youthful and happy attitude—even into old age. You tend to say what you think at the moment of stimulation, but your basic nature is friendly, even gentle. About the only time you flare up is when your basic ideals are attacked. Above all else, you love and cherish your personal freedom and independence, even though you prefer a simple way of life. You suffer when trapped in a discordant environment, and will sacrifice everything rather than be tied to an unpleasant situation, person or place.

You are more complex and difficult to understand, probably, than you realize. Always on your toes, you are friendly, outgoing and gregarious, yet your watchfulness of others amounts almost to mistrust—and can result in the very deception you strive to avoid. Your courage can never be questioned, even though you may seem quiet or even timid to those who don't know you well. You are intelligent and devoted to the *spirit*—if not the practice—of religious belief. You are good at research and study—a reasonable man or woman—with foresight, whose conversational abilities amount almost to eloquence. The opinions you hold are almost always unorthodox.

There's a lukewarm attitude in you toward most family ties. Some difficulty with your father or father-in-law amounts to a kind of torment worse than actual imprisonment. There probably was an early separation from your father. Conversely, you may be separated from your own children—or one of them. Your relationship with brothers and sisters is friendly enough, but many troubles are experienced through them. Two or three marriages (or similar associations) are in store for you. One of these is bad for your position and standing in life, but you will manage to extricate yourself.

While you are in another country or far from home, one of your parents may die. You will travel extensively, and could be exposed to some danger when away from your home. You can anticipate a long and valuable career. Chances are you will end your days peacefully in a distant country.

## CAPRICORN ♑

Your life is based on prudence and caution, yet once embarked on a course of action, you pursue it with dogged determination and persistence. You tend to be quietly melancholy, but you are enormously ambitious whenever your course for a certain goal is set. Among friends you can be forceful and eloquent, even if not very persuasive. Among strangers, however, you seem reticent, quiet—even shy. Your ambition for power and prestige is almost boundless; you often display great courage and are capable of realizing your ambitions, yet achievement itself leaves you unhappy. You are a little different from the norm. This is characterized by a not-unpleasant peculiarity in the way you walk and talk. You may forgive someone who offends or injures you, but you'll never forget it. As an enemy, you can be malicious. As a friend, you are faithful and sincere.

Although you may have received the assistance of your family and the support of friends and business associates, your ultimate success can be attributed almost entirely to your own persistence and hard work. There is more than enough difficulty through brothers and sisters, who often cause considerable sorrow. Unfortunately, additional strife is caused by your family, especially your father, where marriage is concerned. Somehow you don't seem to agree and this causes secret trouble and rivalry in your immediate family. You travel a lot, and conceivably could easily face great danger while on some recondite mission.

Your children are few in number, but you tend to pin all your hopes and ambitions on the oldest, thereby creating for him an emotional burden. You tend to view your husband or wife as some kind of obstacle to your large ambitions. You could lose one partner in marriage, yet acquire a considerable amount of wealth from the next. The wife of a man with Capricorn ascending is usually a wonderful career booster who influences him in many correct decisions. But the marriage has more than its share of ups and downs. In virtually every case of Capricorn rising, the love affairs are subject to enormous, far-reaching changes.

Your friends will often be found connected with Mars-type occupations—doctors, soldiers, chemists, marines and sportsmen. There is a likelihood of sudden, upsetting news about them . . . often their unexpected or untimely death. Among this group of friends, one will inadvertently cause you a great deal of strife, perhaps even the temporary loss of your reputation in middle age. Yet in spite of your own groundless worry about health and position in life—and the consequent melancholy to which you are prone—you will overcome most of your setbacks and succeed through sheer persistence and your burning ambition to reach the top of the heap.

## AQUARIUS ♒

This ascending Sign makes you honest and sincere, very idealistic and humanitarian in your outlook. In some ways you are naive, but in love you are exceptionally affectionate and constant. You are fond of scientific research and the liberal arts. In fact, you probably have a great deal of literary or artistic ability—and musical aptitude for all media. Though you prefer to live quietly and have a generally retiring viewpoint, your basic philosophy is heterodox. Aquarius rising is a fixed Sign. Therefore your willpower is stronger than is apparent. In fact, there is a kind of inflexibility about your outlook.

In personality and temperament you are kindly and humane. Even though your temper is brittle and forceful when angered, you cannot bear malice toward anyone or anything. As you probably realize, your association is highly valued because of your innate sense of fairness and the overall endurance of your friendship. You enjoy solitude, but this doesn't mean you are a recluse. Just the opposite. Aquarius likes to be with people. You are cordial, cheerful and high-spirited, despite some undeserved adversity or reversal of fortune. You are enormously patient and hard working, yet your efforts are seldom crowned with the success they deserve. Whatever you do is achieved through your own devotion to a cause. Even this is liable to sudden and unexpected reversals or secret enemies who create serious obstacles. Your best friends will be found among clergymen, lawyers, journalists and doctors. If you come into an inheritance, chances are it will be more trouble—in the long run—than it is worth.

Relatives—especially one brother—is a great source of annoyance, difficulty and trouble, particularly in business affairs, which can adversely affect your reputation. You'll take many long trips on business and in the administration of family interests. Something of a dual or secretive nature is involved in your work. Perhaps there are two or more sources of income, or you may be engaged in highly classified military or government work. Whichever it is, detective-like secrecy is in order. You are required to make many short trips, either for your vocation or on family business. Whatever the route, it is very familiar, even tiresome to you.

Marriage is a virtual certainty, and usually happens early in your life. You have few children and will go to any length to provide for them. There's a good chance that twins might be born, but there is some danger of illness or accident to the oldest child. Your wife or husband has talent and is profitably employed in some artistic endeavor, such as the composition or playing of music creating new art forms, or acting—on stage, television or in motion pictures. Your marriage is blessed with constancy and longevity; the affection of your wife or husband is enduring and sincere. Although it may seem that you are financially secure, it could be money that dangles just beyond your reach through some kind of legalistic maneuvering. Your children, however, will probably come into a sizable inheritance.

You have many good friends, one of whom will come to your rescue when it seems that everything is in danger of being lost. This may happen when you are traveling or while you're in another country. Chances are you will live out your days in this foreign nation.


## PISCES  ♓

You are easily moved, romantic, imaginative and impressionable—all of which are attributes of your ruling planet, Neptune. Your mind is restless, constantly seeking new ideas for the expression of your creative talents. You are changeable, and can exercise whatever authority you may have with firmness—and yet pleasantly. You can succeed through your own efforts in science, literature or the arts. In fact, there is a good chance that you will achieve celebrity status in your field. Still, you are tortured by excessive worry and fanciful notions. Although generous by nature, you tend to pursue pleasure to a point where it might be injurious to others. Your chief ambition seems to be that of enjoying yourself and tasting the good things of life.

You are a good talker with a conversational ability that might rival the gift of eloquence. You are filled with good will and can easily put yourself in the other person's position; in fact, you tend to suffer for the underdog. Conversely, you can remain emotionally aloof from two opposing ideals and render a critical judgment of one or the other with neither bias nor prejudice. Anger doesn't come easily to you, but once moved to wrath you are almost impossible to appease before wrecking some kind of vengeance, however slight.

You are passionate, impressionable and, therefore, tend to seem vacillating. The pleasure of good company is very important, and you are socially successful because of your friendly outgoing nature and cordiality. You are always busy with one thing or another, and could become successful in almost anything that interests you. You are broadminded, knowledgeable in many fields and can probably pursue two occupations at once. Whatever material rewards you realize will be the result of your own hard work and effort, possibly through successful writing or in traveling. However, you will find that you also enjoy the affection and loyalty of friends and relatives, who are fortunately numerous. There is the danger of the premature loss of a brother or sister, and your parents are not able to contribute much in the way of assistance to your future or well being. Whatever is left in the family estate may be spread so thin that it is hardly worth the trouble of administration.

Your children will be much more fortunate. And there will be several children—mostly engaged in work that takes them on extensive trips with frequent changes in residence. If a man, your wife has some kind of chronic ailment or affliction. You may marry twice because the first marriage might cause difficulty with relatives and in-laws.

Paradoxically, one of your strongest enemies in life will turn out to be your staunchest friend. Pisces ascending is fully capable of gaining great public recognition, honors and considerable wealth. Most of your friends are in important positions and able to boost your career.

## YOUR ASCENDING SIGN—FOR ANY YEAR OF BIRTH

These Ascendants are most accurate at 40° N. Latitude, but are valid for anyone born between 25° and 55° N. Latitude. This covers all of the United States, Southern Canada and Northern Mexico.

Pick the date closest to your birthday (June 15 if your birthday is June 12, for example). Also pick the time closest to the actual time of your birth. If you were born on May 5 at 9:00 P.M., see May 1 at 9:35 P.M. (the closest date and time) and you'll find you have Sagittarius Ascending.

### January 1
#### Approximate Time of Birth

| A.M. | | P.M. | |
|---|---|---|---|
| 12:30 | Libra | 1:10 | Taurus |
| 3:05 | Scorpio | 2:50 | Gemini |
| 5:35 | Sagittarius | 5:05 | Cancer |
| 7:50 | Capricorn | 7:30 | Leo |
| 9:25 | Aquarius | 10:05 | Virgo |
| 10:45 | Pisces | | |
| 11:55 | Aries | | |

### February 1
#### Approximate Time of Birth

| A.M. | | P.M. | |
|---|---|---|---|
| 1:05 | Scorpio | 12:50 | Gemini |
| 3:35 | Sagittarius | 3:05 | Cancer |
| 5:50 | Capricorn | 5:30 | Leo |
| 7:25 | Aquarius | 8:05 | Virgo |
| 8:45 | Pisces | 10:30 | Libra |
| 9:55 | Aries | | |
| 11:10 | Taurus | | |

### January 15
#### Approximate Time of Birth

| A.M. | | P.M. | |
|---|---|---|---|
| 2:05 | Scorpio | 12:10 | Taurus |
| 4:35 | Sagittarius | 1:50 | Gemini |
| 6:50 | Capricorn | 4:05 | Cancer |
| 8:25 | Aquarius | 6:30 | Leo |
| 9:45 | Pisces | 9:05 | Virgo |
| 10:55 | Aries | 11:30 | Libra |

### February 15
#### Approximate Time of Birth

| A.M. | | P.M. | |
|---|---|---|---|
| 12:05 | Scorpio | 2:05 | Cancer |
| 2:35 | Sagittarius | 4:30 | Leo |
| 4:50 | Capricorn | 7:05 | Virgo |
| 6:25 | Aquarius | 9:30 | Libra |
| 7:45 | Pisces | | |
| 8:55 | Aries | | |
| 10:10 | Taurus | | |
| 11:50 | Gemini | | |

### March 1
#### Approximate Time of Birth

| A.M. | | P.M. | |
|------|--|------|--|
| 1:35 | Sagittarius | 1:05 | Cancer |
| 3:50 | Capricorn | 3:30 | Leo |
| 5:25 | Aquarius | 6:05 | Virgo |
| 6:45 | Pisces | 8:30 | Libra |
| 7:55 | Aries | 11:05 | Scorpio |
| 9:10 | Taurus | | |
| 10:50 | Gemini | | |

### May 1
#### Approximate Time of Birth

| A.M. | | P.M. | |
|------|--|------|--|
| 1:25 | Aquarius | 2:05 | Virgo |
| 2:45 | Pisces | 4:30 | Libra |
| 3:55 | Aries | 7:05 | Scorpio |
| 5:10 | Taurus | 9:35 | Sagittarius |
| 6:50 | Gemini | 11:50 | Capricorn |
| 9:05 | Cancer | | |
| 11:30 | Leo | | |

### March 15
#### Approximate Time of Birth

| A.M. | | P.M. | |
|------|--|------|--|
| 12:35 | Sagittarius | 12:05 | Cancer |
| 2:50 | Capricorn | 2:30 | Leo |
| 4:25 | Aquarius | 5:05 | Virgo |
| 5:45 | Pisces | 7:30 | Libra |
| 6:55 | Aries | 10:05 | Scorpio |
| 8:10 | Taurus | | |
| 9:50 | Gemini | | |

### May 15
#### Approximate Time of Birth

| A.M. | | P.M. | |
|------|--|------|--|
| 12:25 | Aquarius | 1:05 | Virgo |
| 1:45 | Pisces | 3:30 | Libra |
| 2:55 | Aries | 6:05 | Scorpio |
| 4:10 | Taurus | 8:35 | Sagittarius |
| 5:50 | Gemini | 10:50 | Capricorn |
| 8:05 | Cancer | | |
| 10:30 | Leo | | |

### April 1
#### Approximate Time of Birth

| A.M. | | P.M. | |
|------|--|------|--|
| 1:50 | Capricorn | 1:30 | Leo |
| 3:25 | Aquarius | 4:05 | Virgo |
| 4:45 | Pisces | 6:30 | Libra |
| 5:55 | Aries | 9:05 | Scorpio |
| 7:10 | Taurus | 11:35 | Sagittarius |
| 8:50 | Gemini | | |
| 11:05 | Cancer | | |

### June 1
#### Approximate Time of Birth

| A.M. | | P.M. | |
|------|--|------|--|
| 12:45 | Pisces | 12:05 | Virgo |
| 1:55 | Aries | 2:30 | Libra |
| 3:10 | Taurus | 5:05 | Scorpio |
| 4:50 | Gemini | 7:35 | Sagittarius |
| 7:05 | Cancer | 9:50 | Capricorn |
| 9:30 | Leo | 11:25 | Aquarius |

### April 15
#### Approximate Time of Birth

| A.M. | | P.M. | |
|------|--|------|--|
| 12:30 | Capricorn | 12:30 | Leo |
| 2:55 | Aquarius | 3:05 | Virgo |
| 3:45 | Pisces | 5:30 | Libra |
| 4:55 | Aries | 8:05 | Scorpio |
| 6:10 | Taurus | 10:35 | Sagittarius |
| 7:50 | Gemini | | |
| 10:05 | Cancer | | |

### June 15
#### Approximate Time of Birth

| A.M. | | P.M. | |
|------|--|------|--|
| 12:55 | Aries | 1:30 | Libra |
| 2:10 | Taurus | 4:05 | Scorpio |
| 3:50 | Gemini | 6:35 | Sagittarius |
| 6:05 | Cancer | 8:50 | Capricorn |
| 8:30 | Leo | 10:25 | Aquarius |
| 11:05 | Virgo | 11:45 | Pisces |

### July 1
#### Approximate Time of Birth

| A.M. | | P.M. | |
|------|------|------|------|
| 1:10 | Taurus | 12:30 | Libra |
| 2:50 | Gemini | 3:05 | Scorpio |
| 5:05 | Cancer | 5:35 | Sagittarius |
| 7:30 | Leo | 7:50 | Capricorn |
| 10:05 | Virgo | 9:25 | Aquarius |
| | | 10:45 | Pisces |
| | | 11:55 | Aries |

### September 1
#### Approximate Time of Birth

| A.M. | | P.M. | |
|------|------|------|------|
| 1:05 | Cancer | 1:35 | Sagittarius |
| 3:30 | Leo | 3:50 | Capricorn |
| 6:06 | Virgo | 5:25 | Aquarius |
| 8:30 | Libra | 6:45 | Pisces |
| 11:05 | Scorpio | 7:55 | Aries |
| | | 9:10 | Taurus |
| | | 10:50 | Gemini |

### July 15
#### Approximate Time of Birth

| A.M. | | P.M. | |
|------|------|------|------|
| 12:10 | Taurus | 2:05 | Scorpio |
| 1:50 | Gemini | 4:35 | Sagittarius |
| 4:05 | Cancer | 6:50 | Capricorn |
| 6:30 | Leo | 8:25 | Aquarius |
| 9:05 | Virgo | 9:45 | Pisces |
| 11:30 | Libra | 10:55 | Aries |

### September 15
#### Approximate Time of Birth

| A.M. | | P.M. | |
|------|------|------|------|
| 12:05 | Cancer | 12:35 | Sagittarius |
| 2:30 | Leo | 2:50 | Capricorn |
| 5:05 | Virgo | 4:25 | Aquarius |
| 7:30 | Libra | 5:45 | Pisces |
| 10:05 | Scorpio | 6:55 | Aries |
| | | 8:10 | Taurus |
| | | 9:50 | Gemini |

### August 1
#### Approximate Time of Birth

| A.M. | | P.M. | |
|------|------|------|------|
| 12:50 | Gemini | 1:05 | Scorpio |
| 3:05 | Cancer | 3:35 | Sagittarius |
| 5:30 | Leo | 5:50 | Capricorn |
| 8:05 | Virgo | 7:25 | Aquarius |
| 10:30 | Libra | 8:45 | Pisces |
| | | 9:55 | Aries |
| | | 11:10 | Taurus |

### October 1
#### Approximate Time of Birth

| A.M. | | P.M. | |
|------|------|------|------|
| 1:30 | Leo | 1:50 | Capricorn |
| 4:05 | Virgo | 3:25 | Aquarius |
| 6:30 | Libra | 4:45 | Pisces |
| 9:05 | Scorpio | 5:55 | Aries |
| 11:35 | Sagittarius | 7:10 | Taurus |
| | | 8:50 | Gemini |
| | | 11:05 | Cancer |

### August 15
#### Approximate Time of Birth

| A.M. | | P.M. | |
|------|------|------|------|
| 2:05 | Cancer | 12:05 | Scorpio |
| 4:30 | Leo | 2:35 | Sagittarius |
| 7:05 | Virgo | 4:50 | Capricorn |
| 9:30 | Libra | 6:25 | Aquarius |
| | | 7:45 | Pisces |
| | | 8:55 | Aries |
| | | 10:10 | Taurus |
| | | 11:50 | Gemini |

### October 15
#### Approximate Time of Birth

| A.M. | | P.M. | |
|------|------|------|------|
| 12:30 | Leo | 12:50 | Capricorn |
| 3:05 | Virgo | 2:25 | Aquarius |
| 5:30 | Libra | 3:45 | Pisces |
| 8:05 | Scorpio | 4:55 | Aries |
| 10:35 | Sagittarius | 6:10 | Taurus |
| | | 7:50 | Gemini |
| | | 10:05 | Cancer |

### November 1
#### Approximate Time of Birth

| A.M. | | P.M. | |
|------|------|------|------|
| 2:05 | Virgo | 1:25 | Aquarius |
| 4:30 | Libra | 2:45 | Pisces |
| 7:05 | Scorpio | 3:55 | Aries |
| 9:35 | Sagittarius | 5:10 | Taurus |
| 11:50 | Capricorn | 6:50 | Gemini |
| | | 9:05 | Cancer |
| | | 11:30 | Leo |

### December 1
#### Approximate Time of Birth

| A.M. | | P.M. | |
|------|------|------|------|
| 12:05 | Virgo | 12:45 | Pisces |
| 2:30 | Libra | 1:55 | Aries |
| 5:05 | Scorpio | 3:10 | Taurus |
| 7:35 | Sagittarius | 4:50 | Gemini |
| 9:50 | Capricorn | 7:05 | Cancer |
| 11:25 | Aquarius | 9:30 | Leo |

### November 15
#### Approximate Time of Birth

| A.M. | | P.M. | |
|------|------|------|------|
| 1:05 | Virgo | 12:25 | Aquarius |
| 3:30 | Libra | 1:45 | Pisces |
| 6:06 | Scorpio | 2:55 | Aries |
| 8:35 | Sagittarius | 4:10 | Taurus |
| 10:50 | Capricorn | 5:50 | Gemini |
| | | 8:05 | Cancer |
| | | 10:30 | Leo |

### December 15
#### Approximate Time of Birth

| A.M. | | P.M. | |
|------|------|------|------|
| 1:30 | Libra | 12:55 | Aries |
| 4:05 | Scorpio | 2:10 | Taurus |
| 6:35 | Sagittarius | 3:50 | Gemini |
| 8:50 | Capricorn | 6:06 | Cancer |
| 10:25 | Aquarius | 8:30 | Leo |
| 11:45 | Pisces | 11:05 | Virgo |

# 7

# The Influence of Mercury

In delineating the interpretations for the eight planets in each of the twelve Signs, there will (with the single exception of Mercury—for which we've devised a shortcut) be a table at the end of each chapter showing where the planets were at the time of your birth. With the faster moving planets, Venus and Mars, it may be necessary to know the time of day you were born in order to know *exactly* when the planets changed Signs. However, if you were born one day *after* or *before* the dates given in the tables, you are within the designated Sign(s).

The basic horoscope, again, is a circle divided into twelve equidistant spokes—or a dozen (roughly) equal parts.

This will not be a mathematically *precise* horoscope, but it is an easy beginning—one that will quickly teach you the basics and allow you to refine your chart later on. For purposes of illustration, we'll use the *natural* order of the Zodiac here—with Aries ♈ on the Ascendant (the Vernal or Spring Equinox—about March 21); Cancer ♋ on the Nadir (the Summer Solstice—about June 21); Libra ♎ on the (right) descendant (the Autumn Equinox—approximately September 20); Capricorn ♑ on the Midheaven (Winter Solstice—about December 21).

These are called the Cardinal points of the chart, or the "angles," whether Cardinal Signs occupy these points or not. (If you have Aries ascending, this is what your chart looks like. If Taurus is your Ascendant, begin with *that* Sign on the Eastern or *left* side of the chart, and so on.)

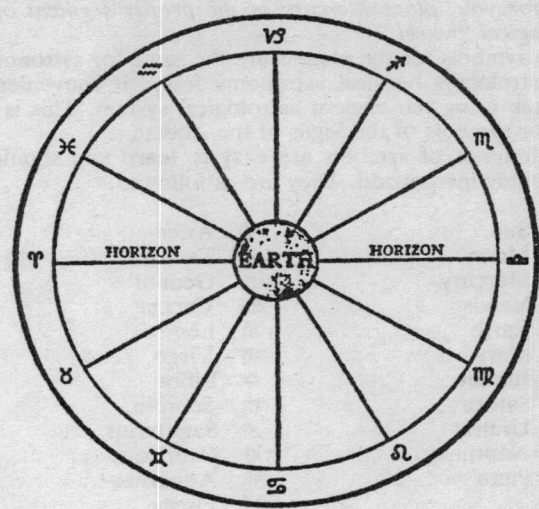

In the short time that it will take you to learn to cast an exact mathematical horoscope, you will include such refinements as the exact degree of the Sign on each house cusp, and the exact degree and minute of celestial arc for every planet. For the moment, the simplest way to know how 75 percent of your chart reads and looks is to put each planet in its correct position by Sign.

From our viewpoint on Earth, Mercury moves faster than any other celestial body except the Moon. Its orbit around the Sun is described once in every 88 days, which means that it would require almost an entire additional book just to list the dates Mercury changed Signs.

There is, however, a shortcut method for you to determine where Mercury was at your birth. This small planet is so close to the Sun that it can only be in one of three Signs. Each Sign is 30 degrees apart, and Mercury is *never* more than 28 degrees from Sol! It *must*, therefore, be either in your Sun Sign or the Sign preceeding or following it.

*By reading all three, you'll quickly get the "feel" of the one that suits you most exactly. This is good basic training in the art of astrological synthesis. Once you've decided which is right for you, place Mercury in the proper segment of the astrological "wheel."*

The symbols for the planets are the same for astronomers *and* astrologers because astronomy found it convenient to continue using the ancient astrological system. This is also true for symbols of the Signs of the Zodiac.

Both series of symbols are easy to learn and should be thoroughly memorized. They are as follows:

| | | | |
|---|---|---|---|
| ☉ | Sun | ♈ | Aries |
| ☽ | Moon | ♉ | Taurus |
| ☿ | Mercury | ♊ | Gemini |
| ♀ | Venus | ♋ | Cancer |
| ⊕ | Earth | ♌ | Leo |
| ♂ | Mars | ♍ | Virgo |
| ♃ | Jupiter | ♎ | Libra |
| ♄ | Saturn | ♏ | Scorpio |
| ♅ | Uranus | ♐ | Sagittarius |
| ♆ | Neptune | ♑ | Capricorn |
| ♇ | Pluto | ♒ | Aquarius |
| | | ♓ | Pisces |

(The *Signs* are inserted in *counterclockwise* direction around the wheel as shown on page 161.)

Although this shortcut method will give you a rudimentary approach to horoscope making the *precision* calculation of your chart would require a series of expensive technical books: (a) A table of houses (b) At least four ephemerides—books of planetary positions from 1890 to 1975 (c) A table of proportional logarithms (d) A book of longitudes and latitudes for the U.S. (e) A book on longitudes and latitudes for the world. By sacrificing 25 percent accuracy you will herein save on all these books.

Until recently the outermost known planet, Pluto, was considered to be as small as the *innermost* known planet, Mercury. Closer observation of Pluto revealed that it is more than four times as large as Earth. Its year amounts only to 248 of our years and its average distance from the Sun is about 3,675,000,000 miles, compared to Earth's 93 million. Light, traveling at 186,000 miles a second, reaches Mercury about two minutes after leaving the Sun. Eight minutes later this same light will illuminate the Earth. Continuing its flight outward from our local star, this light will reach Pluto in eight *hours*. (Four *years* later it reaches the nearest star.)

Speed, smallness and proximity to the Sun are Mercury's chief characteristics—physically, at any rate. The Sun is eight million times larger than Mercury. To the ancient people of the Earth, Mercury was known as Thoth, Hermes, or "The Messenger of the Gods." The symbol of this planet is a young man flying with wings on his heels. He carries a caduceus, an insignia, of olive wood, with a pair of wings at the end and two serpents entwined around the rod. Essentially this is a good representation of the influence of Mercury and of Mercurial-type people, largely Geminians and Virgoans—or those with many planets in these Signs: logic, quality, youthfulness and speed.

Generally speaking, Mercury governs understanding and sight. It rules arms, hands, lungs, the tongue and the nervous system. The influence of Mercury in each of the twelve Signs is as follows:

## MERCURY IN ARIES ☿ ♈

You love literature and literary people; you like to read and write, and will often change your mind about the same situation when seen from a different vantage point, either in time or space. You are generally restless, fiery, impulsive, argumentive and a good debater. Your expressions, either in writing, thought or speech, are fast—*mercurial*. You are eager, earnest and expressive. You are quick to demonstrate your ideas in an interesting, unique, liberal, clever and inventive manner. But you probably realize your lack of the sober, plodding, scientific way of method and order. You are too restless, and liable to skip from one thing to another, unless Mercury is close to being either in Taurus or Pisces.

## MERCURY IN TAURUS ☿ ♉

Although you tend to be somewhat obstinate, you are generally pleasant and easygoing. You possess a highly practical and determined mind, particularly in educational situations or where your interests coincide with the necessity for mental development and training. Generally you have good judgment, a sociable, friendly and affectionate disposition and respect for religion, music, poetry and art. You probably have an excellent memory and can keep plugging determinedly in any kind of mental activity. There are times when you display almost uncontrollable flashes of anger or irritation. You are fond of the opposite sex and of all recreations and pleasure. Although your likes and dislikes are strong and you may be ruled by your own views of things (which tend to remain fixed), you acquire money through an established income and will probably end up with your own good share of material possessions.

## MERCURY IN GEMINI  ☿  ♊

This is a "natural" Sign for Mercury. You probably travel around a lot and find yourself doing a fair amount of studying and reading. You may quickly change from one profession or occupation to another, or else find yourself doing two things at once. You'd probably make a good executive, lawyer or politician. You like to acquire knowledge of any kind. You have an inventive, ingenious, fast-on-the-trigger, clever and resourceful mentality. Generally you tend to be generous and magnanimous, full of good humor and sympathy; and you are unbiased in your attitude toward other people and places. You need to accept things as they are. This is one of the few almost totally unbiased Signs of Mercury.

## MERCURY IN CANCER  ☿  ♋

You have a fine sense of rhythm which expresses itself either physically or mentally. If in the former fashion, you may excel in dancing or athletics; if in the latter, in poetry or music. You are socially disposed, quiet, good-natured and socially graceful. Your world outlook is broad and comprehensive; you understand many things that go on in the world, and this faculty by itself probably makes you rather changeable. You love to travel, especially by water, and could easily gain through this medium. You are inclined to be lucky through members of the maternal side of your family, or inherit from your mother. At any rate, you will gain financially through affairs and occupations associated with property or land. You are discreet, tactful, have a good memory and tend to be diplomatic. Because you are sensitive and impressionable, you are most easily influenced by kindness and consideration.

## MERCURY IN LEO  ☿  ♌

You have a flair for managing, directing or controlling others in communication, health or labor. Chances are you will achieve a responsible, prominent position in one of these areas. You love children, the theater, art and music. In any mental activity you are able to concentrate and persevere—very often to the detriment of your other duties or endeavors. You tend to be self-independent and casual, with a love of pleasure. At the same time, you are basically kind and easygoing—as well as positive and strong-willed. You have an intuitive mind and high ideals, and cannot bring yourself to compromise them. You can be quick-tempered and fiery, confident, determined and ambitious. Generally your mind and willpower are sympathetic, expansive and progressive.

## MERCURY IN VIRGO  ☿  ♍

You tend to be skeptical and critical, with a finely discriminating mind and outlook. Before you are convinced of anything, you must see, know and understand the subject thoroughly. This makes you a good student, writer and detailer. You like math, literature or mental activities that tax your ingenuity, planning and dexterity. You may have innate oratorical skill or ability as a linguist. Diet, hygiene and healing are high on your list of interests. You tend to be serious and quiet and have a great love of studying and memorizing. Basically, you tend to be rather intellectual, but are never showy about it; in fact, you may be known for your reticence. Whatever you learn through your studies you can put to practical everyday use, but you tend to take on too much, to have too many projects going at once. Your achievements, although solid and enduring, probably will not bring widespread publicity or fame. For example, you can master the art of successfully writing about topics that are neglected, overlooked or unpopular—and do this in a practical utilitarian way—but for one reason or another the *sensational* type of success someone else might achieve by doing the same job somehow eludes you.

## MERCURY IN LIBRA  ☿  ♎

In marriage or any other partnership, you tend to have a kind of mental or intellectual comradeship rather than one of an emotional nature. Even so, you may marry someone who is related to you in some way—or who is your social and financial inferior. This position of Mercury is excellent for music, art, poetry, education and intellectual stimulation. You have a finely developed intuitive faculty, and love a good social life, friends, refined pleasures, the theater and children. Whatever sort of educational pursuit you may be engaged in, you work best—even in reading, studying and writing—with someone else. In *partnership*. Association and partnership, either through your own choice or by necessity, is an integral part of your life. You are capable of excellent reasoning and judgment, and love making delicately balanced comparisons. You have a gentle, loving nature, with a refined outlook and a liberal mind.

## MERCURY IN SCORPIO  ☿  ♏

You are resourceful, inventive, secretive and could have a volatile temper. You can follow any kind of pursuit with such intensity and concentration that nothing can elude you. You tend to be both sarcastic and witty, with an excellent command of the language and a highly active mind. You like to solve problems, dig beneath the surface of natural or unnatural mysteries to find the root cause of things. Yet you are obstinate, difficult to convince and exceptionally fond of your own opinions. You can be moved to intense indignation or rage by an injustice, whether it is real or whether you have only imagined it. By the same token, you will plunge into any undertaking or cause you love with tremendous zeal and enthusiasm. You think and act in reckless, forceful and sarcastic ways. You could also be too much a lover of the opposite sex. Your neighbors, relatives and often your friends are a source of friction and trouble. You enjoy pleasure and social activities, love various mystical and occult subjects. You are curious, suspicious and highly critical, yet resourceful and fond of gathering knowledge. You are proud of your shrewd mentality.

## MERCURY IN SAGITTARIUS  ☿  ♐

You are just as active mentally as you are physically (if not more so); you are extremely changeable, and will jump from one thing to another or undertake the study of two different subjects at once. You like science, philosophy and religion, and probably have found yourself with two jobs or occupations at once. Failing that, you tend to change jobs frequently. Even if you have received a good, solid education, the effects will not become evident during your early years; often success comes your way later in life. You will probably travel a lot and take many short trips. These travels will have something to do with your brothers and sisters, writing or education. You tend to be a little too candid, to say exactly what is on your mind. You are often rebellious, independent and impulsive, yet by nature you are sincere, ambitious and far-sighted. You love freedom of thought and freedom of speech and cannot tolerate censorship of any kind. You love nature and appreciate all that is beautiful, as well as being fond of animals and sports, generally. Although you are changeable, you want justice all around, and are philosophical, generous and like to exercise authority.

## MERCURY IN CAPRICORN  ☿  ♑

You are cautious, prudent and painstaking where the development of your mind is involved. You seem to be constantly on the move, industriously pursuing your interests in philosophy, business, science or chemistry. You give the impression of restlessness or discontent with the way things are going, and are likely to be suspicious about the motivations of others. You have an innate curiosity and a natural diplomacy that hides some of your worst faults—mainly a sharply critical attitude—which you are especially careful to conceal. Your penetrating intellect, however critical and changeable, is often tactfully curious about those things that involve your career and ambitions. You are basically conservative, practical and observant. Your general outlook is quite serious and often keenly discriminating toward those who oppose you. Whether you realize it or not, you have the organizational ability of a born executive.

## MERCURY IN AQUARIUS   ☿   ♒

You express your interest in the affairs of others and therefore probably have a long list of friends—not all of whom
are as broad or humanitarian in their outlook as you. Your
high idealism doesn't always influence the less developed
social consciousness of others. In you there is a general
attraction for study, specifically science, invention, sociology or some kind of organizational work. You have excellent powers of reason and concentration for any task at hand.
You have broad humanitarian interests and are undoubtedly
familiar with the great books and writers of the present and
past. You enjoy profound philosophical discussions with intel-
lectuals and people of broad experience. You are truly original
as well as discriminating, and you exercise a keen judgment of
human nature—particularly its frailties. Although your refined
consciousness is broad and you are a deep thinker with
humanitarian ideals, the chances are you may be somewhat
ahead of your contemporaries and they could consider you
eccentric in some way. Your weakness is that you must have
friends and life conditions on your own terms. You become
so involved with the activities of others that you may neglect
your own ambitions, your hopes and dreams for the future. Go
ahead, *be* original, but beware of seeming *too* unorthodox.

## MERCURY IN PISCES   ☿   ♓

You are sympathetic to and understanding of the needs of
others, yet you are liable to use this sympathy as an excuse
or justification for your own lack of confidence. You tend to
feel unworthy, to fear challenge and to shirk responsibility.
These are grave mistakes. Learn to recognize the fact that
your knowledge doesn't necessarily come from books. You
are exceptionally intuitive and psychic. You understand without knowing *why* you do and are therefore inclined to
denigrate your own capabilities and knowledge. You are
interested in hospitals or similar institutions, and have a
good judgment of human nature. You absorb data quickly
and have a retentive memory. You are imaginative, absorbing and impressionable. You love travel by water, and take
great pleasure in studying mystical and occult subjects. Either directly or indirectly through these, you can be of far
greater help to others than to yourself.

# 8

## The Influence of Venus

The second planet out from the Sun is Earth's "sister," Venus. This beautiful, mysterious world was designated by all ancient civilized people as the "goddess of fertility," femininity and beauty. Venus is (interchangeably) Aphrodite. Immanuel Velikovsky, who claims that evolution occurs amid catastrophe, and not gradually, as some believe, claims that less than 4,000 years ago Venus was ejected from the gaseous atmosphere of Jupiter and roamed the solar system as a brilliant comet for several centuries before settling into its present stable planetary orbit. In Greek mythology, Aphrodite (Venus) was born from the head of Zeus (Jupiter).

Until Velikovsky's early predictions about the high temperature of Venus were recently proven by America's space probes, astronomers believed our near neighbor was a cold (probably dead) planet. Although our sister world possesses an opaque atmosphere (and has no natural satellite), it now appears that Life is indeed possible there.

Astrologically, Venus is akin to the Moon in that both influence the emotions, the refined and gentler characteristics of men and women. People born with a well-aspected Venus, especially if it is on or in the Ascendant, as calculated in Chapter 6, are usually graceful, refined, charming and physically attractive.

Both Libra and Taurus are associated with Venus, and her influence is easily detected among people with the Sun, Moon or Ascendant in these Signs. Those with Venus as their planetary "ruler," i.e., those who have Taurus or

Libra as their Ascendant, are noticeably sociable, considerate and kind-hearted.

Still . . . it is possible that the good qualities bestowed by Venus can be offset by powerfully adverse aspects. When this is the case, the native seeks selfish pleasures at the expense of higher interests. He is apt to live on a self-centered, emotional level, seeking cheap amusement, eating and drinking too much, and so on.

The general accent of Venus is on partnership, friendship, harmony and agreeableness. She expresses her influence on your personality and character in good humor, love and generosity. But most of all in harmony.

One of the most important uses of the horoscope, as you will quickly see after making chart comparisons, is the matter of harmony or discord between individuals of the same or opposite sex. Venus figures very prominently in any such comparison. Generally, Venus, Jupiter and the Sun are considered highly beneficial influences, and Saturn and Mars are usually considered as obstacles. The favorable aspects are the sextile (60 degrees or two Signs apart) and the trine (120 degrees or four Signs apart). Depending on the planets involved, the conjunction or no distance between them can be either disadvantageous or beneficial.

If, in the horoscopes of a man and woman, Venus and Mars are in conjunction, they will be strongly attracted physically to each other. This is true for almost *any* aspect between the planet of war and the planet of love—the sextile, trine, and often the opposition or 180 degrees (i.e., planets in opposite Signs). Any of the foregoing harmonious contacts, especially among the Sun, Jupiter, Venus and Mars in the charts of a man and woman are evidence of physical attraction, affection and love. Thus if a man has the Sun in Scorpio and a woman has her Venus on his Sun, a mutually harmonious resonance is automatically in operation between them.

Conversely, if Saturn (the planet of constriction and discipline) in a woman's chart is in conjunction, opposition or square to Mars in a man's chart, the opposite effect will manifest.

You will soon learn the validity of these effects by putting the rules to the ironbound test of crucial experiments. The great Swiss psychriatrist, Carl Jung, examined the horoscopes of his patients as a shortcut aid to diagnosis of root causes of mental and emotional disturbances. He could also predict unerringly either harmony or conflict between any two personalities simply by examining their horoscopes and making critical comparisons.

In order to demonstrate the reliability of astrology as a workable tool in predicting harmony or discord between individuals, a crucial test was set up wherein he examined the planetary patterns in the horoscopes of 483 married couples, 966 individuals in all. For his control group he used 966 horoscopes of people who were not married or even acquainted—a purely random selection. He did not know which was which, except that 1,932 horoscopes were stapled together and mixed so that only by the rules of astrology could he determine the married couples from those who were not married.

Dr. Jung scored an amazing 97 percent in choosing the married couples because of the harmonious contacts among Venus, Jupiter, Mars, the Sun and the Moon. The fact that he chose 6 percent of the unacquainted couples as being married was an interesting error. Two couples of the random group Jung had mistaken as lovers eventually *did* meet and were subsequently married!

At the time of the completion of the experiment, Jung wrote: *"The statistical material shows that a practically as well as a theoretically improbable chance combination occurred, which coincides in the most remarkable way with traditional astrological expectations.*

*"That such a coincidence could occur at all is so improbable and so incredible that nobody could have dared predict anything like it. It really does look as if the statistical material had been manipulated and arranged to give the appearance of a positive result."*

As you set up your own chart, memorize the positions of each planet (i.e. the Sign it is in) and what it means. Later, as you set up the charts of other people—using the same rules—look for the harmonious relationships between the major "benefics," in your chart and that of anyone else you know. If you have Venus in Gemini, you will generally be attracted to mercurial people—writers, speakers, anyone in communications—and especially those who have the Sun, Moon or Mercury in Gemini. Wherever Venus or the Moon are located in your chart, this is where your emotions are most strongly attracted.

You'd hardly expect a (Mars-ruled) warrior or soldier to express the finer, more *harmonious* attributes of Venus. But anyone who has ever studied the astrology of ex-President Dwight Eisenhower knows he was born with the Moon in the blunt, aggressive, militant Sign Scorpio. And yet he expressed that kindly, accommodating, unifying nature which only his Libra Sun could bestow.

Probably the finest illustration of this quality was made by that outspoken Sagittarian statesman and philosopher, Winston Churchill, when he said of Eisenhower:

*"He showed the capacity for making great nations march together more truly united than they have ever been before."*

This is indeed the finest expression of a Venusian nature. Peace, accommodation and harmony. In General Eisenhower's case, it was coupled with and balanced by the iron-hard discipline of the Scorpio Moon.

*At the end of this chapter you will find a listing of Venus' positions from 1890 to 1970.*

## VENUS IN ARIES  ♀  ♈

You are an interesting mixture of harmoniousness and aggressiveness. You can be alternately as meek as a lamb or as mad as a hornet. You are impulsive and ardent in love, strongly attracted to the opposite sex and generous with your affections. You probably have a great attraction for the artistic forms of physical exercise such as ballet, ice and roller skating—possibly gymnastics or even trapeze artistry. You tend to be generous in giving gifts and in the way you spend your money and tip. You are so open-hearted and charitable, your sympathies so easily touched, that you respond instantly to any appeal for help, financial or otherwise. Naturally these characteristics tend to make you very popular. Among your many friends there may be one of the opposite sex to whom you respond quickly and ardently. This could result in a too-early, too-hasty marriage—one that you may later regret because you didn't take time to study all the potential adversities and personality differences. Since you are so romantic (*"in love with love," so to speak*), you may be blinded by your idealism and victimized by an unworthy imitation of the real thing.

## VENUS IN TAURUS ♀ ♉

All things being equal, you will probably inherit money through some sort of legacy, a business partnership or by marriage, although your nuptials could be in for postponement. Like the majority of people, you have no objection to money, but *you* are fond of it because it means ease, comfort and pleasure for you and yours. You like to share these things with your friends. You tend to be more emotionally than mentally inclined. You'd rather *feel* than think, and therefore tend to rely more on your hunches and intuitions. There is some danger here of giving too much of yourself; this may not be in your best interests. Your emotions and feelings are deep and enduring. You tend to be rather fixed and difficult to sway once your mind is made up about something or someone. You are a staunch conservative in your social life and pleasures. No one is likely to find you among the *avant-garde*, either creatively, socially or sexually. The old established, accepted and proven ways seem best. Custom, formality and correct approach are very careful points with you. You are very precise about this. Your love nature is deep, affectionate, faithful and lasting.

## VENUS IN GEMINI ♀ ♊

You are probably known as a gay, romantic traveler with many friends and acquaintances. Your intellect and emotions are refined and clear, but apt to be dualistic. You tend to flirt, to have several love affairs going at once, thus causing jealousy and bringing you a good deal of grief. Yet you bounce right back and start all over again. You are an excellent conversationalist, and have a broad (but often superficial) knowledge of many different subjects. Chances are you make your money from more than one job or occupation—or that you change jobs frequently. Music, art, writing, teaching and drama come easy for you if you have the educational background. Even without extensive formal education, you are able to get ahead in the world because of your original, inventive and intuitive abilities. Venus in Gemini makes you outgoing, friendly, sociable, good-natured, refined—and with a love of games and light mental recreation. This brings you among many people who admire and probably share a deep affection for you. In turn, you flirt and reciprocate this love, and at the same time (paradoxically) insist on faithfulness and loyalty from each of your emotional attachments! Your inconstancy may lead you into marriage with a distant relative, but you're liable to be married two or more times. You derive great pleasure from teaching, writing, speaking and traveling to do these things. If Venus is well-aspected, there is great affection for you among neighbors, co-workers, brothers, sisters and relatives.

## VENUS IN CANCER   ♀ ♋

You have a strong protective desire to shield your loved ones, yet you need the security of being loved *yourself.* Unfortunately, this does not always develop for you. Unseen obstacles are put in the way of marriage, either because of a lack of money, the wrong job or profession or the objections of parents. Still, you are strongly attracted and attached to domesticity and probably have a strong affection for your mother, your home and the feeling of comfort and security it gives you. You are sincere and sentimental, imaginative, kindhearted and responsive to the emotions of others. You have a basically loving nature, receptive and sympathetic. You will probably have several secret love affairs and at least one marriage or alliance with someone considerably older or younger than yourself. This could very likely be with someone involved in mysticism or occultism of some kind. You are basically interested in psychic research, mystical religion and anything of a mysterious nature. You may have certain *psi* talents as well. With Venus in Cancer you tend to develop alliances or friendships with those who are on a lower rung of the social ladder. You may also become involved in an unpopular, obscure or lowly job. Yet, strangely enough, you can profit from any occupation connected with liquids or liquid refreshments. There also is a good indication that you will gain through your parents or profit by dealings in land or houses.

## VENUS IN LEO   ♀ ♌

You are somewhat ostentatious, a natural showman. Chances are good that you will benefit through any occupation connected with the theater, pleasure and amusement—such as singing, music or acting. You tend to dramatize your emotional experiences and to respond impulsively, spontaneously, to whatever gives you positive stimulation. You enjoy basking in the Sun (sometimes the "sun" of your own personality). You will benefit through people of good social connections and through your executive superiors, and achieve much happiness through children and young people. You are able to speculate successfully and to gain through inheritance, investment, and/or royalties. You enjoy friends, entertainment, pleasures and amusements of all kinds, especially where members of the opposite sex are concerned. You are generally kind, charitable, generous and liberal. You are also sincere, sympathetic and a warm lover. Fully appreciating the physical joys of life and often indulging in them, you run the risk of becoming effete through overindulgence. This could mean, if you're not careful, the complete discharge of your emotional batteries, resulting in a jaded insensitivity and disinterest.

## VENUS IN VIRGO ♀ ♍

You need the security of being loved by someone with a high regard for your emotions; you want to feel respected and have your love treated as the delicate and rare thing it is. Unfortunately, however, you are apt to become involved with someone who runs roughshod over your feelings and treats you with either coldness or outright cruelty. You have a deceptively quiet exterior and a deeply sympathetic nature. There is some secret in your love life—possibly an affair with someone who is chronically ill, a doctor, a nurse or someone who works in a subordinate position. In any event, you are likely to experience disappointment in love, or delay in marriage caused by two affairs at once. You should be extremely cautious in financial speculation, but you might profit through joint investment with your marriage or business partner. A basic weakness of Venus in Virgo is a certain lack of discretion. You are liable to become involved romantically with someone of an unsavory reputation, thereby leaving yourself open to scandal. It would be wise to form associations only with people you know to be honest, kind and reliable.

## VENUS IN LIBRA ♀ ♎

You are likely to live in a private world of peace, beauty and harmony. You are susceptible to kindly overtures and will respond with refined affection to those who inspire it. You are highly sympathetic and your love nature is rich, direct and idealistic. You tend to see the good in everything, yet you are sensitive, sometimes disillusioned, and easily hurt. Always, you search for truth, justice and more harmony; you love knowledge and are especially fond of art, music and refined pleasures. All amusements and gay social gatherings are a source of attraction. You prefer associates and friends who have some reputation in the fields of art, music, journalism or who have achieved high academic standards and are socially recognized. Your personality attracts many people because of your innate desire for a well-ordered existence, for harmony and peace again. Venus in Libra is an excellent position. It promises many friends, popularity, a good marriage and children who are musically or artistically talented. Partnerships and marriage are fortunate for you, and there is an excellent chance you will gain materially through others, as well as through the application of your own talents.

## VENUS IN SCORPIO ♀ ♏

Yours is an intense, possessive, often jealous love nature. You are highly demonstrative and a volatile lover. Your passions may rule you rather than vice versa. You love luxury, and delight in pleasures of a sensational nature. Although you are powerfully attracted to the opposite sex, there is the strong likelihood of interminable delays in love, courtship and marriage. And there will be enormous difficulties to overcome with your marriage partner; disagreeable fights, jealousy, vindictiveness, and the possible death of your spouse. You like to travel, to speculate, even to scheme over ways you can capitalize on marriage or alliances with members of the opposite sex. You have a tendency to make friends with those of an antisocial nature or even those who have criminal tendencies—or with those whose interests are occult or mystical. You are generally a free and lavish spender, generous with those whose company you enjoy. You are likely to earn your living (in one way or another) through those things associated with the water Signs, Cancer, Scorpio and Pisces. Although there will be great delays in your profiting through a will, legacy, marriage or partnership, you will eventually reap some sort of financial reward from the deceased. Only through control of your intense emotions can you avoid many of the unpleasant experiences in life.

## VENUS IN SAGITTARIUS  ♀  ♐

You love your personal freedom and independence, and want above all to travel and explore exotic places; you love the unobtainable and could cause yourself a lot of unhappiness thereby. You tend to be ambiguous in your affections— loving two or more members of the opposite sex at the same time. You are not, however, maliciously disloyal. It is simply that you love romance in faraway places. Generally your nature is refined, altruistic, generous, outgoing, imaginative, gay and lighthearted. You may have an income from two different sources, possibly through writing, publishing, or traveling as well as from religious or philosophical interests. You are attracted to outdoor sports, long voyages, animals (especially horses), art and natural beauty. Because of your susceptibility to the opposite sex, you could be attracted to and involved in two or more marriages. One of these will be to someone from a foreign country or at a great distance from your home. This will, in these times, necessitate a great deal of long-distance telephoning and voluminous correspondence. Your friends will be people of importance, power and/or good social standing. Your involvements and adventures are usually a result of blindly following the dictates of your emotions. Venus in Sagittarius makes you impressionable, far-sighted, generous, prophetic and loyal in your intentions if not in actual practice. You are inclined toward literary, philosophical, benevolent and spiritual development.

## VENUS IN CAPRICORN  ♀  ♑

In affairs of the heart you are very careful of appearances or how things might affect your social status or honor. Although you are prudent, cautious and diplomatic, you are also inclined to marry for social or business considerations rather than to follow the dictates of your finer emotions. This is bound to cause coldness or a lack of interest in your spouse, who is likely to be either wealthy or from a different strata of social life. At any rate, this partner is or will be very discriminating, dour and serious. There may be a wide difference in your ages. Yet you are adaptable to adversities and tend to look on them as challenges. You may have a tendency to seem calculating, cold and indifferent yourself, yet by sheer grit, enterprise, willpower and hard work you will manage to gain the respect of older people and your employer or supervisor. It is almost certain that you'll be elevated to a position of responsibility and entrusted with authority. You will profit by your popularity among business and social acquaintances, make many friends in important positions, and realize many advantages, including career advancement, through them. You are likely to travel in foreign countries and to inherit valuable real estate.

## VENUS IN AQUARIUS ♀ ♒

This position of Venus indicates that most of your hopes, dreams, wishes and aspirations will eventually be fulfilled. In love you are earnest, sincere and faithful, yet you will, at one time or another, find yourself involved in secret affairs. You may either marry or remarry in middle or later life. You will experience some bizarre, sudden, strange and unexpected changes in love affairs. One of these will be with someone of an entirely different background—one who is eccentric in the extreme. The person you marry will be of a different age. You are entirely capable of having purely platonic friendships with the opposite sex without romantic involvement, but this is not recommended. You enjoy refined amusements, cultural pursuits and philosophical as well as intellectual stimulation. Although your outlook tends to be candid and sincere, you are likely to keep many of your opinions to yourself. You make friends easily—even with total strangers—and are able to enjoy a wide spectrum of friends, both from the top *and* the bottom of the social stratum. You have a vast capacity for the enjoyment of social life and other pleasures. You are so outgoing, broad and altruistic in your viewpoint that you attract many people who want something from you, but who refuse to give of themselves in turn.

## VENUS IN PISCES ♀ ♓

You are one of those who, fortunately or otherwise, have such a sympathetic nature that you can instantly feel and understand the sufferings of others. You tend to be rather careless or even fickle in romance. As a result, you are likely to be married more than once or to form some kind of secret alliance or affair with someone who isn't quite good enough for you. If there is a square or opposition aspect to Venus from other planets, you'll have a difficult time acquiring money—or you may lose money in a swindle, fraud or deception which you might cause yourself. Yet you are basically kindhearted and deeply sympathetic, with a tendency to help the disadvantaged and downtrodden—even if it means assisting by volunteer work in some sort of institution or hospital. You are psychic, sensitive, idealistic and highly emotional. Anywhere there is suffering or injustice, you are likely to volunteer assistance. Although you may not be lucky in love, you accept your lot in life with resignation and gain what pleasure you can from secret affairs.

## TO FIND THE POSITION OF VENUS AT YOUR BIRTH

| 1890 | Date | Zodiacal Sign |
|------|------|---------------|
| Jan. | 1 | Sagittarius |
| Jan. | 2 to Jan. 25 | Capricorn |
| Jan. | 26 to Feb. 18 | Aquarius |
| Feb. | 19 to Mar. 14 | Pisces |
| Mar. | 15 to Apr. 7 | Aries |
| Apr. | 8 to May 1 | Taurus |
| May | 2 to May 26 | Gemini |
| May | 27 to June 20 | Cancer |
| June | 21 to July 15 | Leo |
| July | 16 to Aug. 10 | Virgo |
| Aug. | 11 to Sept. 6 | Libra |
| Sept. | 7 to Oct. 7 | Scorpio |
| Oct. | 28 to Dec. 31 | Sagittarius |

| 1891 | Date | Zodiacal Sign |
|------|------|---------------|
| Jan. | 1 to Feb. 5 | Sagittarius |
| Feb. | 6 to Mar. 5 | Capricorn |
| Mar. | 6 to Apr. 1 | Aquarius |
| Apr. | 2 to Apr. 26 | Pisces |
| Apr. | 27 to May 22 | Aries |
| May | 23 to June 16 | Taurus |
| June | 17 to July 10 | Gemini |
| July 11 | to Aug. 4 | Cancer |
| Aug. | 5 to Aug. 28 | Leo |
| Aug. | 29 to Sept. 21 | Virgo |
| Sept. | 22 to Oct. 15 | Libra |
| Oct. | 16 to Nov. 8 | Scorpio |
| Nov. | 9 to Dec. 2 | Sagittarius |
| Dec. | 3 to Dec. 26 | Capricorn |
| Dec. | 27 to Dec. 31 | Aquarius |

| 1892 | Date | Zodiacal Sign |
|------|------|---------------|
| Jan. | 1 to Jan. 20 | Aquarius |
| Jan. | 21 to Feb. 13 | Pisces |
| Feb. | 14 to Mar. 9 | Aries |
| Mar. | 10 to Apr. 4 | Taurus |
| Apr. | 5 to May 4 | Gemini |
| May | 5 to Sept. 7 | Cancer |
| Sept. | 8 to Oct. 7 | Leo |
| Oct. | 8 to Nov. 2 | Virgo |
| Nov. | 3 to Nov. 27 | Libra |
| Nov. | 28 to Dec. 22 | Scorpio |
| Dec. | 23 to Dec. 31 | Sagittarius |

### 1893

| | | |
|------|------|---------------|
| Jan. | 1 to Jan. 15 | Sagittarius |
| Jan. | 16 to Feb 8 | Capricorn |
| Feb. | 9 to Mar. 4 | Aquarius |
| Mar. | 5 to Mar. 28 | Pisces |
| Mar. | 29 to Apr. 22 | Aries |
| Apr. | 23 to May 16 | Taurus |
| May | 17 to June 9 | Gemini |
| June | 10 to July 4 | Cancer |
| July | 5 to July 28 | Leo |
| July | 29 to Aug. 22 | Virgo |
| Aug. | 23 to Sept. 16 | Libra |
| Sept. | 17 to Oct. 11 | Scorpio |
| Oct. | 12 to Nov. 6 | Sagittarius |
| Nov. | 7 to Dec. 4 | Capricorn |
| Dec. | 5 to Dec. 31 | Aquarius |

### 1894

| | | |
|------|------|---------------|
| Jan. | 1 to Jan. 8 | Aquarius |
| Jan. | 9 to Feb. 12 | Pisces |
| Feb. | 13 to Apr. 2 | Aquarius |
| Apr. | 3 to May 5 | Pisces |
| May | 6 to June 2 | Aries |
| June | 3 to June 29 | Taurus |
| June | 30 to July 24 | Gemini |
| July | 25 to Aug. 18 | Cancer |
| Aug. | 19 to Sept. 12 | Leo |
| Sept. | 13 to Oct. 6 | Virgo |
| Oct. | 7 to Oct. 30 | Libra |
| Oct. | 31 to Nov. 23 | Scorpio |
| Nov. | 24 to Dec. 17 | Sagittarius |
| Dec. | 18 to Dec. 31 | Capricorn |

| 1895 | Date | Zodiacal Sign |
|------|------|---------------|
| Jan. | 1 to Jan. 10 | Capricorn |
| Jan. | 11 to Feb. 3 | Aquarius |
| Feb. | 4 to Feb. 27 | Pisces |
| Feb. | 28 to Mar. 23 | Aries |
| Mar. | 24 to Apr. 17 | Taurus |
| Apr. | 18 to May 12 | Gemini |
| May | 13 to June 7 | Cancer |
| June | 8 to July 6 | Leo |
| July | 7 to Aug. 13 | Virgo |
| Aug. | 14 to Sept. 12 | Libra |
| Sept. | 13 to Nov. 6 | Virgo |
| Nov. | 7 to Dec. 8 | Libra |
| Dec. | 9 to Dec. 31 | Scorpio |

### 1896

| | | |
|------|------|---------------|
| Jan. | 1 to Jan. 3 | Scorpio |
| Jan. | 4 to Jan. 29 | Sagittarius |
| Jan. | 30 to Feb. 23 | Capricorn |
| Feb. | 24 to Mar. 18 | Aquarius |
| Mar. | 19 to Apr. 12 | Pisces |
| Apr. | 13 to May 6 | Aries |
| May | 7 to May 31 | Taurus |
| June | 1 to June 24 | Gemini |
| June | 25 to July 19 | Cancer |
| July | 20 to Aug. 13 | Leo |
| Aug. | 14 to Sept. 5 | Virgo |
| Sept. | 6 to Sept. 29 | Libra |
| Sept. | 30 to Oct. 24 | Scorpio |
| Oct. | 25 to Nov. 18 | Sagittarius |
| Nov. | 19 to Dec. 13 | Capricorn |
| Dec. | 14 to Dec. 31 | Aquarius |

### 1897

| | | |
|------|------|---------------|
| Jan. | 1 to Jan. 6 | Aquarius |
| Jan. | 7 to Feb. 1 | Pisces |
| Feb. | 2 to Mar. 4 | Aries |
| Mar. | 5 to July 7 | Taurus |
| July | 8 to Aug. 5 | Gemini |
| Aug. | 6 to Aug. 31 | Cancer |
| Sept. | 1 to Sept. 26 | Leo |
| Sept. | 27 to Oct. 20 | Virgo |
| Oct. | 21 to Nov. 13 | Libra |
| Nov. | 14 to Dec. 7 | Scorpio |
| Dec. | 8 to Dec. 31 | Sagittarius |

*1898* Use table for *1890* and subtract one day from the given
       dates. In other words, Venus entered Capricorn on January 1
       instead of January 2.
*1899* Use list for *1891* and subtract one day from the given dates.
*1900* Use list for *1892* and subtract one day from the given dates.
*1901* Use list for *1893* and subtract one day from the given dates.
*1902* Use list for *1894* and subtract one day from the given dates.
*1903* Use list for *1895* and subtract one day from the given dates.
*1904* Use list for *1896* and subtract one day from the given dates.
*1905* Use list for *1897* and subtract one day from the given dates.
*1906* Use list for *1890*.
*1907* Use list for *1891*.
*1908* Use list for *1892*.
*1909* Use list for *1893*.
*1910* Use list for *1894*.
*1911* Use list for *1895*.
*1912* Use list for *1896*.
*1913* Use list for *1897*.
*1914* Use list for *1890* and subtract one day from the given dates.
*1915* Use list for *1891* and subtract one day from the given dates.
*1916* Use list for *1892* and subtract one day from the given dates.
*1917* Use list for *1893* and subtract one day from the given dates.
*1918* Use list for *1894* and subtract one day from the given dates.
*1919* Use list for *1895* and subtract one day from the given dates.
*1920* Use list for *1896* and subtract one day from the given dates.
*1921* Use list for *1897* and subtract one day from the given dates.
*1922* Use list for *1890* and subtract one day from the given dates.
*1923* Use list for *1891* and subtract one day from the given dates.
*1924* Use list for *1892* and subtract one day from the given dates.
*1925* Use list for *1893* and subtract one day from the given dates.
*1926* Use list for *1894* and subtract one day from the given dates.
*1927* Use list for *1895* and subtract one day from the given dates.
*1928* Use list for *1896* and subtract one day from the given dates.
*1929* Use list for *1897* and subtract one day from the given dates.
*1930* Use list for *1890* and subtract two days from the given dates.
*1931* Use list for *1891* and subtract two days from the given dates.
*1932* Use list for *1892* and subtract two days from the given dates.
*1933* Use list for *1893* and subtract two days from the given dates.
*1934* Use list for *1894* and subtract two days from the given dates.
*1935* Use list for *1895* and subtract two days from the given dates.
*1936* Use list for *1896* and subtract two days from the given dates.
*1937* Use list for *1897* and subtract two days from the given dates.
*1938* Use list for *1890* and subtract three days from the given dates.
*1939* Use list for *1891* and subtract three days from the given dates.
*1940* Use list for *1892* and subtract three days from the given dates.
*1941* Use list for *1893* and subtract three days from the given dates.
*1942* Use list for *1894* and subtract three days from the given dates.

*1943* Use list for *1895* and subtract three days from the given dates.
*1944* Use list for *1896* and subtract three days from the given dates.
*1945* Use list for *1897* and subtract three days from the given dates.
*1946* Use list for *1890* and subtract three days from the given dates.
*1947* Use list for *1891* and subtract three days from the given dates.
*1948* Use list for *1892* and subtract three days from the given dates.
*1949* Use list for *1893* and subtract three days from the given dates.
*1950* Use list for *1894* and subtract three days from the given dates.
*1951* Use list for *1895* and subtract three days from the given dates.
*1952* Use list for *1896* and subtract three days from the given dates.
*1953* Use list for *1897* and subtract three days from the given dates.
*1954* Use list for *1890* and subtract four days from the given dates.
*1955* Use list for *1891* and subtract four days from the given dates.
*1956* Use list for *1892* and subtract four days from the given dates.
*1957* Use list for *1893* and subtract four days from the given dates.
*1958* Use list for *1894* and subtract four days from the given dates.
*1959* Use list for *1895* and subtract four days from the given dates.
*1960* Use list for *1896* and subtract four days from the given dates.
*1961* Use list for *1897* and subtract four days from the given dates.
*1962* Use list for *1890* and subtract four days from the given dates.
*1963* Use list for *1891* and subtract four days from the given dates.
*1964* Use list for *1892* and subtract four days from the given dates.
*1965* Use list for *1893* and subtract four days from the given dates.
*1966* Use list for *1894* and subtract four days from the given dates.
*1967* Use list for *1895* and subtract four days from the given dates.
*1968* Use list for *1896* and subtract four days from the given dates.
*1969* Use list for *1897* and subtract four days from the given dates.
*1970* Use list for *1890* and subtract five days from the given date.

| *1971* | Date | Zodiacal Sign | *1972* | Date | Zodiacal Sign |
|--------|------|---------------|--------|------|---------------|
| Jan. | 1 to Jan 7. | Scorpio | Jan. | 1 to Jan. 16 | Aquarius |
| Jan. | 8 to Feb. 5 | Sagittarius | Jan. | 17 to Feb. 10 | Pisces |
| Feb. | 6 to Mar. 4 | Capricorn | Feb. | 11 to Mar. 7 | Aries |
| Mar. | 5 to Mar. 29 | Aquarius | Mar. | 8 to Apr. 3 | Taurus |
| Mar. | 30 to Apr. 23 | Pisces | Apr. | 4 to May 10 | Gemini |
| Apr. | 24 to May 18 | Aries | May | 11 to June 11 | Cancer |
| May | 19 to June 12 | Taurus | June | 12 to Aug. 6 | Gemini |
| June | 13 to July 6 | Gemini | Aug. | 7 to Sept. 7 | Cancer |
| July | 7 to July 31 | Cancer | Sept. | 8 to Oct. 5 | Leo |
| Aug. | 1 to Aug. 24 | Leo | Oct. | 6 to Oct. 30 | Virgo |
| Aug. | 25 to Sept. 17 | Virgo | Oct. | 31 to Nov. 24 | Libra |
| Sept. | 18 to Oct. 11 | Libra | Nov. | 25 to Dec. 18 | Scorpio |
| Oct. | 12 to Nov. 5 | Scorpio | Dec. | 19 to Dec. 31 | Sagittarius |
| Nov. | 6 to Nov. 29 | Sagittarius | | | |
| Nov. | 30 to Dec. 23 | Capricorn | | | |
| Dec. | 24 to Dec. 31 | Aquarius | | | |

| 1973 | Date | Zodiacal Sign |
|------|------|---------------|
| Jan. | 1 to Jan. 11 | Sagittarius |
| Jan. | 12 to Feb. 4 | Capricorn |
| Feb. | 5 to Feb. 28 | Aquarius |
| Mar. | 1 to Mar. 24 | Pisces |
| Mar. | 25 to Apr. 18 | Aries |
| Apr. | 19 to May 12 | Taurus |
| May | 13 to June 5 | Gemini |
| June | 6 to June 30 | Cancer |
| July | 1 to July 25 | Leo |
| July | 26 to Aug. 19 | Virgo |
| Aug. | 20 to Sept. 14 | Libra |
| Sept. | 15 to Oct. 9 | Scorpio |
| Oct. | 10 to Nov. 5 | Sagittarius |
| Nov. | 6 to Dec. 7 | Capricorn |
| Dec. | 8 to Dec. 31 | Aquarius |

**1974**

| Jan. | 1 to Jan. 29 | Aquarius |
|------|------|----------|
| Jan. | 30 to Feb. 28 | Capricorn |
| Mar. | 1 to Apr. 6 | Aquarius |
| Apr. | 7 to May 4 | Pisces |
| May | 5 to May 31 | Aries |
| June | 1 to June 25 | Taurus |
| June | 26 to July 21 | Gemini |
| July | 22 to Aug. 14 | Cancer |
| Aug. | 15 to Sept. 8 | Leo |
| Sept. | 9 to Oct. 2 | Virgo |
| Oct. | 3 to Oct. 26 | Libra |
| Oct. | 27 to Nov. 19 | Scorpio |
| Nov. | 20 to Dec. 13 | Sagittarius |
| Dec. | 14 to Dec. 31 | Capricorn |

**1975**

| Jan. | 1 to Jan. 6 | Capricorn |
|------|------|----------|
| Jan. | 7 to Jan. 30 | Aquarius |
| Jan. | 31 to Feb. 23 | Pisces |
| Feb. | 24 to Mar. 19 | Aries |
| Mar. | 20 to Apr. 13 | Taurus |
| Apr. | 14 to May 9 | Gemini |
| May | 10 to June 6 | Cancer |
| June | 7 to July 9 | Leo |
| July | 10 to Sept. 2 | Virgo |
| Sept. | 3 to Oct. 4 | Leo |
| Oct. | 5 to Nov. 9 | Virgo |
| Nov. | 10 to Dec. 7 | Libra |
| Dec. | 8 to Dec. 31 | Scorpio |

| 1976 | Date | Zodiacal Sign |
|------|------|---------------|
| Jan. | 1 to Jan. 2 | Virgo |
| Jan. | 2 to Jan. 26 | Sagittarius |
| Jan. | 27 to Feb. 19 | Capricorn |
| Feb. | 20 to Mar. 15 | Aquarius |
| Mar. | 16 to Apr. 8 | Pisces |
| Apr. | 9 to May 2 | Aries |
| May | 3 to May 26 | Taurus |
| May | 27 to June 20 | Gemini |
| June | 21 to July 14 | Cancer |
| July | 15 to Aug. 8 | Leo |
| Aug. | 9 to Sept. 1 | Virgo |
| Sept. | 2 to Sept. 26 | Libra |
| Sept. | 27 to Oct. 20 | Scorpio |
| Oct. | 21 to Nov. 14 | Sagittarius |
| Nov. | 15 to Dec. 9 | Capricorn |
| Dec. | 10 to Dec. 31 | Aquarius |

**1977**

| Jan. | 1 to Jan. 4 | Aquarius |
|------|------|----------|
| Jan. | 5 to Feb. 2 | Pisces |
| Feb. | 3 to June 6 | Aries |
| June | 7 to July 6 | Taurus |
| July | 7 to Aug. 2 | Gemini |
| Aug. | 3 to Aug. 28 | Cancer |
| Aug. | 29 to Sept. 22 | Leo |
| Sept. | 23 to Oct. 17 | Libra |
| Oct. | 18 to Nov. 10 | Virgo |
| Nov. | 11 to Dec. 4 | Scorpio |
| Dec. | 5 to Dec. 27 | Sagittarius |
| Dec. | 27 to Dec. 31 | Capricorn |

**1978**

| Jan. | 1 to Jan. 20 | Capricorn |
|------|------|----------|
| Jan. | 21 to Feb. 13 | Aquarius |
| Feb. | 14 to Mar. 9 | Pisces |
| Mar. | 10 to Apr. 2 | Aries |
| Apr. | 3 to Apr. 27 | Taurus |
| Apr. | 28 to May 22 | Gemini |
| May | 23 to June 16 | Cancer |
| June | 17 to July 12 | Leo |
| July | 13 to Aug. 8 | Virgo |
| Aug. | 9 to Sept. 7 | Libra |
| Sept. | 8 to Dec. 31 | Scorpio |

| 1979 | Date | Zodiacal Sign |
|---|---|---|
| Jan. | 1 to Jan. 7 | Scorpio |
| Jan. | 8 to Feb. 5 | Sagittarius |
| Feb. | 6 to Mar. 3 | Capricorn |
| Mar. | 4 to Mar. 29 | Aquarius |
| Mar. | 30 to Apr. 23 | Pisces |
| Apr. | 24 to May 18 | Aries |
| May | 19 to June 11 | Taurus |
| June | 12 to July 6 | Gemini |
| July | 7 to July 30 | Cancer |
| July | 31 to Aug. 24 | Leo |
| Aug. | 25 to Sept. 17 | Virgo |
| Sept. | 18 to Oct. 11 | Libra |
| Oct. | 12 to Nov. 4 | Scorpio |
| Nov. | 5 to Nov. 28 | Sagittarius |
| Nov. | 29 to Dec. 22 | Capricorn |
| Dec. | 23 to Dec. 31 | Aquarius |

| 1980 | | |
|---|---|---|
| Jan. | 1 to Jan. 16 | Aquarius |
| Jan. | 17 to Feb. 9 | Pisces |
| Feb. | 10 to Mar. 6 | Aries |
| Mar. | 7 to Apr. 3 | Taurus |
| Apr. | 4 to May 12 | Gemini |
| May | 13 to June 5 | Cancer |
| June | 6 to Aug. 6 | Gemini |
| Aug. | 7 to Sept. 7 | Cancer |
| Sept. | 8 to Oct. 4 | Leo |
| Oct. | 5 to Oct. 30 | Virgo |
| Oct. | 31 to Nov. 24 | Libra |
| Nov. | 25 to Dec. 18 | Scorpio |
| Dec. | 19 to Dec. 31 | Sagittarius |

| 1981 | | |
|---|---|---|
| Jan. | 1 to Jan. 11 | Sagittarius |
| Jan. | 12 to Feb. 4 | Capricorn |
| Feb. | 5 to Feb. 28 | Aquarius |
| Mar. | 1 to Mar. 24 | Pisces |
| Mar. | 25 to Apr. 17 | Aries |
| Apr. | 18 to May 11 | Taurus |
| May | 12 to June 6 | Gemini |
| June | 7 to June 30 | Cancer |
| July | 1 to July 24 | Leo |
| July | 25 to Aug. 18 | Virgo |
| Aug. | 19 to Sept. 12 | Libra |
| Sept. | 13 to Oct. 8 | Scorpio |
| Oct. | 9 to Nov. 5 | Sagittarius |
| Nov. | 6 to Dec. 7 | Capricorn |
| Dec. | 8 to Dec. 31 | Aquarius |

| 1982 | Date | Zodiacal Sign |
|---|---|---|
| Jan. | 1 to Jan. 22 | Aquarius |
| Jan. | 23 to May 2 | Capricorn |
| May | 3 to Apr. 6 | Aquarius |
| Apr. | 7 to May 4 | Pisces |
| May | 5 to May 30 | Aries |
| May | 31 to June 25 | Taurus |
| June | 26 to July 20 | Gemini |
| July | 21 to Aug. 14 | Cancer |
| Aug. | 15 to Sept. 7 | Leo |
| Sept. | 8 to Oct. 2 | Virgo |
| Oct. | 3 to Oct. 26 | Libra |
| Oct. | 27 to Nov. 18 | Scorpio |
| Nov. | 19 to Dec. 12 | Sagittarius |
| Dec. | 13 to Dec. 31 | Capricorn |

| 1983 | | |
|---|---|---|
| Jan. | 1 to Jan. 5 | Capricorn |
| Jan. | 6 to Jan. 29 | Aquarius |
| Jan. | 30 to Feb. 22 | Pisces |
| Feb. | 23 to Mar. 19 | Aries |
| Mar. | 20 to Apr. 13 | Taurus |
| Apr. | 14 to May 9 | Gemini |
| May | 10 to June 6 | Cancer |
| June | 7 to July 10 | Leo |
| July | 11 to Aug. 28 | Virgo |
| Aug. | 29 to Oct. 5 | Leo |
| Oct. | 6 to Nov. 9 | Virgo |
| Nov. | 10 to Dec. 6 | Libra |
| Dec. | 7 to Dec. 31 | Scorpio |

| 1984 | | |
|---|---|---|
| Jan. | 1 | Scorpio |
| Jan. | 2 to Jan. 25 | Sagittarius |
| Jan. | 26 to Feb. 19 | Capricorn |
| Feb. | 20 to Mar. 14 | Aquarius |
| Mar. | 15 to Apr. 7 | Pisces |
| Apr. | 8 to May 2 | Aries |
| May | 3 to May 26 | Taurus |
| May | 27 to June 20 | Gemini |
| June | 21 to July 14 | Cancer |
| July | 15 to Aug. 7 | Leo |
| Aug. | 8 to Sept. 1 | Virgo |
| Sept. | 2 to Sept. 24 | Libra |
| Sept. | 25 to Oct. 20 | Scorpio |
| Oct. | 21 to Nov. 15 | Sagittarius |
| Nov. | 16 to Dec. 9 | Capricorn |
| Dec. | 10 to Dec. 21 | Aquarius |

| 1985 | Date | Zodiacal Sign |
|------|------|---------------|
| Jan. | 1 to Jan. 4 | Aquarius |
| Jan. | 4 to Feb. 2 | Pisces |
| Feb. | 3 to June 6 | Aries |
| June | 7 to July 6 | Taurus |
| July | 7 to Sept. 2 | Gemini |
| Sept. | 3 to Sept. 28 | Cancer |
| Sept. | 29 to Aug. 22 | Leo |
| Aug. | 23 to Nov. 9 | Libra |
| Nov. | 10 to Dec. 3 | Scorpio |
| Dec. | 4 to Dec. 27 | Sagittarius |
| Dec. | 28 to Dec. 31 | Capricorn |

| 1986 | Date | Zodiacal Sign |
|------|------|---------------|
| Jan. | 1 to Jan. 15 | Capricorn |
| Jan. | 16 to Feb. 9 | Aquarius |
| Feb. | 10 to May 9 | Pisces |
| May | 10 to Apr. 2 | Aries |
| Apr. | 3 to Apr. 26 | Taurus |
| Apr. | 27 to May 21 | Gemini |
| May | 22 to June 15 | Cancer |
| June | 16 to July 11 | Leo |
| July | 12 to Aug. 7 | Virgo |
| Aug. | 8 to Sept. 7 | Libra |
| Sept. | 8 to Dec. 31 | Scorpio |

| 1987 | Date | Zodiacal Sign |
|------|------|---------------|
| Jan. | 1 to Jan. 7 | Scorpio |
| Jan. | 8 to Feb. 4 | Sagittarius |
| Feb. | 5 to May 3 | Capricorn |
| May | 4 to May 28 | Aquarius |
| May | 29 to Apr. 22 | Pisces |
| Apr. | 23 to May 17 | Aries |
| May | 18 to June 11 | Taurus |
| June | 12 to July 5 | Gemini |
| July | 6 to July 30 | Cancer |
| July | 31 to Aug. 23 | Leo |
| Aug. | 24 to Oct. 10 | Libra |
| Oct. | 11 to Nov. 3 | Scorpio |
| Nov. | 4 to Nov. 28 | Sagittarius |
| Nov. | 29 to Dec. 22 | Capricorn |
| Dec. | 23 to Dec. 31 | Aquarius |

| 1988 | Date | Zodiacal Sign |
|------|------|---------------|
| Jan. | 1 to Jan. 15 | Aquarius |
| Jan. | 16 to Feb. 9 | Pisces |
| Feb. | 10 to May 6 | Aries |
| May | 7 to Apr. 4 | Taurus |
| Apr. | 5 to May 17 | Gemini |
| May | 18 to May 28 | Cancer |
| May | 29 to Aug. 6 | Gemini |
| Aug. | 7 to Sept. 7 | Cancer |
| Sept. | 8 to Oct. 4 | Leo |
| Oct. | 5 to Oct. 29 | Virgo |
| Oct. | 30 to Nov. 23 | Libra |
| Nov. | 24 to Dec. 17 | Scorpio |
| Dec. | 18 to Dec. 31 | Sagittarius |

| 1989 | Date | Zodiacal Sign |
|------|------|---------------|
| Jan. | 1 to Jan. 10 | Sagittarius |
| Jan. | 11 to Feb. 3 | Capricorn |
| Feb. | 4 to Feb. 27 | Aquarius |
| May | 1 to May 23 | Pisces |
| May | 24 to Apr. 16 | Aries |
| Apr. | 17 to May 11 | Taurus |
| May | 12 to June 4 | Gemini |
| June | 5 to June 29 | Cancer |
| June | 30 to July 25 | Leo |
| July | 26 to Aug. 18 | Virgo |
| Aug. | 19 to Sept. 12 | Libra |
| Sept. | 13 to Oct. 8 | Scorpio |
| Oct. | 9 to Nov. 5 | Sagittarius |
| Nov. | 6 to Dec. 10 | Capricorn |
| Dec. | 10 to Dec. 31 | Aquarius |

| 1990 | Date | Zodiacal Sign |
|------|------|---------------|
| Jan. | 1 to Jan. 16 | Aquarius |
| Jan. | 17 to May 3 | Capricorn |
| May | 4 to Apr. 6 | Aquarius |
| Apr. | 7 to May 4 | Pisces |
| May | 5 to May 30 | Aries |
| May | 31 to June 25 | Taurus |
| June | 26 to July 20 | Gemini |
| July | 21 to Aug. 13 | Cancer |
| Aug. | 14 to Sept. 7 | Leo |
| Sept. | 8 to Oct. 2 | Virgo |
| Oct. | 3 to Oct. 26 | Libra |
| Oct. | 27 to Nov. 18 | Scorpio |
| Nov. | 19 to Dec. 12 | Sagittarius |
| Dec. | 13 to Dec. 31 | Capricorn |

**9**

## The Influence of Mars

The Red Planet is probably the source of more speculation among Terrestrial scientists than any other Solarian world. It is the first post-lunar body on which our Apollo space-ships are scheduled to land. Its two mysterious "moons," Phobos and Diemos, are believed by many of our finest astronomers and planetary physicists—including the greatest living cosmologist, Dr. Fred Hoyle of Cambridge, as well as Russia's illustrious planetary physicist, Dr. I. S. Shklovsky—to be artificial "space cities,"* Probably the most arresting fact about these two "steeds" of Mars is that *ancient* astrologers knew of their existence, sizes, speeds and altitudes from the Red Planet. In fact, modern astronomers gave them their ancient names.

In astrology, Mars symbolizes energy, action, heat, aggression and power. Its symbol, used by astronomers and astrologers alike, is a glyph (a symbolic figure) for a shield and a spear (♂). Psychologists and doctors recognize the masculinity of Mars: they use the *same* symbol to denote the male—and Venus' symbol (♀) to denote the female.

Mars is associated with and rules two Signs, Aries and Scorpio. Since the discovery of Pluto, however, some astrologers have designated "the god of the underworld," Pluto, as the sole ruler of Scorpio.

As with the remarkably accurate early predictions he made about Venus, Dr. Immanuel Velikovsky of *Worlds in Collision* fame was again vindicated by the recently telemetered pic-

*See *Astrology: The Space-Age Science*.

tures of the *cratered* Martian surface. In the early 1950s he predicted that Mars would be found to be "more Moon-like than Earth-like" due to a tremendous interplanetary exchange of meteors that occurred several thousand years ago. The facts proved him out.

The character and influence of this mysterious red world are viewed in a universally consistent way—even among widely divergent cultures that supposedly had no contact in ancient days. In the astrology of the Hebrews, Egyptians, Aztecs, Chinese, Incas, Polynesians, Indians and Icelandic peoples, Mars was a planet of war, a fearful red god who caused earthquakes, volcanic eruptions, rains of meteors and myriad terrifying phenomena.

Through centuries of refinement in modern astrology, Mars has been observed to symbolize animal strength and energy, ambition and desire in the horoscope. He influences for good or ill, depending on whether other aspects applying to him are adverse or beneficial. Generally those who are strongly under the Mars influence are bold, enterprising, positive and have a love of leadership. They are usually excellent with mechanical devices and highly inventive. They despise being ordered around; their fierce ambitions often drive them to the head of any enterprise in which they are engaged.

Mars reaches its perigee (closest possible approach to Earth) station every 15 years. At this distance of 34 million miles, the Red Planet shines more brilliantly than Venus, "the Morning (or Evening) Star."

Force, courage and strength are attributed to Mars; also the color red, and the iron in our blood. Aries and Mars are very nearly synonymous, because Mars is the "ruling" planet of the first Sign.

*To find where Mars was at your birth, consult the table at the end of this chapter.*

## MARS IN ARIES ♂ ♈

Aries is often referred to as "the Sign of self" because it is the natural first house of the horoscope and indicates the Ascendant, or physical body; Mars placed here (even if Aries is *not* your Ascendant) makes you enterprising, independent and likely to look after your own interests first and foremost. *You* are "Number One." You are also original, courageous and dynamic as well as egotistical. You tend to act on the impulse of the moment, and hate any kind of limitation, bond or restriction that ties you down or prevents your free-wheeling, enterprising, pioneering nature from fully expressing itself—either in action or thought. You have a hot temper, and could often explode into violent wrath. Although you usually simmer down as quickly as you flare up, you may be accident-prone, with a high chance of injury to your head and face. You are positive, blunt, confident and sometimes combative. Yet you are also industrious, enthusiastic, idealistic and liberal. It is difficult for you to conceal your real feelings from others. Your candor can often be a source of embarrassment or trouble. You are a born adventurer with a youthful vitality that lasts into later years. You love active sports and sharply enjoy all kinds of pleasure. Your confidence is so great and your ego so pronounced that you'll carry out your plans not only without help or encouragement, but often against tremendous obstacles and discouragement.

## MARS IN TAURUS  ♂  ♉

You're going to acquire a substantial amount of money and worldly goods, but not without effort. You drive steadily and faithfully toward your goals, usually the acquisition of money and the physical comforts of life, to which you may add "love." If Mars is well-aspected here (i.e., you have planets in the earth or water Signs), you'll *handle* great sums of money, and probably *inherit* a large amount of your own as well. You are persistent, tactful, diplomatic, confident and determined to achieve your personal ambitions. You have a good mind, organizational ability, and are farsighted enough to anticipate the outcome of the forces you manage to set on a certain course. You will probably gain substantially through your job or profession, and enjoy excellent earning power; but you're just as likely to be a free spender in pursuit of the things you enjoy. You have an almost magical ability to carry your ideas and plans into actual materialization; you can create almost anything you visualize. But if there are several adverse aspects to your Mars in Taurus (i.e. if you have many planets in fire or air Signs), you are inclined to have fits of temper and depression caused by sudden losses of money and business reversals. During adverse periods you are almost literally as mad as a bull—irritable, rash and violent. No doubt you'll marry, but it may not be the bed of roses you had anticipated.

## MARS IN GEMINI ♂ ♊

You are very active, mentally restless and inclined to try changing situations to suit yourself. You probably have a high degree of mechanical aptitude and inventiveness. You are both practical and ingenious, but probably like action for its own sake. If the aspects to and from Mars are good, you might become an excellent lawyer, writer, lecturer and/or teacher. This position of Mars makes you agile, both mentally and physically. You have a strong desire to excel in education, and could become a good debater because of your blunt, forceful and aggressive mental attitudes. Your keen perception and insight are a result of your sharp mind, but you need to learn the value of concentration. If badly aspected by other planets (in the water or earth Signs), Mars in Gemini can make you extremely indecisive and often accident-prone with the likelihood of injuring or breaking your shoulder, arms or hands. Nervousness causing excessive smoking may result in pain in your lungs. Generally speaking, the adverse aspects to Mars cause fighting and ill-will or separation from your brothers, sisters and relatives, trouble with neighbors and difficulty in writing, travel and education. Otherwise you are extremely practical, incisive and quick to make proper assessment of conditions and to arrive at correct conclusions.

## MARS IN CANCER ♂ ♋

Chances are you'll have to wear glasses at some time in your life—or else you may develop some kind of eye trouble. You feel it necessary to *fight* for security; you are torn between your loyalty to home and hearth, your respect for authority, on one hand, and your rebellious urge for complete freedom and independence on the other. You are too changeable, and need to develop a more solid foundation for your enterprising spirit. This probably manifested itself early in life through trouble or open clashes with your mother. You may have been separated from her, either through estrangement or her early death. You can profit greatly from your independent, original ventures which may involve physical prowess, long trips and voyages. If Mars is adversely aspected, that is, by planets in fire Signs and air Signs, you may have an unhappy home and marriage relationship, with many changes of residence. You are likely to develop stomach ulcers or other gastric disorders unless you learn to cultivate a calmer, more harmonious outlook. Developing a sense of humor can be enormously helpful for your future happiness. Be especially careful when buying a home because it may be in danger of natural catastrophe, especially by water. Generally, you are hard-working, ambitious, courageous, sometimes rash, and likely to hold grudges for a long time after someone offends you. Try not to be so irritable and touchy; above all, avoid those sudden temperamental outbursts. You have a lot going for you.

## MARS IN LEO  ♂  ♌

Mars here tends to enhance your love of power, sense of grandeur and ego. You are strongly attracted to dangerous or strenuous sports, and adventures in tropical climates. You are forceful, dynamic and have enormous creative energy, if directed in the right channels. No doubt you have above average muscular strength, and a strong heart. Although your vitality is high, you may often run the danger of accidents, cuts, burns and fevers. This is generally a result of your love of hazardous work or play. You are fully able to gain the trust and confidence of superiors and will probably reach a position of authority, responsibility, trust or management. You rush into romantic situations with no thought of the outcome. You let your emotions run wild in love affairs, and are usually ardent, warmhearted, and passionate. Although you can be generous, reasonable, liberal and enthusiastic, with a keen sense of justice, you also like to present overwhelming arguments, and could be regarded as defiant, too aggressive and forceful for your own good. Generally speaking, you are friendly and outgoing, affectionate and sociable. Your chief gains in life will be through the good offices of high-placed executives and businessmen. Yet you are also gifted with a good sense of timing and are a keen judge of proper investment and speculation. In short, you are a born—and often lucky—gambler. Government appointments and public affairs are excellent areas for your forceful, enterprising talents. You tend to interpret all events solely in terms of yourself, or as they affect you. Although you are magnetic and attractive to some, remember that others may be put off by your inordinate force and passion.

## MARS IN VIRGO  ♂ ♍

Your path to basic security lies in your ability to relegate your activities to a systematized formula. You desire your fair amount of prestige, fame and power, but Mars in Virgo often places serious obstacles in your way. You may face many reversals, setbacks and failures of an unusual or peculiar nature before ultimate success crowns your efforts. No doubt you have realized or will realize many moderately successful results from your bold and original scientific innovations or inventions. This success could be amplified if your efforts were directed toward orthodox business, foreign trade or ordinary commerce. You possess excellent reserve strength and energy, and although you quietly pursue your own methods and means of accomplishment, you are strong-willed, shrewd, acquisitive, mentally active and diplomatic. If in someone else's employ, you rarely display your innate ingenuity, but always make of yourself a valuable, almost indispensible employee. You are a fast thinker, discriminating and tactful, but liable to bring about your own illnesses through overwork. You tend to be very careful in matters of diet and hygiene, but could, nevertheless, suffer occasionally from digestive troubles. You are likely to become deeply involved with workers, service employees and/or labor in general. There is some danger of quarreling with friends, and a resulting estrangement from them. This may result from violently opposing viewpoints in labor disputes. Whenever transiting Mars is badly aspected in your chart, you tend to become grouchy, irritable, stubborn, rash, grudge-holding and secretive. During these times, play it cool and avoid overworking yourself in order to avoid illness, the loss of friends, co-workers and/or subordinates.

## MARS IN LIBRA  ♂ ♎

You possess powerful social urges, and want to make a favorable impression on the public. Usually you do, and it could easily be one of youthful vitality and creative power.

You enjoy and need people and bask in popularity and a gay social life. Members of the opposite sex are usually a source of great attraction to you and you become involved in one romance after another, often to your own detriment. You are enterprising, like to speculate, and enjoy refined pleasures and amusements. Your ability to study and observe life is highly developed. Your inner vision is clear, your intuition is keen and your nature generally gentle. Yet you often display a surprisingly brittle temper. This is one of the positions from which Mars bestows a strong tendency for passionate and impulsive love affairs. You are not only powerfully attracted to, but also influenced by, the opposite sex. You will be disappointed in love more than once, and one of these emotional adversities may delay your marriage. Even so, there is good testimony here of an early marriage, although perhaps much strife, argument and unhappiness may surround this partnership. You are likely to have many friends in professional fields: lawyers, clergy, scientists, businessmen, artists and musicians. You can expect strong resistance in business from jealous competitors, but happily will survive intact from each of these clashes. Both openly and secretly, you will encounter envy, bitter criticism and keen competition from others to try to surpass your successes. Either liberally or formally, you will eventually acquire a good education—usually later in life. This increased knowledge and experience will enhance your judgment and foresight. You are almost certain to produce children with highly advanced intellectual abilities. You have a great need for social approbation—and will probably earn it.

## MARS IN SCORPIO ♂ ♏

The motto you live by may well be: "Get results—or else!" You are hard-driving, self-starting, vigorous, determined, positive and tough. You'll drive yourself longer and harder than anyone who works for you, yet you are not an easy boss. You are magnetic, rough, and you wear well once your confidence is gained, but you devote too little time to relaxation or pleasure. Whatever you do, it is done with your own peculiar brand of intensity. You possess a great deal of creative power, but have strong passions and need to exercise self-control and to discipline your volcanic emotions. Your attraction for dangerous jobs could result in your

entrance into hazardous conditions that cause accidents—
or you may meet an unexpectedly violent death. You love
a mystery and like to dig beneath the surface of things until
you find satisfactory answers. Moreover, this intense curiosity does not always follow orthodox lines; you are likely to
become involved in mystical religions, psychical research
and kindred subjects. You'll profit from long trips and through
marriage as well as association with the opposite sex. *Whatever*
project you undertake, it is done with purposeful action and
intensity. Your immediate and direct objective is always to
obtain concrete results. No shillyshallying. You are hard-
working, practical and know exactly how to accomplish your
aims. To others you may seem to be something of a cold
fish, caring little or nothing for the feelings of people in
general—secretive, sarcastic, selfish and vengeful. Unless
other aspects in your chart such as Venus, Jupiter or the
Sun in the earth or water Signs offset this, there is probably
a lot of truth to that. You are good with tools and could
profit in any profession where cold courage is a requisite.
You'd make an excellent surgeon, oil driller, deep sea diver,
fighter or body-contact sportsman. You possess great
magnetism.

## MARS IN SAGITTARIUS ♂ ♐

You have a carefree, courageous, independent and original
outlook, with a daring "don't-give-a-damn" attitude for the
opinions of those in powerful positions. You love all kinds
of activity for its own sake—both physical and mental. You
are gifted with tremendous foresight amounting almost to
prophetic ability. You are fiercely independent and idealistic, and would rather fly than crawl, yet you are always
being faced with the fearful attitude of the conservative-
minded; that everything must be learned by ritual and rote—
starting at the very bottom. You don't quite see it this way
and are not afraid to say so. You love travel and high
adventure, yet you want to influence the major trends of
your generation (and may very well succeed!). Generally,
you are impulsive; you tend to act rashly or say whatever
pops into your mind. Because you're able to see through
pomp and phoniness, and are usually correct in your judgments, this makes your quarry uneasy and angry. You are,
however, candid, liberal, ambitious and generous. You are

also inventive, ingenious and fond of outdoor sports, all forms of athletics and strenuous exercise. You probably have a keen admiration for military and naval tactics as well as for the spartan life of the professional warrior. Your active, inventive mentality keenly enjoys good-natured debates and arguments among friends. You'll profit through inheritance, friends and/or marriage. But the indications are that more than one marriage is in store for you. Under adverse influences such as Saturn in Pisces, Cancer, Scorpio or any of the three earth Signs, Mars in Sagittarius brings trouble through orthodox religious leaders and groups, unhappy relationships with brothers, sisters, neighbors and relatives and danger in your method of livelihood. Learn to curb your tendency for candid, skeptical, unorthodox or iconoclastic appraisals of established values.

## MARS IN CAPRICORN ♂ ♑

You work long and hard, often shoulder responsibilities which do not rightfully belong to you, yet you assume these burdens with patience, ambition and good will. You are a slow but intuitive learner and retain whatever knowledge you gain. You are destined to achieve recognition and honors for your faithful devotion and hard work. Early in your life you probably had some kind of affair with someone considerably older or of an inferior position or station in life—or both. Basically, you are very courageous, and highly stimulated by bold adventure. You are confident and self-reliant, perhaps too much so. Scorning proper precautions may result in accidents or injury, particularly to your knees or lower legs. You are best suited for success in public life due to your organizing, executive ability; you want plenty of space for the breadth of the plans you have in mind. You are hard-working, acquisitive, enterprising and so ambitious that you're bound to succeed in whatever you undertake. Naturally, these characteristics will attract influential and powerful people who will give you a boost. You'll probably travel a lot, deal in foreign trade and profit through science and commerce. In order to acquire the wealth you desire, you do not hesitate to risk your capital in speculation. Whether you engineer it or not, one of the most important turning points in your life will be your marriage. It will have a profound effect on your social standing and future stability. Mars in Capricorn is not especially auspicious for your relationship with one parent—probably your father. This could mean disagreement and separation—or the divorce of your parents, or the early death of one of them. If Mars is really heavily afflicted by adverse aspects from other planets at your birth, you may experience pretty much the opposite of most of the foregoing promises. In any event, your courage, persistence and ambition *are* capable of overcoming great obstacles.

## MARS IN AQUARIUS  ♂  ♒

Although unorthodox, you seek justice for all and will battle courageously for the rights of minorities. You are a fearless debater and an excellent reasoner. Invariably, you are able to find one rather obscure, unique peg from which to hang your arguments. Although you are altruistic and seek only the betterment of others in the public domain, you have an abrupt, often rash and impulsive way of presenting your ideas. This is because you are sensitive, idealistic and highly impatient with the inability of most people to see things as clearly as you do. You are a scientific, fast-talking intellectual, often too far ahead of your contemporaries. You are a truly independent and original thinker and planner—enterprising and ambitious. Rarely do you change your attitude or position, but once this does happen it is a radical, complete and irreversible switch. You are a good lecturer and debater, convincing and powerful. You are able to marshal your facts, present crystal-clear arguments and quickly arrive at your conclusions. Privately you are refined and sincere, a person who attracts friends through your interest in them and your solid abilities. Projects for the public good and welfare constitute areas where you can achieve recognition and financial success. You are interested in electronics or electrical machinery (computers and such), and are probably very original, inventive and intrigued by space programs. You are attracted to literature, philosophy, science and borderline sciences. Your able, responsible character makes you a natural executive for a city, state or federal office. Mars in Aquarius also suits you, as has been indicated, for philanthropies and welfare work as well as for a medical or surgical vocation.

## MARS IN PISCES  ♂ ♓

Although you are strongly influenced by others, and often indecisive, easily depressed and indolent, you are fully capable of much achievement when working quietly and alone. You've probably experienced an extra share of misfortune and trouble, which you strive courageously to overcome. While you will fight valiantly for the rights of others, you tend to neglect your own right to be free and strong. The tendency here is to allow yourself to be ruled by your sympathies and emotions. You are often frustrated in your need for approval and desire for popularity. In ordinary jobs, particularly those connected with private or public institutions, you can achieve a great deal of success. Mars in Pisces is an indication of delays in marriage, disappointment in love affairs and a duality in your affections. You tend to display excessive emotion or passion while at the same time striving to achieve harmony and avoid open conflicts. Some dissipation is indicated here, possibly through excessive use of alcohol or super-stimulated emotions. You are bound to develop friendships with powerful or influential people at some time in your life, and will (temporarily, at least) receive their help and gain financially from them. You need to exercise extreme caution in dealing with liquids of any kind; also with opiates, gas and anesthetics. Water is a potential danger, either through scalding or drowning. You tend to waste your time with fruitless dreams and should cultivate the ability to act on your keen intuition in order to bring these dreams into reality. You are almost determined to avoid concentrating on one thing at a time. This alone prevents the solid achievement of which you are capable. You are probably plagued by your constantly shifting views, emotions, plans for the future and occupation.

To find where Mars was (by Sign) at the time of your birth, consult the following table, then insert this symbol (♂) in its proper place in the horoscope blank.

# TO FIND THE POSITION OF MARS AT YOUR BIRTH

| 1900 | Date | Zodiacal Sign |
|------|------|---------------|
| Jan. | 1 to Feb. 28 | Aquarius |
| Mar. | 1 to Apr. 7 | Pisces |
| Apr. | 8 to May 16 | Aries |
| May | 17 to June 26 | Taurus |
| June | 27 to Aug. 9 | Gemini |
| Aug. | 10 to Sept. 26 | Cancer |
| Sept. | 27 to Nov. 22 | Leo |
| Nov. | 23 to Dec. 31 | Virgo |

| 1901 | | |
|------|------|---------------|
| Jan. | 1 to Mar. 1 | Virgo |
| Mar. | 2 to May 10 | Leo |
| May | 11 to July 13 | Virgo |
| July | 14 to Aug. 31 | Libra |
| Sept. | 1 to Oct. 14 | Scorpio |
| Oct. | 15 to Nov. 23 | Sagittarius |
| Nov. | 24 to Dec. 31 | Capricorn |

| 1902 | | |
|------|------|---------------|
| Jan. | 1 | Capricorn |
| Jan. | 2 to Feb. 8 | Aquarius |
| Feb. | 9 to Mar. 17 | Pisces |
| Mar. | 18 to Apr. 26 | Aries |
| Apr. | 27 to June 6 | Taurus |
| June | 7 to July 20 | Gemini |
| July | 21 to Sept. 4 | Cancer |
| Sept. | 5 to Oct. 23 | Leo |
| Oct. | 24 to Dec. 19 | Virgo |
| Dec. | 20 to Dec. 31 | Libra |

| 1903 | | |
|------|------|---------------|
| Jan. | 1 to Apr. 19 | Libra |
| Apr. | 20 to May 30 | Virgo |
| May | 31 to Aug. 6 | Libra |
| Aug. | 7 to Sept. 22 | Scorpio |
| Sept. | 23 to Nov. 2 | Sagittarius |
| Nov. | 3 to Dec. 11 | Capricorn |
| Dec. | 12 to Dec. 31 | Aquarius |

| 1904 | Date | Zodiacal Sign |
|------|------|---------------|
| Jan. | 1 to Jan. 19 | Aquarius |
| Jan. | 20 to Feb. 26 | Pisces |
| Feb. | 27 to Apr. 6 | Aries |
| Apr. | 7 to May 17 | Taurus |
| May | 18 to June 30 | Gemini |
| July | 1 to Aug. 14 | Cancer |
| Aug. | 15 to Oct. 1 | Leo |
| Oct. | 2 to Nov. 19 | Virgo |
| Nov. | 20 to Dec. 31 | Libra |

| 1905 | | |
|------|------|---------------|
| Jan. | 1 to Jan. 13 | Libra |
| Jan. | 14 to Aug. 21 | Scorpio |
| Aug. | 22 to Oct. 7 | Sagittarius |
| Oct. | 8 to Nov. 17 | Capricorn |
| Nov. | 18 to Dec. 27 | Aquarius |
| Dec. | 28 to Dec. 31 | Pisces |

| 1906 | | |
|------|------|---------------|
| Jan. | 1 to Feb. 4 | Pisces |
| Feb. | 5 to Mar. 16 | Aries |
| Mar. | 17 to Apr. 28 | Taurus |
| Apr. | 29 to June 11 | Gemini |
| June | 12 to July 27 | Cancer |
| July | 28 to Sept. 12 | Leo |
| Sept. | 13 to Oct. 29 | Virgo |
| Oct. | 30 to Dec. 16 | Libra |
| Dec. | 17 to Dec. 31 | Scorpio |

| 1907 | | |
|------|------|---------------|
| Jan. | 1 to Feb. 4 | Scorpio |
| Feb. | 5 to Apr. 1 | Sagittarius |
| Apr. | 2 to Oct. 13 | Capricorn |
| Oct. | 14 to Nov. 28 | Aquarius |
| Nov. | 29 to Dec. 31 | Pisces |

## 1908

| Date | | Zodiacal Sign |
|---|---|---|
| Jan. | 1 to Jan. 10 | Pisces |
| Jan. | 11 to Feb. 22 | Aries |
| Feb. | 23 to Apr. 6 | Taurus |
| Apr. | 7 to May 22 | Gemini |
| May | 23 to July 7 | Cancer |
| July | 8 to Aug. 23 | Leo |
| Aug. | 24 to Oct. 9 | Virgo |
| Oct. | 10 to Nov. 25 | Libra |
| Nov. | 26 to Dec. 31 | Scorpio |

## 1909

| | | |
|---|---|---|
| Jan. | 1 to Jan. 9 | Scorpio |
| Jan. | 10 to Feb. 23 | Sagittarius |
| Feb. | 24 to Apr. 9 | Capricorn |
| Apr. | 10 to May 25 | Aquarius |
| May | 26 to July 20 | Pisces |
| July | 21 to Sept. 26 | Aries |
| Sept. | 27 to Nov. 20 | Pisces |
| Nov. | 21 to Dec. 31 | Aries |

## 1910

| | | |
|---|---|---|
| Jan. | 1 to Feb. 22 | Aries |
| Feb. | 23 to Mar. 13 | Taurus |
| Mar. | 14 to May 1 | Gemini |
| May | 2 to June 18 | Cancer |
| June | 19 to Aug. 5 | Leo |
| Aug. | 6 to Sept. 21 | Virgo |
| Sept. | 22 to Nov. 6 | Libra |
| Nov. | 7 to Dec. 19 | Scorpio |
| Dec. | 20 to Dec. 31 | Sagittarius |

## 1911

| | | |
|---|---|---|
| Jan. | 1 to Jan. 31 | Sagittarius |
| Feb. | 1 to Mar. 13 | Capricorn |
| Mar. | 14 to Apr. 22 | Aquarius |
| Apr. | 23 to June 2 | Pisces |
| June | 3 to July 15 | Aries |
| July | 16 to Sept. 5 | Taurus |
| Sept. | 6 to Nov. 29 | Gemini |
| Nov. | 30 to Dec. 31 | Taurus |

## 1912

| Date | | Zodiacal Sign |
|---|---|---|
| Jan. | 1 to Jan. 30 | Taurus |
| Jan. | 31 to Apr. 4 | Gemini |
| Apr. | 5 to May 27 | Cancer |
| May | 28 to July 16 | Leo |
| July | 17 to Sept. 2 | Virgo |
| Sept. | 3 to Oct. 17 | Libra |
| Oct. | 18 to Nov. 29 | Scorpio |
| Nov. | 30 to Dec. 31 | Sagittarius |

## 1913

| | | |
|---|---|---|
| Jan. | 1 to Jan. 10 | Sagittarius |
| Jan. | 11 to Feb. 18 | Capricorn |
| Feb. | 19 to Mar. 29 | Aquarius |
| Mar. | 30 to May 7 | Pisces |
| May | 8 to June 16 | Aries |
| June | 17 to July 28 | Taurus |
| July | 29 to Sept. 15 | Gemini |
| Sept. | 16 to Dec. 31 | Cancer |

## 1914

| | | |
|---|---|---|
| Jan. | 1 to May 1 | Cancer |
| May | 2 to June 25 | Leo |
| June | 26 to Aug. 14 | Virgo |
| Aug. | 15 to Sept. 28 | Libra |
| Sept. | 29 to Nov. 10 | Scorpio |
| Nov. | 11 to Dec. 21 | Sagittarius |
| Dec. | 22 to Dec. 31 | Capricorn |

## 1915

| | | |
|---|---|---|
| Jan. | 1 to Jan. 29 | Capricorn |
| Jan. | 30 to Mar. 9 | Aquarius |
| Mar. | 10 to Apr. 16 | Pisces |
| Apr. | 17 to May 25 | Aries |
| May | 26 to July 5 | Taurus |
| July | 6 to Aug. 18 | Gemini |
| Aug. | 19 to Oct. 7 | Cancer |
| Oct. | 8 to Dec. 31 | Leo |

## 1916

| | | |
|---|---|---|
| Jan. | 1 to May 28 | Leo |
| May | 29 to July 22 | Virgo |

| *1916* | *Date* | *Zodiacal Sign* |
|---|---|---|
| July | 23 to Sept. 8 | Libra |
| Sept. | 9 to Oct. 21 | Scorpio |
| Oct. | 22 to Dec. 1 | Sagittarius |
| Dec. | 2 to Dec. 31 | Capricorn |

*1917*

| | | |
|---|---|---|
| Jan. | 1 to Jan. 9 | Capricorn |
| Jan. | 10 to Feb. 16 | Aquarius |
| Feb. | 17 to Mar. 26 | Pisces |
| Mar. | 27 to May 4 | Aries |
| May | 5 to June 14 | Taurus |
| June | 15 to July 27 | Gemini |
| July | 28 to Sept. 11 | Cancer |
| Sept. | 12 to Nov. 1 | Leo |
| Nov. | 2 to Dec. 31 | Virgo |

*1918*

| | | |
|---|---|---|
| Jan. | 1 to Jan. 10 | Virgo |
| Jan. | 11 to Feb. 25 | Libra |
| Feb. | 26 to June 23 | Virgo |
| June | 24 to Aug. 16 | Libra |
| Aug. | 17 to Sept. 30 | Scorpio |
| Oct. | 1 to Nov. 10 | Sagittarius |
| Nov. | 11 to Dec. 19 | Capricorn |
| Dec. | 20 to Dec. 31 | Aquarius |

*1919*

| | | |
|---|---|---|
| Jan. | 1 to Jan. 26 | Aquarius |
| Jan. | 27 to Mar. 6 | Pisces |
| Mar. | 7 to Apr. 14 | Aries |
| Apr. | 15 to May 25 | Taurus |
| May | 26 to July 8 | Gemini |
| July | 9 to Aug. 22 | Cancer |
| Aug. | 23 to Oct. 9 | Leo |
| Oct. | 10 to Nov. 29 | Virgo |
| Nov. | 30 to Dec. 31 | Libra |

*1920*

| | | |
|---|---|---|
| Jan. | 1 to Jan. 31 | Libra |
| Feb. | 1 to Apr. 23 | Scorpio |
| Apr. | 24 to July 10 | Libra |

| *1920* | *Date* | *Zodiacal Sign* |
|---|---|---|
| July | 11 to Sept. 4 | Scorpio |
| Sept. | 5 to Oct. 18 | Sagittarius |
| Oct. | 19 to Nov. 27 | Capricorn |
| Nov. | 28 to Dec. 31 | Aquarius |

*1921*

| | | |
|---|---|---|
| Jan. | 1 to Jan. 4 | Aquarius |
| Jan. | 5 to Feb. 12 | Pisces |
| Feb. | 13 to Mar. 24 | Aries |
| Mar. | 25 to May 5 | Taurus |
| May | 6 to June 10 | Gemini |
| June | 20 to Aug. 2 | Cancer |
| Aug. | 3 to Sept. 18 | Leo |
| Sept. | 19 to Nov. 6 | Virgo |
| Nov. | 7 to Dec. 25 | Libra |
| Dec. | 26 to Dec. 31 | Scorpio |

*1922*

| | | |
|---|---|---|
| Jan. | 1 to Feb. 18 | Scorpio |
| Feb. | 19 to Sept. 13 | Sagittarius |
| Sept. | 14 to Oct. 30 | Capricorn |
| Oct. | 31 to Dec. 11 | Aquarius |
| Dec. | 12 to Dec. 31 | Pisces |

*1923*

| | | |
|---|---|---|
| Jan. | 1 to Jan. 20 | Pisces |
| Jan. | 21 to Mar. 3 | Aries |
| Mar. | 4 to Apr. 15 | Taurus |
| Apr. | 16 to May 30 | Gemini |
| May | 31 to July 15 | Cancer |
| July | 16 to Aug. 31 | Leo |
| Sept. | 1 to Oct. 17 | Virgo |
| Oct. | 18 to Dec. 3 | Libra |
| Dec. | 4 to Dec. 31 | Scorpio |

*1924*

| | | |
|---|---|---|
| Jan. | 1 to Feb. 19 | Scorpio |
| Feb. | 20 to Mar. 6 | Sagittarius |
| Mar. | 7 to Apr. 24 | Capricorn |
| Apr. | 25 to June 24 | Aquarius |
| June | 25 to Aug. 24 | Pisces |

| 1924 | Date | Zodiacal Sign |
|------|------|---------------|
| Aug. | 25 to Oct. 19 | Aquarius |
| Oct. | 20 to Dec. 18 | Pisces |
| Dec. | 19 to Dec. 31 | Aries |

### 1925

| | Date | Zodiacal Sign |
|------|------|---------------|
| Jan. | 1 to Feb. 4 | Aries |
| Feb. | 5 to Mar. 23 | Taurus |
| Mar. | 24 to May 9 | Gemini |
| May | 10 to June 25 | Cancer |
| June | 26 to Aug. 12 | Leo |
| Aug. | 13 to Sept. 28 | Virgo |
| Sept. | 29 to Nov. 13 | Libra |
| Nov. | 14 to Dec. 27 | Scorpio |
| Dec. | 28 to Dec. 31 | Sagittarius |

### 1926

| | Date | Zodiacal Sign |
|------|------|---------------|
| Jan. | 1 to Feb. 8 | Sagittarius |
| Feb. | 9 to Mar. 22 | Capricorn |
| Mar. | 23 to May 3 | Aquarius |
| May | 4 to June 14 | Pisces |
| June | 15 to July 31 | Aries |
| Aug. | 1 to Dec. 31 | Taurus |

### 1927

| | Date | Zodiacal Sign |
|------|------|---------------|
| Jan. | 1 to Feb. 21 | Taurus |
| Feb. | 22 to Apr. 16 | Gemini |
| Apr. | 17 to June 5 | Cancer |
| June | 6 to July 24 | Leo |
| July | 25 to Sept. 10 | Virgo |
| Sept. | 11 to Oct. 25 | Libra |
| Oct. | 26 to Dec. 7 | Scorpio |
| Dec. | 8 to Dec. 31 | Sagittarius |

### 1928

| | Date | Zodiacal Sign |
|------|------|---------------|
| Jan. | 1 to Jan. 18 | Sagittarius |
| Jan. | 19 to Feb. 27 | Capricorn |
| Feb. | 28 to Apr. 7 | Aquarius |
| Apr. | 8 to May 16 | Pisces |
| May | 17 to June 25 | Aries |
| June | 26 to Aug. 8 | Taurus |
| Aug. | 9 to Oct. 2 | Gemini |
| Oct. | 3 to Dec. 19 | Cancer |
| Dec. | 20 to Dec. 31 | Gemini |

| 1929 | Date | Zodiacal Sign |
|------|------|---------------|
| Jan. | 1 to Mar. 10 | Gemini |
| Mar. | 11 to May 12 | Cancer |
| May | 13 to July 3 | Leo |
| July | 4 to Aug. 21 | Virgo |
| Aug. | 22 to Oct. 5 | Libra |
| Oct. | 6 to Nov. 18 | Scorpio |
| Nov. | 19 to Dec. 28 | Sagittarius |
| Dec. | 29 to Dec. 31 | Capricorn |

### 1930

| | Date | Zodiacal Sign |
|------|------|---------------|
| Jan. | 1 to Feb. 6 | Capricorn |
| Feb. | 7 to Mar. 16 | Aquarius |
| Mar. | 17 to Apr. 24 | Pisces |
| Apr. | 25 to June 2 | Aries |
| June | 3 to July 14 | Taurus |
| July | 15 to Aug. 27 | Gemini |
| Aug. | 28 to Oct. 20 | Cancer |
| Oct. | 21 to Dec. 31 | Leo |

### 1931

| | Date | Zodiacal Sign |
|------|------|---------------|
| Jan. | 1 to Feb. 15 | Leo |
| Feb. | 16 to Mar. 29 | Cancer |
| Mar. | 30 to June 9 | Leo |
| June | 10 to July 31 | Virgo |
| Aug. | 1 to Sept. 16 | Libra |
| Sept. | 17 to Oct. 29 | Scorpio |
| Oct. | 30 to Dec. 9 | Sagittarius |
| Dec. | 10 to Dec. 31 | Capricorn |

### 1932

| | Date | Zodiacal Sign |
|------|------|---------------|
| Jan. | 1 to Jan. 17 | Capricorn |
| Jan. | 18 to Feb. 24 | Aquarius |
| Feb. | 25 to Apr. 2 | Pisces |
| Apr. | 3 to May 11 | Aries |
| May | 12 to June 21 | Taurus |
| June | 22 to Aug. 3 | Gemini |
| Aug. | 4 to Sept. 19 | Cancer |
| Sept. | 20 to Nov. 12 | Leo |
| Nov. | 13 to Dec. 31 | Virgo |

### 1933

| | Date | Zodiacal Sign |
|------|------|---------------|
| Jan. | 1 to July 5 | Virgo |
| July | 6 to Aug. 25 | Libra |

| 1933 | Date | Zodiacal Sign |
|------|------|---------------|
| Aug. | 26 to Oct. 8 | Scorpio |
| Oct. | 9 to Nov. 18 | Sagittarius |
| Nov. | 19 to Dec. 27 | Capricorn |
| Dec. | 28 to Dec. 31 | Aquarius |

### 1934

| | | |
|------|------|---------------|
| Jan. | 1 to Feb. 3 | Aquarius |
| Feb. | 4 to Mar. 13 | Pisces |
| Mar. | 14 to Apr. 21 | Aries |
| Apr. | 22 to June 1 | Taurus |
| June | 2 to July 14 | Gemini |
| July | 15 to Aug. 29 | Cancer |
| Aug. | 30 to Oct. 17 | Leo |
| Oct. | 18 to Dec. 10 | Virgo |
| Dec. | 11 to Dec. 31 | Libra |

### 1935

| | | |
|------|------|---------------|
| Jan. | 1 to July 28 | Libra |
| July | 29 to Sept. 15 | Scorpio |
| Sept. | 16 to Oct. 27 | Sagittarius |
| Oct. | 28 to Dec. 6 | Capricorn |
| Dec. | 7 to Dec. 31 | Aquarius |

### 1936

| | | |
|------|------|---------------|
| Jan. | 1 to Jan. 13 | Aquarius |
| Jan. | 14 to Feb. 21 | Pisces |
| Feb. | 22 to Mar. 31 | Aries |
| Apr. | 1 to May 12 | Taurus |
| May | 13 to June 24 | Gemini |
| June | 25 to Aug. 9 | Cancer |
| Aug. | 10 to Sept. 25 | Leo |
| Sept. | 26 to Nov. 13 | Virgo |
| Nov. | 14 to Dec. 31 | Libra |

### 1937

| | | |
|------|------|---------------|
| Jan. | 1 to Mar. 12 | Scorpio |
| Mar. | 13 to May 13 | Sagittarius |
| May | 14 to Aug. 7 | Scorpio |
| Aug. | 8 to Sept. 29 | Sagittarius |
| Sept. | 30 to Nov. 10 | Capricorn |
| Nov. | 11 to Dec. 20 | Aquarius |
| Dec. | 21 to Dec. 31 | Pisces |

| 1938 | Date | Zodiacal Sign |
|------|------|---------------|
| Jan. | 1 to Jan. 29 | Pisces |
| Jan. | 30 to Mar. 11 | Aries |
| Mar. | 12 to Apr. 22 | Taurus |
| Apr. | 23 to June 6 | Gemini |
| June | 7 to July 21 | Cancer |
| July | 22 to Sept. 6 | Leo |
| Sept. | 7 to Oct. 24 | Virgo |
| Oct. | 25 to Dec. 10 | Libra |
| Dec. | 11 to Dec. 31 | Scorpio |

### 1939

| | | |
|------|------|---------------|
| Jan. | 1 to Jan. 28 | Scorpio |
| Jan. | 29 to Mar. 30 | Sagittarius |
| Mar. | 21 to May 23 | Capricorn |
| May | 24 to July 20 | Aquarius |
| July | 21 to Sept. 23 | Capricorn |
| Sept. | 24 to Nov. 18 | Aquarius |
| Nov. | 19 to Dec. 31 | Pisces |

### 1940

| | | |
|------|------|---------------|
| Jan. | 1 to Jan. 2 | Pisces |
| Jan. | 3 to Feb. 16 | Aries |
| Feb. | 17 to Mar. 31 | Taurus |
| Arp. | 1 to May 16 | Gemini |
| May | 17 to July 2 | Cancer |
| July | 3 to Aug. 18 | Leo |
| Aug. | 19 to Oct. 4 | Virgo |
| Oct. | 5 to Nov. 19 | Libra |
| Nov. | 20 to Dec. 31 | Scorpio |

### 1941

| | | |
|------|------|---------------|
| Jan. | 1 to Jan. 3 | Scorpio |
| Jan. | 4 to Feb. 16 | Sagittarius |
| Feb. | 17 to Apr. 1 | Capricorn |
| Apr. | 2 to May 15 | Aquarius |
| May | 16 to July 1 | Pisces |
| July | 2 to Dec. 31 | Aries |

### 1942

| | | |
|------|------|---------------|
| Jan. | 1 to Jan. 10 | Aries |
| Jan. | 11 to Mar. 6 | Taurus |
| Mar. | 7 to Apr. 25 | Gemini |

| 1942 | Date | Zodiacal Sign |
|------|------|---------------|
| Apr. | 26 to June 13 | Cancer |
| June | 14 to July 31 | Leo |
| Aug. | 1 to Sept. 16 | Virgo |
| Sept. | 17 to Oct. 31 | Libra |
| Nov. | 1 to Dec. 14 | Scorpio |
| Dec. | 14 to Dec. 31 | Sagittarius |

### 1943

| | | |
|------|------|---------------|
| Jan. | 1 to Jan. 25 | Sagittarius |
| Jan. | 26 to Mar. 7 | Capricorn |
| Mar. | 8 to Apr. 16 | Aquarius |
| Apr. | 17 to May 26 | Pisces |
| May | 27 to June 6 | Aries |
| June | 7 to Aug. 22 | Taurus |
| Aug. | 23 to Dec. 31 | Gemini |

### 1944

| | | |
|------|------|---------------|
| Jan. | 1 to Mar. 27 | Gemini |
| Mar. | 28 to May 21 | Cancer |
| May | 22 to July 11 | Leo |
| July | 12 to Aug. 28 | Virgo |
| Aug. | 29 to Oct. 12 | Libra |
| Oct. | 13 to Nov. 24 | Scorpio |
| Nov. | 25 to Dec. 31 | Sagittarius |

### 1945

| | | |
|------|------|---------------|
| Jan. | 1 to Jan. 4 | Sagittarius |
| Jan. | 5 to Feb. 13 | Capricorn |
| Feb. | 14 to Mar. 24 | Aquarius |
| Mar. | 25 to May 1 | Pisces |
| May | 2 to June 10 | Aries |
| June | 11 to July 22 | Taurus |
| July | 23 to Sept. 6 | Gemini |
| Sept. | 7 to Nov. 10 | Cancer |
| Nov. | 11 to Dec. 25 | Leo |
| Dec. | 26 to Dec. 31 | Cancer |

### 1946

| | | |
|------|------|---------------|
| Jan. | 1 to Apr. 21 | Cancer |
| Apr. | 22 to June 19 | Leo |
| June | 20 to Aug. 8 | Virgo |
| Aug. | 9 to Sept. 23 | Libra |
| Sept. | 24 to Nov. 5 | Scorpio |

| 1946 | Date | Zodiacal Sign |
|------|------|---------------|
| Nov. | 6 to Dec. 16 | Sagittarius |
| Dec. | 17 to Dec. 31 | Capricorn |

### 1947

| | | |
|------|------|---------------|
| Jan. | 1 to Jan. 24 | Capricorn |
| Jan. | 25 to Mar. 3 | Aquarius |
| Mar. | 4 to Apr. 10 | Pisces |
| Apr. | 11 to May 20 | Aries |
| May | 21 to June 30 | Taurus |
| July | 1 to Aug. 12 | Gemini |
| Aug. | 13 to Sept. 30 | Cancer |
| Oct. | 1 to Nov. 30 | Leo |
| Dec. | 1 to Dec. 31 | Virgo |

### 1948

| | | |
|------|------|---------------|
| Jan. | 1 to Feb. 11 | Virgo |
| Feb. | 12 to May 17 | Leo |
| May | 18 to July 16 | Virgo |
| July | 17 to Sept. 2 | Libra |
| Sept. | 3 to Oct. 16 | Scorpio |
| Oct. | 17 to Nov. 25 | Sagittarius |
| Nov. | 26 to Dec. 31 | Capricorn |

### 1949

| | | |
|------|------|---------------|
| Jan. | 1 to Jan. 3 | Capricorn |
| Jan. | 4 to Feb. 10 | Aquarius |
| Feb. | 11 to Mar. 20 | Pisces |
| Mar. | 21 to Apr. 29 | Aries |
| Apr. | 30 to June 9 | Taurus |
| June | 10 to July 22 | Gemini |
| July | 23 to Sept. 6 | Cancer |
| Sept. | 7 to Oct. 26 | Leo |
| Oct. | 27 to Dec. 25 | Virgo |
| Dec. | 26 to Dec. 31 | Libra |

### 1950

| | | |
|------|------|---------------|
| Jan. | 1 to Mar. 27 | Libra |
| Mar. | 28 to June 10 | Virgo |
| June | 11 to Aug. 9 | Libra |
| Aug. | 10 to Sept. 24 | Scorpio |
| Sept. | 25 to Nov. 5 | Sagittarius |
| Nov. | 6 to Dec. 14 | Capricorn |
| Dec. | 15 to Dec. 31 | Aquarius |

| 1951 | Date | Zodiacal Sign |
|------|------|---------------|
| Jan. | 1 to Jan. 21 | Aquarius |
| Jan. | 22 to Feb. 28 | Pisces |
| Mar. | 1 to Apr. 9 | Aries |
| Apr. | 10 to May 20 | Taurus |
| May | 21 to July 2 | Gemini |
| July | 3 to Aug. 17 | Cancer |
| Aug. | 18 to Oct. 3 | Leo |
| Oct. | 4 to Nov. 23 | Virgo |
| Nov. | 24 to Dec. 31 | Libra |

| 1952 | | |
|------|------|------|
| Jan. | 1 to Jan. 19 | Libra |
| Jan. | 20 to Aug. 26 | Scorpio |
| Aug. | 27 to Oct. 11 | Sagittarius |
| Oct. | 12 to Nov. 20 | Capricorn |
| Nov. | 21 to Dec. 29 | Aquarius |
| Dec. | 30 to Dec. 31 | Pisces |

| 1953 | | |
|------|------|------|
| Jan. | 1 to Feb. 7 | Pisces |
| Feb. | 8 to Mar. 19 | Aries |
| Mar. | 20 to Apr. 30 | Taurus |
| May | 1 to June 13 | Gemini |
| June | 14 to July 28 | Cancer |
| July | 29 to Sept. 13 | Leo |
| Sept. | 14 to Oct. 31 | Virgo |
| Nov. | 1 to Dec. 19 | Libra |
| Dec. | 20 to Dec. 31 | Scorpio |

| 1954 | | |
|------|------|------|
| Jan. | 1 to Feb. 8 | Scorpio |
| Feb. | 9 to Apr. 11 | Sagittarius |
| Apr. | 12 to July 2 | Capricorn |
| July | 3 to Aug. 23 | Sagittarius |
| Aug. | 24 to Oct. 20 | Capricorn |
| Oct. | 21 to Dec. 3 | Aquarius |
| Dec. | 4 to Dec. 31 | Pisces |

| 1955 | | |
|------|------|------|
| Jan. | 1 to Jan. 14 | Pisces |
| Jan. | 15 to Feb. 25 | Aries |
| Feb. | 26 to Apr. 9 | Taurus |

| 1955 | Date | Zodiacal Sign |
|------|------|---------------|
| Apr. | 10 to May 25 | Gemini |
| May | 26 to July 10 | Cancer |
| July | 11 to Aug. 26 | Leo |
| Aug. | 27 to Oct. 12 | Virgo |
| Oct. | 13 to Nov. 28 | Libra |
| Nov. | 29 to Dec. 31 | Scorpio |

| 1956 | | |
|------|------|------|
| Jan. | 1 to Jan. 13 | Scorpio |
| Jan. | 14 to Feb. 27 | Sagittarius |
| Feb. | 28 to Apr. 13 | Capricorn |
| Apr. | 14 to June 2 | Aquarius |
| June | 3 to Dec. 5 | Pisces |
| Dec. | 6 to Dec. 31 | Aries |

| 1957 | | |
|------|------|------|
| Jan. | 1 to Feb. 27 | Aries |
| Feb. | 28 to Mar. 16 | Taurus |
| Mar. | 17 to May 3 | Gemini |
| May | 4 to June 20 | Cancer |
| June | 21 to Aug. 7 | Leo |
| Aug. | 8 to Sept. 23 | Virgo |
| Sept. | 24 to Nov. 7 | Libra |
| Nov. | 8 to Dec. 22 | Scorpio |
| Dec. | 23 to Dec. 31 | Sagittarius |

| 1958 | | |
|------|------|------|
| Jan. | 1 to Feb. 2 | Sagittarius |
| Feb. | 3 to Mar. 16 | Capricorn |
| Mar. | 17 to Apr. 26 | Aquarius |
| Apr. | 27 to June 6 | Pisces |
| June | 7 to July 20 | Aries |
| July | 21 to Sept. 20 | Taurus |
| Sept. | 21 to Oct. 28 | Gemini |
| Oct. | 29 to Dec. 31 | Taurus |

| 1959 | | |
|------|------|------|
| Jan. | 1 to Feb. 9 | Taurus |
| Feb. | 10 to Apr. 9 | Gemini |
| Apr. | 10 to May 31 | Cancer |
| June | 1 to July 19 | Leo |
| July | 20 to Sept. 4 | Virgo |

| 1959 | Date | Zodiacal Sign |
|---|---|---|
| Sept. | 5 to Oct. 20 | Libra |
| Oct. | 21 to Dec. 2 | Scorpio |
| Dec. | 3 to Dec. 31 | Sagittarius |

### 1960

| | | |
|---|---|---|
| Jan. | 1 to Jan. 13 | Sagittarius |
| Jan. | 14 to Feb. 22 | Capricorn |
| Feb. | 23 to Apr. 1 | Aquarius |
| Apr. | 2 to May 10 | Pisces |
| May | 11 to June 19 | Aries |
| June | 20 to Aug. 1 | Taurus |
| Aug. | 2 to Sept. 20 | Gemini |
| Sept. | 21 to Dec. 31 | Cancer |

### 1961

| | | |
|---|---|---|
| Jan. | 1 to May 5 | Cancer |
| May | 6 to June 27 | Leo |
| June | 28 to Aug. 16 | Virgo |
| Aug. | 17 to Sept. 30 | Libra |
| Oct. | 1 to Nov. 12 | Scorpio |
| Nov. | 13 to Dec. 23 | Sagittarius |
| Dec. | 24 to Dec. 31 | Capricorn |

### 1962

| | | |
|---|---|---|
| Jan. | 1 to Jan. 31 | Capricorn |
| Feb. | 1 to Mar. 11 | Aquarius |
| Mar. | 12 to Apr. 18 | Pisces |
| Apr. | 19 to May 27 | Aries |
| May | 28 to July 8 | Taurus |
| July | 9 to Aug. 21 | Gemini |
| Aug. | 22 to Oct. 10 | Cancer |
| Oct. | 11 to Dec. 31 | Leo |

### 1963

| | | |
|---|---|---|
| Jan. | 1 to June 2 | Leo |
| June | 3 to July 26 | Virgo |
| July | 27 to Sept. 11 | Libra |
| Sept. | 12 to Oct. 24 | Scorpio |
| Oct. | 25 to Dec. 4 | Sagittarius |
| Dec. | 5 to Dec. 31 | Capricorn |

| 1964 | Date | Zodiacal Sign |
|---|---|---|
| Jan. | 1 to Jan. 12 | Capricorn |
| Jan. | 13 to Feb. 19 | Aquarius |
| Feb. | 20 to Mar. 28 | Pisces |
| Mar. | 29 to May 6 | Aries |
| May | 7 to June 16 | Taurus |
| June | 17 to July 29 | Gemini |
| July | 30 to Sept. 14 | Cancer |
| Sept. | 15 to Nov. 5 | Leo |
| Nov. | 6 to Dec. 31 | Virgo |

### 1965

| | | |
|---|---|---|
| Jan. | 1 to June 28 | Virgo |
| June | 29 to Aug. 19 | Libra |
| Aug. | 20 to Oct. 3 | Scorpio |
| Oct. | 4 to Nov. 13 | Sagittarius |
| Nov. | 14 to Dec. 22 | Capricorn |
| Dec. | 23 to Dec. 31 | Aquarius |

### 1966

| | | |
|---|---|---|
| Jan. | 1 to Jan. 29 | Aquarius |
| Jan. | 30 to Mar. 8 | Pisces |
| Mar. | 9 to Apr. 16 | Aries |
| Apr. | 17 to May 27 | Taurus |
| May | 28 to July 10 | Gemini |
| July | 11 to Aug. 24 | Cancer |
| Aug. | 25 to Oct. 11 | Leo |
| Oct. | 12 to Dec. 3 | Virgo |
| Dec. | 4 to Dec. 31 | Libra |

### 1967

| | | |
|---|---|---|
| Jan. | 1 to Feb. 11 | Libra |
| Feb. | 12 to Mar. 31 | Scorpio |
| Apr. | 1 to July 18 | Libra |
| July | 19 to Sept. 9 | Scorpio |
| Sept. | 10 to Oct. 22 | Sagittarius |
| Oct. | 23 to Nov. 30 | Capricorn |
| Dec. | 1 to Dec. 31 | Aquarius |

### 1968

| | | |
|---|---|---|
| Jan. | 1 to Jan. 8 | Aquarius |
| Jan. | 9 to Feb. 16 | Pisces |
| Feb. | 17 to Mar. 26 | Aries |

| 1968 | Date | Zodiacal Sign |
|------|------|---------------|
| Mar. | 27 to May 7 | Taurus |
| May | 8 to June 20 | Gemini |
| June | 21 to Aug. 4 | Cancer |
| Aug. | 5 to Sept. 20 | Leo |
| Sept. | 21 to Oct. 8 | Virgo |
| Oct. | 9 to Dec. 28 | Libra |
| Dec. | 29 to Dec. 31 | Scorpio |

### 1969

| | | |
|------|------|---------------|
| Jan. | 1 to Feb. 24 | Scorpio |
| Feb. | 25 to Sept. 20 | Sagittarius |
| Sept. | 21 to Nov. 3 | Capricorn |
| Nov. | 4 to Dec. 13 | Aquarius |
| Dec. | 14 to Dec. 31 | Pisces |

### 1970

| | | |
|------|------|---------------|
| Jan. | 1 to Jan. 23 | Pisces |
| Jan. | 24 to Mar. 6 | Aries |
| Mar. | 7 to Apr. 17 | Taurus |
| Apr. | 18 to June 1 | Gemini |
| June | 2 to July 17 | Cancer |
| July | 18 to Sept. 2 | Leo |
| Sept. | 3 to Oct. 19 | Virgo |
| Oct. | 20 to Dec. 5 | Libra |
| Dec. | 6 to Dec. 31 | Scorpio |

### 1971

| | | |
|------|------|---------------|
| Jan. | 1 to Jan. 23 | Scorpio |
| Jan. | 24 to Mar. 12 | Sagittarius |
| Mar. | 13 to May 3 | Capricorn |
| May | 4 to Nov. 6 | Aquarius |
| Nov. | 7 to Dec. 26 | Pisces |
| Dec. | 27 to Dec. 31 | Aries |

### 1972

| | | |
|------|------|---------------|
| Jan. | 1 to Feb. 10 | Aries |
| Feb. | 11 to Mar. 27 | Taurus |
| Mar. | 28 to May 12 | Gemini |
| May | 13 to June 28 | Cancer |
| June | 29 to Aug. 15 | Leo |
| Aug. | 16 to Sept. 30 | Virgo |
| Oct. | 1 to Nov. 15 | Libra |
| Nov. | 16 to Dec. 30 | Scorpio |
| Dec. | 31 | Sagittarius |

| 1973 | Date | Zodiacal Sign |
|------|------|---------------|
| Jan. | 1 to Feb. 12 | Sagittarius |
| Feb. | 13 to Mar. 26 | Capricorn |
| Mar. | 27 to May 8 | Aquarius |
| May | 9 to June 20 | Pisces |
| June | 21 to Aug. 12 | Aries |
| Aug. | 13 to Oct. 29 | Taurus |
| Oct. | 30 to Dec. 24 | Aries |
| Dec. | 25 to Dec. 31 | Taurus |

### 1974

| | | |
|------|------|---------------|
| Jan. | 1 to Feb. 27 | Taurus |
| Feb. | 28 to Apr. 20 | Gemini |
| Apr. | 21 to June 9 | Cancer |
| June | 10 to July 27 | Leo |
| July | 28 to Sept. 12 | Virgo |
| Sept. | 13 to Oct. 28 | Libra |
| Oct. | 29 to Dec. 10 | Scorpio |
| Dec. | 11 to Dec. 31 | Sagittarius |

### 1975

| | | |
|------|------|---------------|
| Jan. | 1 to Jan. 21 | Sagittarius |
| Jan. | 22 to Mar. 3 | Capricorn |
| Mar. | 4 to Apr. 11 | Aquarius |
| Apr. | 12 to May 21 | Pisces |
| May | 22 to July 1 | Aries |
| July | 2 to Aug. 14 | Taurus |
| Aug. | 15 to Oct. 17 | Gemini |
| Oct. | 18 to Nov. 25 | Cancer |
| Nov. | 26 to Dec. 31 | Gemini |

### 1976

| | | |
|------|------|---------------|
| Jan. | 1 to Mar. 18 | Gemini |
| Mar. | 19 to May 16 | Cancer |
| May | 17 to July 6 | Leo |
| July | 7 to Aug. 24 | Virgo |
| Aug. | 25 to Oct. 8 | Libra |
| Oct. | 9 to Nov. 20 | Scorpio |
| Nov. | 21 to Dec. 31 | Sagittarius |

### 1977

| | | |
|------|------|---------------|
| Jan. | 1 to Jan. 2 | Sagittarius |
| Jan. | 2 to Feb. 9 | Capricorn |
| Feb. | 10 to Mar. 20 | Aquarius |
| Mar. | 21 to Apr. 27 | Pisces |

## 1977

| Date | | Zodiacal Sign |
|---|---|---|
| Apr. | 28 to June 6 | Aries |
| June | 7 to July 17 | Taurus |
| July | 18 to Sept. 1 | Gemini |
| Sept. | 2 to Oct. 26 | Cancer |
| Oct. | 26 to Dec. 31 | Leo |

## 1978

| | | |
|---|---|---|
| Jan. | 1 to Jan. 26 | Leo |
| Jan. | 27 to Apr. 10 | Cancer |
| Apr. | 11 to June 14 | Leo |
| June | 15 to Aug. 4 | Virgo |
| Aug. | 5 to Sept. 19 | Libra |
| Sept. | 20 to Nov. 2 | Scorpio |
| Nov. | 3 to Dec. 12 | Sagittarius |
| Dec. | 13 to Dec. 31 | Capricorn |

## 1979

| | | |
|---|---|---|
| Jan. | 1 to Jan. 20 | Capricorn |
| Jan. | 21 to Feb. 27 | Aquarius |
| Feb. | 28 to Apr. 7 | Pisces |
| Apr. | 8 to May 16 | Aries |
| May | 17 to June 26 | Taurus |
| June | 27 to Aug. 8 | Gemini |
| Aug. | 9 to Sept. 24 | Cancer |
| Sept. | 25 to Nov. 19 | Leo |
| Nov. | 20 to Dec. 31 | Virgo |

## 1980

| | | |
|---|---|---|
| Jan. | 1 to Mar. 11 | Virgo |
| Mar. | 12 to May 4 | Libra |
| May | 5 to July 10 | Scorpio |
| July | 11 to Aug. 29 | Sagittarius |
| Aug. | 30 to Oct. 12 | Capricorn |
| Oct. | 13 to Nov. 22 | Aquarius |
| Nov. | 23 to Dec. 31 | Pisces |

## 1981

| | | |
|---|---|---|
| Jan. | 1 to Feb. 9 | Aquarius |
| Feb. | 10 to Mar. 17 | Pisces |
| Mar. | 18 to Apr. 25 | Aries |
| Apr. | 26 to June 6 | Taurus |
| June | 7 to July 19 | Gemini |

## 1981

| Date | | Zodiacal Sign |
|---|---|---|
| July | 20 to Sept. 2 | Cancer |
| Sept. | 3 to Oct. 21 | Leo |
| Oct. | 22 to Dec. 16 | Virgo |
| Dec. | 17 to Dec. 21 | Libra |

## 1982

| | | |
|---|---|---|
| Jan. | 1 to Aug. 3 | Libra |
| Aug. | 4 to Sept. 20 | Scorpio |
| Sept. | 21 to Nov. 1 | Sagittarius |
| Nov. | 2 to Dec. 12 | Capricorn |
| Dec. | 13 to Dec. 31 | Aquarius |

## 1983

| | | |
|---|---|---|
| Jan. | 1 to Jan. 17 | Aquarius |
| Jan. | 18 to Feb. 22 | Pisces |
| Feb. | 23 to Apr. 5 | Aries |
| Apr. | 6 to May 16 | Taurus |
| May | 17 to June 29 | Gemini |
| June | 30 to Aug. 13 | Cancer |
| Aug. | 14 to Sept. 29 | Leo |
| Sept. | 30 to Oct. 18 | Virgo |
| Oct. | 19 to Dec. 31 | Libra |

## 1984

| | | |
|---|---|---|
| Jan. | 1 to Jan. 12 | Libra |
| Jan. | 13 to Aug. 17 | Scorpio |
| Aug. | 18 to Oct. 5 | Sagittarius |
| Oct. | 6 to Nov. 13 | Capricorn |
| Nov. | 14 to Dec. 25 | Aquarius |
| Dec. | 26 to Dec. 31 | Pisces |

## 1985

| | | |
|---|---|---|
| Jan. | 1 to Feb. 2 | Pisces |
| Feb. | 3 to Mar. 15 | Aries |
| Mar. | 16 to Apr. 26 | Taurus |
| Apr. | 27 to June 10 | Gemini |
| June | 11 to July 26 | Cancer |
| July | 27 to Aug. 10 | Leo |
| Aug. | 11 to Oct. 27 | Virgo |
| Oct. | 28 to Dec. 14 | Libra |
| Dec. | 15 to Dec. 31 | Scorpio |

| 1986 | Date | Zodiacal Sign |
|------|------|---------------|
| Jan. | 1 to Feb. 2 | Scorpio |
| Feb. | 3 to Mar. 28 | Sagittarius |
| Mar. | 29 to Oct. 9 | Capricorn |
| Oct. | 10 to Nov. 26 | Aquarius |
| Nov. | 27 to Dec. 31 | Pisces |

| 1987 | | |
|------|------|---------------|
| Jan. | 1 to Jan. 8 | Pisces |
| Jan. | 9 to Feb. 20 | Aries |
| Feb. | 21 to Apr. 5 | Taurus |
| Apr. | 6 to May 21 | Gemini |
| May | 22 to July 6 | Cancer |
| July | 7 to Aug. 22 | Leo |
| Aug. | 23 to Oct. 8 | Virgo |
| Oct. | 9 to Nov. 24 | Libra |
| Nov. | 25 to Dec. 31 | Scorpio |

| 1988 | | |
|------|------|---------------|
| Jan. | 1 to Jan. 8 | Scorpio |
| Jan. | 9 to Feb. 22 | Sagittarius |
| Feb. | 23 to Apr. 6 | Capricorn |
| Apr. | 7 to May 23 | Virgo |
| May | 24 to July 13 | Pisces |
| July | 14 to Dec. 31 | Aries |

| 1989 | Date | Zodiacal Sign |
|------|------|---------------|
| Jan. | 1 to Jan. 19 | Aries |
| Jan. | 20 to Mar. 11 | Taurus |
| Mar. | 12 to Apr. 29 | Gemini |
| Apr. | 30 to June 16 | Cancer |
| June | 17 to Aug. 3 | Leo |
| Aug. | 4 to Sept. 19 | Virgo |
| Sept. | 20 to Nov. 4 | Libra |
| Nov. | 5 to Dec. 18 | Scorpio |
| Dec. | 19 to Dec. 31 | Sagittarius |

| 1990 | | |
|------|------|---------------|
| Jan. | 1 to Jan. 29 | Sagittarius |
| Jan. | 30 to Mar. 11 | Capricorn |
| Mar. | 12 to Apr. 20 | Aquarius |
| Apr. | 21 to May 31 | Pisces |
| June | 1 to July 12 | Aries |
| July | 13 to Aug. 31 | Taurus |
| Sept. | 1 to Dec. 14 | Gemini |
| Dec. | 15 to Dec. 31 | Taurus |

**10**

### The Influence of Jupiter

Jupiter is the fifth planet out from the Sun. It is a colossal-sized world about which little is known by astronomers. Formerly, it was believed that beneath its great banded gaseous atmosphere, an 18,000-mile-thick layer of ice encrusted its surface. It has *recently* been discovered that Jupiter (larger by far than all other planets and moons in the solar system combined!) actually *radiates* about three times as much heat as it *receives* from the Sun. This has raised the question of whether or not Jupiter is a small, cool star rather than a large, hot planet. While the average distance of Mars to the Sun is 141 million miles, Jupiter's mean distance from our star (the Sun) is about 483 million miles . . . a huge empty space exists between Mars and Jupiter. This gap is filled with cosmic rubble and meteoric debris (the asteroid belt) where in all likelihood another planet once orbited. Ancient mythology believed that that planet's name was "Vulcan," a world associated with such explosive violence that its very name has come down to us through the ages, and applies to *volcanoes*.

Jupiter is 120 times larger than the Earth, with an equatorial diameter of 89,329 miles compared to Earth's 8,000. This giant planet orbits the Sun once in about 12 Earth years (11.80 years, to be exact). In spite of its tremendous size, Jupiter makes one complete spin around its axis in 9 hours and 55 minutes compared to Earth's 24 hours. The giant of the solar system may well be the parent of most of the "inner" planets—Mars, "Vulcan" (the asteroid belt), Earth, Venus and Mercury. Jupiter has 12 moons, four of which

Galileo discovered, in 1610, when he first trained his telescope on them. The two largest moons, Ganymede and Callisto, are each larger than Mercury! Jupiter's atmospheric envelope is multicolored and streaked parallel to its equator. This is caused by the tremendous velocity of its axial spin.

Many large oval spots of various colors (probably gases of different densities in the atmosphere) have been observed from time to time. The most noteworthy is the Great Red Spot which is 8,000 miles wide and 30,000 miles long. It does not follow Jupiter's rotation, but tends to drift irregularly. Astronomers cannot explain it. But if Dr. Immanuel Velikovsky's cataclysmic theories continue to be vindicated at their present rate, the Great Red Spot may well be proved to be the remaining scar resulting from the "comet" Venus being torn from the Jovian atmosphere!

In astrology, Jupiter is called "the greater fortune," and Venus "the lesser fortune." Both planets seem to generate good luck in whatever Sign or house of the horoscope they are found. With only a little practice and experience, you'll notice that you tend to like people whose Sun Sign is the same as the Sign your Jupiter occupies—and vice versa. (By the same token, if Venus in a man's chart is in the same Sign as Mars in a woman's chart, a strong mutual attraction is evident. This is also true for Mars-Moon conjunctions, Venus-Ascendant conjunctions and Sun-Venus conjunctions. The charts at the end of each chapter will generally enable you to determine these a harmonious contacts.) "Jovial" is the word to describe Jupiterians (also those with Sagittarius ascending). People with a strong Jupiter influence are compassionate, sociable, optimistic, honest and straightforward. They are dignified, liberal, logical, confident and determined. It is well to remember that you have Jupiter (and every other planet) placed *somewhere* in your chart. Wherever it is, it will usually bring you good luck in those areas governed by that Sign.

*Check the end of this chapter for the position of Jupiter at your birth.*

## JUPITER IN ARIES ♃ ♈

One way or another, you are something of a pioneer, and love to travel and broaden your mind. You tend to be overly confident, brave, and a lover of sports, but *not* usually as a spectator. You are ambitious, but once success is within your grasp you are liable to switch your goal to some other pursuit. You are likely to hold down two jobs or engage in two occupations at once. This position of Jupiter encourages expansiveness and extravagance, which attributes are likely to make you very attractive to others. You are easy to reason with, a generous, honest, idealistic and philosophical person with many influential friends and sincere admirers. You are generally respected and usually fortunate in all your dealings. Anything that heightens your mental powers, or takes you traveling, has a strong appeal for you. You have a natural inclination for philosophy (unorthodox religion), literature and science. You are ambitious, optimistic, progressive and reasonable, fully capable of holding down the most responsible positions, particularly in relation to military matters or those wherein you are able to exercise authority and gain prestige. Insurance, investment and speculation are generally fortunate unless Jupiter is adversely affected by planets in the water and earth Signs. You are also lucky through children, young people, religious associates, law, travel and exporting. Virtually all your success is a result of your own efforts and qualifications—also of your marriage, domestic conditions and social standing.

## JUPITER IN TAURUS  ♃  ♉

Inasmuch as Jupiter signifies abundance and expansion, and Taurus is the natural house of money, your financial condition could be easy for you—too easy. You enjoy the pleasures of life so much you are apt to spend freely and engage in extravagances beyond your means. Your general tendency is to go overboard in whatever you do: spending money, eating, drinking, partying, etc. The opposite sex is good for you and you may meet many friends therein at church or religious social gatherings. You tend to be philosophical and generous, but your views on religion are fixed and dogmatic. You are generally reserved, peaceful, firm, affectionate and faithful. Although you are something of a bibliophile, and may have a good collection of books on religion, philosophy and travel, you prefer to stay close to home, except when you are forced to travel for education, business or health reasons. You love your home environment for the comfort and ease it affords and do not see any percentage in changing things or moving around a great deal. You tend to overemphasize your ability to provide for others, and may promise a lot more than you're actually able to deliver. You make some good starts, but tend to be rather lackadaisical, easygoing, without the drive or ability to tie things up as you had originally planned. Still, you are a great believer in justice and equality, with a harmonious, affectionate disposition.

## JUPITER IN GEMINI  ♃  ♊

Although somewhat impractical, you are blessed with a good sense of humor, a generally gay outlook and a ready flow of conversation, correspondence and exchange of ideas. You are compelled to keep in touch with other people, but are likely to be rather disorganized and to scatter your mental and nervous energies. You need to develop the power of concentration and learn to stick to one thing at a time. You are idealistic and inspirational, but often too changeable, restless and uncertain. Two marriages are indicated here; one of them may be with a close associate, a neighbor or someone related to you. However it turns out, you're bound to run into trouble through your travels (which may be extensive), writing and relatives—all of which affect your marriage. Jupiter in Gemini is a born philosopher-communicator; you may graduate from writing to publishing, especially of far-sighted religious subjects, science and invention. If Jupiter is badly aspected in your chart (i.e. if Mars or Saturn are in earth or water Signs), difficulties with your publisher, or publishing, may result from unpopular or unprofitable ventures. Nevertheless, you are one of the most interesting, sincere and voluble friends anyone could want.

## JUPITER IN CANCER  ♃  ♋

You have an interesting, seemingly paradoxical view of life—one that combines an admixture of intellectual and emotional good will toward all. You are fiercely patriotic and have a strong attachment to your own home (and home town) and the love of your mother. Even so, you thoroughly enjoy long travels, for education and just plain pleasure—especially near large bodies of water. Yet you always return to your home base. You like to eat and drink and may have a tendency to put on extra weight. You enjoy making money—as well as spending it on those you love. Your generosity, expansiveness and good will are well known. You are creative, imaginative and curious about the psychic, the occult and mysterious fields. You enjoy fine culture, art, music and the standard forms of creative excellence established by the old masters rather than the *avant-garde*. You enjoy a good social life, and are known to be kindly, sympathetic, humane and charitable—whether or not your friends happen to be on the same social and economic scale. Jupiter in Cancer indicates a peaceful, happy and honorable demise, either in a distant country or far from where you were born. You are benevolent, good-humored, and likely to acquire a large share of the world's material blessings, which you generously share with your family, whether they deserve it or not. You are proud of your ancestry and loyal to your loved ones.

## JUPITER IN LEO  ♃  ♌

You admire power, prestige and grandeur. You are a sincere and ardent lover, high-minded, loyal, courageous and generous. You have little trouble in gaining popularity, and are likely to fall in love with and marry someone who is highly influential—perhaps a celebrity, or someone who leads you into extravagance. You are lucky in love, speculation, and through children. You enjoy a healthy vitality, a strong constitution and the willpower and determination to hold positions of trust and responsibility. You are generally compassionate, good-natured, courteous, broad-minded and noble. You can profit greatly from long trips in association with diplomatic, educational or religious affairs. All forms of finer culture appeal to you; art, music, religion, philosophy and science. You thoroughly enjoy reaping the rewards (and honors) for your efforts. You like being the center of attention and achieving positions of social and professional prominence. You will profit financially from wise investments as well as from speculation. Fortunately, you are blessed with willpower, excellent judgment, foresight and wisdom. With your keen intuition and sense of diplomacy, you could rise in public esteem and hold a prominent government position. Your biggest drawback may be a tendency to "hold court" or expect people to treat you as "visiting royalty." But in love matters your affections are sincere and deep. You will probably be blessed with children, and those who know you will realize that you are not at all pompous in reality.

## JUPITER IN VIRGO ♃ ♍

You have an almost uncanny knack for turning small interests into profitable hobbies. This ability may be a substitute for a normal emotional give-and-take, which your discriminating nature tends to throttle. You *want* to let yourself go—to enjoy the pleasure of children, amusement and speculation, but you "prudently" tend to look for nonexistent troubles. You tend, too, toward the study of natural laws, particularly where they apply to diet and hygiene. You are probably pro-labor, but employees find it difficult to impose on you. You exercise great care in your choice of friends and acquaintances. Jupiter in the mental Sign of Virgo increases your powers of discrimination, practicality, prudence and discretion. You tend to be intellectually materialistic, with an innate talent for philosophical studies and scientific investigations. You are generally honest, smart, analytical and strongly critical. You need to let down your hair a little, loosen up and become less stiff and formal. Speculation, however, is not your forte. You may be able to dope out the market and invest wisely and moderately, but should avoid any sudden plunge or you're bound to come a cropper. You are lucky with co-workers and employees, fortunate in longterm investments, literature and commercial ventures— and in business generally. You will undoubtedly be promoted into higher economic and social strata than you ever anticipated earlier in life. Your business activities will take you to foreign countries where you may meet your spouse-to-be. This person is somewhat eccentric, possibly not as successful as you, or not your intellectual equal.

## JUPITER IN LIBRA ♃ ♎

When well aspected—that is, by other planets in fire and air Signs, Jupiter in Libra is excellent evidence for extremely happy and profitable partnerships; this means an exceptionally good marriage blessed with fine, talented children who will bring you great credit and joy. You possess an extraordinary ability for making friends and for creating peace and harmony from anger and chaos. You have a generous, pleasing personality, one that is obviously sincere, mild, moderate, obliging, and so sociable that you try to please everyone at once. You probably have musical or artistic talent and like all sorts of cultural and intellectual stimulation. You love travel, are highly liberal and understanding, compassionate and charitable. You will enjoy and profit from the theater, places of amusement and speculation in various forms of art and entertainment. You have a hidden "hunger" for public approbation and praise. Your biggest gains will accrue through marriage, partnership, associations and undertakings that hinge on broad popular appeal. Above all else, you are dedicated to the proposition that justice, mercy, peace and harmony should prevail everywhere. (Would that there were millions more like you!)

## JUPITER IN SCORPIO  ♃ ♏

You like all sorts of secrets, and close association with those you believe to be in a position of power or strong influence. You are a defender of the underdog and liable to cultivate the friendship of highly eccentric occultists—even those who have criminal connections. You are not always aware of this at the outset, but you eventually manage to ferret out professional and personal secrets and are not always above using your information to the detriment of someone else's good name. You can justify or rationalize any of your actions and have enormous pride in facing down challenges and overcoming minor disasters—many of which you create yourself. You are exceptionally fortunate (or intuitive) in choosing the right investments, and you demonstrate your faith by backing small stocks or enterprises that eventually bloom into gigantic corporations which pay large dividends. You manage to take many trips, some of them under the auspices of higher executives, with some of whom you may be involved in secret dealings. You manage to acquire considerable prestige in your field, and among your colleagues, which could lead to a position of power. This serves to strengthen your ambition, perseverance, generosity and ability to undergo considerable hardship and deprivation—if you feel the aim is worthwhile. You have a paradoxical compulsion to range between constructive and destructive acts and thoughts. Generally, you have an active, confident, discriminating and shrewd mind, a love of mystery, mysticism, occultism and weird experiences during your travels. When Jupiter is adversely aspected (i.e. by planets in the air and fire Signs), beware of false friends, unwise speculation and the envy of those in powerful positions. You possess inordinate pride and should be careful about confiding the secrets of others or spending too lavishly the money received from legacies or dividends.

## JUPITER IN SAGITTARIUS  ♃  ♐

Sagittarius is "ruled" by Jupiter, so this is his natural Sign, wherein Jupiter tends to bestow good fortune and success in most of your undertakings. You have a sharp, intuitive mind, a generally happy and expansive spirit and a love of higher education, although your own may be somewhat less formal owing to your dislike of hidebound, formalized procedures. Somehow you feel that sitting in a classroom interferes drastically with your education. You will benefit most from broad travels, particularly voyages overseas. You are philosophical, far-sighted, candid in your opinions, generous, kindly and high-minded. You tend to be the leader in your circle of friends and associates, and will often come into great honors and praise. Jupiter in Sagittarius is an excellent position for harmonious association with educational institutions, travel agencies, religious organizations, philosophical bodies and publishing houses. You are tolerant, sympathetic, broadminded, somewhat prophetic, eminently fair and sportsmanlike, with an excellent sense of humor. You have a general liking for outdoor sports and entertainment. Your overall expansiveness gives you a love of speculation, and unbounded faith in your ultimate good luck, which usually works the way you had expected. Regardless of the difficulties you encounter, you always manage to land on your feet. You are idealistic and well-nigh incorruptible; once you've decided on the morally right thing to do, you will fight to the bitter end to defend your ideal.

## JUPITER IN CAPRICORN  ♃ ♑

You are something of a paradox in that you are pulled by your desire for absolute independence on one hand and for security on the other. You are apt to plunge courageously into a situation, fully intending to fight to the bitter end, but when obstacles arise and you realize the dangers involved, your initial resolution will dissolve as through it had never been. You tend to be serious, deliberate, inventive and capable of solid, practical achievements. Your education is likely to be liberal and practical, not necessarily orthodox. You have your own way of gaining knowledge, and might easily participate in the practical advancement of political, scientific, religious or philosophical knowledge. Although quietly intelligent, you are often too cautious to come out and give your views, which probably tend to range between conservative and liberal. (You seem to have one foot in each camp.)

Jupiter in Capricorn is good testimony for an executive position at some time or other in your life. You are almost certain to achieve success in a position of authority or command. You possess a fine capacity for leadership, but need to overcome a too-cautious attitude and a tendency to care too much about what others are liable to think of you. You have the ambition (if not the complete confidence) and organizational ability to reach the top in almost any governmental or other public career. Anything connected with foreign affairs or international commerce is a fertile field for your constructive, practical abilities. You'd *like* to pioneer in new fields and be different, but your respect for tradition and the status quo, by contrast, generates a deep sense of insecurity. This same principle applies to your many impulses to be generous or to shake off your fears and to travel. Loosen up and disregard the opinions of those in authority. They have problems of their own. Be careful!

## JUPITER IN AQUARIUS  ♃ ♒

You possess a great deal of charm, combined with a broadly liberal viewpoint. In the best, most mature and creative sense of the word, you are a true, jovial humanitarian. You sincerely want everyone else to be happy and to enjoy the best there is in life. Yet you are often cold or indifferent to the normal, everyday matters that are a necessary part of living. This is because you are supremely idealistic, with an unusual progressive and independent outlook. Your personality has an enormous influence on friends and associates. You are open, friendly, easy to meet and truly interested in other people—the more you know the better. Your friends are faithful and sincerely affectionate. You are probably a living example of the adage: *"If you want to have a friend, BE one."*

You are keenly interested in and gain great pleasure from all kinds of public work, whether it involves institutions, political movements, labor or charitable activity. You are generally refined, far-sighted, at times even visionary. Your congenial attitude and your sympathetic and compassionate nature is jarred by strife, discord or lowly antagonism. You probably have a reputation for being helpful, optimistic, genteel and urbane. Whatever good you desire for the majority of people, you will work hard to bring it about. You will lend or donate your money and time, join organizations that share your broad, liberal philosophical and humanitarian aims and views. You are inclined to follow unusual, sometimes eccentric, lines of thought and study. You like to study the classic and ancient arts, mysticism, science, music and literature from all the ages. You often undergo strange experiences through certain off-beat friends and associates. You will profit well in your profession, particularly if it is connected with congressional or government activity or some form of work for the public good.

## JUPITER IN PISCES  ♃  ♓

You are strongly idealistic and tend to suffer personally at the injustices you see experienced by others. Although you are charitable, kind and sympathetic, you often overlook your *own* misfortunes. You are generally sociable, and possess many outstanding talents which you are apt to play down or overlook. You are unassuming, hospitable, fond of (and kind to) animals. You are most likely to profit from friends and associates who recognize your willingness to extend sympathy and help to the poor, the ill and those who otherwise suffer misfortune. You are likely to achieve a great deal of recognition, praise and honor for your work with sanitariums, laboratories, hospitals and similar institutions. You can also achieve success with the earthy and watery elements—in land, houses, mining or shipping.

You are strongly spiritual, highly idealistic, emotional, sensitive and imaginative in a positive way. You have probably experienced many precognitive dreams and similar evidences of your *psi* talents. This may have stimulated your curiosity and interest in psychic and occult phenomena. It is a good bet that you belong to one or more organizations for research into the investigation of psychic, mystical, occult or arcane phenomena. There is some danger that you will attract a member of the opposite sex whose sole aim is to take advantage of your kind and sympathetic nature. You may do considerable traveling by water in the course of your life's work. Learn to confide your secret ambitions, dreams, visions and feelings in someone you can trust and respect. You have a tendency to suffer inwardly while wearing a smile and allowing the world to believe you are supremely happy and contented.

To find where Jupiter was (by Sign) at the time of your birth, consult the following table, then insert this symbol (♃) in its proper place in the horoscope blank.

## TO FIND THE POSITION OF JUPITER AT YOUR BIRTH

| Date | Zodiacal Sign |
| --- | --- |
| Dec. 26, 1899 to Jan. 18, 1901 | Sagittarius |
| Jan. 19, 1901 to Feb. 6, 1902 | Capricorn |
| Feb. 7, 1902 to Feb. 19, 1903 | Aquarius |
| Feb. 20, 1903 to Feb. 29, 1904 | Pisces |
| Mar. 1, 1904 to Aug. 8, 1904 | Aries |
| Aug. 9, 1904 to Aug. 31, 1904 | Taurus |
| Sept. 1, 1904 to Mar. 7, 1905 | Aries |
| Mar. 8, 1905 to July 20, 1905 | Taurus |
| July 21, 1905 to Dec. 4, 1905 | Gemini |
| Dec. 5, 1905 to Mar. 9, 1906 | Taurus |
| Mar. 10, 1906 to July 30, 1906 | Gemini |
| July 31, 1906 to Aug. 18, 1907 | Cancer |
| Aug. 19, 1907 to Sept. 11, 1908 | Leo |
| Sept. 12, 1908 to Oct. 11, 1909 | Virgo |
| Oct. 12, 1909 to Nov. 11, 1910 | Libra |

| Date | Zodiacal Sign |
|------|---------------|
| Nov. 12, 1910 to Dec. 9, 1911 | Scorpio |
| Dec. 10, 1911 to Jan. 2, 1913 | Sagittarius |
| Jan. 3, 1913 to Jan. 21, 1914 | Capricorn |
| Jan. 22, 1914 to Feb. 3, 1915 | Aquarius |
| Feb. 4, 1915 to Feb. 11, 1916 | Pisces |
| Feb. 12, 1916 to June 25, 1916 | Aries |
| June 26, 1916 to Oct. 26, 1916 | Taurus |
| Oct. 27, 1916 to Feb. 12, 1917 | Aries |
| Feb. 13, 1917 to June 29, 1917 | Taurus |
| June 30, 1917 to July 12, 1918 | Gemini |
| July 13, 1918 to Aug. 1, 1919 | Cancer |
| Aug. 2, 1919 to Aug. 26, 1920 | Leo |
| Aug. 27, 1920 to Sept. 25, 1921 | Virgo |
| Sept. 26, 1921 to Oct. 26, 1922 | Libra |
| Oct. 27, 1922 to Nov. 24, 1923 | Scorpio |
| Nov. 25, 1923 to Dec. 17, 1924 | Sagittarius |
| Dec. 18, 1924 to Jan. 5, 1926 | Capricorn |
| Jan. 6, 1926 to Jan. 17, 1927 | Aquarius |
| Jan. 18, 1927 to June 5, 1927 | Pisces |
| June 6, 1927 to Sept. 10, 1927 | Aries |
| Sept. 11, 1927 to Jan. 22, 1928 | Pisces |
| Jan. 23, 1928 to June 3, 1928 | Aries |
| June 4, 1928 to June 11, 1929 | Taurus |
| June 12, 1929 to June 26, 1930 | Gemini |
| June 27, 1930 to July 16, 1931 | Cancer |
| July 17, 1931 to Aug. 10, 1932 | Leo |
| Aug. 11, 1932 to Sept. 9, 1933 | Virgo |
| Sept. 10, 1933 to Oct. 10, 1934 | Libra |
| Oct. 11, 1934 to Nov. 8, 1935 | Scorpio |
| Nov. 9, 1935 to Dec. 1, 1936 | Sagittarius |
| Dec. 2, 1936 to Dec. 19, 1937 | Capricorn |
| Dec. 20, 1937 to May 13, 1938 | Aquarius |
| May 14, 1938 to July 29, 1938 | Pisces |
| July 30, 1938 to Dec. 28, 1938 | Aquarius |
| Dec. 29, 1938 to May 10, 1939 | Pisces |
| May 11, 1939 to Oct. 29, 1939 | Aries |
| Oct. 30, 1939 to Dec. 19, 1939 | Pisces |
| Dec. 20, 1939 to May 15, 1940 | Aries |
| May 16, 1940 to May 25, 1941 | Taurus |
| May 26, 1941 to June 9, 1942 | Gemini |
| June 10, 1942 to June 29, 1943 | Cancer |

| *Date* | *Zodiacal Sign* |
|---|---|
| June 30, 1943 to July 25, 1944 | Leo |
| July 26, 1944 to Aug. 24, 1945 | Virgo |
| Aug. 25, 1945 to Sept. 24, 1946 | Libra |
| Sept. 25, 1946 to Oct. 23, 1947 | Scorpio |
| Oct. 24, 1947 to Nov. 14, 1948 | Sagittarius |
| Nov. 15, 1948 to Apr. 11, 1949 | Capricorn |
| Apr. 12, 1949 to June 26, 1949 | Aquarius |
| June 27, 1949 to Nov. 29, 1949 | Capricorn |
| Nov. 30, 1949 to Apr. 14, 1950 | Aquarius |
| Apr. 15, 1950 to Sept. 14, 1950 | Pisces |
| Sept. 15, 1950 to Dec. 1, 1950 | Aquarius |
| Dec. 2, 1950 to Apr. 20, 1951 | Pisces |
| Apr. 21, 1951 to Apr. 27, 1952 | Aries |
| Apr. 28, 1952 to May 8, 1953 | Taurus |
| May 9, 1953 to May 23, 1953 | Gemini |
| May 24, 1954 to June 11, 1955 | Cancer |
| June 12, 1955 to Nov. 16, 1955 | Leo |
| Nov. 17, 1955 to Jan. 17, 1956 | Virgo |
| Jan. 18, 1956 to July 6, 1956 | Leo |
| July 7, 1956 to Dec. 11, 1956 | Virgo |
| Dec. 12, 1956 to Feb. 18, 1957 | Libra |
| Feb. 19, 1957 to Aug. 5, 1957 | Virgo |
| Aug. 6, 1957 to Jan. 12, 1958 | Libra |
| Jan. 13, 1958 to Mar. 19, 1958 | Scorpio |
| Mar. 20, 1958 to Sept. 6, 1958 | Libra |
| Sept. 7, 1958 to Feb. 9, 1959 | Scorpio |
| Feb. 10, 1959 to Apr. 23, 1959 | Sagittarius |
| Apr. 24, 1959 to Oct. 4, 1959 | Scorpio |
| Oct. 5, 1959 to Feb. 29, 1960 | Sagittarius |
| Mar. 1, 1960 to June 9, 1960 | Capricorn |
| June 10, 1960 to Oct. 24, 1960 | Sagittarius |
| Oct. 25, 1960 to Mar. 14, 1961 | Capricorn |
| Mar. 15, 1961 to Aug. 11, 1961 | Aquarius |
| Aug. 12, 1961 to Nov. 3, 1961 | Capricorn |
| Nov. 4, 1961 to Mar. 24, 1962 | Aquarius |
| Mar. 25, 1962 to Apr. 3, 1963 | Pisces |
| Apr. 4, 1963 to Apr. 11, 1964 | Aries |
| Apr. 12, 1964 to Apr. 21, 1965 | Taurus |
| Apr. 22, 1965 to Sept. 20, 1965 | Gemini |
| Sept. 21, 1965 to Nov. 16, 1965 | Cancer |
| Nov. 17, 1965 to May 4, 1966 | Gemini |

| Date | Zodiacal Sign |
|------|---------------|
| May 5, 1966 to Sept. 26, 1966 | Cancer |
| Sept. 27, 1966 to Jan. 15, 1967 | Leo |
| Jan. 16, 1967 to May 22, 1967 | Cancer |
| May 23, 1967 to Oct. 18, 1967 | Leo |
| Oct. 19, 1967 to Feb. 26, 1968 | Virgo |
| Feb. 27, 1968 to June 14, 1968 | Leo |
| June 15, 1968 to Nov. 14, 1968 | Virgo |
| Nov. 15, 1968 to Mar. 29, 1969 | Libra |
| Mar. 30, 1969 to July 14, 1969 | Virgo |
| July 15, 1969 to Dec. 15, 1969 | Libra |
| Dec. 16, 1969 to Apr. 29, 1970 | Scorpio |
| Apr. 30, 1970 to Aug. 14, 1970 | Libra |
| Aug. 15, 1970 to Dec. 31, 1970 | Scorpio |
| Jan. 1, 1971 to Jan. 14, 1971 | Scorpio |
| Jan. 15, 1971 to June 5, 1971 | Sagittarius |
| June 6, 1971 to Sept. 11, 1971 | Scorpio |
| Sept. 12, 1971 to Dec. 31, 1971 | Sagittarius |
| Jan. 1, 1972 to Feb. 6, 1972 | Sagittarius |
| Feb. 7, 1972 to July 24, 1972 | Capricorn |
| July 25, 1972 to Sept. 25, 1972 | Sagittarius |
| Sept. 26, 1972 to Dec. 31, 1972 | Capricorn |
| Jan. 1, 1973 to Feb. 23, 1973 | Capricorn |
| Feb. 24, 1973 to Dec. 31, 1973 | Aquarius |
| Jan. 1, 1974 to Mar. 8, 1974 | Aquarius |
| Mar. 9, 1974 to Dec. 31, 1974 | Pisces |
| Jan. 1, 1975 to Mar. 18, 1975 | Aquarius |
| Mar. 19, 1975 to Dec. 31, 1975 | Aries |
| Jan. 1, 1976 to Mar. 26, 1976 | Aries |
| Mar. 27, 1976 to Aug. 23, 1976 | Taurus |
| Aug. 24, 1976 to Oct. 16, 1976 | Gemini |
| Oct. 17, 1976 to Dec. 31, 1976 | Taurus |
| Jan. 1, 1977 to Apr. 3, 1977 | Taurus |
| Apr. 4, 1977 to Aug. 20, 1977 | Gemini |
| Aug. 21, 1977 to Dec. 31, 1977 | Cancer |
| Jan. 1, 1978 to Apr. 12, 1978 | Gemini |
| Apr. 12, 1978 to Sept. 5, 1978 | Cancer |
| Sept. 6, 1978 to Dec. 31, 1978 | Leo |
| Jan. 1, 1979 to Mar. 1, 1979 | Leo |
| Mar. 2, 1979 to Apr. 20, 1979 | Cancer |
| Apr. 21, 1979 to Sept. 29, 1979 | Leo |
| Sept. 30, 1979 to Dec. 31, 1979 | Virgo |

| Date | Zodiacal Sign |
|------|---------------|
| Jan.   1, 1980 to Oct. 27, 1980 | Virgo |
| Oct.  27, 1980 to Nov. 27, 1980 | Libra |
| Nov.  28, 1980 to Dec. 26, 1982 | Scorpio |
| Dec.  27, 1982 to Jan. 19, 1984 | Sagittarius |
| Jan.  20, 1984 to Feb.  6, 1985 | Capricorn |
| Feb.   7, 1985 to Feb. 20, 1986 | Aquarius |
| Feb.  21, 1986 to Mar.  2, 1987 | Pisces |
| Mar.   3, 1987 to Mar.  8, 1988 | Aries |
| Mar.   9, 1988 to July 21, 1988 | Taurus |
| July  22, 1988 to Nov. 30, 1988 | Gemini |
| Dec.   1, 1988 to Mar. 11, 1990 | Cancer |
| Aug.  19, 1990 to Aug. 12, 1991 | Leo |

# 11

## The Influence of Saturn

Because of its halo of rings, Saturn is generally considered the most beautiful planet in the solar system. To this day, astronomers cannot agree on what these beautiful discs are composed of or how thick they are; estimates range from ten miles to eight inches. When seen edge-on, the rings flatten out and become entirely invisible. There has been recent speculation that Saturn is not the only Solarian planet surrounded by rings. Earth may also have its retinue of gossamer rings, some astronomers theorize, but they supposedly are not visible from the surface. On the face of it, this seems unlikely.

Saturn is the second largest of all the planets; slightly flattened, its equatorial diameter is 75,021 miles. From pole to pole, however, it measures 67,805 miles. Not counting the Asteroid Belt between Jupiter and Mars, Saturn is the sixth planet out from the Sun, at a mean distance of 887,200,000 miles from its parent star. Saturn's orbital period around the sun is 29½ Earth years—and like Jupiter's 12-year period this increment corresponds with many terrestrial cycles, indicating that there may indeed be a possible connection (between Saturn and our Earth). Also like Jupiter, gigantic Saturn spins on its axis at a tremendous velocity for so massive a body—10 hours and 38 minutes is the length of the Saturnian day. Undecipherable, but seemingly artificial, radio waves have been received from both Jupiter and Saturn, and recorded at most of the world's radio observatories. Until 1967 Saturn was believed to have only nine moons, but now a tenth—called Themis—has been discovered and verified. The combined width of Saturn's three rings is 41,500 miles across. The outer or first ring is a little over 10,000 miles wide. After that there is Cassini's Division, a dark band in which there is little or none of the material which makes up the rings; this is probably about 3,000 miles wide. The second ring is about 16,000 miles across. The innermost "crepe" ring (because it looks like dress material) is 11,500 miles wide.

The innermost edge of the rings arcs about 7,000 miles above the surface of Saturn, which is also a multicolored, banded giant like Jupiter. If they could be seen from the surface, Saturn's rings would be a spectacular sight . . . perhaps even more spectacular if viewed from one of its moons—Titan, Hyperion, Phoebe or Themis. Titan, the largest of Saturn's moons, is also one of the largest satellites in the solar system, with a possible diameter of almost 4,000 miles.

Since the earliest known records of ancient astrologers, Saturn has been equated to adversity and relegated to the status of a *malefic* planet. Saturn's principle (its general influence) is the exact opposite of Jupiterian expansion and joviality. Saturn represents cold, contraction, seriousness, stability, discipline and practicality. No nonsense here. The typical Saturn-*ruled* individual (one with Capricorn rising), however, doesn't lack a sense of humor at all. He is inclined to make wry, witty, cryptic observations that to the discerning mind are incisive, apropos and often hilarious. Saturn sometimes causes temporary denial of the things promised in the horoscope by Jupiter or Venus. Yet in retrospect (a Saturnian condition) you often discover that your greatest obstacles present challenges that, when overcome, give you lasting strength and character that an easy path would not have offered. With good aspects in your chart, Saturn will incline you toward prudence, caution, diplomacy, seriousness, stability, conservatism, practicality, intellectual depth and good managerial or organizational ability. Physically, Saturn governs the knees, teeth, bones and inner ear.

*Find the position of Saturn at your birth by checking the list at the end of this chapter.*

## SATURN IN ARIES ♄ ♈

As you already know, the early part of your life is the most difficult. From this base of obstacles and adversity you can build the strength of character to surmount anything that may confront you for the remainder of your life. You are ambitious and determined to succeed; you desire responsibility, authority, dignity and respect, but often lack the confidence necessary to grasp the opportunity firmly when it presents itself. Yet your preseverence and hard work will ultimately be crowned with success. It does not come easily, however. Sometimes it may seem as though you fall two steps behind for every forward stride. But Saturn, often symbolized as the bearded, scythe-carrying "Father Time" will work *for* you over the years. Just as you may have felt you were deliberately "jinxed" in your youth, each year now brings you greater wisdom, less struggle and the increased prestige you've always wanted. One of your chief difficulties may be marital trouble caused by a jealous or insecure mate. On the other hand, you're not exactly easy to live with; you have a tendency to flare into anger when you are opposed, and you can be highly argumentative and cantankerous. Left to your own devices, however, you tend to reason things out and see the light of logic through quiet contemplation. Although it is possible that you may lack the depth of mind you assume, you're eventually going to win the admiration and respect of those in a position to do you the most good.

## SATURN IN TAURUS ♄ ♉

You tend to be rather too stolid, and to develop great fears about losing money, love, and the comfort and security they bring. With discipline, economy and wise investment, combined with a certain amount of frugality, you will manage, though, to acquire enough material goods in the form of houses, land and securities to satisfy yourself. You tend to nurse grudges, have a quick and brittle temper and can be stubborn and resentful. Face the fact that you're going to have money trouble with relatives and could lose some of your hard-earned gains. This is a touchy situation; you're liable to place your trust in people who are unscrupulous and blame those who hold your best interests foremost.

Before you're able to straighten out the resulting unhappy domestic scene, there will be losses and trouble caused by these relatives. You can gain a great deal of satisfaction and relaxation from working in or with the earthy things: raising or breeding stock, studying botany, gardening or farming. You tend to keep your personal troubles bottled up and can be reserved, diplomatic and prudent in your relationships. Generally, you are of a kindly, quiet and considerate disposition, thoughtful, determined and able to function well under emotional pressure and other adverse conditions.

## SATURN IN GEMINI    ♄  ♊

You have an ingenious, practical interest in all that goes on around you—in the present as well as with regard to prospects for the future. You have a built-in talent for deep intellectual achievements in writing, publishing, mathematics or science. You may have a tendency to skip from one thing to another—being equally serious about each subject, topic or study—then just dropping and forgetting about them. You are liable to experience difficulty and much sorrow in your dealings with relatives, and many obstacles, or misfortune, in short trips and traveling. You are clever and observant, resourceful, adaptable and serious-minded. Neighbors, relatives (and friends at one time or another) will succeed in placing the yoke of restraint or heavy responsibility on you, severely limiting your personal freedom and independence. You may tend to delude yourself by seeing things as you'd *like* them to be. This can cause you to become easily depressed because you are usually motivated by the finest ideals and may experience disillusionment through others. You can overcome many such setbacks by studying and applying positive philosophical attitudes. Emerson is a good example of Saturn in Gemini

## SATURN IN CANCER    ♄  ♋

You are inclined to be ultrasensitive, fearful because you lack the security (either now or in the past) of the love of your parents. There is some difficulty, sorrow or anxiety indicated in your home life, through children and parent-image attachments you form—either consciously or unconsciously. You are rather changeable and lack the confidence to stand independently and break away from a stultifying past. You revere experience, age and authority because it represents the anchor and stability whose lack you feel so keenly. You want assurance, guidance—almost as a child who is overindulged and made to feel that his parents don't love him enough to care what he does. You have a powerful drive to appease those in authority or who are older, in the vain hope that these people will extend the love and security of which you feel deprived. You often tend to be discontented, dissatisfied, jealous, anxiety-ridden and changeable.

You may change your residence, your job, your interests and moods, but it always stems from the same problem—insecurity—the early denial of parental love and affection. You may marry someone older, a serious hard-working person who stimulates your active interest in helping to operate a good economical household. You will derive much satisfaction and happiness through psychic studies and occultism, but are liable to be emotionally affected by discordant conditions created by other people.

## SATURN IN LEO ♄ ♌

This position of Saturn can affect the heart and cause you some sorrow in love affairs and through children. You seek to compensate by hard work for an apparent inability to derive pleasure from amusements. But this merely serves to create the additional dangers of overwork, overtaxing your heart and impairing your general health. (Psychologists could learn a great deal simply from observing how people with Saturn in Leo develop complex emotional difficulties when it comes to expressing the love they must eventually feel for someone.) There is a powerful blockage here, and you may seek an outlet for your thwarted feelings in an illicit alliance with someone unworthy of you. This is almost certain to create trouble with those who are inferior in some way. You are ambitious, determined, have a hair-trigger temper and strong spiritual inclinations. You are an odd combination of courageousness and prudence. You are generous, have a strong will, but may be a victim of too severe and limiting religious discipline as a child. Try to loosen up and reveal your true feelings; you're liable to be happily surprised at the response.

## SATURN IN VIRGO ♄ ♍

Good, careful investment in real estate will almost assuredly pay off for you, but the first half of your life is liable to be plagued by obstacles, sorrow, ill health, and difficulties that could bring you to the brink of a nervous breakdown. Although you may tend to exaggerate the slight ailments with which you are plagued, you probably experience severe headaches and possible constipation. You are generally reserved, rather humble and self-effacing, discreet, extra careful and so anxious and cautious that you cause a general rundown and tired feeling in yourself through your negative thinking. You are very serious, prudent, reserved and quiet. You also tend to be watchful, ready for quick flight, mistrustful of others, doubting, anxious, gloomy, worried and easily depressed. This is an unfortunate combination for a happy marriage, and unless you make a determined effort to see the bright side of every situation, you are certain to cause troubles, misfortune and general unhappiness in any partnership or marriage. You have a good mind, and could easily excel in scientific studies of health, hygiene or literature.

## SATURN IN LIBRA ♄ ♎

If you happen to be a woman you are likely to be quite attractive, but Saturn, the celestial taskmaster, will take his good old time in finding the right marriage partner for you. Somehow, there is disappointment here—a lack of warmth, love or enthusiasm in your marriage. More than one marriage is indicated for you. Business partnerships also cause difficulty. Much as you desire and work for harmony, peace and good public relations, you develop enemies, some of whom are likely to be women rather than men.

You have refined tendencies, a liking for the better things of life—music, art, the theater and socializing—but you often become involved in controversial subjects and heated arguments. Your relations with other people are not at all what you want them to be. You seek order, harmony and justice, but run into emotional turmoil instead. The deepest love affair in your life may have ended in loss and heartbreak. There is some trouble in your employment, and there are separations from some people you love. Still, this Sign is excellent evidence of fine mental machinery in a person well-equipped for a career in law or science. The image you project to that part of the world you want most to impress is entirely too serious. Be careful of broken contracts and protect any documents pertaining to your home or land.

## SATURN IN SCORPIO ♄ ♏

When you apply your somewhat simmering volcanic nature toward achievement in the sciences, geology, archeology or researching new knowledge, you may overcome your willful, passionate, jealous nature. You are forever searching out better avenues for expressing your hidden talents. With proper training and self-discipline, you can easily develop great intellectual depth. Ordinarily you proceed with shrewdness and caution, yet you are resourceful, extremely independent and passionate. You are inclined to make sudden decisions that often surprise even yourself, but once embarked on a course of action you *will* doggedly pursue your plan to the bitter end—even when you can clearly see your own destruction looming at that end. It is as though you are unable to help yourself; but the obsessions can just as easily be checked and rechanneled, because you possess great willpower.

You are acquisitive, cautious, resourceful and calculating. You are able to overcome enormous obstacles, and, through sheer persistence, attention to detail, cleverness and patience, you can reach great pinnacles of success. One of your chief drawbacks is trouble with the opposite sex; you tend to take on secret love affairs and the burden of knowing the innermost secrets of people who confide in you. You often act in haste, drive yourself into troubled waters and live to regret your impulsiveness. Learn to accept that what is done is done and that no amount of mental or emotional rehashing will change the past. The trick is to learn from your mistakes—not to repeat them. You are fascinated by mysteries, secrets and occult studies and may have such a powerful intuitive faculty that it borders on *psi* ability.

## SATURN IN SAGITTARIUS ♄ ♐

You are gifted with powerful hunches, strong intuition and accurate prophetic talents. You are therefore far-sighted, visionary, and able to foresee the logical outcome of long-range scientific and social developments. You carry yourself with dignity, and gain the esteem of others through your talents and mental abilities. Although you enjoy approbation, *self*-respect comes even higher on your list of priorities. You are deeply philosophical and sincerely religious, perhaps in a rather paradoxical "liberal-orthodox" sense. You are very serious about how the game of life is played; the stress, however, is not so much on material success, and recognition, as on the moral issues involved—one might almost say the "sportsmanship" of adhering to certain rules of discipline.

Those who stand in your way do not realize how sensitive you are or how deeply hurt you can become by the slings and arrows, the cutting antagonism and severe criticism of harsh opposition. By allowing yourself the luxury of resentment against these censures, you delay the promotion and ultimate recognition you rightfully deserve. It is almost certain that you will experience the tarnishing of your reputation at some time in life. Your honor and ethics will be unjustly questioned and aired in public. You will be unable to combat these setbacks with abstract philosophy or "tried and true" methods of communicating your real stands and objectives. They're bound to be misinterpreted. You are generally kind and considerate, broad and humanitarian in your views and absolutely fearless and outspoken when you are involved with the politics of economy or the promotion of sound governmental fiscal policy. You need the firm feeling of conviction that your undertakings are essentially ethical and morally right as well as practical. You want to inspire others, but may wind up simply insisting that everyone practice outdated "virtues" that have little relevance to modern society unless you broaden your outlook.

## SATURN IN CAPRICORN ♄ ♑

Your chief characteristic is your ability to achieve in spite of great odds. You are constantly aware of your keen desire to lift yourself to great heights. Your ambition knows no bounds, and you will persist in hard work, the cultivation of those who can help, and diplomacy and tact until you achieve the success you have set out to win. You work so hard and play so seldom that you are liable to chronic illnesses and may even come close to a nervous breakdown through overwork, worry and anxiety. Try not to repress your emotions or stifle your occasional desire for fun and relaxation. Know that despite all adversity your failures are actually minor victories because you learn from every mistake and will succeed in the long pull.

You have a reserved, serious exterior, excellent reasoning abilities and a determinedly stubborn faith in yourself. This is an unbeatable combination, yet your acquisitiveness and rather materialistic outlook make you suspicious, fearful, melancholy, overly cautious and often deeply dissatisfied with your progress. You tend to form attachments with those who are your intellectual inferiors, and often members of the opposite sex. Unless Saturn is well-aspected in your horoscope, i.e., with the Sun, Venus or Jupiter either four Signs away (in trine) or two Signs (sextile), you may be plagued with unfaithful or unreliable friends. Marriage could bring unexpected trouble and sorrow in your home life. You possess good managerial and executive abilities, are well qualified to handle responsibility and could easily operate your own business (which you'd much rather do than take orders or work for someone else).

## SATURN IN AQUARIUS  ♄  ♒

You have many friends and aquaintances who will last a lifetime. Among these people, there is someone with whom you'll form a lasting romantic attachment. You enjoy being attractive to the opposite sex and are serious, friendly, sociable and quite good natured generally. You tend to be courteously reserved, thoughtful, considerate and (outwardly) tractable. Whenever you become involved in anything that attracts your interest, you take straightforward action and are able to express yourself knowledgeably and impressively. Like Saturn in the other fixed Signs, Scorpio, Leo and Taurus, Saturn in Aquarius leads you to far more fortunate circumstances in later life than during your early years. You learn rapidly and will further refine your thinking processes through experience, observation and study. The longer you practice broadly progressive policies, the more profound your mind will become and the more clearly your insight and intuition will be developed.

You are especially adept in the arts and in science, but are likely to adopt the orthodox path to learning *and* development. However, this does not prevent your seeing things in their broadest context and often in an entirely original and inventive manner. With quiet, steady determination and faithful application of the wisdom you acquire, you will reap high financial rewards, either professionally or through employment in a large company or corporation. Your sincerity, reasonableness and intelligence will win you the recognition and lovable friends you value so highly.

SATURN IN PISCES  ♄  ♓

You are fortunate if Saturn in Pisces is beneficially aspected—i.e., by the Sun, Jupiter or Venus in any of the earth or water Signs—and well placed in your horoscope. If so, you are able to help yourself by study, meditation, volunteer work in hospitals, prisons and mental institutions and welfare work for the poor. Do not simply accept what you consider to be your lot in life—many obstacles and difficulties if Saturn happens to be adversely aspected (usually by Mars in a fire or air Sign) in your chart. Events may occur, though, that are completely beyond your ability to deal effectively with them. You are often faced by and forced to deal with the totally unexpected and completely undesirable in life. Even when you manage to work your way into a position of dignity, esteem or prestige, it takes all the will power and determination you can muster just to hold your own there. You are often the cause of your own unhappiness and bad luck, however. You are highly emotional, strongly sympathethic and likely to feel as though others are in worse condition. You have a strong, desiring nature, but need to encourage within yourself the ability to see things optimistically, with a continuously firm attitude. Of course you have suffered mishaps, sadness, loss of love, sorrow and tragedy that may deeply affect you emotionally. Only *you* can help yourself, however—by developing *ambition:*

"All competent men should have some ambition, for ambition is like the temper in steel. If there's too much the product is brittle, if there's too little the steel is soft; and without a certain amount of hardness a man cannot achieve what he sets out to do."—Dwight D. Eisenhower.

## TO FIND THE POSITION OF SATURN AT YOUR BIRTH

| Date | Zodiacal Sign |
|------|---------------|
| Oct. 27, 1897 to Jan. 20, 1900 | Sagittarius |
| Jan. 21, 1900 to July 18, 1900 | Capricorn |
| July 19, 1900 to Oct. 16, 1900 | Sagittarius |
| Oct. 17, 1900 to Jan. 19, 1903 | Capricorn |
| Jan. 20, 1903 to Apr. 12, 1905 | Aquarius |
| Apr. 13, 1905 to Aug. 16, 1905 | Pisces |
| Aug. 17, 1905 to Jan. 7, 1906 | Aquarius |
| Jan. 8, 1906 to Mar. 18, 1908 | Pisces |
| Mar. 19, 1908 to May 16, 1910 | Aries |
| May 17, 1910 to Dec. 14, 1910 | Taurus |
| Dec. 15, 1910 to Dec. 14, 1910 | Aries |
| Jan. 20, 1911 to July 6, 1912 | Taurus |
| July 7, 1912 to Nov. 30, 1912 | Gemini |
| Dec. 1, 1912 to Mar. 25, 1913 | Taurus |
| Mar. 26, 1913 to Aug. 24, 1914 | Gemini |
| Aug. 25, 1914 to Dec. 6, 1914 | Cancer |
| Dec. 7, 1914 to May 11, 1915 | Gemini |
| May 12, 1915 to Oct. 16, 1916 | Cancer |
| Oct. 17, 1916 to Dec. 7, 1916 | Leo |
| Dec. 8, 1916 to June 23, 1917 | Cancer |
| June 24, 1917 to Aug. 11, 1919 | Leo |
| Aug. 12, 1919 to Oct. 7, 1921 | Virgo |
| Oct. 8, 1921 to Dec. 19, 1923 | Libra |
| Dec. 20, 1923 to Apr. 5, 1924 | Scorpio |
| Apr. 6, 1924 to Sept. 13, 1924 | Libra |
| Sept. 14, 1924 to Dec. 2, 1926 | Scorpio |
| Dec. 3, 1926 to Mar. 29, 1929 | Sagittarius |
| Mar. 30, 1929 to May 4, 1929 | Capricorn |
| May 5, 1929 to Nov. 29, 1929 | Sagittarius |
| Nov. 30, 1929 to Feb. 22, 1932 | Capricorn |
| Feb. 23, 1932 to Aug. 12, 1932 | Aquarius |
| Aug. 13, 1932 to Nov. 18, 1932 | Capricorn |
| Nov. 19, 1932 to Feb. 13, 1935 | Aquarius |
| Feb. 14, 1935 to Apr. 24, 1937 | Pisces |

| *Date* | *Zodiacal Sign* |
| --- | --- |
| Apr. 25, 1937 to Oct. 17, 1937 | Aries |
| Oct. 18, 1937 to Jan. 13, 1938 | Pisces |
| Jan. 14, 1938 to July 5, 1939 | Aries |
| July 6, 1939 to Sept. 21, 1939 | Taurus |
| Sept. 22, 1939 to Mar. 19, 1940 | Aries |
| Mar. 20, 1940 to May 7, 1942 | Taurus |
| May 8, 1942 to June 19, 1944 | Gemini |
| June 20, 1944 to Aug. 1, 1946 | Cancer |
| Aug. 2, 1946 to Sept. 18, 1948 | Leo |
| Sept. 19, 1948 to Apr. 2, 1949 | Virgo |
| Apr. 3, 1949 to May 28, 1949 | Leo |
| May 29, 1949 to Nov. 19, 1950 | Virgo |
| Nov. 20, 1950 to Mar. 6, 1951 | Libra |
| Mar. 7, 1951 to Aug. 12, 1951 | Virgo |
| Aug. 13, 1951 to Oct. 21, 1953 | Libra |
| Oct. 22, 1953 to Jan. 11, 1956 | Scorpio |
| Jan. 12, 1956 to May 13, 1956 | Sagittarius |
| May 14, 1956 to Oct. 9, 1956 | Scorpio |
| Oct. 10, 1956 to Jan. 4, 1959 | Sagittarius |
| Jan. 5, 1959 to Jan. 9, 1962 | Capricorn |
| Jan. 10, 1962 to Dec. 16, 1964 | Aquarius |
| Dec. 17, 1964 to Mar. 2, 1967 | Pisces |
| Mar. 3, 1967 to Apr. 28, 1969 | Aries |
| Apr. 29, 1969 to Dec. 31, 1970 | Taurus |
| Jan. 1, 1971 to June 18, 1971 | Taurus |
| June 19, 1971 to Dec. 31, 1971 | Gemini |
| Jan. 1, 1972 to Jan. 10, 1972 | Gemini |
| Jan. 11, 1972 to Feb. 21, 1972 | Taurus |
| Feb. 22, 1972 to Dec. 31, 1972 | Gemini |
| Jan. 1, 1973 to Aug. 1, 1973 | Gemini |
| Aug. 2, 1973 to Dec. 31, 1973 | Cancer |
| Jan. 1, 1974 to Jan. 7, 1974 | Cancer |
| Jan. 8, 1974 to Apr. 18, 1974 | Gemini |
| Apr. 19, 1974 to Dec. 31, 1974 | Cancer |
| Jan. 1, 1975 to Sept. 17, 1975 | Cancer |
| Sept. 18, 1975 to Dec. 31, 1975 | Leo |
| Jan. 1, 1976 to Jan. 14, 1976 | Leo |
| Jan. 15, 1976 to June 5, 1976 | Cancer |
| June 6, 1976 to Dec. 31, 1976 | Leo |
| Jan. 1, 1977 to Nov. 17, 1977 | Leo |
| Nov. 18, 1977 to Dec. 31, 1977 | Virgo |

| Date | | Zodiacal Sign |
|------|---|---------------|
| Jan. 1, 1978 to Jan. 5, 1978 | | Virgo |
| Jan. 6, 1978 to July 26, 1978 | | Leo |
| July 27, 1978 to Dec. 31, 1978 | | Virgo |
| Jan. 1, 1979 to Dec. 31, 1979 | | Virgo |
| Jan. 1, 1980 to Sept. 21, 1980 | | Virgo |
| Sept. 22, 1980 to Nov. 29, 1982 | | Libra |
| Nov. 30, 1982 to May 7, 1983 | | Scorpio |
| May 8, 1983 to Aug. 24, 1983 | | Libra |
| Aug. 25, 1983 to Nov. 17, 1985 | | Scorpio |
| Nov. 18, 1985 to Feb. 13, 1988 | | Sagittarius |
| Feb. 14, 1988 to June 10, 1988 | | Capricorn |
| June 11, 1988 to Nov. 12, 1988 | | Sagittarius |
| Nov. 13, 1988 to Feb. 6, 1991 | | Capricorn |

**12**

# The Influence of Uranus

Uranus, the seventh planet out from the Sun, is an eccentric banded giant with a diameter of 33,219 miles—more than four times as large as Earth. Discovered in 1781 by Sir William Herschel, Uranus' mean distance from the Sun is one billion, seven hundred and eighty-four million, eight hundred thousand (1,784,800,000) miles. Although Herschel is officially credited for discovering the planet that once briefly bore his name, it was first seen and recorded by an *astrologer* on five different occasions almost a century before. John Flamstead, the first Astronomer Royal of England (and builder of the Observatory at Greenwich), was actually a first-rate astrologer who timed the laying of the observatory cornerstone by horoscopy and recorded five notations of Uranus before the year 1690—long before its "official" discovery.

Uranus is unique in the solar system in that its axis is inclined at the peculiar angle of 98 degrees from the plane of its orbit. In effect, it lies somewhat on its side. Uranus rotates on its axis in 10 hours and 48 minutes, and takes 84 years and four days to complete one orbit around the Sun. Due to its extreme axial tilt, however, the Sun seems to stand directly above each pole at the opposite ends of its orbit. During the period when the Sun is "above" its South pole, the entire Northern hemisphere of Uranus lies in total darkness for almost 20 Earth years at a time—and vice versa.

Uranus has five known satellites, all of which orbit in the plane of the planet's equator. Their names are taken from the writings of Shakespeare and Alexander Pope: "Miranda," from *The Tempest;* "Oberon" and Titania," from *A Midsummer Night's Dream;* "Umbriel," from *The Rape of the Lock;* and "Ariel," also from *The Tempest.*

Since the discovery of Uranus, it has been observed by astrologers to correlate with science, astrology, electricity, broad humanitarian movements, the production of earthquakes and events that occur with unexpected swiftness. Since Uranus takes 84 Earth years to complete one solar orbit, it spends about seven years in each Sign of the Zodiac.

People born with Uranus strongly placed in their horoscope, particularly the Ascendant (First House) or Midheaven (Tenth House), or powerfully aspected in any way, are usually inventive and attracted to what seems odd or peculiar to most other people; they may appear eccentric in some ways, often curious and are actually far ahead of their time. These people are so intuitive, imaginative and far-sighted that they can perceive ways and means to improve on almost anything that crosses their path. They are gifted with an uncanny imagination and a strong, constructive social consciousness. Uranus type people usually practice equality, liberty and democracy.

Paradoxically, Uranus is considered "strange," "cold," "airy," "magnetic," "positive," "malefic," "dry," and "occult," yet it "rules" science in general and astrology in particular; it is considered to be "electric," and often prompts us to act without rhyme or reason. Uranus represents the unexpected, the unpremeditated, and all things futuristic, revolutionary and visionary.

*Find the position of Uranus at your birth in the listing at the end of this chapter.*

## URANUS IN ARIES  ♅  ♈

Although you may not intentionally be so, you are apt to be blunt, rude, brusque or radically untactful in your relations with others. You have the feeling that *you know* all that is necessary to know and are too impatient to consider the dull, plodding (often actually erroneous) theories of others. You frequently find yourself involved in heated arguments which result in the loss of your friends. You have certain rather cold, scientific ideas about stimulating the intellectual or mental abilities of young children before they are exposed to the myriad superstitions and myths of a "disorganized" society. You have a well-developed, pioneering, inventive ability, originality and resourcefulness. Coupled with a practical knowledge of business and finance, you could be a one-person unbeatable team. You tend to be rash, impulsive and forceful, extremely positive that you are in the right. You are bubbling with enthusiasm, intellectual vigor and often repressed physical activity. Nothing can dampen your great love for freedom and independence. You like to move around, travel, change your residence and *possibly* to work out totally new electronic and fluidic technological ideas or the most advanced and novel methods of accomplishing anything new or original in the age of space. Regardless of your age, it is an excellent idea to pursue additional education, be it formal or liberal.

## URANUS IN TAURUS   ♅   ♉

You are apt to gain financially through original real estate and land enterprises. You are probably quite fortunate in partnership transactions and associations with progressive practical organizations that encourage innovation, ingenuity and invention, at which you are clever. If beneficially aspected, that is, if the Sun, Moon, Jupiter or Venus are in the earth or water Signs, Uranus in Taurus is a good indication for a happy and prosperous marriage, although this position *usually* brings about strife, arguments and the jealousy of your marriage partner. You are inclined to be somewhat intuitive, psychic or far-sighted. Your natural ingenuity, originality and resourcefulness are capable of meeting and overcoming almost all obstacles that fate or circumstances place in your path. You are headstrong, fully determined to achieve your goals despite any opposition, and likely to be tractable, broadminded and easygoing at one time, then switch unexpectedly to a rigidly stubborn and intractable attitude. It is best to use your innate originality during quiet times to find ways of working at an even pace with cool deliberation most of the time, rather than ploughing ahead in fits and starts. Give your sense of what is practical an opportunity to influence your decisions.

## URANUS IN GEMINI  ♅  ♊

You are naturally endowed with a good, logical, inventive mind, a love of study and a strong attraction for advanced thinking in all the sciences. You could become an excellent logician, an electronics expert with new, original and extremely advanced ideas, or a space age writer or communicator —or an engineer in any of these new areas. All the sciences, anything original, novel or new in concept immediately gains your favorable attention. Your ingenuity, hair-trigger responses and unusual methods of expression may cause you to be branded as something of an eccentric. You are versatile, have a facility with languages and attract unusual friends in the arts and sciences. You enjoy people and also making new friends and traveling among or with literary and advanced scientific thinkers. There may have been some difficulty with your education; you are not likely to have successfully concluded orthodox examinations for your degree(s), despite your strong interest in the sciences—or perhaps because of it. This could result in unfair, unfavorable criticism of your work later in life. You are probably talented with ESP, *psi* and clairvoyant abilities. There may have been sudden separations from your brothers, sisters and relatives—or difficulty through neighbors when you were younger. You will continue to be attracted to off-beat subjects, unusual phenomena, new ideas and scientific as well as literary reforms.

## URANUS IN CANCER  ♅  ♋

Even though you may love your home and children and want to enjoy the security and comfort of a good life, you encounter many difficulties on the domestic scene that will eventually bring sorrow or estrangement. You have novel and original ideas as well as unique methods of expressing your views, particularly in regard to civic activities, congressional, legislative or municipal affairs. You are intensely and actively patriotic and probably belong to one or more organizations fervently supporting the government. Yet you like to travel and probably have a strong preference for ocean voyages.

The difficulties you are likely to encounter during emotionally charged litigations concerning your home, property or land can result in financial loss and physical illness, notably some kind of stomach trouble such as ulcers. You are emotionally high-strung and very sensitive; events that others might simply shrug off as unimportant cause you a great deal of sorrow. You are too easily moved by apparent injustices to yourself or others. You have some *psi* ability and much of the sensitivity that the water Sign Cancer bestows, but your sensitivities are so close to the surface that you may appear touchy, cranky, impatient with others, restless and suddenly changeable—or liable to some form of radical behavior that seems peculiar and eccentric to your friends and associates. Make it a habit to get off by yourself occasionally to refresh and recharge these emotionally sensitive batteries.

## URANUS IN LEO  ♅  ♌

You hanker for (and will probably achieve) a distinguished professional career, one that is unique or exceptional in some way. You *are* more than normally progressive, and have a strong desire to display your leadership and ingenuity in an executive position controlling advances in scientific programs. You experience sudden, strange eventualities in love affairs and often suffer unexpected sorrow, loss and estrangement in conditions involving your affections. There are abrupt endings to your relationships, many of which are caused by some of your rather odd attractions and prejudices. Although you may practice physical moderation, your mind is never still, always churning up new, original schemes.

You plunge headlong into the most dangerous, exhilarating adventures and excitement you can find. There are times when you almost deliberately seem to court the wrath of friends and business associates with your complete disregard for conventional behavior, your arrogance and rebelliousness. It is virtually impossible to reason with you during such periods because you become fiery tempered, passionately fixed in your opinions and impossibly eccentric. Your force is soon abated, however, and, like a straw fire, it is often subdued as abruptly as it began. Try to anticipate these outbursts and plan in advance to keep them under tight control. Working on another new idea or invention is one good way to accomplish this. Otherwise, you have great leadership abilities.

## URANUS IN VIRGO  ⛢ ♍

Your chief source of professional satisfaction and profit may be derived from a public career in government or in local civic groups. You also have a keen interest in the newer developments in world health, hygiene and antipollution measures. You have hidden talent in the manufacturing or production of devices to purify air, water and soil. You will gain recognition by following these and allied occupations. You have a built-in talent for mechanistic problems and could easily become a teacher or be naturally successful as an employment guidance expert or actual employer of others—particularly in the fields of biochemistry, electronics or the medical sciences. You are attracted to scientific curiosities, archeological "imponderables" and "erratic" artifacts from ancient history.

You tend to be rather fixed in your outlook, but impress people with a quiet exterior. Inwardly, you are seething with intellectual curiosity; your mind is set on being original, unencumbered and subtle. Although you are independent and eccentric, Uranus in Virgo accentuates your adept intellectual abilities and your devotion to the cause of greater health and comfort for everyone.

## URANUS IN LIBRA  ⛢ ♎

Although you are drawn to artistic, musical, literary and scientific pursuits, you are liable to generate the animosity of open enemies who may formerly have been good friends. If Uranus is well-aspected, that is, if you have the Sun, Moon, Mercury, Venus or Jupiter in fire or air Signs, you will gravitate toward friendship with intellectually stimulating and scientifically inclined people. You are generally far-sighted and intuitive. You have an excellent imagination and a vaulting ambition. Your mental chemistry is good; you reason well and think clearly, but may be somewhat eccentric or unusual in your choice of friends and associates.

You are rather restless, have a brittle temper and dislike the intervention of associates or partners in your pet projects, which might very well be in aerospace or advanced electronics.

You are inventive and ingenious, and possess a great deal of personal magnetism, all of which brings you into strange and often unexpected relationships with the opposite sex. Through at least one of these, you are likely to stun everyone with a completely unannounced or unusual kind of marriage. This may prove to be a most unfortunate decision in your life, inasmuch as it could lead to insurmountable marital difficulties, quarrels, separation, estrangement or divorce. In an extreme case, you are liable to lose your spouse through death. This is *not* a favorable position for harmonious marriage or partnership unless you devote all your efforts toward making it so.

## URANUS IN SCORPIO ♅ ♏

In this position, if Uranus is very badly aspected—with Mars or Saturn, say, in Aries, Leo or Sagittarius, you are susceptible to sudden accidents, danger on or in water, or the threat of physical damage by electrical devices. When well-aspected by planets in earth and water Signs however, Uranus in Scorpio bestows great concentrative powers, strength of mind, determination and willpower. Generally with Uranus in Scorpio, your sheer persistence and spirit are exceptionally resistant, unbreakable by most exterior forces. You have a deeply ingrained love of innovation, and of new and original methods of mechanical and electronic invention.

You drive toward personal advancement in sudden, long bursts of sheer creative energy and will defy any and all who oppose your methods or suggest that you stick to standardized procedures and orthodox methods. You are nearly always at odds with people who live by "accepted" teachings. You are outspoken, sharp, stubborn, secretive, rebellious, blunt, aggressive, courageous, audacious and shrewd. Fortunately, some of our greatest inventions and long-range achievements have come from those with the courage, vision and ability of Uranus in Scorpio. Your relationship with the opposite sex is often volatile and uncontrollable. You tend to change suddenly from a platonic friendship to a passionate physical affair without quite knowing how or why. It also works the other way around. Your greatest asset is the depth and originality of your mind. Use it.

## URANUS IN SAGITTARIUS ♅ ♐

You may run into difficulty occasionally with those who are scientifically or religiously orthodox, and may even experience trouble through foreign travels and business abroad. But you have a deep love of true science and possess a broad, humanitarian philosophy that may make organized religion and its practitioners seem very plodding and dull. You are strongly inclined to keep abreast of scientific and technological developments, such as supersonic jets and space voyages—any new method of long-distance travel, for that matter. You avoid the orthodox, the conventional, and strike out in new directions to pioneer the unknown. You seek philosophical and rational understanding of the cosmos, and don't care whether or not you are personally or physically secure from danger in the process. Above all, you insist on absolute liberty—freedom of speech and movement.

You are open-hearted, generous, adventurous, daring and progressive. Although you may have been uncomfortable in academic surroundings and the discipline required by rigid studies, you instinctively understand that is the road to broader knowledge, and affords the scope that only higher education can give—cultivation of the higher intellectual and spiritual side of your candid, spontaneous nature. You may be given to precognitive dreams; you have powerful intuition and could possess a strongly visonary, far-sighted imagination. You often have sharp premonitions of coming events that work out in the most uncanny way. It would serve you well to develop this faculty.

## URANUS IN CAPRICORN ♅ ♑

During those times when Uranus in your basic horoscope is perturbed by adverse (temporary) transits of Saturn, Mars or Mercury, you tend to become uneasy, restless and impulsive. At these times, you tend to act without thinking; you become stubborn, erratic, radical and eccentric. Generally, however, Uranus in Capricorn is an excellent antidote to the dourness, conservatism, reserve and overserious attitude of this Cardinal earthy Sign. You delight in creating new methods and progressive innovations in business. You have a good balanced sense of independence, ambition, intensified perseverance and good executive abilities. You refuse to shrink from newer, bolder enterprises. You tend to treat all people alike, regardless of their station in life, the job they hold or what their intellectual or educational qualifications may be. Your attitude is generally equitable and democratic, both to your employees and to your superiors. You can and probably will handle positions of responsibility, authority and/or power.

This position of Uranus is excellent testimony for ultimate success in positions of public trust, particularly in the operation or management of huge power or electrical generating plants, on a televison station or network, with an electronics firm or in the manufacturing of new and unusual forms of transportation. You are able to anticipate and foresee the necessities of the coming years, the conditions of people generally and their needs long in advance. You are not afraid to make radical departures from established procedures in order to achieve a desired goal. You possess a well-balanced, penetrating and profound mind with excellent logic and vision.

## URANUS IN AQUARIUS  ♅  ♒

This is the natural position of Uranus because this eccentric planet rules Aquarius and they are mutually compatible. Your many and varied friends are often regarded as engaged in unusual or off-beat occupations or somewhat extraordinary jobs. You have a naturally obliging, friendly, pleasing personality and usually attract refined, humanitarian, sociable, freedom-loving people such as you are yourself. Some of your most dearly cherished beliefs, however, at least *tend* to be peculiar or eccentric. By some kind of strange mental chemistry, you are actually able to equate your great love of freedom and independence with your work—and ultimate success—in electronics, space technology, anything of a mechanical, logistic computer or scientific nature. You enjoy the association of others in your field and are generally attracted to large organizations, humanitarian social movements, advanced kinds of communications networks, government offices or business or fraternal societies.

You can achieve great satisfaction and success through association with other people. You just like to be "where the people are," particularly those who are prominent in public life. You are a born innovator, highly inventive, with a strong dash of the visionary. You quickly comprehend the most complex social problems, grasp ideas and convey them in terms others can understand. You are resourceful, ingenious, original, and powerfully intuitive—you have a good, active mentality.

## URANUS IN PISCES ♅ ♓

This is one of the most difficult and yet strongly psychic positions of Uranus. You have a tendency to become involved in all sorts of occult activity, and to associate with unusual, psychic or eccentric people. You experience strange phenomena, and though you are not by any means unbalanced, you may often be subject to visions or other strange impressions and even experiences. This frequently results in dreams of a prophetic nature. You have the knack for sensing things before they occur—for seeing things that are about to happen. Unfortunately, they usually manifest rather negatively—in the most dire, dismal and foreboding sort of expectations imaginable. Try to see things from the bright side rather than anticipating doom and disaster, or fearing the death of loved ones.

You have excellent ability to invent new methods of treatment for old and often "incurable" ills. Develop your latent powers of healing, study and advance your knowledge of biochemistry in order to employ your talents in a positive and helpful way. Don't be discouraged at times of sudden, unexpected misfortune or reversals. This is par for the course for an adversely aspected Uranus—particularly with Mars or Saturn in one of the fire Signs—and *always* works to your advantage in the long run if you are willing to learn.

To find the Sign Uranus occupied at the time of your birth, consult the following table:

## TO FIND THE POSITION OF URANUS AT YOUR BIRTH

| Date | Zodiacal Sign |
|------|---------------|
| Sept. 11, 1898 to Dec. 19, 1904 | Sagittarius |
| Dec. 20, 1904 to Jan. 30, 1912 | Capricorn |
| Jan. 31, 1912 to Sept. 4, 1912 | Aquarius |
| Sept. 5, 1912 to Nov. 11, 1912 | Capricorn |
| Nov. 12, 1912 to Mar. 31, 1919 | Aquarius |
| Apr. 1, 1919 to Aug. 16, 1919 | Pisces |
| Aug. 17, 1919 to Jan. 21, 1920 | Aquarius |
| Jan. 22, 1920 to Mar. 30, 1927 | Pisces |
| Mar. 31, 1927 to Nov. 4, 1927 | Aries |
| Nov. 5, 1927 to Jan. 12, 1928 | Pisces |
| Jan. 13, 1928 to June 6, 1934 | Aries |
| June 7, 1934 to Oct. 9, 1934 | Taurus |
| Oct. 10, 1934 to Mar. 28, 1935 | Aries |
| Mar. 29, 1935 to Aug. 6, 1941 | Taurus |
| Aug. 7, 1941 to Oct. 4, 1941 | Gemini |
| Oct. 5, 1941 to May 13, 1942 | Taurus |
| May 14, 1942 to Aug. 29, 1948 | Gemini |
| Aug. 30, 1948 to Nov. 11, 1948 | Cancer |
| Nov. 12, 1948 to June 9, 1949 | Gemini |
| June 10, 1949 to Aug. 23, 1955 | Cancer |
| Aug. 24, 1955 to Jan. 27, 1956 | Leo |
| Jan. 28, 1956 to June 8, 1956 | Cancer |
| June 9, 1956 to Oct. 31, 1961 | Leo |
| Nov. 1, 1961 to Jan. 11, 1962 | Virgo |
| Jan. 12, 1962 to Aug. 8, 1962 | Leo |
| Aug. 9, 1962 to Sept. 27, 1968 | Virgo |
| Sept. 28, 1968 to May 20, 1969 | Libra |
| May 21, 1969 to June 23, 1969 | Virgo |
| June 24, 1969 to Nov. 22, 1974 | Libra |
| Nov. 23, 1974 to May 2, 1975 | Scorpio |
| May 3, 1975 to Sept. 8, 1975 | Libra |
| Sept. 9, 1975 to Nov. 16, 1981 | Scorpio |
| Nov. 17, 1981 to Feb. 14, 1988 | Sagittarius |
| Feb. 15, 1988 to May 26, 1988 | Capricorn |
| May 27, 1988 to Dec. 2, 1988 | Sagittarius |
| Dec. 3, 1988 to Dec. 31, 1992 | Capricorn |

**13**

## The Influence of Neptune

Moving outward from the Sun, the eighth world one en-
counters is the nebulous, most perfectly spherical of all the
planets, Neptune. Discovered mathematically through the
joint efforts of English, French and German astronomers,
named Adams, Leverrier and Galle, on September 23, 1846,
Neptune exhibited its influence by perturbing the orbit of its
planetary neighbor, Uranus. Neptune is about four times
the size of the Earth—27,700 miles in diameter—and is very
slightly oblate. Like the other giant outer planets, Neptune
rotates quite rapidly on its axis; its day is 15 hours and 48
minutes long and its year equals 164.79 Earth years; in other
words it takes about 165 years to orbit the Sun. Its distance
from the Sun is 2,796,700,000 miles, on the average.

Neptune possesses two satellites. Triton, discovered in
1846, is the largest known moon in the entire solar system.
Larger than the planets Mars or Venus, it is nearly 5,000
miles in diameter, and at 219,000 miles from Neptune is
considerably closer than our own Moon is to the Earth. The
second satellite, Nereid, was discovered by Gerard Kuiper
in 1949, and ranges between three to five million miles from
its mother planet. As one proceeds outward from the Sun,
the planets in their orbits move progressively more slowly.
Neptune takes more than 13 years to pass through each Sign
of the Zodiac. At a distance of almost three billion miles
Neptune cannot be resolved by astronomers to more than a
disc with no visible markings, even by the finest Earthbound
telescopes.

Pluto has recently been discovered to be almost exactly

247

the same size as Neptune. Consequently, instead of being regarded as an escaped moon of Neptune, Pluto is thought more likely to have been a stray comet or planet captured by the solar system in fairly recent (cosmological) times. The eccentricity of its orbit is greater than any other planet in the solar system. Its closest passage to the Sun (its perihelion) is almost three billion miles; its longest distance (its aphelion) is nearly five billion miles. Yet there are certain times when Pluto, the "outermost" planet, approaches almost 50 million miles *closer* to the Sun than does Neptune. Ever since it was discovered in 1930, astrologers have been equating Pluto with atomic energy, large group movements, the underworld, "rulership" of the Sign Scorpio, etc. Because of the comparatively brief period in which Pluto has been observed and studied, and because of its great distance from the earth, it seems unlikely at this point that one can confidently make reliable correlations between terrestrial events and Pluto's influence. At least we can't accurately do so until a far longer period of study has been devoted to it. For this reason, and because Pluto takes more than 20 years to pass through just one Sign of the Zodiac (retrograding in motion much of this time) it will require considerable study before astrologers can state with authority what Pluto's influence will be, say, in Aquarius, Capricorn or Pisces, between 120 and 140 years from now, or in any individual horoscope.

Neptune—our final planet here—is the ruling planet of Pisces, and therefore governs the feet, as you will learn in the next chapter. Neptunian-type people are usually found to be deeply involved in mystical religion, psychism, dream interpretation, spiritualism, mediumship or telepathy. When under adverse aspects, Neptunians are inclined to pretend (and believe) that something is true when in fact it is visionary or dreamlike. They make good promoters, advertising people and (when under powerfully adverse conditions) confidence men and women. When positively aspected, Neptunians psychically reach the highest essence of understanding and sympathy; they gain and possess sure knowledge of events and people—not as they may seem to be, but as they actually are. Neptune represents inner perception, extrasensory ability, ethereal feeling and almost spiritlike sensitivity. This planet is related to liquids and gases, alcohol, drugs, anesthetics and chemicals. When born strongly under

Neptune (i.e., with many planets either harmoniously or adversely aspecting it), people have an affinity for liquid refreshments, love to be by the ocean, to work with chemicals or in some capacity be connected with the petroleum industry.

*Find the position of Neptune at your birth in the list at the end of this chapter.*

## NEPTUNE IN ARIES  ♆  ♈

You are impelled in the direction of reforming the existing establishment, through a politically active career or public life on the national level. You have some novel ideas concerning the medical profession or spiritual or religious matters, and often receive flashes of inspiration on ways and means of alleviating human suffering and the conditions of the poor or disadvantaged. You possess intuition, understanding, sympathy and a generally affectionate and benevolent nature. You have highly original ideas, probably prompted by your psychic or spiritual experiences. Your sensory apparatus is acute and your emotions and feelings intense. You are attracted to psychic research and secret or mystical societies. You are bound to achieve a great deal of acclaim or popularity in at least one of the various fields of occultism, and will eventually accept a leading role in some popular form of mystical religion—one that takes you traveling. You may have to be wary of a tendency for habituation simply to gratify your physical senses or sensational desires. This includes such plebian pleasures as excessive smoking or the more dangerous indiscriminate use of various forms of stimulants.

## NEPTUNE IN TAURUS  ♆  ♉

You have a strong leaning toward luxury, ease and mysticism. Although you can be quite sensual, you are usually easygoing, good-hearted and patient. You are generally friendly, but fiery and enthusiastic about the things you believe. In fact this position of Neptune is likely to make you short-tempered when others disagree about your rigid belief in psychic and similar phenomena. You have a good chance of achieving business success and profiting through private or secret organizations and speculation.

You are fortunate in your friendships and affections

and in marriage. Although you gain by investment, you have a keen insight into the emptiness of sheer material wealth, and are likely to preach a doctrine of mental and spiritual advancement. You have a certain knack for simplifying complex scientific data, and for making basic truths interesting to the majority. Yet you tend to lack confidence in conventional ways, and often disregard or flaunt orthodox methods of carrying on a successful business. You are something of a visonary, able to foresee the outcome of human progress and achievement many years in advance. You are attracted to the artistic, beautiful and spiritual aspects of life, and have a highly developed aesthetic sense, a tendency, again, toward mysticism and the occult, and a love for what is unusual, curious, odd or antique.

## NEPTUNE IN GEMINI  Ψ  ♊

You have a natural flair for science, mechanics, writing or anything requiring manual dexterity. You are able to express yourself with ingenuity and resourcefulness, particularly through mechanical or electrical devices and in language or mathematics. You are highly imaginative and possess a sensitive, creative mentality. You have a keen interest in mystical studies, unusual forms of liberal education, poetry and dramatic theater. You often have precognitive dreams and *déjà vu* experiences. You are impressionable, and an excellent conversationalist with a profound understanding of symbolism and good facility with languages. You are congenial, sociable, generally friendly and sympathetic.

During periods when Neptune is under adverse aspects— either natally or by transit (particularly where transiting Neptune is in conjunction with or opposition to your natal Mars or Saturn), you are liable to be confused and in a generally muddled state of mind. You're liable then to believe wild rumors and to misunderstand honest reports. When afflicted, Neptune in Gemini results in mental diffusion and the misunderstanding of promises, or deceit with contracts or in agreements. These are periods when you are mentally restless, hypersensitive and impressionable; you become involved with odd or strange friends and caught up in unconventional romances. This leads to difficulty with your family, your friends, and neighbors—and often with a brother or sister. Otherwise you have a good, prophetic mind and varied mental talents.

## NEPTUNE IN CANCER ♆ ♋

You have a great love of travel, particularly of ocean cruises. In a rather dual sense, you also crave the comforts of domesticity and love your home and family. At one time or another some very unusual and weird circumstances and experiences will develop mysteriously in your home—events so strange that they will force an important change in your residence.

You possess highly developed spiritual faculties combined with an idealistic, refined and delicate personality. Your emotions are intense; you are impressionable and have a strong imagination. You either have (or have had) great understanding and sympathy for your mother, who may have taught you to love and respect Nature and science, and helped you develop along lines of spiritual communication.

Under adverse aspects, (i.e., planets in fire and air Signs) Neptune in Cancer makes you discontented, restless, changeable, excessively sensitive and impressionable. You may become involved in deception in the home. Strange or peculiar conditions in your domestic life could cause excessive anxiety, pessimism and a highly agitated physical condition—usually resulting in stomach troubles or related illness. One way or another, you'll experience a powerful drive for radical change.

## NEPTUNE IN LEO ♆ ♌

If in your natal chart you have the misfortune of Neptune adversely aspected in Leo (i.e., with many planets in water or earth Signs) you tend to express yourself rashly and impulsively; you're likely to squander your money and physical energies and to allow your feelings and emotions to override your sense of reason. This gives you an inordinate love of pleasure, which results in difficulty controlling your physical desires.

When Neptune is well-aspected (i.e., by the Sun, Moon, Mercury, Venus or Jupiter in fire Signs or air Signs), however, your mind and emotions are keen, intense and convey impressions of human emotions that are sharp and clear. You are considerate, conscientious and spiritually inclined; also generous, visionary and intuitive, with a charitable sympathetic nature. You tend to be dignified, ambitious, benevolent, warm-hearted and reserved.

This position of Neptune is likely to cause disappointment or deception in love, or heartache through the loss of someone you love deeply and the crushing of your affections. You experience exceptional, highly unconventional conditions in your love life. You are often exposed to mysterious, almost indescribably peculiar sensations and feelings. You are deeply attached to your children and enjoy the theater, refined outdoor sports, swimming, socializing and the fine arts.

## NEPTUNE IN VIRGO    Ψ   ♍

Your disposition is generally kind, patient, gentle and reliable. You tend to be shy and reserved in dealing with strangers, but when it comes to the rather paradoxical mixture of practicality and subjectivity, you shine like a beacon. You are probably good at math and have a strongly spiritual or mystical streak, with a deep understanding of occult phenomennd a strong intellectual bent toward mystical or spiritual matters.

You have an unusual approach to medical problems, diet and hygiene. You often express an odd or peculiar set of theories concerning employment, labor and/or medicine. You have a deep and abiding love for all small living creatures, whether they are fish, fowl, plant or animal. You may often be found nursing sick shrubs or flowers, feeding birds or fish or taking care of cats and dogs. You can excel in positions where trust, reliability and attention to detail are important requirements.

## NEPTUNE IN LIBRA    Ψ   ♎

When Neptune in Libra is under adverse (transiting) influences by other (malefic) planets, you develop an enormous, invariably unwarranted attraction to the opposite sex. During these times you are apt to cry too easily—for little or no discernible reason. You develop too powerful emotions of sympathy and intensity of feeling. Any association or affair you may have will trigger some mysterious or peculiar reactions.

When under favorable aspects by other planets in fire or air Signs (either natal or transiting), however, Neptune brings you admiration, a good social life, love, partnership, popularity and a good marriage. You are keenly poetic, artistic and musically inclined, with an excellent imagination and a deeply compassionate and tender nature. You love peace, harmony, economic and social equality and justice. You like the theater, are fascinated by magic and mystical traditions, and have a general admiration for science and the arts or motion pictures and television. You are strongly attached to a partner, and hardly ever consider doing anything unless it is with someone you are attracted to, or with a sociable group.

## NEPTUNE IN SCORPIO  Ψ  ♏

You have a deep and abiding love of the occult sciences. You have a quick, flaring temper and a strong attraction for what you consider to be secret or recondite arts. You are reticent, extremely secretive at times; you are reserved, and possess a persistent, determined nature. Your feelings and judgments are broad, deep and intense.

You have an excellent capacity for invention and innovation and for devising quicker and better methods of accomplishing things. Your scope of interests is broad, and you probably have a keen attraction for biochemistry, practical psychometry and the meaning of the many strange dreams you've experienced most of your life, particularly during your youth. This is an excellent position for Neptune in regard to financial gain through legacy, but you should be aware that some kind of treachery or deceit will accompany your windfall. Be careful of a tendency you may have for overindulgence in food and drink, and try to exercise some control over your rather excessive love of luxury and sensationalism.

## NEPTUNE IN SAGITTARIUS  Ψ  ♐

You have an almost insatiable desire to travel—everywhere—and as often as possible. Neptune in Sagittarius endows you with long-range prophetic ability, and a highly developed talent for insight into the motivations of other people. You are liable to have sudden inspirations, or vivid dreams in which you actually perceive visions that eventually prove to be true. You possess superb creative ability along the lines of editorial work and journalism; you like literature, foreign travel and the improvement of conditions in other countries which are often either Latin or Spanish-speaking.

You have advanced, peculiar notions about religion, the human soul, recondite philosophy—and the "new" world of *psi* talents as well as a liking for research into ephemeral, spiritual realms of knowledge. This may be true even though you are actively engaged in making your living in science, art or the business world. You may at times experience trouble during your travels in or through other countries as a result of your sometimes offbeat ideas or different religious views. There are times when you become restless and get an urge to travel—for no discernible reason whatsoever. Try to curb a slight tendency you develop at times to be emotionally oversensitive, as a result of strange, indefinite feelings brought on by bad dreams. Concentrate on your positive mental and emotional talents.

## NEPTUNE IN CAPRICORN  ♆  ♑

You are generally cautious and careful; you possess the kind of mind that considers all the possible repercussions before taking final action. This results in business acumen. You have insight that could well bring you success from stock or bond investments in liquids such as oil, chemicals, beverages, etc. Your reasoning is sound and your faith is strong; once you arrive at a decision and become convinced that your projected path to a certain goal is *the* correct one, you follow it with remarkable courage, and a lack of fear that seems to those who know you well to indicate that you've completely changed character and tossed all caution to the winds. Big business and large financial transactions appeal to you. You are also able to manage or direct private and public institutions.

You have a keen interest in psychic and clairvoyant phenomena, and, if other favorable planetary aspects in your chart agree (i.e., planets in earth and water Signs), you tend to profit through music and art rather than to appreciate it aesthetically. You are often quite serious, and can become morose and depressed, or go through severe peri-

| July | 24, | 1929 | to | Oct. | 3, | 1942 | Virgo |
|------|-----|------|----|------|----|------|-------|
| Oct. | 4, | 1942 | to | Apr. | 18, | 1943 | Libra |
| Apr. | 19, | 1943 | to | Aug. | 2, | 1943 | Virgo |
| Aug. | 3, | 1943 | to | Dec. | 22, | 1955 | Libra |
| Jan. | 1, | 1950 | to | Dec. | 24, | 1955 | Libra |
| Dec. | 25, | 1955 | to | Mar. | 11, | 1956 | Scorpio |
| Mar. | 12, | 1956 | to | Oct. | 19, | 1956 | Libra |
| Oct. | 20, | 1956 | to | June | 15, | 1957 | Scorpio |
| June | 16, | 1957 | to | Aug. | 6, | 1957 | Libra |
| Aug. | 7, | 1957 | to | Jan. | 4, | 1970 | Scorpio |
| Jan. | 5, | 1970 | to | May | 2, | 1970 | Sagittarius |
| May | 3, | 1970 | to | Nov. | 6, | 1970 | Scorpio |
| Nov. | 7, | 1970 | to | Jan. | 18, | 1984 | Sagittarius |
| Jan. | 19, | 1984 | to | June | 22, | 1984 | Capricorn |
| June | 23, | 1984 | to | Nov. | 21, | 1984 | Sagittarius |
| Nov. | 22, | 1984 | to | Dec. | 31, | 1992 | Capricorn |

**14**

## How the Stars Influence
## Your Health

Some of the latest discoveries of space-age medics have upset the notion of "biological clocks"—a belief that the cycles and rhythms of all living things are somehow "built into" all organisms. That old belief is no longer taken as true. Space-age studies have shown that extraterrestrial forces regulate almost all natural rhythms.

Thanks to an entirely new kind of research, we know now that these rhythms correlate to and are caused by extraterrestrial forces, much of it in the form of magnetism. This force is so powerful that it is used to twist, cut and form huge chunks of cold steel; industrially it is called *magnaforming*. If magnetism (an invisible force, remember) can do this to cold steel weighing tons, it must have an effect on living tissue. Kenneth S. MacLean, M.D., a New York gynecologist and cytologist (cell expert), has been healing everything from stiff muscles to crippling arthritis with a powerful electromagnetic field.

Professor Robert J. Uffen of the University of Western Ontario has gone even further. He is convinced that "magnetism is the key to Life's origin on Earth."

When Dr. Robert O. Becker, an orthopedic surgeon at State University in New York, applied this theory to individuals in hard testing, he discovered the human biomagnetic field. With his colleagues, he mapped out this field in great detail. "Celestial force fields," he said, "can and do exert an influence upon human beings and are responsible for behavioral changes."

Dr. Becker is reluctant to use the word "astrology" to

prompted heretofore undreamed-of studies of space medicine by the National Aeronautics and Space Administration.

The Hebrew Medical Journal *Harofé Haivri* (Volume One, 1963) was instrumental in attracting thousands of modern doctors to consider at least a partial reevaluation of astrology on human health conditions. In an article by Benjamin L. Gordon, M.D. of Atlantic City, New Jersey, titled "The Impact of Astrology on Medicine," ancient Babylonian, Hebrew, Greek, Egyptian and Chaldean medical knowledge was impartially reviewed, and cited as a major source of modern clinical studies relating the Sun, Moon, and planets to human health and disease conditions.

THE MOON, ruler of Cancer, fourth Sign of the Zodiac, affects the breasts, stomach (also the emotions) and functions of the body. It is probably no accident or coincidence that the most advanced ancient civilizations independently agreed on the nature and influence of each celestial body. Unlike the blazing golden Sun, the cold silvery Moon was believed to rule the left eye of a man and the right eye of a woman. Luna seems to affect the hereditary chain of molecules called RNA (ribonucleic acid). RNA has been scientifically shown to affect the memory. It has long been known to astrologers that people born to the sign of Cancer or otherwise strongly under the lunar influence have exceptionally good memories. Now we find that RNA is the stuff from which memory is made. Here is additional justification for the repeated claim that emotional and mental imbalance or derangement is connected with the Moon's influence (the term "lunatic" is related here). Diseases under the Lunar influence are asthma (disorders in the body's mucous membranes), ulcers and other stomach illnesses, abscesses and tumors.

MERCURY, ruler of Gemini and Virgo, governs the nervous system, physical sense perception, respiration and the bioelectrical field (synapses and dendrites at the nerve endings). This ancient "messenger of the gods" is the fast-moving planet associated with nervous disorders: over-excitement, neurasthenia, indecision and restlessness. Those who are born with the Sun, Ascendant or several planets in Gemini or Virgo are strongly affected by Mercury's retrograde periods, when it *appears* to move backward—a phenomenon relative to the Earth's and Mercury's orbits.

VENUS, ruler of Taurus and Libra, governs the neck, throat, larynx, esophagus, kidneys and the internal reproductive system. Being the planet of balance, it rules the inner ear and affects emotional responses to musical harmony, equilibrium and artistic sensibilities (again depending on its position by Sign and house and the aspects to and from other planets). Look to the position of Venus and her aspects to the Sun, Moon or Ascendant for clues to inflammation of the throat such as tonsilitis as well as kidney disease, goiter and other lymphatic ailments.

MARS is the ruler of Aries and the co-ruler, or lower octave of Scorpio. The adverse position and/or relationship of Mars to the Sun, Saturn or Jupiter in a horoscope indicates deliberation, lack of muscular coordination and weakness. When computer studies are made of the relationship between muscular dystrophy and the adverse influence of Mars in the horoscopes of the stricken, science may well have leapfrogged all *cures* and discovered a method of *prevention*. The best current method is to *time* a child's birth in order to benefit from the good aspects to and from Mars. Mercury has a great deal to do with muscular coordination; both palsy and muscular dystrophy result from adverse aspects between the Sun, Mars and Mercury at birth. Mars rules your strength, vigor, courage and animal vitality. When adversely aspected by transiting planets superimposed against the natal chart, the Red Planet produces a *concentrated* biomagnetic field in the body, inducing fever as well as the transformation of calories and carbohydrates into heat and energy. Mars is intimately associated with the red blood corpuscles, with hemorrhaging from injuries, with accidents and operations. All wounds, all genital and muscular disorders, are under the nominal signature of Mars. This also applies to all contagious and infectious diseases.

JUPITER is the ruler of Sagittarius and the lower octave of Pisces. This banded giant of the solar system is now recognized by planetary physicists as a small sun rather than a huge planet. During the past few years scientists have been compiling evidence indicating that the known comets (as well as the outer planets: Neptune, Uranus and Pluto) may actually have originated from the immense body of this "planet of abundance," as the Romans and Greeks called it.

Jupiter is larger than all other Solarian planets combined. Due to some totally unexplained paradox, as I've mentioned before, Jupiter radiates more than two and a half times more energy than he receives from the Sun. According to the observations of medical astrologers, many centuries before the time of Hippocrates, Jupiter's designation as the planet of abundance was determined by his position in the charts of millions of human beings. Jupiter rules the liver and cellular nutrition, and therefore the building of new flesh and blood.

It has been demonstrated countless times that those who have Jupiter on the Ascendant (the Eastern horizon) at birth, usually have some difficulty with weight control; this part of the horoscope represents the physical body—and Jupiter symbolizes abundance. Psychologically, Sagittarians and Jupiter-ruled people are usually of the "jovial" type (this is a purely astrological term)—expansive and gregarious. Their diseases are usually high blood pressure, diabetes and illnesses caused by congestion—a general overrichness of the physical system. Interestingly enough, this can also include liver trouble, gout or even high cholesterol count.

SATURN is the most beautiful ringed ruler of Capricorn. Its principle is contraction, precisely opposing Jupiterian expansion. Saturn is the perfect symbol for what Dr. Lloyd Graham of Grant's Pass, Oregon, calls a negative biomagnetic field—(the human body's electrical charge) at its most intense. "Whatever Jupiter promises, Saturn denies," is a good rule of thumb, when both planets are equally or heavily aspected in a health horoscope. Generally, however, if Jupiter is more favorably aspected by Venus or the Sun, the health of the native is excellent.

In spite of its concentric rings and beautiful colors, Saturn, when under transiting adverse aspects, causes a *decentrated* (cold) energy field in the human body. Saturn is also responsible for impediments to inner physical functions, causing obstructions, sluggishness and poor circulation. According to Saturn's position by house, Sign, and aspects to other planets, either natally or by transit, the slowing down of any physiological process may be determined. Saturn is a major cause of constipation, rheumatism and similar complaints. Because of the physiologically and mentally constricting influence of this planetary ruler of Capricorn, Saturn often produces melancholy, emotional depression and the kind of fear that weighs heavily on a person. The result is a wholly negative attitude—one that might easily thwart all attempts at a fast cure. Psychological depression *can*, usually, be traced to a *temporary* (transiting) bad aspect made by Saturn. Even amateur astrologers can easily predict when it will be over by noting how long it takes Saturn to move several degrees "out of orb" of a bad aspect. It is important to remember that our bad periods and cycles are largely caused by adverse traits of the planets to sensitive points *in* our horoscopes. Just remember that 90 degrees (square) and 180 degrees (opposition) are adverse, while 60 degrees (sextile) and 120 degrees (trine) are beneficial. Everything passes.

It's no accident that we consider the serious, dour, sad or melancholy person or mood as "saturnine." This is another purely astrological term—and one that has been with us from the most ancient times.

The late Dr. William Davidson of Chicago wrote that "Medical astrology, as astro-diagnosis, is of the profoundest use to nearly everyone. It is the key to the idiosyncrasies of the body . . . you'll find that your horoscope can be a greater contribution to your health than you suspect. It shows you not only how to keep well, how to prevent disease, but also what approach to take for the cure of it. For the professional, it is priceless."

# 15

## Space-Time Forecasting

Does the future rather than the past determine present events? Does the Sun have a 36-year "beat" or pulse which affects the world economy? Is it possible to forecast the major twists and turns of the stock market?

According to an exotic new formula that has been used successfully for more than a decade, the answer to all three questions is a strong affirmative. Space-Time Forecasting has been astonishingly accurate since it was launched in 1965.

The financial shock waves of 1973 and 1974 were predicted more than a year in advance by STF experts who also foresaw President Nixon's attempts to keep wholesale prices from exploding.

It seems only logical that those who can predict the vagaries of the stock market (especially on a long-range basis) would try to make money for themselves instead of selling their services to other people. That's how it would *seem*—IF it were true that everyone involved in economic studies is dominated only by the desire to get rich. Of course, hundreds of stockbrokers and financial advisers would have you buried in their mailings if they could. Stacks of fancy letters advise you how to make all kinds of money in coal, steel, plastics, cereals, hogbellies, electronics, soybean oil—you name it.

There are, however, exceptions to this rule.

The unusual, little-known system which has proven consistently accurate in calling every economic change is Space-Time Forecasting, the brainchild of Louis and Muriel

Hasbrouck. This charming, erudite couple has a wide and versatile background in astrology and other disciplines. Their base of operations is their large mid-Manhattan apartment, and they *do* seem to be more interested in proving that man responds to cosmic rhythms than in making a killing in the market. Yet, according to their intensely loyal band of subscribers, the Hasbroucks have indeed developed the key to the basic cause of all economic ups and downs. And they do it well in advance.

They don't advertise or solicit in any way, but since STF was established in 1964 they have enjoyed a slow, steady increase of subscribers to their unorthodox service. The only way subscribers learn of the Hasbroucks is by word of mouth, which is pretty good evidence that they're not fly-by-nighters or irresponsible gypsies out to mulct a credulous public. In fact, they're extremely wary of any kind of sensationalism and tend to avoid personal publicity. They don't need it.

One reason for this is the fact that other investment counselors subscribe to Space-Time Forecasts and use it freely to flavor and color their own forecasts, which take on a greater feeling of accuracy and authenticity as a result. The Hasbroucks know this and seem quietly pleased by it. A former McGraw-Hill executive, who is highly successful with his own educational-games company, admits, "They've been enormously helpful to me with long-term forecasts of great accuracy and usefulness. But I was really amazed when they predicted the very dates when the eruption of Mount Etna in Sicily would take place. They also timed the Alaskan and Nicaraguan earthquakes."

How do they manage such forecasts? The Hasbroucks admit they use certain planetary configurations to develop their predictions, but they are quick to point out that their system is much more complex than traditional astrology. It took them almost three decades of intensive, independent research before they developed Space-Time Forecasting.

And of all the contrary opinions in the fine art of financial speculation, the most contrary of all is that *The Future Shapes the Present!*

"Our main objective is not to exploit the market," says Muriel Hasbrouck, a multi-talented former journalist from Toronto who was once a ghost writer for famed astrologer Evangeline Adams. "We're using our system in order to get people interested in its underlying principles."

Exactly what *are* the underlying principles for the strange doctrine that the present is not shaped by past events, but "pulled" by the future? First of all, Space-Time Forecasting involves some hard-to-define concepts, mainly the rhythmical influence of solar activity on the mind of man, hence all human activity, including the national and world economy.

Their years of private study and research finally paid off with the correlation of a regular 36-year pulse in the economic-emotional cycle—one that stretches centuries into the past and enables them to predict major economic trends of the foreseeable future. In 1959 (years before they launched STF) the Hasbroucks foresaw a dollar devaluation in the early 1970s and "the dissolution of the international monetary system into a formless suspension of regional blocks. . . ."

But STF isn't based entirely on traditional astrology. "There are however, nine expressions of the four astrological elements, fire, earth, air and water," Louis Hasbrouck explained. "These yield the 36-year rhythm of Space-Time Forecasting. Our system is basically a bridge between *accepted* science—in this case Einstein's Unified Field Theory—and the still *un*-accepted science of astrology."

Whether the theory of astro-relativity is right or wrong, it's difficult to overlook STF's years of accurately forecasting every major economic trend. And the explanation of the "mechanics" of the system has a compelling kind of logic. As Louis puts it, "The Sun is the *only* living thing—the center of all life in our solar system. It generates an enormous field of energy in all directions; it stretches invisibly toward us from its main line of concentration along the equatorial belt of the Sun. The fields of the planets themselves agitate and change the solar field, which produces regular periods called 'waves.' We don't call them cycles."

The Space-Time graph looks like the rhythmic "heartbeat" of the Sun. And Louis Hasbrouck is correct in considering the Sun (a medium-sized star) as the "only living thing" in the solar system. The whole theory makes sense once STF subscribers can visualize the Sun as a living, pulsating entity, and the planets as "disturbers" of its field.

"Sometimes when you walk near your TV set," Hasbrouck said, "your own biomagnetic field causes the sound or picture to blur. Well, that's a small example of how one field interferes with another."

Their chief argument with science is that scientists refuse

to allow any place in nature for the influence of man's *mental* activities. In spite of the broad interest in parapsychology, science is still largely dominated by the idea that human mental and emotional activity is beyond the scope of hard scientific research.

"The hell it is," Hasbrouck snorted. "What we're doing—by accurately forecasting economic trends—is demonstrating that human thoughts and feelings are every bit as much affected by changes in solar and planetary activity as the Earth's atmosphere, radio waves or any number of other natural phenomena. And we prove it by showing that the stock market, agriculture, industry, etcetera, are directly affected by the way people *think* and behave. We've shown that man is physically *and* psychically integrated with the solar and interplanetary field. How could anything that was formed from the same stuff that makes up the solar system be divorced from it?"

A Yale graduate, class of 1911, Hasbrouck was an Air Force pilot during World War I and an Air Corps officer in World War II. He was also formerly a mining engineer and set himself up as a construction engineer in New York before becoming interested in the stock market. Before the market crash that preceded the Great Depression of the 1930s, he practiced investment and finance in New York and later became an independent investment counselor. When the great financial debacle struck in 1929, he figured it was time to learn what makes markets change, and what natural laws, if any, were at work behind these changing economic trends.

He admits he made "a lot of money as an investment counsellor during the 1920's without knowing anything about the market at all. Hell, nobody knew *anything* then, and I lost my shirt in 1929 because none of the experts knew just what the hell was going on."

Would-be subscribers to STF who expect to find a couple of exotic gypsies in some storefront operation or a couple of aging stargazers peering over weird charts are invariably surprised by what they find. Great interest in the Hasbroucks' system has been demonstrated by major corporations—Boeing Aircraft Corporation and United Airlines, for example. One of their most influential and enthusiastic clients was so impressed with Space-Time's ability to forecast the exact times of solar flares and geomagnetic storms that he introduced the Hasbroucks to some high government officials (who now have their system under close study).

And because they can accurately forecast "proton events," (solar flares that cause atmospheric and geomagnetic disturbances) and geophysical activity such as earthquakes and volcanic eruptions, their system is being studied by the NASA Space Center in Colorado and by the National Center for Atmospheric Research in Boulder, Colorado. One reason for this keen interest was their annual long-range forecast for 1972 and 1973 (issued in 1971) when they picked the first week of August, 1972, as the time for a truly enormous outburst of solar activity. When the Sun erupted violently right on schedule, most scientists—particularly astrophysicists—were totally unprepared for anything even close to its intensity.

"When you sort them out," said Muriel Hasbrouck, "our 'signals' coincide with solar flares, geomagnetic storms and—to a lesser extent—earthquakes. This is a pretty clear indication that all natural phenomena are interrelated. The reason we can *time* these events so accurately is because the planetary movements are known with great exactness, therefore we can locate them in time and space."

"It took years of study," Louis added, "to satisfy our curiosity about this basic concept, and still more years to develop a workable system that would, through practical use, prove our point. There are, of course, other, more irregular solar disturbances."

Based on the accuracy of their system, the Hasbroucks have been accepted and registered by the Federal Communications Commission as "Economic Trend Forecasters"—a special classification.

For the relatively inexpensive fee of $300, the couple issues a detailed long-range forecast of what the national and world economy will do each year. But subscribers get much more. They also receive a bimonthly Supplemental Forecast which is mailed out in the beginning and middle of each month (to correlate current minor trends with the annual forecast and to give key dates for changes).

In a cultivated tenor voice, Hasbrouck observed that "the *only* way we can prove our system is correct to a large enough segment of the investment crowd is by predicting on a long-range basis the actual behavior of people—en masse."

(He is getting wider recognition among old Yale classmates and other alumni as the years go by.)

As a younger woman, Muriel Hasbrouck made a long and intensive study of the basic elements of astrology and did graduate work in comparative philosophy. She authored one of the most accurate and impressive books ever written on the astrological influence of the *decanates* (the division of each 30-degree Zodiacal Sign into three segments of ten degrees).

By working in close harmony, blending their knowledge and talents, the Hasbroucks discovered a method of predicting the precise time when radio transmissions would be disturbed. It was tested by the Bell Telephone Laboratories in 1940, and later evolved into the system used by John H. Nelson of RCA, Inc., then the world's largest long-distance communications network.

The idea was to predict the exact time when solar flares would erupt and stir up ionospheric storms in the highest reaches of the Earth's atmosphere. These storms scramble and destroy short-wave radio transmissions which (before the time of communications satellites) were bounced off the ionosphere to reach beyond the curvature of the earth to a distant receiving station.

An important scientific debacle erupted in the late 1950s when RCA announced that planets' positions were responsible for weather and other phenomena. The executives at RCA however, were far from enthusiastic about endorsing astrology. "John Nelson," they said, "is our Weather Propagation Analyst, sort of a scientific weather engineer who predicts radio weather for us according to the positions of the planets and the angles formed among them. These positions coincide so closely with sunspots and magnetic solar storms which ruin radio transmission . . . that they constitute an entirely new study."

In spite of this evidence and astrology's gradually increasing acceptance, sciencedom remains a stubborn holdout: "The planets are too far away to have any influence on the Earth. . . ."

Directly, or indirectly? "They're only partly right," Muriel Hasbrouck responded demurely. "We can't prove the planets *directly* affect us or influence the economy. But we do know they disturb the solar field, which *does* have a direct influence. This is very subtle, but it's reflected in the mass psychology."

The Sun's enormous field pulses in all directions through space as it radiates rhythmically up and down the scale of all the intensities and wavelengths of energy—known and unknown. Its main lines of force are concentrated along a line extending from the solar equatorial belt—somewhat like a gigantic but invisible version of the rings of Saturn. The primary strength of the field is concentrated along the belt of the ecliptic where most of the planets orbit.

This solar field stretches for enormous distances, and probably reaches beyond the outermost known planets; it is profoundly influenced both by the interplanetary field and the systems' combined center of gravity. Swimming around the Sun in their allotted orbits, the planets' own fields create a kind of "wake," which results in minor changes in solar radiation that affects everything on Earth.

"The crests and troughs of these energy waves can be timed," Louis Hasbrouck said. "They coincide with all the major turning points in economic history—and also with changes in public moods."

As the solar field reaches the Earth it alters the geomagnetic field and powerfully influences human moods and behavior, individually and collectively. "Changes in the solar field affect us all at the same time," says Muriel, "but in different ways because each individual was born into the field at a different time."

This difference in time and place of birth causes the subtle changes of personality and character found even among twins. How did ancient astrologers discover this fact?

"I don't know *how* they did it," Louis responded, "but when a baby is born, we know that it comes—for the first time—and on its own, into a larger field of energy. And *that* field at *that* time has certain qualities which are different at other times. Even the air we breathe can be positively or negatively ionized."

RCA's John Nelson once dismissed natal astrology as unscientific. He's now a respected member of the American Federation of Astrologers.* By independent observation, he

*The headquarters of the AFA at Six Library Court, S.E., Washington, D.C. 20003 is the oldest, largest and most democratic astrological body in the nation. Members are classified as Student, Professional or Teacher. Two of these classifications are thoroughly tested by a board of elected profes-

learned that the same angles among planets which were considered adverse by ancient astrologers are also bad for solar and radio weather. These rediscovered adverse angles are 45, 90 and 180 degrees, respectively. They coincide with serious upheavals on the Sun and in the Earth's ionosphere. The traditionally "beneficient" planetary angles of ancient astrology—30, 60 and 120 degrees—are associated with moderate solar activity and "good radio weather."

"Every basic element," says Louis Hasbrouck, "is composed of electric field charges. Every living thing is actually an electrical transformer. Since we all live in the Earth's field—and the food and water we consume, even the air we breathe, is composed of these same elements—we're part of the whole living picture. The entire planetary energy field is forever changing and affecting everything within its influence."

To demonstrate how the present is attracted or "pulled" by conditions existing in the future, the Hasbroucks demonstrated a recurrent 36-year wavelength, or "beat" of the Sun, which affects the world economy by influencing mass human consciousness. By a strange "coincidence" the ancient Hindu and Hebrew World Horoscope was also divided into subcycles of 36 years each. This is a pretty good indication that ancient scholars and scientists were highly advanced in areas we moderns are just beginning to discover.

Edward R. Dewey, president of the Foundation for the Study of Cycles, is probably the foremost scientific expert in this field. He cites four reasons why external forces influence the mind of man and therefore all human activities:

1. Almost everything fluctuates.
2. Many things fluctuate in cycles or waves.
3. Many of these waves repeat so regularly, so dominantly, that they cannot possibly be accidental or ascribed to mere "chance."
4. If the wave or cycle is *not* repeating by chance, then something, some force, must "trigger" it.

---

sional members. If the applicant passes these tests, he or she receives a Certificate of Competency. It is only by years of experience, study and hard work that AFA-accredited practitioners are equipped to serve the public. Anybody seeking the services of a qualified Professional astrologer (or a local AFA affiliate group) may apply directly to its headquarters on Capitol Hill.

"When the force (or forces) that trigger the wave are discovered, "we will have solved our mystery. I picture the space in which we live as filled with forces that alternately stimulate and depress all human beings—make them more or less optimistic, or make them more or less fearful. These forces don't *control* us, they merely *influence* us."

But *does* the future shape history—and especially the present? It seems paradoxical, but as long as the Hasbroucks are successfully predicting future trends, their theory is valid and their system merits serious consideration—no matter how arbitrary their interpretation of it may seem, at least until something better comes along.

As it now stands, Space-Time is the *only* economic system that uses astrology and the only one that would dare to make its kind of predictions. As one of their rather well-to-do subscribers remarked, "The failure of economics to become a real science is directly because the economists failed to realize that there are natural rhythmic forces from the cosmic environment to which humans naturally respond."

Considering the fantastic increase in world population, increasing scarcity of agricultural products and the general capriciousness of weather patterns, Space-Time Forecasting (or something very much like it) will be absolutely essential in the near future.

The acceptance of the reality and potency of these celestial forces will be one of the great advances in scientific history.

**15**

## Fate vs. Free Will

Using the rule of Occam's Razor (i.e., the simplest explanation is usually the most accurate), the reason for the general academic reluctance to adopt serious studies of astrology is not generated by a lack of acceptable evidence, but largely because the majority of us suspect that there is something fatalistic about it. In a sense, the idea of complete freedom is a fetish in this country, and at this time in history. We refuse, many of us, to think about any limitations on our freedom.

In the memory banks of the world's most sophisticated computers, and in all of us (scientist and layman alike) there seems to be a powerful aversion to anything that could change our accepted view of Life—particularly human consciousness and its essential meaning. *Any* kind of change is uncomfortable, but when it affects our basic concepts we tend to regard it as a revolutionary threat.

To refuse to consider the evidence for cosmic influence on our world is against all the stated principles of science. This stance is irrational, perhaps neurotic. But so is the fear that generates the irrationality. Most laymen tend to overlook the fact that scientists are human beings cursed (or blessed) with the same kind of prejudices and bias, as any other cross-section of humanity.

One powerful argument in favor of the astrological thesis that we are strongly influenced by celestial forces is that human events tend to occur in various kinds of cycles. Accordingly, we can therefore expect a reversal of present scientific attitudes to the idea that humanity's destiny hinges on *exogenous forces*. This would simply be the conclusion of one cycle and the beginning of another.

Suppose that at an indeterminate future date, when a network of the largest computer memory banks in the world exists, someone decides to ask a central input station a crucial question about human subjective consciousness and free will. I submit that, given all the data, a computer will respond that human beings have only a fractional control over their destiny.

To discipline the mind so that thinking is channeled in a desired direction indicates a certain amount of freedom of choice. Left to its own "free and normal" functioning, the brain (or mind) operates somewhat like ordinary light, i.e., a seemingly indiscriminate rambling off in all directions. An ordinary electric light, for example, radiates on many wavelengths at once. Technically this kind of light is called "incoherent."

A laser beam, on the other hand, is a fine example of disciplined or "coherent" light. Trillions of photons from a laser are traveling on the same wavelengths—"in step," so to speak—like a battalion of soldiers in precision marching across a bridge. Long before Roman legions conquered the Mediterranean world, military men knew what happened when troops marched across a bridge in synchronized motion. Ultimately this regular pounding either weakened or demolished the bridge. To avoid this, soldiers were ordered to break step and walk in a kind of random, chaotic fashion, thus neutralizing the effect of a regular beat.

Whenever any purposeful efforts, be they marching troops, beams of intensely coherent light, or concentrated human thought, are used for a clearly defined ultimate purpose, we have excellent examples of the kind of discipline that strongly supports the case for free will. Randomness and chaos, on the other hand, characterize a *lack* of free choice, either in science, social psychology or in our personal lives.

Even a cursory study of human history makes our cherished belief in free will an elusive matter at best. The fact that a chemist can unfailingly predict the result of combining two parts hydrogen to one part oxygen to produce water is perfect proof of the existence of a natural law which unfailingly *permits* it. It has never been even loosely determined to what degree humans are governed by exogenous forces. The entire idea of outside influence is usually shrugged off as violently contradictory to the beliefs we so dearly cherish. The great majority of people throughout known history seem to have blindly accepted the dogma that each man is a free agent, entirely capable of exercising, if not willing to exercise, his freedom of choice.

This belief has never been scientifically challenged. All authority, both secular and clerical, promotes and supports it. Orthodox science, which, like logic, is only one of the avenues approaching reality, aids and abets the universally accepted notion that all human beings have a God-given free will, and that animals function solely by instinct (whatever that is).

The mere mention of the credibility of the opposite idea triggers all the time-worn clichés (and often brings down the wrath) of the sizable majority. It seems to be in the vested interest of leaders in every age of history to support the belief that man has a divine free choice in all his affairs, and that what he makes of his life is entirely his own responsibility.

There's a certain "necessity" about this. World leaders, law enforcement officials, the clergy and most people seem to distrust human nature and fear the consequences if it should ever be proved that we are *not* entirely self-determining creatures. It's a paradoxical situation, an irrational stance.

We should have *some* faith in our institutions! That which we call civilization seems to work—more or less. But on the other hand, so do, for example, those colonies of industrious insects: ants, bees and termites, which operate by "instinct." They don't engage in self-destructive wars, a fact that may explain our relative dominance over them, because conflict, struggle and strife have resulted in most of mankind's greatest advances.

Egyptian astrologers were familiar with the cycles of civilization. (The phoenix was their symbol of death—and resurrection from the ashes of the old.) They weren't such believers in divinely given free will.

Item: Whenever this concept of free will is closely examined, some rather unnerving facts emerge. Certainly the freedom of a young soldier drafted into service during wartime is sharply curtailed. What are the chances of a child born blind to become a brain surgeon, for example? What chance has a low-grade moron of becoming a business executive—or for that matter, of leading a well-ordered life? It may be symbolic that, aside from the death penalty, the worst punishment our society metes out to its law offenders is imprisonment—the curtailing of physical freedom. In all of us there is a distinct dread of having our freedom taken away. This is reflected in the constitutions of the world's democracies. It is as though all humans instinctively, subconsciously recognize the flimsiness of the idea of personal independence. To lose what little we have is a tragic event.

Even "unreasoning" animals will fight to avoid being caged or trapped. On the other hand, there are times when we willingly trade some of our freedom for a seemingly greater long-range benefit.

As far as we know, no one has ever been known to request his or her existence. Life is thrust on us. Each comes into a world not of his making and (to a greater or lesser degree) is impelled along a life path by forces both tangible and intangible. With magnificent hindsight we understand the inevitability of someone else's life—given a certain set of circumstances to begin with. We can't, however, be objective about ourselves. The question is, what are the known, visible or tangible forces? I submit that it is rather like Newton's Third Law of Motion—applied to human events. (For every action there is an opposite and equal reaction.)

Most of us have only the faintest idea that this law could exist. Each decision we make is boobytrapped with conditions over which we have no control. Thus the man who is weary of commuting to his office, but hates to live in the city, and still has to make a living, obviously cannot get off the treadmill. The skeins are wound even tighter if he hates his job or happens to be frustrated in some other area of his life.

"But there are escape mechanisms," the old argument states: "There are any number of 'outs' for anyone who wants to use them. He can play golf—or take a vacation. He can quit his job and go into another field—or simply do some hard drinking."

Choose any solution. Theoretically, the alternatives are almost infinite. The trick of fate is that he can "choose" no more than one at a time—and usually brings about certain other *inevitable* conditions as a result of his choice.

There is simply no way of knowing with certainty whether our choices are truly free or if they are the inevitable, predictable outcome of everything that has happened before. If there is one thing most astrologers, astronomers, chemists, politicians and clergymen unilaterally agree on it is the theorem: "Man possesses a free will." Yet some of the most learned men of all ages were essentially astrologers who could cast the horoscopes of infants and accurately foretell the kind of human beings those babies would become. Not in vague, general terms, but in specific detail, such as personality, intelligence, talents, accomplishments, ailments and (most important) the motivating force of the deeper individuality.

Consider evolution and the statement, "Man is a free agent endowed with high intelligence and conscience—and is therefore accountable for all his acts." In essence, this has been the attitude of orthodox authority of every age in every land. It seems to be a crucial necessity. If *any* Establishment (itself buffeted by invisible forces it neither recognizes nor understands) were to concede that intangible forces *might* be shaping man's destiny, the fear is that the status quo would be forced to make changes that might lead to its downfall.

Again, evolution. The residue of 19th Century materialism and Victorianism has sullied the world outlook of several generations. These views, originally the "Divine Right" of kings, and now the very idea of authority itself, are mutually exclusive alternatives, currently being questioned by the new generation.

It is relevant that this particular world cycle was predicted by many sages, seers and astrologers. History possesses a certain inevitability. To those who understand it, the occurrences we call great world events do *not* come as a shock. The assassination which led to World War I (and ultimately to World War II and the Cold War) was predictable. In fact, it *was* prophesied. To some it is a horrible thought that the future might be a foregone conclusion. Yet there are many clear predictions about coming events in the world.

We reject them because they imply that we have little or nothing to say about the future. If he'd known about it in advance, how could President Franklin D. Roosevelt have prepared America for a space race or a manned voyage to Mars? How serious was this prospect to anyone in authority before or during World War II? Yet these are modern *realities*, the existence of which was curtained by a couple of decades of time

And yet we can see the historic necessity of one great event triggering another, of Soviet Russia's launching of Sputnik I and the subsequent technological contest. There's a certain *inevitability* about all sequences of events; they occur in a certain order due to ironclad necessity. America *couldn't* have been defeated by Japan or Germany, just as it was impossible for Hitler to have successfully invaded Russia. The tides of history were against him.

You don't have to be an astrologer to foresee the radical changes wrought by the present questioning of all institutions. Fewer and fewer people believe there are matters that should *not* be questioned. There are few sanctuaries left for the True Believer; the bulwarks of materialism and Victorianism are disintegrating. In the next ten years the world will change more than it has during the past two hundred. Predictably so.

Consider Teilhard de Chardin: "It is an extraordinary thing. Scientists for the last hundred years have been examining, with unheard of subtlety and daring, the mysteries of material atoms and the living cell. They have weighed the electron and the stars. They have dissected hundreds of thousands of specimens of the vegetable and animal world. They are striving with infinite patience to link the human form anatomically to that of the other vertebrates. They endeavor to examine the springs of human psychology, or to isolate the laws governing the exchanges of products and services in the growing complexity of our society. Now in the midst of these great labours, almost nobody has yet decided to put the main question: 'But what exactly is the phenomenon of man?' That is to say in rather more precise terms: 'What is the place and purpose of this extraordinary power of thought in the development of the world of experience?' " (Pierre Teilhard de Chardin's *The Vision of the Past*.)

More evolution: the materialistic scientific establishment would have us believe that certain molecular ingredients were formed by some mysterious process in the backwaters of Earth's primordial seas—and that, as a result of natural forces, Life simply evolved into ever more complex living organisms—*without* teleological direction—*without* intelligence or purpose. Such a stance makes Life a monstrous accident.

Man is peculiarly adapted to the electromagnetic-gravitational field in the Earth, Sun, Moon and planets. There is no certainty that he can exist with the alien astrology of a different planet.

This evolution is a tricky thing. Did some of those ancient amino acid and carbon molecules possess the free choice necessary for them to "decide" to evolve into what is currently the most sophisticated form of vertebrate life on Earth? No one is prepared to state what the bees or ants might "think," but it is obvious that they *are* industrious, that they *are* social and tend to group together. Instinct, or free will? No answer has yet been found. Man also seeks the companionship of his own kind.

Each spring teeming throngs of young people at Fort Lauderdale, Florida, gather along a narrow stretch of beach about one hundred yards long. An empty beach stretches for miles on either side of this mass of humanity.

Fish travel in schools, wolves in packs, cattle in herds and lions in prides. Considering the law of self-preservation, it is probably safe to assume that every living creature possesses a faculty somewhat like the human ego. Seals, walruses and sea elephants battle each other over possession of a harem. Business executives cling to precarious positions while the younger men try to stake out their own precarious claim in the corporate structure. Humanity probably has more in common with other species than it suspects.

If those primordial molecules did *not* decide to evolve, then Life as we know and understand it is eternally *acted upon* by invisible, as yet unknown forces which shape its destiny, create its myriad forms, and once pushed Homo sapiens into his present precarious position of world dominance.

According to the ever-changing cycle or style of this age, man is a self-determining creature, capable of bringing order out of the shimmering cauldron of history. Communists in Russia and China really believe they have pulled it off. Like a good novel, history has the characteristic of inevitability. Officially America has thrown off the yoke of colonialism and proclaims itself a model of democracy for the rest of the world. This is entirely relative. We consider ourselves liberators; many countries believe we are oppressors and that the Reds point toward ordered freedom. The odd thing about these basically humanitarian revolutions are (a) that each has subsequently inflicted on weaker nations the same conditions they fought to overthrow and (b) that long before they occurred, all revolutions were predicted by someone, somewhere. Any predictable event is charged with the aura of inevitability. Neither a nation nor its leaders and people have any choice in a truly unavoidable situation; a sky diver might just as well try to "fall" upward!

When science states that if you do thus and so, *this* condition must inevitably follow, and then it works out as predicted, you are dealing with an inflexible natural law. If astrologers through the ages have noted a tendency for wars to follow eclipses where "malefic" planets were in evil aspect to the eclipse—and then those wars happened on schedule—our *collective* free will probably adds up to not much above zero.

Yet these are the actual conditions with which we are faced and under which we are forced to live. We're able to accept an obvious fact if it is not too troublesome or painful. But all of us *are* swept along by the tides of history. No one is immune to the peculiar influence of his own age.

One interesting corollary in astrology is the tendency for each generation to typify the influence of positions of the outer (more ponderous) planets. Neptune is a huge, banded-atmosphere planet four times the size of Earth and takes nearly 165 years to perform one orbit of the Sun. In terrestrial nature there are many cycles of 165 years to correlate with Neptune's orbit. By the same token, Uranus, another banded giant of a planet, exerts its influence on several generations. Uranus takes 84 years and four days to complete one cycle of the Sun. Saturn's 29½-year solar orbit coincides with hundreds of terrestrial cycles. And Jupiter, the giant of the solar system, larger than all other planets combined, has the clearest relationship to Earthly cycles. Its 11.80-year orbital period also conforms to the major Sunspot cycle, which is widely known to influence barometric changes, ionospheric disturbances and the commodity and stock market.

The fact that many of these planetary cycles are interlaced has created some difficulty for astro-economists like Lt. Cmdr. David Williams in sorting out the correlations for impatient skeptics. It took mankind long eons to trace the connection between planetary orbits and the things influenced by each body. Since the discovery of Pluto in 1931, many interesting studies are being made of its influence. By far the most intriguing was made by Spengler in his *Cycles of Civilization*. Pluto's orbit of the Sun takes about 250 years. Tracing this increment far back into ancient Chinese civilization, Spengler found that the overthrow of one dynasty took place when Pluto was at its perigee (closest approach to the Sun) *station* every 125 years. A century and a quarter later, when Pluto was at its aphelion station, conditions began changing for yet another dynastic change, when Pluto once more came to its closest solar approach.

Moreover, the capital of China was continually reestablished every 250 years (right on the "click" of the planetary dial, so to speak), first in northern China, and then in southern China, for as far back as Chinese records of civilization are available.

Astrologers since ancient times have known what Dr. Richard Head of the National Aeronautics and Space Administration's Electronics Research Center is just discovering: that Jupiter's colossal mass is largely responsible for great solar magnetic storms, especially every 12 years when the giant planet comes closest to the Sun. Solar flares and magnetic storms cause enormous changes in our ionosphere. In 1965 the National Engineering Science Co. reported that ionospheric disturbances also affected the troposphere, and thus *all* lower atmospheric conditions (as astro-meteorologists since Hipparchus have claimed).

Furthermore, the cavity between the Earth's surface and the ionosphere is regarded by scientists these days as a completely resonant system: its characteristic resonance is about one-eighth of a second, the exact time it takes for light to speed once around the Earth.

As Electronics science editor Red Pay pointed out in the May 15, 1967, issue of *Technology Week*, this resonant frequency is thus 8 cps (eight cycles per second), which is congruent with that of the Alpha rhythm of the human brain. The geomagnetic field, therefore, provides the "fine tuning mechanism for this characteristic frequency."

Dr. Robert O. Becker, orthopedic surgeon at Syracuse Veterans Administration Hospital and New York's Upstate Medical Center, has discovered that human behavior is predictably affected by changes in this frequency, by fluctuations in the geomagnetic field (which subtly but powerfully affects the human biomagnetic field), and by the angular positions of the planets in their orbits.

Dr. Becker regards ancient astrological theories concerning unseen celestial and terrestrial forces not simply as superstitious nonsense, but as the basis for a new super-science of the future. As *Technology Week* stated: "The positions of the planets probably play a much larger part in human affairs than anyone previously supposed. From this point of view, one of the most important reasons for sending man to the Moon is to see what happens to his behavior after chronic exposure to a very low magnetic field."

As long ago as 1962, Dr. Becker warned an international space symposium of grave dangers to astronauts when they invaded the interplanetary environment with its wildly fluctuating electromagnetic fields.

One of the most important aspects of science is the fact that increased knowledge seems to give us proportionate control over the forces of Nature. Relatively speaking, we have not even begun to ask the correct questions. We cling to out-moded, obviously superstitious beliefs, one of which is that man is solely responsible for all that happens in history. Both Toynbee's and Spengler's studies have shown the real extent of man's control of history. As long as we accept an egocentric view of life, our control of Nature will remain minimal, at best.

If humanity actually did control such forces, history would *never* be changed by droughts, earthquakes, ice ages, floods or widespread disease. If we cannot perceive a cause-effect mechanism to the limitations on our freedom, we are unwilling to accept life as it is.

A hurricane stops a sailing we had planned; we accept the necessity of that. The Cold War prevents us from visiting China or Cuba; we accept that. Earth's deadly radiation belts thwart the efforts of astronauts to travel to the planets. We accept these limitations because they are tangible—and so huge that we cannot possibly control them.

And yet, humanity is enclosed by many more invisible cages—intangible prisons. With hard realism, most of us must eventually reconcile ambitions and goals with personal abilities. Men are *not* all created equal, however much we may want to hold this truth to be evident. Many potential financiers are forced by conditions beyond their control to make a living as clerks. Millions of us are frozen at various rungs on what we call the ladder of success. The style of this materialistic age is such that almost everyone wants to reach the top. The harsh reality is that only a relative few manage to achieve "success" (which means many things to many people).

No one who has ever explained, fairly and fully, to the talented boy who wants to become a fine writer, artist, or musician why he winds up as a hack—or worse yet, apparently destroys his own talent. Charles E. Luntz' book, *Vocational Guidance by Astrology* gives a good picture of the life potential in every horoscope. Each chart has, by definition, a great deal of inevitability and a comparatively slim margin for error. Acceptance of a relative kind of predestination is not as unwholesome as we may have come to believe. Knowing the truth about ourselves and where we can go from *there* is far more important than the blind belief that we are the lords of creation.

To sum up: there are some areas of free choice; this varies among individuals and in different departments of life. Properly calculated and accurately interpreted, the horoscope will reveal the areas of your greatest freedom of choice, as well as the most constricted, or compulsive, territory in your natal chart—and therefore your life.

Predictably, the next important breakthrough in human knowledge, after the *psi* faculty has been explored and charted, will be a universal study of the impinging forces of the universe—and how much control we really have over our destiny.

This is bound to result in increased freedom and greater control over our lives, but the fact will probably remain that a large number of aspects in our lives are simply waiting there to be experienced. This could be for good or ill; it all depends on how much of the free will you were born with you'll decide to use.

Once you've set up the rudimentary chart this book describes, see how many planets are sextile (two Signs apart) or trine (four Signs apart); how many are in square (three Signs apart) or opposition (six Signs apart). Of course, you won't know the exact *degree* of each planet, or the degrees of the signs on the house cusps, but with many trine and sextiles (as well as conjunctions, i.e., planets together), you will find you have a greater freedom of choice, and go through life much more easily, than those with many planets in opposition or square aspect; the latter are known by astrologers to create obstacles and conflict.

However, it is an observable (albeit paradoxical) fact that obstacles are regarded by people with strong willpower as challenges to be overcome. Historically, the greatest achievers were people with many squares and oppositions in their horoscopes. The secret seems to be that they had many planets in the fixed Signs, Taurus, Leo, Scorpio and Aquarius. And since these Signs are in *all* horoscopes, the chances are that you have one or more planets in these stabilizing Signs.

# SIGNET Books You'll Want to Read

☐ **LIVE YOUR LIFE BY THE NUMBERS:** *Your Guide to Numerology* by Sylvia DiPietro. This fascinating guide makes the ancient study of numerology available to the modern reader. Discover valuable insights and make the numbers in your life add up to health, wealth, and happiness.                    (170474—$5.99)

☐ **STARPOWER:** *An Astrological Guide to Supersuccess* by Jacqueline Stallone with Mim Eichler. With a Foreword by Sylvester Stallone. In this eye-opening book, packed with celebrity gossip, Jacqueline Stallone shares the astrological advice that helped lead her son Sylvester to fabulous wealth and success.
                                                                (168437—$4.95)

☐ **THE CRYSTAL HANDBOOK** by Kevin Sullivan. Put Crystal Consciousness to work for you! The A-to-Z guide to the psychic energies of more than 100 cosmic crystals, gems, minerals, and healing stones.                   (154916—$4.99)

☐ **THE MYSTICAL TAROT** by Rosemary Ellen Gulley. Your step-by-step guide to the Tarot's ancient and mysterious symbols.                          (168003—$5.99)

☐ **INTIMATES THROUGH TIME** by Jess Stearn. In this fascinating account of reincarnation and its influence on human nature, find out how people come together out of the past in groups to work out the unresolved conflicts of their previous lives and how those who were once intimate are forever united through eternity.
                                                                (175301—$4.99)

Prices slightly higher in Canada

# SYDNEY OMARR'S 1995 DAY-BY-DAY ASTROLOGICAL GUIDES
## 18 Months of Daily Horoscopes From
## July 1994 to December 1995

Let America's most accurate astrologer show you what the signs of the zodiac and Pluto's welcome transit into Sagittarius will mean for you in 1995! Sydney Omarr gives you invaluable tips on your love life, your career, your health—and your all-round good fortune.

☐ **Capricorn**—December 22–January 19          (181166—$3.99)

☐ **Taurus**—April 20–May 20                    (181131—$3.99)

☐ **Virgo**—August 23–September 22              (181123—$3.99)

☐ **Sagittarius**—November 22–December 21       (181239—$3.99)

☐ **Scorpio**—October 23–November 21            (181220—$3.99)

☐ **Aquarius**—January 20–February 18           (181174—$3.99)

☐ **Libra**—September 23–October 22             (181247—$3.99)

☐ **Leo**—July 23–August 22                     (181212—$3.99)

☐ **Cancer**—June 21–July 22                    (181190—$3.99)

☐ **Gemini**—May 21–June 20                     (181158—$3.99)

☐ **Aries**—March 21–April 19                   (181204—$3.99)

☐ **Pisces**—February 19–March 20               (181182—$3.99)